PERSPECTIVES O[N]

C000083769

AIR POWER IN ITS WIDER CONTEXT

Edited by
Stuart Peach

Defence Studies (Royal Air Force),
Joint Services Command Staff College Bracknell

LONDON : THE STATIONERY OFFICE

© Crown Copyright 1998
Published with the permission of the
Ministry of Defence on behalf of the
Controller of Her Majesty's Stationery Office.

Applications for reproduction should be made in writing to The Copyright Unit, Her Majesty's
Stationery Office, St. Clements House, 2-16 Colegate, Norwich, NR3 1BQ.

The opinions, conclusions and recommendations expressed or implied within are solely those of
the authors and do not necessarily represent the views of the Ministry of Defense or those of
the Royal Air Force.

The views expressed in this volume are those of the authors and do not reflect the official policy or
position of the United States Air Force, Department of Defense or US Government.

Published by The Stationery Office and available from:

The Publications Centre
(Mail, telephone and fax orders only)
PO Box 276, London SW8 5DT
General enquiries 0171 873 0011
Telephone orders 0171 873 9090
Fax orders 0171 873 8200

The Stationery Office Bookshops
123 Kingsway, London WC2B 6PQ 0171 430 1671 Fax 0171 831 1326
68-69 Bull Street, Birmingham B4 6AD 0121 236 9696 Fax 0121 236 9699
33 Wine Street, Bristol BS1 2BQ 0117 9264306 Fax 0117 9294515
9-21 Princess Street, Manchester M60 8AS 0161 834 7201 Fax 0161 833 0634
16 Arthur Street, Belfast BT1 4GD 01232 238451 Fax 01232 235401
The Stationery Office Oriel Bookshop The Friary, Cardiff CF1 4AA
01222 395548 Fax 01222 384347
71 Lothian Road, Edinburgh EH3 9AZ (counter service only)

Customers in Scotland may mail, telephone or fax their orders to:
Scottish Publications Sales, South Gyle Crescent, Edinburgh EH12 9EB
0131 622 7050 Fax 0131 622 7017

The Stationery Office's Accredited Agents
(see Yellow Pages)
and through good booksellers

Printed in the United Kingdom for The Stationery Office JA5476 C40 6/98

FOREWORD

By the Chief of the Air Staff
Air Chief Marshal Sir Richard Johns
GCB CBE LVO ADC FRaes RAF

The basic nature of war does not change; it remains extremely violent, dangerous and unpredictable. What does change, however, is the way we plan to conduct warfare. This century has witnessed an evolution from total war waged by great powers pitted against one another to a world of complex crises contained within uneasy peace or involving variable intensities of war fighting.

Although powered flight is less than a century old, the development of air power technology has dramatically influenced the conduct of contemporary warfare as it has enormous utility throughout the spectrum of conflict. It can operate independently of land and naval forces for strategic impact in tandem with diplomacy, sanctions or other forms of coercive pressure. Equally air power can contribute either directly or indirectly to the conduct of joint and multi-national operations.

Many commentators suggest that we are undergoing a 'revolution in military affairs', as we enter the information age. If we are to exploit this information and take the best advantage of the adaptability of air power, we may need to re-examine the military labels, concepts and doctrine of the Cold War era. But in so doing, we must learn the vital lessons of aviation history and not exaggerate our expectations of technology. We have to understand the limits of available and developing technology and that the future of air power will stand or fall not by promises and abstract theory, but by its relevance to political objectives and its ability to secure them at a cost affordable to the government of the day. So as we look forward to a complex and uncertain future, it behoves us to be realistic and careful in our claims and promises. Such is the setting for this book.

PERSPECTIVES ON AIR POWER

In 1994, my predecessor formed an air power workshop to examine the dynamics affecting air warfare. The result was 'The Dynamics of Air Power' first published in 1996, as a volume which broke new ground in our thinking. This companion volume sets the foundation for describing air power within the wider context of contemporary warfare – conflicts that now embrace the development of new concepts involving matters such as space, coalition warfare and legal issues.

The book has been developed from a series of workshops held in the Centre for Defence Studies, London, during 1997. I am grateful to the academics, independent analysts and military officers who have given so much of their time to the completion of this volume. Not everyone will agree with the views expressed, nor should opinions be taken as representing Ministry of Defence or Royal Air Force policy. Nevertheless, one of the primary aims of this volume is to stimulate debate, and discussion should not be limited to those whose job it is to apply air power – others with an interest in joint and combined operations must have their say if the issues are to be adequately discussed.

This book is a significant step forward in our thinking on contemporary air power and I commend it in equal measure to theorists, practitioners and commentators – and, indeed, to anyone interested in the study of armed conflict in general.

Richard Johns.

CONTENTS

Part 1

Political Context:

Part 2

Technological Context:

Part 3

Military Context:

LIST OF FIGURES

ILLUSTRATIONS

PERSPECTIVES ON AIR POWER

GENERAL INTRODUCTION

As the Chief of Air Staff makes clear in his foreword, although still less than a century old, air power has been one of the 'revolutions' in the way we conduct warfare. Now we see air and space power in all their manifestations being employed with great utility around the spectrum of conflict. In addition to its independent application for strategic impact or effect, air and space power can be decisive in support and the key enabler for any joint or combined intervention campaign or expeditionary operation.

And yet, theories and doctrines for air power remain largely in Cold War stasis. Theorists from the early days of the century made exaggerated claims for air power. Claims which created the controversies and baggage of the 1920s and 1930s on both sides of the Atlantic. Although air power made a significant and, on occasion, decisive contribution in all theatres of operation during World War II, the historical controversy surrounding the 'strategic' application of air power continues to excite comment and court controversy.

If air power was one of the first 'military technical revolutions' of this century, the advent of nuclear weapons was another. As the Cold War solidified into bipolar competition, air dropped and then air launched nuclear weapons dominated strategic thinking about air power. Meanwhile small wars went on in the retreat from Empire and the struggle for self-determination. Air power was employed around the globe outwith its perceived 'strategic' role, often using aircraft and weapons for roles and missions for which they were not designed.[1] By the time of the Gulf War, investments made in doctrine, organisation and weapon systems of increasing precision appeared to come together; promises could be fulfilled. But again we should be wary of exaggeration. In this world of complex emergencies, air power proponents take as their thesis that the technology inherent in what

---

1. See Max Hastings, 'The Korean War', London, Michael Joseph, 1995 and Mark Clodfelter, 'Vietnam, The Limits of Air Power', New York 1989 for surveys of the successes and failures of air power in Korea and Vietnam.

many call the 'Revolution in Military Affairs' will propel air and space power even more to the fore to make it the decisive force in the next century. The aim of this book is to place air power in its wider context as part of that debate.

The first volume in this series from the UK Chief of Air Staff's Air Power Workshop, addressed the dynamics at work in the doctrine and use of air power in conventional armed conflict and Peace Support Operations (PSO)[2]. This second volume goes further and attempts through a series of perspectives on issues of the moment to place air power in a political, military and technological context for the Millennium.

In Part I, 'The Political Context', Professor Michael Clarke of King's College, London, begins with an examination of the political context of the modern world and the use of force by and between states. This introductory chapter is more than a scene setter, it sets the whole book in its political context. The author shows how the processes of globalisation and interdependence affect our views of the world and shape the framework of complex emergencies which emerge from the fractures and fissures of intra-state conflict. In western democracies the interplay between the civil and political authorities and the military has always been a complex and at times opaque relationship. In Chapter Two, Dr David Gates looks at the enduring processes at work between the civilian and military authorities and examines how the twin pressures of instant communications systems and the advent of global media organisations are shaping and affecting our response to crisis and conflict. If conflict is becoming more complicated, so too are civil-military relations.

Chapter Three, examines coalition operations from an air power perspective. I look at coalitions which have been successful and some that have not. Several key trends emerge. Command and control arrangements need to be simple with as little overlap as possible. Pundits trade terms such as unity of command and unity of effort; a canter through recent campaigns suggests that neither are easy to achieve and can, on occasion, be misleading. Similar fashions extend to the use of the word interoperability. In terms of coalition operations, I extend the notion that interoperability applies to more than platforms, it is a much wider concept which encompasses cultural and doctrinal interoperability alongside the ability of aircraft to operate together or weapons systems to be employed to synergistic effect. If carefully nurtured, air power coalitions should be able to build on their inherent strengths of common training, doctrine, culture and procedures in a way that land and maritime forces find more difficult; moreover, as we turn to friends and allies the history of air power has developed differently in different nations.

---

2. See 'The Dynamics of Air Power', available via D Def S (RAF), defs-raf@netcomuk.co.uk.

Some see air power as an intrinsically strategic asset, whilst other nations – based on their history and experience – see air power in a different light; essentially in support of land or maritime operations. This chapter, and this section, concludes by offering paradigm for air coalition operations.

If coalitions offer political burden sharing for the exploitation of air power, nations also rely on the importance of the legal framework to ensure legitimacy for intervention in conflicts born of choice. In a ground breaking work in Chapter Four, Dr Adonis Kyriakides, a Cambridge PhD and independent member of the workshop, offers the reader a perspective on the legal framework for all air operations and the considerations for the commander and politician alike. This chapter is not aimed at the legal practitioner, rather to inform the general reader of how international air law has developed and the importance of legal considerations for any use of military force.

In Part II, we look at technology and air power. In Chapter Five, Air Vice-Marshal Professor Tony Mason examines the impact of the microprocessor on air power and associated systems. He postulates that by concentrating on small numbers of the 'right' systems, western nations can make air and space power a more flexible and adaptable instrument of military power for any future conflict. Whilst some commentators – notably outside the Washington Beltway – dispute that a 'Revolution in Military Affairs' is underway, few strategists and commentators would dispute that we live in an information age. In Chapter Six, Peter Emmett looks at air power and information age warfare. In a wide-ranging chapter, he examines both our reliance on commercially available data systems and our reliance upon software-driven technology to offer a thesis on the new economies of force for the next century.

The exploitation of space in support of military operations is a reality. In terms of communications, navigation and surveillance, space systems are ubiquitous; the weaponisation of space is, for some, just around the corner. In his chapter peeking into the future, General Jones outlines the sheer scale of investment in space and postulates that the sheer scale of corporate and commercial interest alone will mean we cannot ignore operations in and mounted from space in any discussion about the application of air and space power.

As the technology of air power expands to new heights of sophistication, the support and logistic requirements to sustain air power need equal prominence in our thinking and our doctrine. In Chapter Eight, Wing Commander David Foster explores the dynamics and complexities of 'fighting and stuff' and relates it to the wider context of deployed operations and complex emergencies to offer a useful paradigm for the future. Regardless of slogans such as 'just in time', agile combat support, or focused logistics, if we cannot support and sustain our intervention operations, they will surely fail.

Nor does this complexity end where diplomacy fails and military force is applied. The interdependence of the modern world applies in equal measure to the application of military force. Increasingly, nations work together in joint operations.

In Part III of the book, we turn to the wider context of the application of air power within the spectrum of conflict. Regardless of the size, shape or complexity of an illustrative model for conflict, few would argue that, as we approach the Millennium, the edges between concepts and doctrine have become blurred and messy. All strategic studies scholars agree, however, on the potential role for coercive action in intervention operations. In Chapter Nine, Dr Philip Sabin of King's College, London, puts the vital element of joint operations into the context of the application of air power and re-examines both the characteristics and the strengths and limitations of air power for the air element of joint operations. He offers a tentative paradigm for the future based firmly on the notion of three separate and independent services serving their specialist environment but in a complex and interdependent context. So if the political scene is set and the context for future operations is bounded, what of air power itself? Do the trends emerging from the Military Technological Revolution or Revolution in Military Affairs, justify the hype? In Chapter Ten, Group Captain Andrew Lambert develops his theory on the psychological impact of air power and builds a model for coercive effect using air power. He draws on post-Cold War examples to draw a distinction between military action for coercive effect and military action for denial.

In Chapter Eleven, Lieutenant Colonel Mark Bucknam explores the dilemma which has long teased the UK doctrine community – whither strategic air operations. As he states, the debate over strategic bombing is alive if not well. After a broad historical sweep across the canvas of strategic bombing, he discards the historical baggage in an attempt to define the characteristics to which the epithet strategic is applied. He leaves the reader with the notion that although the subject may not appear well, if we understand the problem we can, at least, treat the patient – the strategic application of air power is here to stay, whatever label we attach to it.

Finally in Chapter Twelve, Arthur Williamson a PhD student at Cambridge reminds us that the 'dragons' of future conflict are still out there. We can peek into the future and incorporate RMA concepts into future doctrine to underpin our procurement decisions, but the limitations which surround any application of military force, particularly in interventions born of choice and not necessity, must be offered to balance the equation. He does not offer solutions but leaves the reader with the breadth and complexity of the decisions which may lie ahead, for the practitioner and commentator alike.

Group Captain Stuart Peach, Director of Defence Studies (Royal Air Force), Joint Services Command Staff College, Bracknell, 1998

GLOSSARY

AAM	Air to Air Missile
AAR	Air to Air Refuelling
ADIZ	Air Defence Identification Zone
AI	Air Interdiction
ALCM	Air Launched Cruise Missile
AP	Air Publication
ARM	Anti-Radiation Missile
ASTOR	Airborne Stand-Off Radar
ATC	Air Traffic Control
ATO	Air Tasking Order
AWACS	Airborne Warning and Control System
BR	Book of Reference
BVR	Beyond Visual Range
BW	Biological Warfare
C2	Command and Control
C2W	Command and Control Warfare
C3	Command, Control and Communication
C3I	Command, Control, Communication and Intelligence
C4I	Command, Control, Communication, Computers and Intelligence
CAOC	Combined Air Operations Centre
CEP	Circular Error Probable
CFE	Central Forces Europe
CFE	Conventional Forces Europe
CJTF	Combined/Commander Joint Tasks Forces
COG	Centre(s) of Gravity
COIL	Chemical Oxygen-Iodine Laser
COMAO	Composite Air Operation
COS	Chief(s) of Staff
COTS	Commercial off the shelf
CTAPS	Contingency Theatre Automated Planning System
CW	Chemical Warfare
DoD	Department of Defense (US)

ECM	Electronic Counter Measures
EMP	Electro Magnetic Pulse
ESDI	European Security and Defence Identity
ESM	Electronic Support Measure
EW	Electronic Warfare
EZ	Exclusion Zone
FCO	Foreign and Commonwealth Office
FDI	Foreign Direct Investment
FLIR	Forward Looking Infra-Red
FMRAAM	Future Medium Range Air-to-Air Missile
FMS	Foreign Military Sales
GDP	Gross Domestic Product
GLONASS	Global Orbiting Navigation Satellite System
GNP	Gross National Product
GPS	Global Positioning System
GSM	Ground Support Module
HERF	High Energy Radio Frequency
I&W	Indicators and Warning
ICAO	International Civil Aviation Organization
ICJ	International Court of Justice
IFF	Identification Friend or Foe
INS	Inertial Navigation System
IR	Infra Red
IRST	Infra Red Search and Track
IW	Information Warfare
JDAM	Joint Direct Attack Munition
JFACC	Joint Force Air Component Commander
JSOW	Joint Stand Off Weapon
JTIDS	Joint Tactical Information Distribution System
JWID	Joint Warrior Interoperabilty Demonstration
LANTIRN	Low Altitude Navigation and Targeting Infra Red for Night
LOC	Lines of Communication
MAC	Military Air Command
MAD	Mutually Assured Destruction
MASINT	Measurements and Signature Intelligence
MOD	Ministry of Defence
MOOTW	Military Operations Other than War
MPA	Maritime Patrol Aircraft
MTCR	Missiles Technology Control Regime
MTI	Moving Target Indicator
NASA	North American Space Administration

NATO	North Atlantic Treaty Organisation
OB	Order of Battle
PGM	Precision Guided Munition
PJHQ	Permanent Joint Headquarters
PRC	People's Republic of China
PRO	Public Records Office
PSO	Peace Support Operation
QDR	Quadrennial Defence Review
RAAF	Royal Australian Air Force
RMA	Revolution in Military Affairs
ROE	Rules of Engagement
SACEUR	Supreme Allied Commander Europe
SAM	Surface to Air Missile
SAR	Search and Rescue
SDR	Strategic Defence Review
SEAD	Suppression of Enemy Air Defences
SHORAD	Short Range Air Defence
SLEP	Service Life Extension Programme
SMV	Space Manoeuvrable Vehicle
STARS	Surveillance Target Attack Radar System
STOVL	Short Take Off and Vertical Landing
SW	Software Warfare
SWA	South West Africa
TIALD	Thermal Imaging Airborne Laser Designator
TLAM	Tomahawk Land Attack Missile
TMD	Theatre Missile Defence
UAV	Uninhabited Aerial Vehicle
UCAV	Uninhabited Combat Aerial Vehicle
UN	United Nations
UNCLOS	United Nations Convention on the Law of the Sea
UNCOPUS	United Nations Committee on the Peaceful Use of Space
UNGA	United Nations General Assembly
UNPROFOR	United Nations Protection Force
UNSC	United Nations Security Council
UNSCR	United Nations Security Council Resolution
USAF	United States Air Force
USAAF	United States Army Air Force
WWI/II	World War I/II
WEU	Western European Union
WMD	Weapons of Mass Destruction

ABSTRACTS

Chapter 1- Threats and Challenges in the UK's Security Environment –
    Professor M Clarke
Britain is safer today from threats of invasion or from the prospect of having to
fight a war for survival than at any time since a recognisable nation state existed in
these islands. It is however, faced with multiple challenges to the security of the
international order from which this comfortable international position is now
derived. Such challenges pose uniquely difficult choices for policy-makers and
range over instabilities of modern Europe and Asia, to the problems of economic
security for a state such as Britain in an international environment subject to globalisation. In these circumstances, UK Defence Policy is characterised by a high
degree of discretion and choice; it is no longer driven by the imperatives of a
need to defend western Europe from a full scale land attack and all three Armed
Services are facing major reappraisals of their role in a defence policy that will
henceforth be far more a servant to foreign policy. Air power thus, has to be cast
in a political context that is far more sensitive and volatile than in the past. This
raises uncomfortable questions for UK air power theorists concerning the
complexities of multinational operations, the costs of remaining interoperable
with US forces, the role of UK forces in a European context and the question of
maintaining an indigenous strategic role for the RAF itself. Prudence may dictate
traditional answers to such questions; but they cannot remain unaddressed.

Chapter 2 – Air Power and aspects of Civil-Military Relations –
    Dr D Gates
Relations between a state's armed forces and its civil power have always been
convoluted. Armed services reflect the societies that give rise to them, with
changes in the latter inevitably spawning changes in the former, both in their
equipment and ethos. As this chapter seeks to explain, whilst a comparatively new
product of technological advance and particularly dependent upon it, military
air power is acquired, maintained and employed in an environment where

political, economic, socio-cultural and legal factors have also always been of immense importance. Just as the general nature of human society is becoming more complex, so too is the specific issue of military-civil relations.

Chapter 3 – Coalition Air Operations –
Gp Capt S W Peach
Most western nations plan to engage in conflict with allies. Coalition warfare is not a new trend for air power. Air power has always been employed in coalition. In this Chapter, Group Captain Peach examines the definitions and concepts which underlie coalition warfare before looking at the experience of air power in a number of coalition conflicts. From this historical overview, certain trends emerge: simple command and control mechanisms, shared and common views on the end-state for any given operations and a real understanding of the need for interoperability. Above all, however, to succeed in coalition warfare, the essential glue is trust.

Chapter 4 – Air Power and International Air Law –
Dr K A Kyriakides
The central objective of this chapter is to analyse the impact of certain aspects of International Air Law upon air power. To this end, it considers inter alia how air power is affected by the principles of state sovereignty over national airspace and the territorial sea, the uncertainty over the legal definition of the boundary between national/terrestrial airspace and outer space, and the laws regarding the overflight of foreign states by military aircraft. The chapter also summarises the area of international law concerning the inherent right of self-defence, particularly with respect to the interception of intruding military and civil aircraft.

Chapter 5 – The Technology Interaction –
Air Vice-Marshal Professor R A Mason
The impact of the microprocessor in the last generation on information gathering, communications and precision attack has enhanced all air power's traditional roles, enabling them to adapt effectively to the changed circumstances of the post Cold War world. At the same time, surface to air and surface to surface missiles have also benefited. Now, even the richest countries are being compelled to identify the most effective coordination of manned aircraft and uninhabited aerial vehicles (UAVs). With the advent of satellite information and communications and the proliferation of surface to surface missiles, air power has become aerospace power. As the advanced systems become more easily accessible to many states, albeit in smaller numbers, technological superiority will not be a luxury,

but essential in expeditionary and other operations mounted by the Atlantic Community and friends, to offset numerical inferiority, accessibility or vulnerability. The cumulative impact of the new technology is to make aerospace power, on the threshold of the new century, a politically attractive, most cost effective and highly adaptable instrument.

Chapter 6 – Air Power in the Information Age –
    Sqn Ldr P Emmett
The roots of military change in the Information Age involve a new economics of force which draws its primary strength from the computer, including its embedded forms, and from software. More does not equal better in this new era. The aim should be to discover what counts in the moments of danger, and using effective communications, to be capable of operating with minimal information. This requires efficient and adaptable exploitation of the software engine of military technologies. Unless checked, the habits of technological overkill which developed during the Cold War will progressively disadvantage the West as others exploit the new economics of force with greater agility.

Chapter 7 – Air Power in the Space Age –
    Maj Gen W E Jones
As we approach the 21st Century, it becomes increasingly apparent that Space represents a fundamental security commitment that will continue to grow in importance. The international security implications of space exploitation will have significant influence on the expansion of military operations, which leads the author to conclude that space warfare will become reality in the 21st Century. The correlation between the evolution of military space and that of the aeroplane is significant. Dominance of space and the ability to survey across a theatre of operations has evolved to the point of providing a legitimate alternative in the military application of force. This chapter seeks to demonstrate that the degree to which air forces remain relevant in the 21st Century, may be determined by their use within the whole spectrum of interests that influence the socio-economic well-being of a nation. As a result, air power theory must be revised to integrate Space as a continuum of air operations and this may require a fundamental revision of the principals that have underwritten the provision and execution of air forces since the 1940s.

Chapter 8 – Air Operations and Air Logistics –
   Wg Cdr D Foster
Logistics is pivotal in all military operations. When coordination of operations and logistics works it is unseen and unremarkable; failure, on the other hand, highlights the operational cost of shortage and delay – often generating more heat than light, as hurried analysis of mere symptoms is used to apportion blame. In an attempt to focus on the causes and stimulate more measured debate, Wing Commander David Foster examines the fundamentals of the partnership between operations and logistics. He isolates the basic factors that influence effective coordination and draws out principles that may usefully inform the design and operation of future logistic systems.

Chapter 9 – Air Power in Joint Warfare –
   Dr. P Sabin
Technological trends are making 'air power' increasingly difficult to define in this era of 'jointery', but aerospace systems ranging from helicopters to cruise missiles still deserve at least some degree of distinct analytical considerations. They can make several generic contributions to the joint campaign, in terms of observation, interception, surface attack, transport and support. How large a role they will play compared to surface forces depends on a wide variety of factors, including political context, the nature of both sides' military capabilities and the nature of the battle area. A key requirement, especially in air-land warfare, is to ensure that the combination of surface and aerospace forces produces synergy rather than interference. The command and control of the various aerospace assets is very important in this regard, and one must strike the right balance in each case between centralisation and decentralisation and between specialisation and integration. Even if unmanned aerospace systems attain greater prominence in the future, there will still be a very strong case for all three Services to retain their identity within an increasingly joint framework.

Chapter 10 – Air Power and Coercion – An Analysis –
   Gp Capt A P N Lambert
Sceptics will, no doubt, find plenty of reasons why the threatened use of air power against Iraq in February 1998 was immaterial to Saddam Hussein's compliance. The West was actually being manipulated by Saddam. Bombing was hardly persuasive compared with the relaxation of UN sanctions. This was a 'cry wolf' stratagem and, once the West departs, he will resume his delinquency. There are always many reasons to doubt the efficacy of coercion, because it is difficult to interpret the pressures from the perception of the coerced. In reality

however, it only matters if both the coercer believes it to be efficacious and the victim finds coercion a factor in his compliance. This chapter analyses the dynamics at work in the coercive process and offers practical advice for those wishing to employ the full panoply of coercive tools.

Chapter 11 – Strategic Bombing: What is it and is it Still Relevant ? –
   Lt Col M A Bucknam USAF
Debates about strategic bombing are currently alive, if not well. The lack of consensus over the term 'strategic', and disagreements over what separates strategic bombing from other bombing operations, often hinder intelligent debate. As an aid to clear thinking on this subject, Lieutenant Colonel Mark Bucknam presents a broad historical context for understanding strategic bombing. He then goes on to address the continuities and changes in the practice and thinking on the subject. Next, he focuses on the defining characteristics of strategic bombing, and he ends the chapter with a discussion on the future relevance of these characteristics for operations.

Chapter 12 – Challenges Facing Military Power –
   Mr A Williamson
In his chapter, 'Challenges Facing Military Power', Mr Williamson discusses problems which might face the military in the future, be it in humanitarian operations, peace keeping and enforcement roles or war. The sub-title, 'Beyond this place there be Dragons', is a metaphor for the new and as yet unknown hazards which may be awaiting the unwary or unthinking in future conflicts. The chapter does not attempt to offer solutions, but it does suggest that knowledge of past experience can be useful and that air power can offer some unique capabilities to the military.

ACKNOWLEDGEMENTS

In the process of putting this book together, the help and co-operation of the following people has been very much appreciated: for help with the photographs we are grateful to Chris Hobson, Librarian of the Joint Services Command Staff College, to Graham Ford and colleagues for the artwork and graphics and to the Media Services staff at Headquarters Personnel and Training Command for the cover design. Our thanks go also to Group Captain Andrew Lambert who, as the previous Director Defence Studies (RAF), started this project and to Sue Hutchinson for her efficiency in dealing with a myriad of day to day tasks in support of this project. We also wish to thank Squadron Leader Robert Hopkin for acting as a most efficient and effective Secretary to the Air Power Workshops to 'pin' authors down to deadlines and to respect the content of the discussions. Many thanks to all those who have participated in the Workshops, adding invaluable contributions to the concepts and thoughts which have helped to create this book. Last, and above all, a special thank you to Flight Lieutenant Jenny Lynch who has been tireless in her efforts at compiling this volume, liaising with authors, sponsors and printers. Without her unstinting efforts, the process would have surely faltered.

PART I

POLITICAL CONTEXT

CHAPTER 1

THREATS AND CHALLENGES IN THE UK's SECURITY ENVIRONMENT
Professor Michael Clarke

THINKING ABOUT DEFENCE POLICY

THE WAY IN WHICH THE UK has to think about its defence policy has changed rapidly in recent years. Elements of continuity are important and unavoidable. Indeed, in a world of independent sovereign states, some elements of defence policy may appear to be immutable. In a condition of anarchy, where there is no central authority over states in the international system, the possibilities of war between one and another must necessarily always be present.[1] But however true this is in a philosophical sense, it is not much help to defence planners when their international world has changed as much as the UK's has over the last decade. At the practical level of the defence planner, even the first principles of defence policy are now difficult to specify. They certainly cannot be deduced through some self-evident equation.

In these circumstances, defence planners must therefore keep in mind the possibilities of having to fight a major war for survival, but they have to accord it an appropriate priority within a framework that makes many competing demands. The definition of 'an appropriate priority' is an entirely political question. The many 'competing demands' arise out of the international environment of the post-Cold War era and the place that the UK tries to occupy within it. The latter element of this side of the equation is also an entirely political consideration.

Thus, the UK faces a world in which there are few threats but many challenges. To be more specific, the country faces a situation where the existential threat of having to fight a war for the survival of the homeland still exists; in an 'anarchical' world it could not be otherwise. But that threat is distant and, in present circumstances, constitutes a low risk. On the other hand, the UK faces a world in which there are many security challenges in which it may want to employ its defence policy as a major instrument of governmental power.

---

1. The best expression of the condition of 'internal anarchy' is still to be found in, Hedley Bull, *The Anarchical Society*, London, Macmillan, 1977.

Defence decisions will, therefore, be highly discretionary for perhaps the next 10 to 20 years. Governments will feel they have more genuine choices to make over whether, and how, to employ the armed forces than they had during the Cold War. The UK will probably not have to deploy or fight anywhere. But it will almost certainly choose to do so for broader foreign and security policy purposes. This was explicitly foreshadowed in the 1995 and 1996 *Statements on the Defence Estimates* which stated that defence policy is 'designed to support this wider security policy'[2] and that 'our interests are best promoted by the use of a wide range of political, trade and cultural as well as military tools... the use of our armed forces has to be considered alongside, and interwoven with, the use of other instruments.'[3] It was also an assumption clearly articulated in the launching of the Strategic Defence Review in May 1997.[4]

If such statements appear to be no more than recognitions of a simple truth in present circumstances, they nevertheless raise difficult and vital questions over precisely how we should define the declining level of threat, and the increasing incidence of challenges, which might require the use of Armed Forces as part of a UK response.

THREATS TO THE UNITED KINGDOM

All governments must take responsibility for the protection of the country over which they preside; it is one of the basic tests of sovereignty (that a territory has a government which regards itself as having such a responsibility) and of governmental authority (that those claiming to represent government have some practical ability to offer protection over the territory).[5] It is also true that defence planners must try to keep in mind, not worst case scenarios (after all a worst case scenario for the UK would be massive, sudden aggression against this country

---

2. Statement on the Defence Estimates 1995, Cm 2800, London HMSO, 1995, para 202.

3. Statement on the Defence Estimates 1996, Cm 3223, London HMSO 1996, para 102.

4. George Robertson, 'Britain's Defence: Securing Our Future Together', Ministry of Defence Press Release 055/97, 28 May 1997.

5. Many governments do not have the military capacity adequately to defend their own country, and many others who do have reasonable capacity would nevertheless fail if put to a severe test. The importance of this observation, however, is that governments must have some military and/or political ability to offer a level of protection that the population regards as tolerable. If a government's capacity to offer physical protection is perceived to fall below this level then alternative governments, or sub-state groups, are likely to gain popular legitimacy if they can prove themselves capable of offering – by whatever means – more acceptable protection.

from the USA!), but all *credible* eventualities that might threaten the country. Even in a time of general peace, therefore, it is important to consider first, what it is we assume must be defended when we speak of 'our country' or 'the United Kingdom'; and second, which developments in the international environment might have a bearing on our attempts to defend that entity.

Threats to the essential integrity of the United Kingdom should be seen not so much as threats to the territory of the UK or its Dependent Territories, as much as threats to some essential sense of a 'way of life'. After all, if Scots, Welsh or Ulster residents of the UK voted unambiguously for independence, then the Government in London would never fight to keep a united kingdom. Losing territory is not the issue, rather it is *how and why* territory may be lost. Equally, when there seemed to be no alternative to a war with Nazi Germany in 1939, it was not because Hitler threatened the territory of the UK directly (quite the reverse, since he stressed he had no quarrel with Britain and wanted only to be left a free hand in Europe) but rather because he threatened to create a continent that would be deeply antithetical to the British interpretation of freedom, order and development. In other words, though territory is often bound up with the sense of a country's 'way of life', it is not, at least for the British, the essence of the issue. Nor do the British have disputed borders with other neighbouring countries,[6] or significant national minorities from nearby states. Britain's immigrant communities are from the New Commonwealth rather than any unstable part of Europe, and very little that happens in New Commonwealth countries has a major domestic political impact within Britain. Germany, Italy or France, in contrast, can be critically affected via their immigrant communities by events in the Balkans, Turkey or North Africa.

The essence of what the UK wants to protect, therefore, is a mixture, firstly, of some sense of physical safety for residents of this county and the Dependent Territories, and secondly, the preservation of a way of life that is the free choice of these people. Both characteristics are highly impressionistic and impossible to measure. If we lost to foreign terrorists the 4000 or more people we lose in road accidents each year, there would be a political outcry; if we had taken from us the power to exercise governmental autonomy that we now voluntarily give to the European Union, we would probably consider ourselves oppressed; and if a foreign power had made life in the Dependent Territory of Montserrat as difficult as the Soufrie volcano has over the last two years, we would probably consider our

---

6. Disputes over Gibraltar and the Falkland Islands with neighbouring countries (Spain and Argentina) to those Dependent Territories are over their whole political/legal status, not their appropriate territorial boundaries.

honour to be at stake in helping the population of the island. In short, our essential interests that might be under threat, at any given time, are not a matter of logical deduction but rather a process of political perception.

In this respect, the threats to the UK's essential integrity that can be credibly postulated for the next twenty years are a mixture of the distant, the peripheral and the exotic. The distant threat is of a major war against a resurgent Russia. Ignoring what, even in the worst case, the motives of a 'resurgent Russia' could be, Russian military capacities are still considerable but certainly insufficient to launch a major war against the whole of Europe. A resurgent Russia at war within some part of Europe is conceivable, but not a Russia adopting the military objectives of the Soviet-led Warsaw Pact of the Cold War era, where the only plan that made military sense was to attempt a Blitzkrieg across Europe to expel the US from the continent and occupy (among others) the UK, to prevent the US getting back.[7] If Russia became involved in a regional war in Europe, the UK might be involved as part of an allied stand, but this would not be for the sake of our territorial integrity, or even to prevent – as in 1939 – a hostile power dominating Europe. Russian capacities, let alone motives, cannot credibly run that far in the coming era.[8] Moreover, all credible scenarios of Russian economic and military growth imply a long warning period, should these assumptions change. The UK would have some considerable time to address a 'resurgent Russia' which posed a threat to the UK's essential integrity if such a scenario should begin to unfold. At the very least, this means that readiness criteria can be relaxed, certainly in the eventuality of all-out war with Russia. The 'resurgent Russia' threat cannot be entirely ruled out, if only because geography determines that Russia is Europe's territorial superpower, and history determines that relations have been predominantly antagonistic for most of the Twentieth Century. But for the moment this threat must be regarded as a distant prospect.

The peripheral threats to the essential integrity of the UK can be classed as the prospects of ballistic missile attack on the country from those powers who have, or will have, the capability to deliver nuclear, chemical or biological warheads with missiles of a sufficient range. These are presently the US, Russia, and, within

---

7. On the thinking behind this plan, and the lack of sensible alternatives for the Soviet Union, see Michael MccGwire, *Military Objectives in Soviet Foreign Policy*, Washington DC, The Brookings Institution, 1987.

8. Even on the optimistic assumption of a 4% annual growth rate from 2000 to 2015, Russia would still only achieve a GDP of about $1000 billion (in 1996 prices) at the end of that time; about the present, 1997, GDP level for the UK. Any major new investment in military capacities (ie in the context of a 'resurgent' leadership) over that period would detract from the 4% level of annual growth, so diminishing the infrastructure for military development, and so on.

a twenty year time scale, certainly China; perhaps one or more Gulf state (Iran, Saudi Arabia, perhaps Iraq) one North African state (Libya) which may upgrade its missile capacity sufficiently, and perhaps a South Asian state such as India.[9] This list, however, only refers to capabilities. It is very difficult to think of a credible scenario in which a direct ballistic WMD attack on the UK would make any political or military sense, except as a peripheral (though dire) response to some other international crisis that had gone horribly wrong and in which the UK was involved. Again, the possibilities certainly cannot be ruled out and appropriate responses – perhaps some measures of ballistic missile defence, political initiatives to strengthen global non-proliferation, perhaps deterrent postures – might be considered prudent. But none of these possibilities can be rated as a credible, central threat to the integrity of the UK, since this sort of attack could not be regarded as fulfilling any core military purpose for the attacker.

Other threats to the essential interests of the UK could best be described as exotic; that is, possibilities arising in the international sphere that are not traditionally associated with the defence of the realm, but which in the next century might have the potential to undermine significant aspects of Britain's 'way of life' or put at physical risk large sections of the population. Such exotic threats might be the growth of international crime – transiting in and out of the country and using Britain as a base – to such a level that it undermined major institutions or aspects of the British social system; the prospect of persistent environmental catastrophes which compromised agricultural production and British public safety – such as three or four Chernobyl-type nuclear disasters in Europe in quick succession; the possibility of determined terrorist attacks that attempted to cause mass destruction through, for example, the poisoning of water supplies, or surprise biological attacks using the food processing industry. All such exotic threats would have to be posed at levels of magnitude greater than anything so far experienced, and the threat of them would have to be sustained over a period for such eventualities to threaten 'way of life' values or widespread public safety. Nevertheless, they are imaginable and cannot be ruled out.[10] So too, the less exotic but disturbing prospect of a straight breakdown of social order in Britain from within. This could arise perhaps from a combination of mobilised, disaffected minorities,

---

9. Longer term possibilities also include Pakistan, Israel and Syria. See 'Defence: Circles of Fear', *The Economist*, 4 January 1997. See also, David G Weincek, 'Dynamic Arsenals: Missile Threats in and From Asia', Bailrigg Memorandum 22, Lancaster, CDISS, 1997, and Aaron Karp, *Ballistic Missile Proliferation: The Politics and Technics*, Oxford, OUP, 1996.

10. See, David Mepham and Edmund Cairns, 'Security, Inclusion and Defence', *Brassey's Defence Yearbook 1998*, London, Centre of Defence Studies/Brassey's, 1998.

overwhelmed and inadequate policing, a political crisis and major exacerbating economic adjustments or failures. Again, to be credible this scenario would require most of these determinants to be present simultaneously, and for a sustained period.

All such scenarios remain 'exotic' but they are not unimportant, because in reality the population of the UK tends to believe in the relevance of some parts of all of them. International crime is disturbing, the environment is under greater stress, domestic law and order appears to be more precarious, terrorists seem to devise ever more frightening strategies, and so on.[11] In this way, at least, they affect our perception of the British way of life and our view – as taxpayers – of what matters to our personal security. We cannot rule out the prospect that such concerns could become politically obsessive in some circumstances.

Such an analysis of the threat to the UK's essential interests leads to two particular conclusions. Firstly, such threats are not absent, but they are harder to define than at any time in Britain's modern history and since they are distant, peripheral or exotic, no one of them conveys the same imperative as any of the other threats to our essential interests that have arisen during the Twentieth Century. Great Britain, as a country, has never been so safe, at least from external forces. Secondly, in so far as we should accord these threats 'an appropriate priority' in our defence planning, it is not immediately clear what they mean for the majority of the armed forces. Distant threats do not require immediately ready war fighting capabilities for the defence of the country; peripheral threats suggest that ballistic missile defence and/or a deterrent posture and/or a vigorous international arms control policy may be the most appropriate response; and exotic threats suggest that the armed forces can barely be employed at all, unless their roles are radically redefined.

CHALLENGES FOR THE UNITED KINGDOM

If it is difficult to specify threats to the UK with any precision, it is all too easy to offer a long list of potential challenges to the UK's predominantly favourable security environment. The spectre of global general war has receded while the prospect of global disorder and localised conflict looms ever larger. The most relevant potential instabilities suggest themselves readily enough.

---

11. *Gallup Political Index*, published monthly, regularly reports surveys about what concerns the public most or how much they fear for their personal safety.

Within our own continent, the prospects in South Eastern Europe are for continuing conflict, perhaps still in Bosnia, but certainly in the southern part of Former Yugoslavia in Kosovo and possibly Albania, over the future of Macedonia, and possibly involving Greece and Turkey, whose multiple quarrels in the Eastern Mediterranean and Aegean have been escalating for some time.

A series of lesser instabilities exists within what might be termed 'Hungarian Europe' – the 3.5 million Hungarian nationals who find themselves, after the collapse of empire, in neighbouring countries. The 2.6 million in Rumania and Southern Slovakia are of particular importance since they maintain a definite national identity and are concentrated in certain areas. Tensions have lessened over these two communities in the last four years and the Hungarian government has embarked on a series of constructive initiatives, but the minorities still represent a potential nationalist card that can be played by politicians in any of the 'host' countries or in Hungary itself. The Russian littoral states, and regions within the Russian Federation itself – for example in the Transcaucasus – pose a series of potential instabilities. The nationalist reverberations of the collapse of the Soviet Empire are still being felt throughout the continent, and a Russia that is antagonised by NATO expansion, feels pressured or moves to consolidate a natural 'sphere of influence' in its 'near abroad' in anticipation of an expanded NATO, may become embroiled in any number of disputes around its borders. The contemporary problem for the West is not so much trying to guess at a Russian strategy so much as trying to cope with a transitional Russia that has very little strategy at all in its external field.[12] For the West Europeans, Russian-generated crises in the three Baltic States or within Ukraine would represent the most dangerous challenges to their present security environment; as indeed would purely indigenous crises in any of these states.

Crises in North Africa also pose important challenges for the Europeans. Certainly, France, Spain and Italy have greater security concerns to their South than their East and the orientation of their defence policies reflects this. As the escalating crisis in Algeria since 1992 has demonstrated, the Europeans can apparently avoid direct involvement in North Africa, but a general destabilisation of the region, occasioned by the growing crisis of governability in a number of states, can affect the security of the Mediterranean in general.

A factor in the crisis potential of all these areas might be termed the 'overlaying conditions'; developments that are not crises in themselves but which have the

---

12. Vladimir Baranovsky, ed, *Russia and Europe: The Emerging Security Agenda,* Oxford, OUP, 1997, pp 543-554.

power to exacerbate any given crisis, give them a tendency to spill over from one area to another, or to be more difficult to address. Such conditions include environmental stress, over-rapid population growth, uncontrolled migration, crises of governmental authority and/or state collapse, economic breakdown, disinvestment and growing exclusion from the mainstream international economy. It so happens, for example, that the small states most at risk from political insecurity in South East Europe – Serbia, Bosnia, Albania, Macedonia, and not excluding Rumania and Bulgaria – are also facing major economic insecurities. Their security problems are politically driven, but it is no coincidence that they are also some of the economic basket cases of Europe. The societies most at risk in North Africa are subject to demographic pressures, environmental refugees moving into cities which cannot cope, and governmental crises over economic distribution. Despite its superpower status and further potential, Russia itself suffers from a potent mixture of almost all of these factors; economic breakdown, a protracted crisis of government, demographic imbalance as the Southern and Asiatic populations of the Federation burgeon, environmental stresses and a black economy that hinders all attempts to integrate Russia more fully into the Western economic system. All such factors should be included in any analysis of the potential instabilities facing Europe for the next twenty or so years.

Beyond Europe, the UK will be concerned about potential instabilities in the Middle East. Crises or regional wars in this area pose less of a direct problem to the UK itself than to its allies. Indeed, as an oil producer, the UK stands to benefit from a relative advantage in any crisis or war that creates pressure on oil supplies. But partly because of the sensitivity of oil, and for other more politicised reasons, the Middle East carries a high value in allied and 'world order' terms. Any instability that threatens oil supplies poses a genuine short-term problem for the western world. The Gulf and the Arab-Israeli dispute have become more interlinked in recent years than ever before and to this must now be added the politics of West Asia – Russia, Kazakhstan and Transcaucasia – as a factor in Gulf politics, affecting Iran, Iraq, Turkey and oil pipeline routes into Western and Southern Europe.[13]

The UK will also feel an interest in stability in South and East Asia, not because it can be directly affected by any given political crisis in the area, but because of the sheer scale of the impact that major instability in South and East Asia could have on the states of the West. In armed conflicts between 1945 and

---

13. See, Elaine Holoboff, 'Russia's Strategic Pipelines', *Brassey's Defence Yearbook 1997*, London, Centre for Defence Studies/Brassey's, 1997.

1994, for example, Central, South and East Asia have accounted for over 13 million fatalities – almost three times more than the 4.4 million occasioned by conflicts in all other regions of the world combined. Within that Asian total, Central and South Asia accounted for 2.8 million deaths and East Asia for 10.4 million.[14] The environmental stresses of Indian and Chinese industrialisation, as it develops, and the effects it will have both on their immediate neighbours and on the wider ecology is a further factor likely to add both to regional instability and global management concerns. With 40% of the world's population living in South and East Asia, major economic crises in the region have the power to induce a world economic recession. A widespread political or social collapse in China alone, because of the sheer scale of the consequences, would affect European countries in a variety of volatile ways.[15] The UK is unlikely to antici-pate any significant military responses to instability in South and East Asia – certainly not as a defence planning assumption – but the region has to feature in this country's security equation and the prospects of a military response cannot be entirely ruled out, if a capacity were anyway available and if there seemed to be a compelling political advantage in such a reaction.[16]

Beyond such regionally-based calculations, the security challenges faced by the UK also include its economic status and future prospects within the globalised economy. The UK has a more genuinely 'international' economy than most. In absolute GDP terms it remains the fifth or sixth largest in the world with an output of over $1,014 billion.[17] It is strong in service industries, oil and high tech-nology. In comparison with Germany, for example, where home companies raise money directly from German banks – often with bankers sitting on company boards – industry in the UK raises most of its capital on the London stock market. That stock market quotes some 3000 companies which account for 30% of the UK's GNP (Frankfurt quotes 600 companies which account for 10% of Germany's GNP), while the UK remains second only to the US as the world's biggest recipient of all foreign direct investment (FDI). In 1996 the UK was host

---

14. Figures taken from, International Institute for Strategic Studies, *The Military Balance 1997*, London, IISS, 1997. These figures have also been derived from *World Military and Social Expenditures 1996*, Washington DC, World Priorities Inc, 1996.

15. Robert B Zoellick, 'Economics and Security in the Changing Asia Pacific', *Survival*, 39(4), Winter 1997-98.

16. An interesting case for the UK could be the event of a breakdown of order, creating a 'complex political emergency' in North Korea whereby the US looked for an allied response in a peace support operation.

17. Official OECD figures. In GDP per capita terms, or in terms of output competitiveness, however, the UK is ranked somewhere between 12th and 20th in the world.

to some 40% of all FDI into the European Union and, thanks to £3 billion of Japanese investment, was the fastest growing car producer in the Union.[18] Not least, the City of London, fortuitously straddling all the time zones of the world, played host in 1997 to 429 foreign banks, less than half of them European.[19]

All of this speaks of a country that is a significant – if no longer a structural – economic player in the world, characterised by a depth of foreign economic penetration and balanced by a growing financial outreach: a country that has a major stake in international economic growth and a liberal world trading regime; a country that both benefits and suffers to a disproportionate extent from the booms and recessions of the global economy. How far these characteristics can be affected by political instabilities around the world depends on the way the world's economy evolves in the coming decade. If the crisis of the Asian economies indicates that 'directed' state-centric capitalism – of the sort practised in most Asian countries – has reached its limits in this 'information age', then the prospects for the UK economy might be considered generally secure; it would be at the leading edge of a trend towards more porous economies and might derive some economic security from the opening of information markets in the Asian tigers. If, on the other hand, the crisis encourages economic retrenchment in Asia and recession on a global scale, then the UK will be more economically insecure than most.

Beyond questions of economic security, it remains an open question whether the rapid growth of globalisation in the world economy will encourage or suppress military interventions. It may be that the international market will help demilitarise crises by finding economic ways to circumvent the disruptions caused by political instability and punish regions of insecurity by its failure to invest. But it is equally possible that the interdependence of the world economy and the ubiquity of information and the media, though it might discourage full scale war, could nevertheless create greater incentives to small scale military interventions, in the name of conflict prevention, crisis management, reassuring allies or safe-guarding some of the world's common goods. Globalisation is still too novel a phenomenon to make a judgement on this issue. Similarly, it remains to be seen whether the UK will prove to be more vulnerable than its European partners to the possibilities of information warfare (IW).[20] All that is certain is that if IW can

---

18. R Starkes, 'Investment in the UK, 1997', *Direct Foreign Prospective Investors in Britain*, London, Department of Trade and Industry, 1997, pp 4-5.

19. *The Banker/Financial Times*, 27 November 1997, p 8.

20. Andrew Rathmell, 'Information Warfare', *Brassey's Defence Yearbook 1998*, London Centre for Defence Studies/Brassey's 1998. See also Chapter 6, 'Air Power in the Information Age' by Squadron Leader P Emmett.

be directed at major national economic structures, then the UK stands to lose some important economic assets in the City, the service industries, the milieu that attracts FDI and within so many internationalised information systems centred in the UK.

THE INTENSITY OF THE CHALLENGES

Though all this creates an atmosphere of great uncertainty for British defence planners, there is some comfort in the opportunity to rate the intensity of these threats and challenges to the UK, at least to the point that we can ask what is at stake in any given case. The UK is less threatened in a military sense than almost any of its partners save for the US itself. It faces many challenges to its presently benign international environment, possibly in the economic sphere, in which it is more exposed than most of its partners. But it also faces a catalogue of challenges in more politicised ways that might suggest a military response. But since the direct threat level is low, the UK therefore has unprecedented discretion over how it might employ its forces to meet any of the likely security challenges of the next two decades. If intervention in future armed conflicts will be more a matter of choice than necessity, then it is possible to define a number of motives which might weigh in any choice.

One motive to become militarily involved might be the danger of ripple effects stemming from a crisis itself. Economic ripple effects from crises in the Gulf or East Asia are not difficult to imagine, and while military expeditions have the capacity to become part of the problem and further damage an economy, there might be cases where the reassurance and commitment implied by a military intervention would do much to maintain political confidence. In 1991, for example, the opening of the air war against Iraq, far from sending the oil price rocketing and stock markets tumbling, as had been widely predicted, actually contributed to an oil price and stock market stabilisation, since it promised to be the beginning of the end of the crisis.[21] The most obvious form of ripple effect from an area of instability is a flow of refugees and uncontrolled migration. This is a major incentive for many European countries in reacting to crises in South Eastern Europe, but it is not a strong pressure on the UK given its distinctive pattern of immigration.

---

21. Lawrence Freedman and Efraim Karsh, *The Gulf Conflict 1990-1991*, London, Faber, 1993, p 343.

A second motive for military involvement is the need to maintain allied unity and to support the UK's partners. This is a strong motive since the UK has invested a great deal of political capital since 1945 in fostering collective defence responses among the transatlantic community. The NATO alliance represents an excellent vehicle for British diplomacy that gives the country a military influence far in excess of that it would have individually. Allied unity is important to the UK; more so since the transatlantic relationship is manifestly undergoing an important evolution. The UK is also developing closer military links with non-NATO countries both inside and outside Europe. The demonstrable skill of the UK's armed forces in contingencies since 1990, the desire to look for non-American military partners, and the benefits of the use of English – an official language now in 60 countries – has led a number of non-European countries to explore the possibilities of training and co-operation with the UK. The trend for the UK, particularly with the enlargement of NATO and the evolution of its military role, is towards more military partnerships with a wider range of countries. Though none of these should be classed as alliances, they may increase the motives to involvement where a partnership is developing.

A third motive is to contribute to the upholding of regional or world order. This has always been overtly a part of the rationale of UK defence policy and has grown in importance over recent years. The Labour Government elected in May 1997 made it clear from the outset that it intended to pursue an internationalist foreign and defence policy, one that would have a clear 'ethical dimension' and which would give the UK the ability 'to make a difference' in the world. The UK could not behave like a 'global power', but it could be perceived to make a useful – perhaps disproportionate – 'contribution globally'.[22]

A fourth motive is the UK's intention to maintain its permanent seat on the United Nations Security Council, its 'P5 status'. This, too, has increased in relative importance as the composition of the Security Council has become politically sensitive at the UN since 1996. With the prospect that the status of the P5 might be altered, or at least diluted, and given the manifest over-representation of the Europeans on it at present, it is in the interests of the UK to demonstrate that it is more than just a useful member of the UN but rather, one of its core actors. This implies that there will be an increasing incentive for the UK to play its military card in UN missions in the future, since this represents an area of comparative advantage. In particular, the provision of technical military

---

22. See, for example, the speech by the Prime Minister 'The Principles of a Modern British Foreign Policy', 10 November 1997, Foreign and Commonwealth Office, Verbatim Service VS15/97.

support and specialist skills is at a premium in most UN field operations, and few countries can provide them. Among the Europeans, only the UK and France have a wide range of specialist military skills, and though the political price of P5 membership may be expected to increase, their military currency is also being steadily revalued by trends in post-Cold War conflicts.

A final motive is that the UK may become militarily engaged for the sake of altruism, for humanitarian reasons, in response to public opinion and/or to foster a favourable image of the UK abroad. These motives have certainly been powerful since the early-1990s and may continue to be so, but it is not automatic. Public opinion is generally volatile over foreign expeditions (though more supportive in the UK than politicians usually acknowledged over interventions in Bosnia[23] and the media's interest is sporadic. So far, there have been 18 recognised 'complex emergencies' since 1989, defined by the United Nations as a situation where government has collapsed and international action is desirable or urgent.[24] There is every indication that the incidence of such emergencies will grow. But it is not at all certain that the world's media, or the public in the UK, will focus on subsequent cases as much as it has in the past. Nevertheless, humanitarian altruism, the force of public opinion and a powerful media interest can, in the present era of ubiquitous public information, 'kick in' to a policy-making process quickly and powerfully; even though it may just as easily separate itself from policy if conditions change. The immediacy of these pressures is a relatively new burden that policy-makers now have to bear.

AIR POWER IN POLITICAL CONTEXT

In addressing the new security environment all instruments of UK Defence Policy are facing some important conceptual and political choices, and air power is no exception. The UK's role within NATO during the Cold War was so overwhelming in its importance and immediacy that it severely constrained doctrinal thinking in Britain about the meaning and use of air power. A series of major questions lurked in the background during the Cold War period but did not have to be faced – at least not by defence planners – if only because the air power employed by all three Services had vital allied tasks to perform in the event of a

---

23. Richard Sinnot, 'European Public Opinion and Security Policy', *Chaillot Papers*, 28 July 1997, pp 32, 59.

24. They range from obvious cases such as Rwanda or Somalia through Bosnia and Haiti to some more marginal cases such as Georgia, Tajikistan and Azerbaijan.

Warsaw Pact offensive, and these tasks offered few conceptual alternatives. Doctrine was driven essentially by NATO tasks, and tasks were determined by the perception of an external threat.[25] Freed from such constraints, however, all air power analysts – including planners – now have to provide answers to a number of major questions.

The first concerns the innate political sensitivity of all operations the UK is likely to be engaged in during the coming era. The UK may face many more situations where the use of its air power would be militarily appropriate but ruled out for political reasons; and such circumstances will involve agonising policy-making judgements. All military operations are undertaken in the pursuit of some political objective, but such objectives are almost certain to be more sensitive and volatile in the future. If the UK will be using its military resources more to pursue its interests rather than to meet an overt threat, then the political objectives at stake in any operation will be critical. And it is in the nature of political objectives outside overt war scenarios that they tend to shift. In this respect air power carries a heavy symbolism that affects political perceptions. It appears to carry a high value as a coercive instrument, even when its task is not necessarily coercive at all.[26]

This may be either a plus or a minus depending on the intention – but the use of air power is unlikely to have a neutral effect on objectives. Even during the Gulf War of 1991-92, where the objectives of expelling Saddam Hussein from Kuwait were clear and consensual within the coalition, there was a growing disquiet at an initial air campaign that appeared to some commentators to be directed at Iraqi society rather than Iraqi forces; and there was also considerable political pressure to end the war after '100 hours' – premature in a military sense given the escape of two Republican Guard Divisions – because the air attacks on Iraqi forces escaping on the road to Basra were beginning to turn stomachs in the West.[27] In the context of total war in 1944 it is difficult to imagine – even if instant TV pictures had been available at the time – that allied attacks on hapless German forces in the Falaise Gap would have caused any political qualms at all in

25. It is no coincidence, for example that the only RAF doctrinal statement during the Cold War was published in 1957 and allowed to atrophy thereafter. The document was out of print by the mid-1960s and a new doctrinal statement, AP3000, was not published until 1991.

26. See, Michael Clarke, 'Airpower, Force and Coercion', in Andrew Lambert and Arthur Williamson, eds, *The Dynamics of Air Power*, Bracknell, RAF Staff College, 1996, pp 67-85.

27. See for example, 'On their way?' *The Economist*, 9 February 1991. On the ending of the war after 100 hours see, Norman Schwarzkopf, *It Doesn't Take a Hero*, New York, Bantam Books, 1992, p 468, and Freedman and Karsh, *op cit*, pp 402-5.

Washington or London. The political sensitivity of air power was demonstrated in Bosnia even more dramatically. Under the mandate of the UN, the objectives of the international community were constantly shifting and the employment of air power in other than support roles was generally regarded as too politically loaded to be acceptable. The civilian head of the UN operation in Bosnia repeatedly vetoed the force commander's requests for enforcement air operations against Bosnian Serb positions. When NATO took command over the military operations, however, during the second half of 1995, the coercive air campaign had a major effect in transforming the political objectives of the UN powers – led now by the United States – towards the enforcement of a peace settlement agreed under the Dayton Accords.[28]

Air power also carries a relatively high political value in other ways. It represents a major contribution to coalition operations and, in most circumstances, is a prerequisite to the employment of other forces.[29] Among the European NATO allies only the UK and France can offer air power assets that are highly capable across the board. In operations where the US provides the bulk of the relevant air power, these capabilities can buy political influence by being able to slot into a US strategy; in cases where the US may not be involved in the air, they have their own intrinsic political value. In non-war, delicate, situations, however, air power also embodies its own political vulnerabilities. Its very high-tech presence, the symbolism it carries of technological superiority, means that the downing of a single aircraft may be regarded by a weaker opponent as a political victory. In the protracted air campaigns to enforce the no-fly-zones in Northern and Southern Iraq, a major constraint on the operations of allied air forces was the prospect of handing Saddam Hussein just such a victory while nevertheless forcing him to concede on substantive violations of UN resolutions. In these type of situations losses in ground forces, even fatal accidents among international monitors and inspectors, do not carry the same political penalties as losses and accidents among air forces. This was demonstrated at its most stark during the US operation in Somalia where the downing of one aircraft and the outrages heaped on the bodies of its crewmen had a disproportionate effect on domestic politics in the US and among the allies.

In the context of politically delicate operations, in other words, air power cannot help but be significant in anything other than strategic transport and

---

28. See Chantal de Jonge Oudraat, *The UN and International Conflicts*, Cambridge, Mass, MIT Press, 1998 especially the chapter on 'The Use of Force in Bosnia'.

29. See Group Captain Peach's Chapter 3 on Coalition Operations.

communications support roles.[30] Even an observation and monitoring role may carry heavy political significance and run the risk of losses where it is unwelcome on the ground. For the UK, all this implies that its air power capabilities will have an increased political significance in those operations most likely to be undertaken in the coming years; the more so since air power capability represents one of the areas of clear comparative advantage for the UK in relation to its European partners, but it also implies that its political significance will have to be weighed very carefully in any given contingency.

A second major question that the post-Cold War era necessarily highlights concerns the near-certainty of multi-national coalition operations in the future. If the potential motives for UK involvement in international instability listed in the previous section are correct, then the UK will have little incentive – and even less need – to act in circumstances where other allies do not wish to act. This does not absolutely rule out unilateral action; another Falklands operation is conceivable, if very unlikely, and the protection or evacuation of British citizens abroad is always a residual defence responsibility. But it indicates that we should assume all significant military involvements to be as part of a coalition operation.

This issue has taken on some interesting dynamics in recent years. One is that, having built up the habits of operational co-operation with its NATO allies to an unprecedentedly high level over the last 40 years, the UK must now consider more military co-operation with new-NATO and non-NATO allies. The enlargement of NATO will involve more co-operation with the air power arms of former Warsaw Pact states, among others. This makes new demands on co-operative arrangements since the RAF has more training and equipment in common with (say) the Saudi or Malaysian air forces than with the air forces of Poland, Rumania or Hungary. Even when these challenges have been met, the UK will have to be prepared to operate within broad coalitions that would have seemed fanciful only a few years ago. This has two contrasting implications for command and control of air operations and the expectations the UK has of the command structures within which it might be operating. If the US is involved in an air campaign, whether within or outside the NATO framework, then the UK will need the ability to slot into US C^3 technologies which are already at the edge of this country's national technical capabilities. If, on the other hand, UK air power is involved in a non-NATO ad hoc coalition without the US, then the C^3 requirements will tend towards a lowest common denominator which will force the UK

---

30. In-theatre transport, obviously, may be politically significant because of the visibility of air assets used in this way. On the vulnerabilities of it see, 'Power Projection – The Tactical Air Transport Contribution', *Airpower 1996* (Supplement to Air Clues), Air Warfare Centre, 1996, p 78.

to operate below its full technical capacity, or else leave others struggling to keep up if the UK wants to use its full C^3 potential. Technically, the UK is poised between an accelerating US C^3 capacity and the much lower levels of some putative coalition partners, in a circle that is almost impossible to square. The obvious temptation is to respond to the technological push of the US and assume that in any non-US coalition the UK might have to operate its air assets unilaterally, or with just one or two other established NATO partners. But even this involves potentially severe trade-offs since it contradicts two other dynamics of modern coalition operations – mass and synergy.

The problem of projecting mass has taken on a new significance in modern – particularly coalition – operations. Projecting a sufficient quantity of forces in an expeditionary operation is critical, and what constitutes a 'sufficient quantity' is determined increasingly by the political delicacy of the operations. Mass is important for the safety of the force itself. In war, losses are to be expected and risks will be taken. But in operations other than war, risk of losses has to be minimised, so forces cannot be left vulnerable. This is especially the case in peace support operations, where forces on the ground are *deliberately* under-armed as part of an attempt to restore normality, and so need as much over-the-horizon back-up as possible. Mass is also important to give effect to the politically important principle of 'minimum force'. Greater numbers, in a more overt presence, is normally the best way to guarantee that only minimal force will have to be used, making the most of the deterrent effect of the mass of any deployment. Not least, mass is important in coalition operations because it will be related in some way to the political influence each contributor will have within the coalition, or perhaps within the UN, and it will certainly be reflected in the relevant commands that different allies can claim. For the UK, therefore, it means that though its technological C^3 edge may remain adequate to high, in a non-US coalition its capacity for unilateral arrangements will be limited as it will still need to be part of the projection of a sufficient mass of relevant and co-ordinated force to satisfy the political requirements of a likely contingency.

Another dimension of coalition operations is the need to generate complementarity or synergy between air and ground forces.[31] Modern operations – war or non-war – require a complex interaction between air, ground, and often maritime, assets to achieve the superiority and safety required to meet political objectives; to achieve speed of response, surprise, sensitivity to changing political imperatives, maximum application of capabilities, greatest economies of scale,

---

31. See Chapter 9 by Philip Sabin, on the meanings of synergy and complementarity.

and so on. These are not matters of choice but have become modern require-ments. For as with all evolutions of operational tactics, where technology facilitates them and the advantages are clear, forces have little choice but to pursue the synergistic benefits, on the assumption that other comparable forces will be doing the same. It follows that in multinational operations synergy between air and ground forces will be all the more complex and prone to failure where so many different national contingents are involved, even if one or two nations, or one of NATO's command structures, provides the framework. The problems of projecting mass and pursuing symmetry, in other words, pose some expensive opportunity costs for a UK that tries to size and design itself mainly as a junior air power partner of the US; though the political costs of being incapable of being such a partner are also high. The happy compromise position between these two pressures is not obvious.

A final dimension of multinational operations that has become more promi-nent in recent years is the possibility of major contributor nations, such as the UK, having to project relatively small packages of air power long distances and sustain them for some time. RAF operations during the Gulf War benefited from friendly and large air bases in Saudi Arabia and Turkey; in enforcing the no-fly zones in Iraq the RAF continued to operate from Incirlik; and during Bosnia operations a series of convenient NATO bases were readily available. UK air power has had little need – other than for settled post-colonial purposes – of strategic airlift, the ability to move passengers and cargo between operational theatres. But in future air operations under less favourable circumstances are likely to be contemplated and the requirement for simultaneous small air detach-ments in far flung places might grow if the Government is serious about 'making a difference' on a global scale. Air detachments can be supplied by sea, but only after an initial deployment which, in the nature of international instabilities, is likely to be urgent. Projecting small detachments of air power into distant parts of the world is relatively expensive and exposes one of the persistent weaknesses in the spectrum of UK air power, since in the Cold War context tactical airlift was generally sufficient. Strategic airlift assets are of such a specialised nature that it is impossible to 'adapt' them, where available, out of a force structure that is designed for something else. Either they have to be acquired as a result of giving this capability a higher priority, or contingency planning has to be made to employ civil air transport or leasing appropriate aircraft from the US or Russia who operate strategic airlifters.[32]

---

32. The USAF operates the C-5, C141 and C-17, Russia operates the An124. The European Future Large Aircraft project remains a matter of some uncertainty in this respect.

A third major question that air power planners have now to confront is a direct attack on some of the points implied above: what are the implications for UK air power of a major change in the attitude of the United States to military operations in and around Europe? It is a reasonable assumption that it will not be in the UK's foreign policy interests to engage in military operations outside Europe and the Mediterranean – say in the Gulf or South Asia – unless the US heads a coalition; we only go out of area with the US. But it may not work the other way round, since the US may not want to be militarily involved in a European or Mediterranean crisis where the major European allies nevertheless feel they have an interest in becoming engaged. The military dimensions of the grand 'transatlantic bargain' may be changing and UK planners have to consider more tangibly than before what European air power alone might be capable of, and what the UK would contribute to it. This is not to say that the Europeans would not prefer US involvement in all likely military contingencies, or that they are itching to flex their Euro muscles independently. The Bosnia experience after 1992 showed quite the opposite.[33] But the possibility of a purely European allied operation involving significant air power assets within our own continent, whether or not it has the command benefits of being a Combined Joint Task Force, must be taken seriously.

The major military powers in Western Europe are not short of capable combat aircraft; the UK, France and Germany between them field over 1400, Italy some 286 combat aircraft with over 100 more in store; the Netherlands, Belgium and Denmark between them possess over 400 F-16 fighter and fighter/ground attack aircraft.[34] Nor is there an absolute shortage of attack helicopters if the ground forces of France and Germany are taken into account.[35] Britain and France have useful carrier forces, and France, Germany and Britain between them can field over 200 in-theatre lift aircraft – around 8 million ton miles of lift.[36] Even this takes no account of the considerable forces available in Turkey, or from new-NATO and non-NATO Europeans such as Poland, Rumania, Ukraine or Russia. The Europeans cannot substitute for US satellite

---

33. Jane M O Sharp, 'Will Britain Lead Europe?', *The World Today*, December 1997, pp 316-9.

34. This compares well with a Russia that probably fields fewer than 2000 serviceable combat aircraft, despite a CFE ceiling of 3450 aircraft. On the other hand, the US fields over 2800 combat aircraft with another 1000 serviceable in store within the USAF alone and taking no account of maritime aviation or the Marine Corps.

35. Figures taken from, International Institute for Strategic Studies, *The Military Balance 1997-98*, London IISS, 1997.

36. David T Burbach, 'Ready for Action? European Capabilities for Peace Operations', *Breakthrough*, 6(1), Security Studies Program, MIT, Spring 1997, p 14.

intelligence capabilities, or its intelligence processing technology, though they have around 170 reconnaissance and 27 Airborne Early Warning aircraft[37], plenty to maintain surveillance and airborne C^2 over Bosnia where satellite intelligence is anyway less useful, but probably insufficient to mount major operations over something bigger or during simultaneous operations in different theatres. The Europeans are certainly not without logistical air assets though there are major problems in the inherent mobility of fighting units and some sizeable holes in the capabilities of the smaller nations which the US habitually fills in allied operations. Above all, the Europeans lack the command facilities to operate a sophisticated air/ground campaign, even among the major allies, let alone with a more ad hoc grouping.[38] NATO's own – reorganised – Combined Air Operations Centres are in any case not fully modernised for air/ground operations and if the US contribution were taken away, the Europeans would be virtually stranded in anything other than a minor air operation. Big investments would have to be made in European C^3 to address these deficiencies and the ambitions of the Western European Union to do this have, if anything, become more modest since the disappointments of Bosnia for the Europeans between 1993 and 1995.[39] The prospect is that sizeable European air forces would simply be unable to operate in an integrated manner in a situation where the US was not involved.

All these factors point to European air power that would collectively perform less well than its inventory might suggest; a force that, *even if operating as an alliance*, would punch some way below its weight. It might be in the longer term interests of the UK to play a more proactive role among the Europeans to address at least some of these weaknesses, since their persistence will tend towards a greater reliance on UK and French air assets within Europe which may stimulate unrealistic demands, or resentment, if they cannot be met.

A fourth major question that the present international environment poses for air power in the UK concerns the problem of technological innovation. The general problem is the speed with which new and potentially decisive technologies develop, primarily now in the civil sector, and the growing expense of

---

37. Figures derived from a comprehensive attempt at capabilities comparisons reported in, Assembly of the Western European Union, 'The Readiness and Capabilities of Air Forces in WEU Member States', Document 1444, 17 November 1994, p 5.

38. See, Michael Bratby, 'A Review of NATO Airpower', *Brassey's Defence Yearbook 1996*, London, Centre for Defence Studies/Brassey's, 1996, pp 183-6.

39. See, Bart Rosengarten, 'The Role of the Western European Planning Cell', in Anne Deighton, ed, *Western European Union 1954-1997: Defence, Security, Integration*, Oxford, European Interdependence Research Unit, 1997, pp 157-168.

incorporating them into military aerospace technology. The art of military innovation is increasingly becoming that of civil systems *integration and adaptation*.[40] This
poses its own problems in designing procurement systems that are capable of
rapid and economical evolution over the lifetime of a project. In the past, evolving specifications during the design and testing phase of new defence systems
have been one of the prime culprits of late delivery and cost overruns, and it
remains to be seen how effective a 'smart procurement' approach can be in
addressing this problem. But the civilianisation of major aspects of technological
innovation has not only heightened procurement problems; it has created a more
systemic and predictable 'technological seepage' throughout the world. One
response to this would be to assume that there is no choice but to maintain high
technology aerospace systems, even if the number of units were small. But this
would not necessarily be consistent with the needs of mass in coalition operations,
of appropriate equipment for more peace support roles, or the expectation that
small packets of forces might have to be deployed in a range of situations.
Planners face a general dilemma in not being able to afford to keep up with all
aerospace technologies, and in having to back certain horses, based on a second-
guessing of what the UK's putative opponents, and allies, will have within the
mid- to long-term.

The more specific version of this problem for UK defence planners is deciding
whether, and how, to keep up with the revolution in military affairs (RMA) that
has so galvanised the United States. As mentioned above, technical compatibility
with the US is highly desirable for a number of reasons, but unless the RMA
proves to be a complete chimera, it is certain to be expensive and the UK cannot
pursue it in all sectors simultaneously in the way the US does. Any decisions on
which parts of the RMA are worth major UK investments – C^3, intelligence,
stealth technology, information warfare, etc – can only be made on the basis of
some answers to the questions posed above: would the investment be designed to
complement US resources, shadow them, substitute for them on behalf of the
Europeans, enhance operations other than war, enhance multinational coalition
operations, and so forth? UK policy on the RMA, in other words, will be based
on a series of important political assumptions that the UK never explicitly had to
make during the Cold War. If the expense of RMA technologies is as great as
might be expected, it will be impossible (i.e. too expensive) to hold open a range of
technological possibilities for a protracted period in order to maintain as much

---

40. Oliver Morton, 'Defence Technology' (Ch 7) in, The Economist, *Going Digital*, London, Profile
Books, 1996.

discretion as possible. Hard choices will have to be made and their timing will be dictated by progress in the US.

A final major question that the new era raises for UK air power is the extent or the form in which it should maintain an indigenous strategic role. In the NATO battle plan during the Cold War, UK air power intended to play both strategic and tactical roles in every major theatre of anticipated operations; the distinction between tactical and strategic was not particularly important in this context since the plan was driven by the imperatives of an all-out Warsaw Pact attack. In the present era, however, resource choices have to be made, military operations for the UK will be largely matters of choice, and the types of operation for the next few years are more likely to involve supporting the ground forces either in very limited wars or in operations other than war. The distinction between strategic and tactical then becomes important, and resource choices made now cannot quickly be reversed. To some extent, the decision to procure *Tomahawk* cruise missiles and to develop the capacities of Trident missiles to perform in a 'sub-strategic' (nuclear) role offers a hedge to maintain a capacity for strategic bombardment regardless of the evolution of other aspects of the UK's air power. But the issue goes deeper than the capacity to bomb an opposition homeland or military infrastructure. *Air Power Doctrine* puts the 'Strategic Air Offensive Campaign' within the overall context of other campaigns that air power will wage in a war, making the point that Counter-Air is 'The Primary Campaign'.[41]

In this context, however, the notion of a strategic role is more generalised than that used in *Air Power Doctrine*.[42] The question arises as to whether UK air power should be designed to maintain an independent role, capable of indigenous war-fighting operations of all sorts against an opponent's homeland or strategic forces. If it can, it certainly provides an extra dimension to the UK's war-fighting abilities and may, in some situations, be the only military response that is physically possible. But the desirability of this has to be set against the opportunity costs of achieving greater 'jointery', of building combined forces for synergistic operations, and of investing resources in a war-fighting capacity that may remain largely unused for some time. The promise of genuinely multi-role air power weapons is not yet sufficiently realised to mitigate this harsh trade-off very much. And the delicacy of this question in terms of the inter-service rivalry it tends to provoke does not negate its intrinsic importance. Again, the trade-offs that

---

41. *Air Power Doctrine* AP3000, 2nd Edition, London, MOD, 1993, p 41.
42. The most stark expression of this more generalised meaning is offered by Martin van Creveld, *On Future War*, London, Brassey's, 1991, especially pp 198-205.

planners will be forced to make in the future as they allocate resources will be driven to a considerable extent by their answers to the questions outlined in this section.

Air power all over the world is in a state of rapid evolution for reasons that are political, technological, and economic. In some respects, the questions facing the UK are obvious symptoms of this fact. Yet in other ways the UK is an important test case of how these factors *interact*. The UK is a country that is now internationally secure but which attaches a high value to regional and world order, a country that has uniquely close relations with the United States and within the United Nations. It has air power assets that are highly developed but which are small and now in danger of losing their place among the top echelons of air power technology and under economic pressures from demands in the domestic arena. The UK remains an important actor in air power terms but its new international environment raises major questions over how it should most appropriately employ this status. In making its choices the UK will be indicating major directions in the evolution of air power for the military establishments of many other countries who have highly developed, but not superpower, capacities.

CHAPTER 2

AIR POWER AND ASPECTS OF CIVIL-MILITARY RELATIONS
Dr. David Gates

INTRODUCTION

A S THE ULTIMATE INSTRUMENT of a state's power, armed services
have a unique position in both its domestic and foreign affairs. Until the early
19th Century, it was common in Western polities for the supreme military and
political authority to be vested in one person. Although such a fusion of civil and
military roles is best exemplified by soldier-monarchs like Frederick the Great of
Prussia and Napoleon I of France, even in states where there was at least a degree
of democracy the political leadership was also accorded a pivotal part in the
control and use of military power. Thus, as late as 1743, George II exercised his
entitlement to lead Britain's troops in the field, while, to this day, his successors
continue to combine the positions of monarch and commander-in-chief, however
token the latter role might have become. Similarly, whereas the right to declare
war still remains the crown's prerogative in Britain, the authors of the
Constitution of the United States of America saw fit to endow Congress with this
power. Even here, however, it was envisaged that this right – which was, and
arguably remains, the paramount manifestation of sovereignty – was to be exercised at the recommendation of the president, the holder of 'The Executive
Power', who was also deemed to be the legal and titular head of the armed
forces.[1]

From the beginning of the 19th Century onwards, the rise of, on the one hand,
bureaucracies and military officer corps which consisted not of political cronies

---

1. Intermittent Congressional attempts to restrain the president's powers in his capacity as
commander-in-chief culminated in the War Powers Act of 1973. However, its provisions have
been skilfully circumvented on occasion by the executive. Often, the simple expedient of
contrasting the legal concept of 'war' with that of 'armed conflict' has been exploited as a means
by which an executive power can preserve its freedom of action. For instance, when, on 4
November, 1956, he was questioned in the House of Commons over the Suez Crisis, the British
Prime Minister, Sir Anthony Eden, averred: "We are not at war with Egypt. We are in armed
conflict."

and other amateurs but of trained professionals and, on the other, the spread of popular participation in government steadily eroded the powers enjoyed by Western heads-of-state in law, practice, or in both. By the time of the Franco-Prussian War, although Napoleon III, like his opponent, King William I, chose to accompany his army in the field and was still both commander-in-chief and the supreme repository of civil authority within the State, professional military 'advisers' such as General Edmond Leboeuf were increasingly relied upon so far as the actual leadership of the armed services was concerned. Moreover, any influence exerted over these commanders by their political masters was essentially founded on the personal fealty that all good citizens were expected to show their sovereign. As such, it had less to do with their function as strategists, the specific task with which the monarch had entrusted them, than with their broader obligations as loyal servants of the crown. Certainly, in neither his writings nor his work as the Prussian Army's chief-of-staff did Helmuth von Moltke, for instance, evince any sense of subservience to the Prussian political authorities, save to the king himself, to whom he had pledged allegiance. Indeed, when it came to the distribution of rights and responsibilities between the civil and military powers in wartime, Moltke was adamant that "at the moment of mobilisation the political adviser should fall silent, and should take the lead again only when the strategist has informed the king, after the complete defeat of the enemy, that his task has been fulfilled." [2]

This reasoning, however, clashed with that of a second school of thought which was based on the views of that great doyen of military theorists, Carl von Clausewitz. In *Vom Kriege*, he had insisted that war was "not a mere act of policy but a true political instrument, a continuation of political activity by other means." [3] It therefore followed that the military's political overlords should stipulate not only what the objectives behind the use of armed force were, but also how, in so far that it could be controlled, they were to be achieved.

Although there are states in the world where the attitude expressed by Moltke still prevails, modern Western practice is much more in keeping with the Clausewitzian model, with the military seeking guidance from their political masters. Indeed, the political docility of most Occidental armed forces is something which many people rather take for granted. Resting on a complex foundation of material interests interwoven with socio-cultural factors, such as professional ethics and respect for the rule of law, which are frequently more

---

2. Quoted in R. Stadelmann, *Moltke und der Staat* (Krefeld, 1950), p. 206.
3. Carl von Clausewitz, *On War* (Edited by M. Howard and P. Paret, Princeton, 1976), p. 87.

intangible, the amenability of the West's armed forces is a quality which requires careful handling if the existing partnership between the ruled and their rulers is to be preserved. This can be difficult enough in peacetime; in war, which by definition is a revolutionary activity, it can prove a formidable challenge. Above all, the military needs to be set a clear goal that, in theory at least, is attainable and to which their political overlords are prepared to devote the requisite material resources and resolve.

Yet this requires that the often conflicting demands made by, on the one hand, the armed forces and, on the other, their wider community be kept in balance. Clausewitz himself stressed that, whereas "The aims a belligerent adopts and the resources he employs must be governed by the particular characteristics of his own position, ... they will also conform to the spirit of the age and its general character." [4]

Because of the evolving nature of warfare, long before the end of the 19th Century it was becoming increasingly difficult to reconcile the supremacy of policy with the independence of military commanders. Subsequent developments have done nothing to ease this dilemma. Not only has technological change – notably the development of air and spacepower – progressively increased the potential tempo and scope of military operations, leaving field commanders with little, if any, time for political consultations, even if they sometimes possess the means, but also, as monarchical rule has given way to popular government, a breed of politician has arisen which is 'professional' in so far that the people concerned make their living from the world of politics. Such politicians are motivated less by a sense of *noblesse oblige* than by other considerations and have a vested interest in maintaining their voter-appeal. With more importance being accorded to the rights of the individual citizen, growing sensitivities about public opinion and the provisions of international law have gradually conditioned politicians' attitudes to the employment of armed force. This is especially true in the case of so-called 'limited' conflicts, in which it is difficult to argue that supreme national interests are at stake. All military operations are, therefore, bound to be subject to regulation by the political authorities; what remains to be determined is the extent of the control the civil power will seek, and the degree to which the military can and do respond to it. Whilst this clearly has implications for the use of all manner of armed forces, air power, because of its peculiar nature, is likely to be subject to particular scrutiny in this regard.

---

4. *Ibid.*, p. 594.

THE SPECIAL CHARACTERISTICS OF AIR POWER

Air power's capacity to undertake missions which, in theory at least, can extend across the length and breadth of a given theatre and, as they can be conducted in parallel rather than sequentially, across the spectrum of operations endows it with a flexibility that surface forces cannot match. Whilst the Berlin Airlift of 1948-9 is perhaps the best example of the peaceful exploitation of this quality on a large scale for humanitarian purposes, military air assets have more often been employed as instruments of violence. For sure, in many instances, they have been the weapons of first resort, precisely because from the very outset of a conflict they can strike at a range of tactical and strategic targets, switching from one to another with relative ease and speed. Indeed, this attribute led Douhet and other theorists to conclude that air power constituted the offensive weapon *par excellence*.

Berlin Airlift

Yet this very distinction has often made the employment of air power difficult for democratic political authorities to endorse. Just as, from a political standpoint, the presence of main battle tanks in 'peace support' and other 'constabulary' operations might appear incongruous, the mere deployment, let alone active use, of highly capable rotary- or fixed-wing combat aircraft might prove too contro-versial to countenance. For this reason, it is highly improbable that, for instance, the British cabinet would be willing to authorise the utilisation of *Apache* attack helicopters by the security forces in Northern Ireland, even if a persuasive military case could be advanced for their deployment; great importance is attached to the use, or threatened, use, of force being seen to be proportionate, discriminative and in accordance with national and international law.

There are, of course, many governments in the world which are less scrupulous. Indeed, the controversy surrounding the global trade in armaments not only focuses primarily on sales by Western democracies to regimes with a history of human-rights violations, but also tends to crystallise around the export of aerospace equipment especially. Nevertheless, some states actually link the provision of economic aid to developing countries with arms deals, while nobody would dream of restricting the export of, say, farming implements to Rwanda or Zaire, where, in recent years, hundreds of thousands of people have been killed or maimed with machetes, a form of technology that appears innocuous when set against combat aircraft.

These paradoxes, together with the very existence of so-called 'peace enforcement' and other 'constabulary' undertakings, executed, it is often claimed, on behalf of the 'international community', whatever that might be, help illustrate how politicians at best enjoy only imperfect control over the use of violence for political purposes both within the borders of their own respective states and further afield. But certain forms of violence are more intractable than others, particularly when the people confronting them come from a liberal-democratic background. From an intellectual perspective at least, all wars are 'limited' in one sense or another. However, for a number of reasons, the less total a conflict is, the harder it can be for a democracy to wage it. Whilst counter-terrorist operations perhaps best encapsulate this dilemma, foreign wars fought out of choice rather than necessity manifest similar limitations and are likely to prove vexatious. Public reaction to casualties among innocent bystanders and those military personnel who, rather than defending vital national interests, are widely perceived to be filling an optional, altruistic role, can be so adverse that every bomb dropped has the potential to cause an explosion which is as political as it is physical.[5] Indeed, given the speed and reach of modern telecommunications and the influence of the mass media,[6] many democratic politicians increasingly agonise over the use of

---

5. The public response to the bombing of the Al Firdos bunker during the Gulf War is a prime illustration of this dilemma.
6. It is now entirely possible, given the speed of modern telecommunications and the ubiquity of journalists, for a unit commander to be confronted with media questions about a particular raid *before* the aircrew which carried it out have returned to base and been debriefed.

military force to the point where they would like to control the trajectory of every bullet fired, if that were possible.

THE PEACE SUPPORT ENVIRONMENT

The employment of anodyne terminology, notably 'peace enforcement' in place of 'war', has done nothing to ease this problem. On the contrary, it has encouraged the public to apply peacetime standards when gauging the sacrifices to be made for the achievement of a given objective. In the past, whilst great concern was regularly expressed about the possibility of heavy casualties being incurred in land operations especially, the use of air power has been regarded as less controversial in this regard. Indeed, having witnessed the gory stalemate of the trenches of World War I, many interwar-period theorists saw aircraft as offering a means by which such deadlock, with its concomitant casualties, might be avoided. Wars, it was believed, could be decided quickly and relatively cleanly through the avoidance of the sequential operations and relatively prolonged commitments which characterise surface combat. In any event, the loss of a comparative handful of aviators seemed as nothing when set against the sanguinary nature of land battles in particular.

However, as Western attitudes to the use of military force *per se* have altered, and improved technology has opened up new possibilities, even this view continues to undergo modification. In the light of the success of the Allied aerial offensive in the Gulf War and of Operation 'Deliberate Force' in Bosnia in 1995, some commentators have been tempted to believe that air power is not just a formidable coercive instrument but also that it is capable of subduing an opponent without much, if any, assistance from surface forces; air power alone, they argue, can do the job.[7] Yet, although its reach, speed, ubiquity, firepower and flexibility offer the promise of quick results, these can often prove ephemeral unless they are consolidated and exploited by surface forces. There can be other drawbacks to the employment of air power, too; for aviators are not immune from the dangers inherent in combat. The televised spectacle of captured Western aircrew being abused by their Iraqi interrogators during the Gulf War, and of dead American aviators being dragged through the streets of Mogadishu during the UN operation in Somalia, highlighted a serious flaw in the assumption that air power is a means by which wars can be waged and decided cheaply. For cheap-

---

7. See, for instance, D.B. Rice, *The Air Force and US National Security: Global Reach – Global Power* (Dept. of the Air Force, Washington DC, 1991).

ness is relative. Although somewhat eclectic in attaching value to life, Western liberal-democratic societies have, generally speaking, made the avoidance of bloodshed of paramount concern. Admirable though this might be, it does, rather ironically, fly in the face of war's uniquely human aspects. *Homo Sapiens* is, after all, the only species that engages in war, and our willingness to do so is essentially dependent upon not physical but moral strength. As Clausewitz observed in *Vom Kriege*, "Since war is not an act of senseless passion but is controlled by its political object, the value of this object must determine the sacrifices to be made for it in *magnitude* and also in *duration*. Once the expenditure of effort exceeds the value of the political object, the object must be renounced and peace must follow." [8]

The Inter-Agency process in action

In wars of choice in particular, it is all too easy for the value of the political object to be surpassed long before substantial costs have been incurred. Indeed, asymmetries in vulnerability as well as power can determine a conflict's outcome. Even in the Gulf War, where significant Western interests were at stake, the Iraqis seem to have hoped to thwart the Allied coalition less by defeating it in 'the mother of all battles' than by rendering the price of victory unacceptably high; it

8. Clausewitz, *op. cit.*, p. 92.

was calculated that the Americans especially – who made up the very heart of the alliance – would falter once a certain pain threshold had been reached.[9]

Mercifully, Allied casualties in the Gulf War were kept to a remarkably low level, undermining Saddam Hussein's expectations. But losses need not be at all significant in absolute terms for the public to begin to question the relative value of the political object at stake. Certainly, the events in Mogadishu helped put paid to the American presence in Somalia, while, in 1995, so politically sensitive did the fate of a single US pilot, Captain Scott O'Grady, become that it was to jeopardise the Americans' involvement in Operation 'Deny Flight', if not their endeavours to manage the Balkan crisis as a whole. His F-16 brought down by a surface-to-air missile, Captain O'Grady was in danger of falling into the hands of hostile Serbs. As yellow ribbons began to appear all over the USA, not only did the incident necessitate the issuing of several soothing statements by President Clinton himself, it also provoked a rescue mission which involved the insertion into Serb-held territory of a team of 43 marines, ferried and supported by some 40 aircraft, in order to retrieve just one man. With the mission successfully completed, no less a figure than the president himself telephoned the captain's family to advise them of his safe return. Whilst one can only sympathise with Captain O'Grady and with his relations, friends and colleagues in their ordeal, and whilst stranded aircrew should clearly be rescued whenever it is safe and practical to do so, both the extraordinary apprehension that the fate of a solitary aviator provoked and the lengths gone to secure his safe return are testimony to the potency of vociferous public opinion and to the susceptibility of elected politicians to the leverage that such sentiment can exert.

That rulers can be influenced by the ruled in this fashion is arguably nothing more than a manifestation of democratic accountability. But what we are really witnessing here is the vulnerability of politicians to what was once described by one prominent statesman as the 'wars of televised suffering'.[10] Further, since war is all about a willingness to endure pain as well as inflict it, there is another side to this phenomenon. Even very limited aims cannot always be achieved without the making of substantial sacrifices. Yet there is a growing reluctance within the Western liberal democracies at least to sustain *any* casualties except perhaps in circumstances where there is no alternative, as in cases of resistance to external aggression. So far as the West is concerned, however, the foreseeable politico-

---

9. See 'The Glaspie Transcript,' in *The Gulf War Reader: History, Documents, Opinions* (Edited by M.L. Sifry and C. Cerf, New York, 1991), pp. 122-33; and N. Cigar, 'Iraq's Strategic Mindset and the Gulf War: Blueprint for Defeat,' *Journal of Strategic Studies*, Vol. 15 (1992), 5.

10. D. Hurd, 'Is Colin Powell the Man of the Hour?' *Sunday Telegraph*, 12 September, 1995, p. 31.

Captain Scott O'Grady

strategic environment is one in which participation in armed conflict is likely to be a matter of choice, not necessity. Under these conditions, it is probable that any initial decision to become involved and the detailed nature of that commitment will be strongly influenced by considerations which carry less weight when supreme national interests are at stake.

This process has already manifested itself on a number of occasions since the end of the Cold War. The West's decision to intervene vigorously in Bosnia, for example, was a long time in coming, while the ongoing commitment of outside forces to the work of preserving the region's fragile peace remains doubtful. In other crises elsewhere, notably in Africa, Ngorno Karabakh and Tajikistan, even limited interference proved fleeting, or was rejected from the very beginning as impracticable or unjustifiable. As to the Cold War itself, two of its attributes are noteworthy. First, whereas the West essentially elected to wage the conflicts it has participated in since the Iron Curtain was torn down, the Cold War was one of necessity, not choice. Second, the so-called 'proxy' wars in Korea, Vietnam and Afghanistan aside, the Cold War was a bloodless conflict so far as the superpowers were concerned. The *principal* challenge, as the first SACEUR, General Eisenhower, recognised from the outset,[11] was sustaining morale and economic vitality, which were related processes, over a prolonged period, while acquiring and preserving adequate military strength for an armed confrontation which might not – and, in the event, did not – materialise. This imposed as many demands on politicians as it did on the armed forces themselves, and it was largely because of its superior civil-military relations that the West emerged triumphant. Although the allocation of sufficient resources to defence had to be justified and maintained – a process which proved difficult at times – and whilst the posture of nuclear deterrence intermittently strained civilian morale, the West succeeded in overcoming these problems whereas the USSR did not; she lost the Cold War without a shot being fired in anger.

The point here is that the sacrifices called for by the Cold War were primarily *material* ones. For the affluent West at least, these were more affordable, while both sides evidently found them preferable to the alternative, a conflict which could only have resulted in scores of millions of casualties and unimaginable destruction. The mutual reliance on military *power*, rather than *force*, within the framework of the East-West confrontation permitted such a choice to be made. However, amidst the disarmament race and the demands for a financial 'peace dividend' which have followed the Cold War, allocating resources to defence, rather than to welfare or even to reductions in taxation, has become a far more daunting and less popular political mission which is increasingly warranted in terms of preserving employment, manufacturing skills and exports. Although the defence sector of the Western economy is an important constituency containing many votes, in the prevailing climate there is a danger that military capabilities, which take years to acquire or regenerate once lost, will fall victim to political expediency. Moreover, the current politico-strategic environment is likely to prove more troublesome for Occidental statesmen and women than that of the Cold War in so far that it not only calls for the material sacrifices which preserving military muscle demand but also the intermittent employment of that strength. [12]

---

11. See, for example, C.J. Bartlett, *The Global Conflict: The International Rivalry of the Great Powers, 1880-1990* (London, 1994), pp. 305-6.

12. Of late, this has been particularly striking in the case of Germany and Japan. Both of these countries have devoted considerable resources to amassing military *power*, yet have been loath to actually employ armed *force*. In the case of the Gulf campaign, for example, they both preferred to donate huge sums of money to the Allied war effort rather than combat units. Whilst constitutional constraints are the ostensible explanation for this phenomenon, these legal restraints are of course merely symptomatic of broader, inveterate concerns about military power within German and Japanese society. Even the participation of the *Bundeswehr* in its very first military engagement – Operation 'Deliberate Force' in September, 1995 – was heavily circumscribed, despite being a NATO undertaking which had the blessing of the UNO.

Although the principal peacetime role of armed services remains deterrence, the retention of military capabilities is increasingly justified in terms of the *political* importance attached to being able to intervene forcibly on the world stage, particularly under the auspices of the UN and other international organisations. Yet the amount of political influence which can be derived from the possession of armed might is ultimately determined by the practical utility of that military power; and, when it comes to active coercion, bloodshed, on one or both sides, is unavoidable. However, so great is the West's sensitivity to casualties, at least in wars of choice, that it has imparted considerable momentum to the quest for machines which might take over roles normally fulfilled by human beings. This trend is particularly noticeable in the air power arena. As the O'Grady case highlighted, aircrew, mounted on high-technology steeds, are the knights of modern warfare; their defeat or capture can be a *coup* with greater political than military significance. Increasingly, instead of manned aircraft, 'smart' missiles are being used to assail well-protected targets, particularly at crucial times in the electoral cycle when the death or capture of aviators might prove disproportionately costly in domestic political terms.[13]

TECHNOLOGY AND THE MANNED PLATFORM DILEMMA

We are also witnessing attempts to develop a generation of sophisticated uninhabited aerial vehicles which, by exploiting virtual-reality systems and other ingenious software, could supersede platforms with vulnerable human operators. Again, this process can only be carried to a certain point before it becomes counterproductive: violence is, after all, one of the defining characteristics of war, and a conflict in which both sides relied exclusively upon machines would be a travesty if only because, as an exclusively human activity, war has psychological as well as physical dimensions.[14] Moreover, if the distribution of power between military forces and their political masters can be contentious, the scope for controversy in relationships between humankind and intelligent machines is still greater. Whilst the dawn of a new generation of 'smart' weapons that, once

---

13. A good illustration of this occurred in 1996 when, eight weeks before the US presidential elections, President Clinton authorised punitive action against Iraq following her occupation of the Kurdish safe haven of Sulaymaniyah. The attacks consisted, not of raids by manned aircraft, but of the firing of two salvos of cruise missiles at targets in southern Iraq.
14. For a discussion of some of the issues this gives rise to, see D. Gates, 'Air Power and the Theory and Practise of Coercion,' *Defense Analysis*, Vol. 13/3 (1997), 239-54.

released, can themselves distinguish between targets and choose which ones to strike raises questions as to exactly who (or what) is calling the tune, one sees similar problems vividly enough in the realm of civil aviation, where automation has occasionally seemed to smack of a brave new world in which humankind has lost discrimination and control. Indeed, nowadays, as aircrew seek to interact with flight-control computers and other sophisticated artificial-intelligence devices, a remark picked up regularly by flight-deck voice-recorders in civil airliners is: "What's it doing *now?*"

Certainly, the public's intuitive initial reaction to air crashes tends to take the form of questions about the safety of the type of aircraft involved; the competence of the crew is usually taken for granted. In fact, numerous accidents have been caused by pilot error, many of them arising from human attempts, usually incorrectly, to correct mistakes which the plane's flight-control computer has been perceived to have made. Against this background, it can be assumed that, in peacetime at least, the regulatory authorities of almost every state will want to ensure that unmanned aerial vehicles, particularly 'stealthy' combat versions, do not interfere with the safe running of airlines, commerce and the everyday lives of citizens. If the restraints on the flying of remote-controlled model planes are anything to judge by, governmental controls over uninhabited platforms are likely to be still stricter than those applying to crewed aircraft.

So far as Europe is concerned, the use of uninhabited aerial vehicles is still in its infancy and the implications for air-traffic control, for example, have not yet been fully explored. Advanced robotics clearly have a contribution to make to warfare in general, and we should be wary of Luddite attitudes to such technology. However, the exploitation of uninhabited systems is likely to further complicate civil-military relations. In any event, reduced human vulnerability at the cost of increased reliance on exotic technology might easily prove a mixed blessing. The B-2 Stealth Bomber is the ultimate example of this approach. Its very sophistication makes it as expensive as it is militarily awesome. If, however, by some mischance, such a plane were to be destroyed in combat, particularly in a 'peace enforcement' operation, or some other war of choice, the loss of such a prestigious, expensive weapons-platform could well have devastating political repercussions, even if the crew were to escape death or capture. On the other hand, the successful use of such superior technology against far less capable adversaries could provoke moral indignation in certain quarters and apprehension in others. Even the use of comparatively primitive technology against seemingly helpless opponents can arouse widespread revulsion and condemnation. The fashion in which the international media portrayed the carnage wrought by Allied aircraft, including relatively old-fashioned A-10s, among the retreating and essentially defenceless Iraqis along the Basra road at the climax of the Gulf War is a good illustration of how what many might see as a legitimate act of war can so easily become simple murder in the eyes of others; even some of the aircrew involved in the attacks expressed their misgivings over what was being perpetrated.

THE ETHICS OF INTERVENTION

That aircrew and other military personnel can find themselves obliged to carry out distasteful assignments on the orders of their senior officers and political masters highlights the conflicts which can occur between an individual's sense of personal and professional ethics. Indeed, the question of what constitutes the legitimate exercise of power looms large in both civil-military relations and those within the hierarchy of a state's armed forces. The gradual acceptance of concepts of international law which impinge on the prosecution of armed conflict and thus encroach on the sovereignty of belligerents has exacerbated the difficulties this can give rise to, as has the increasingly intrusive nature of media coverage. Mindful of the potential for broader repercussions, politicians have often endeavoured to impose constraints on their armed services' actions by means of, for example, rules of engagement, which stipulate under what circumstances they are permitted to use force and in what fashion. In the execution of strategic bombing campaigns especially, we also see many instances of politicians determining what targets can and cannot be attacked. During Operation 'Rolling Thunder' in the Vietnam War, for instance, President Johnson once asserted that "the US Air Force cannot even bomb an outhouse without my approval." [15] However, in the absence of physical restraints, such as 'dual-key' systems, which might prevent a weapon being used but cannot influence targeting, claims like this one are founded on mere assumptions and trust. [16] In fact, steadily improving technology has put tremendous destructive power literally at the fingertips of individual aircrew and other military personnel. That they, and it, will necessarily remain under control, particularly when subjected to the stresses and strains of

---

15. Quoted in W. C. Westmoreland, *A Soldier Reports* (New York, 1980), p. 119.
16. This problem is exacerbated whenever the sovereignty of an individual party is effectively compromised through, for example, coalition operations. Be it in peace or war, a 'host' nation can only enjoy imperfect control over the forces of its allies. For a discussion of, for instance, British political control over USAF units stationed within the United Kingdom, see D. Gates, 'American Strategic Bases: The Agreements Governing Their Use,' *Comparative Strategy*, Vol. 8 (1989), 99-123.

combat conditions, cannot be taken for granted. Much depends upon the education and training of the military, and upon the respective roles they perceive themselves and politicians as having in their society. Equally, however, fear, injury, deprivation and frustration have often proved the solvents of discipline. Rules of engagement, for example, have frequently stoked up resentment, having been seen as the instruments of unduly meddlesome politicians who, ensconced in some comfortable office far from the fighting, have no real appreciation of the nature of combat and do not share its dangers. This can place an intolerable burden of responsibility on military personnel in the thick of the action, many of whom are of very junior standing. In the opinion of one young fighter pilot in Vietnam, for instance, the rules of engagement were "created by US leaders to cover themselves; then each subordinate commander added a few more rules to cover himself; and pretty soon everyone was covered – except the fighter pilot, and he had to know all the rules." [17]

When Georges Clemenceau opined that "War is much too serious a thing to be left to the generals," political interference in military operations was, in the main, still confined to the provision of broad directives at the strategic level. Throughout the 19th and early 20th Centuries, as the interests of the great powers expanded across the globe and their armed forces became commensurably bigger, so too did potential zones of conflict (indeed, this process culminated in *world* war, not least because of the development of air power). However much political or military authority he might have possessed in theory, it ceased to be practicable for one man, even a soldier-monarch, to control forces single-handedly, if only because the means available for the dissemination of orders did not lend themselves to the regulation of the minutiae of warfare. Despatches, laboriously written by hand, could take days, weeks or even months to reach a given theatre, by which time the situation at the front could have altered dramatically. Even new technology, such as telegraphs and telephones, which, if available, could speed up communications, were unsuitable for the transmission of large volumes of information to large numbers of recipients.

As long as central political control ineluctably remained as limited as it was remote, the devolution of considerable power to commanders in the field was unavoidable. However, with the growth and refinement of electronic communications, including radio, the theoretical capacity for the micromanagement of

---

17. Quoted in R.J. Drake, 'The Rules of Defeat: The Impact of Aerial Rules of Engagement on USAF Operations in North Vietnam, 1965-68,' (Thesis, School of Advanced Airpower Studies, Maxwell, Alabama, 1993), p. 13.

conflicts by not just military leaders using 'electronic hilltops' but also their political overlords steadily increased. As long ago as 1855, General Pélissier, commander of the French forces in the Crimea, was reduced to impotent rage by Napoleon III, who, exploiting a newly-laid cable, repeatedly interfered in his operations by means of telegrams. "Your Majesty must free me from the narrow limits to which he has assigned me", the wretched general insisted, "or else allow me to resign a command impossible to exercise in co-operation with our loyal allies at the somewhat paralysing end of an electric wire." [18] With the growth of 'real time' intelligence, politicians and senior commanders now enjoy an unprecedented capacity to 'reach down' into the activities of their subordinates in the field. Yet, at the same time, this and other technological advances are also empowering front-line military personnel such as aircrew. For forces equipped with advanced technology, notably those of the USA, striking a balance between the devolution of power and its centralisation could prove increasingly difficult. One wonders what rules of engagement are likely to be issued to, say, the crews of B-2 Stealth Bombers or the airborne lasers which, mounted in modified Boeing 747s, the USAF plans to employ to destroy ballistic missiles while they are still in their boost-phase and over the country of launch. Whilst the airborne laser programme has fairly been described as being "as revolutionary as the invention of gunpowder or the Manhattan project," [19] its implications in terms of international and civil-military relations seem similarly momentous. Indeed, local and theatre commanders appear to be reacting to the trend with a parallel phenomenon of 'reach back' to clarify higher commanders' intent and create an audit trail particularly in case something goes wrong.

THE DECISION/ACTION CYCLE AND COMMAND AND CONTROL

To be sure, various aspects of ballistic missile defence – among them, the need to trade space for time in order that decisions can be taken – beg some very thorny political questions, many of which have a bearing on the theoretical use of air power *per se*. One of the perceived advantages afforded by air power is its comparative speed. It can, effectively, concertina time, enabling not only locations

---

18. Quoted in B.D. Gooch, *The New Bonapartist Generals in the Crimean War: Distrust and Decision-Making in the Anglo-French Alliance* (Den Hague, 1959), p. 218.
19. 'Boeing, Lockheed-Martin, TRW win Airborne Laser Contract,' *Boeing News Release*, Washington DC, 12 November, 1996, p. 1.

but also decisions to be reached rapidly. On the other hand, the sheer pace of aerial warfare threatens to leave its practitioners with few choices. Certainly, one can ill afford to cede the initiative; to wait in the air is to risk defeat. In fact, the adage that "the best defence is to attack," is nearly always applicable to air operations. However, whilst this makes the use of pre-emption extremely tempting if not essential, the initiation of hostilities should remain a political, not a military, decision. But this, in turn, requires that the political authorities have the time, information and capability to authorise military action. As the Russians in the Cold War clearly recognised, this can be an exploitable weakness. Today, with spies, surveillance satellites and other intelligence-gathering systems scrutinising every move that putatively hostile armed forces make, it can be very difficult for a would-be attacker to achieve strategic surprise. Nevertheless, he might acquire the same practical advantages if his opponent's political leadership can be neutralised in some fashion. Though it could be achieved by, say, the assassination of key figures, such decapitation need not be by violent means. A sense of complacency, perhaps brought about by alternating acts of brinkmanship and conciliation, could be sufficient to bring about the paralysis of an opponent's defences. For no matter how convinced the military might be that they are about to be assailed, there would be very little that they could do in terms of mobilising their forces for action without the endorsement of their political overlords. Yet this might not necessarily be forthcoming. Any decision-making process requires, firstly, intelligence and, then, sufficient time for its evaluation. A shortage of time can result in the first satisfactory, rather than the best possible, course of action being pursued. Moreover, the implementation of any decision essentially depends upon the quality and extent of command and control. Indeed, in polities where the armed services are kept firmly under political direction, either a break in the decision-making process or an inappropriate outcome to that process can leave the state very vulnerable to an attack which might prove as decisive as it is sudden.

There is no simple solution to this conundrum. Politicians can either endeavour to retain control over the armed services, or they can cede at least some of it in the form of standing instructions, rules of engagement and so on. These, however, can prove to be hostages to fortune. The intermittent debate about member states placing units at the disposal of the Secretary General of the UNO illustrates what a contentious issue this is. The notion of some kind of UN standing force for use in contingencies has never found much favour, while, in the various 'peace support' operations that have occurred, most, if not all, contributors have maintained national control over their military personnel one way or another. Even within the context of NATO's integrated military command, politicians have been reluctant to relinquish jurisdiction over their respective countries' forces, at least so far as operations in peacetime are concerned. Indeed, although the theory surrounding the Combined Joint Task Force concept sounds plausible enough, past experience with multinational forces suggests that, in practice, such a body is likely to be hamstrung by not just inter-operability problems but also by disputes over accountability and control. For all the talk about the USA permitting the WEU to make use of NATO assets, for example, one cannot really envisage a situation in which the US Congress would be prepared to give European political and military authorities *carte blanche* in the employment of American military equipment, infrastructure and, probably, some specialist personnel. After all, the SACEUR is a serving American officer largely so that the NATO command hierarchy is not at odds with the provisions of the US Constitution, notably Article II, Section 2, which stipulates that the "President shall be Commander-in-Chief".

Politics is the exercise of power and, in any environment, be it an office or an air base, is an integral part of human affairs. Whilst legal provisions and other measures might seek to regulate and legitimise our relationships, these are themselves only enforceable if there is sufficient power behind them. This can be moral, physical, or both. Indeed, so much in civil-military relations, for instance, depends upon a willingness to accept the legitimacy of the rule of law and other forms of accountability. Although in the West this is established practice, it should not be taken for granted. All power can be abused, and occasionally military figures have defied or usurped their political masters. Even Clausewitz himself was accused of insubordination when, unable to acquiesce in, let alone support, his king's foreign policy, he resigned his commission, eventually going so far as to side with his country's enemy in what he believed to be a just war. Other military figures have also asserted that they understand their people's true needs better than any civil authority and have acted accordingly. But there is also scope for the abuse of power both by politicians in the way that they treat the armed services under their control and within the forces themselves. This includes the rotation or selection of officers in accordance with domestic political concerns rather than with military needs, qualifications or experience; promotion policies founded on political leanings rather than on martial skill; and sexual or racial harassment, positive discrimination or favouritism. Indubitably, the training and general education of the military is a key component in the creation and preservation of satisfactory civil-military relations. Yet this does not take place in a vacuum; the nature of society as a whole, and its receptiveness to external influences, are also of importance. After all, armed forces tend to mirror the societies which spawn them.

'OWNING' AIR POWER

In fact, because some societies are far wealthier and more developed than others, the acquisition of air power has not occurred in a uniform fashion. Not only does the production of sophisticated aircraft remain the preserve of a handful of countries, they also require skilled, highly educated people to fly and service them. Since advanced combat aircraft and all the paraphernalia that they need for their operation and maintenance are prohibitively expensive, many states are obliged to rely on simpler, cheaper, if less flexible alternatives, such as missiles, which are easier to procure and operate. Moreover, numerous countries which can afford to purchase advanced aircraft have no indigenous aerospace industries. This makes them potentially lucrative export markets for those that do. The 'cutting edge' nature of the technology involved can, furthermore, give it a central position in national science and research policies, while the numerous skilled jobs generated by the sector can be of immense importance to regional and national economies. As a result, the capacity to develop and build aircraft like the *Eurofighter* can have significance which transcends simple strategic considerations.

The need for qualified technicians to construct and service aerospace platforms makes appreciable demands on a country's education and training facilities. Certainly, the perception that the 'military-industrial complex' consumes, to the detriment of the wider economy, too many of the best available engineering and science graduates can be a widespread and damaging one. Moreover, the armed forces can find such skilled workers difficult and costly to recruit and retain. This has encouraged some governments to rely increasingly on private contractors rather than on military personnel to fulfil maintenance and other support roles. Financially advantageous though this sometimes proves, it can result in the military effectiveness of the armed forces being compromised. For example, there have been occasions on which inept servicing has led to aircraft being damaged and grounded, while the willingness and capacity of civilian staff to work in war zones is not always apparent. Nor does the public always show much sympathy for the armed forces' need to practice. Low-flying aircraft especially are a common source of complaint, yet adequate training is essential if aviators are to perfect the skills they need to carry out their wartime assignments. Whereas everybody wants disarmament but, because of the employment implications, they do not want to see the closure of their local military base or armaments factory, training is invariably something which, everyone believes, would be better done in some other neighbourhood. Air forces are particularly unwelcome in this regard, since they often exercise in regions which are some considerable distance from their home base. They are therefore perceived as bringing nothing to the locality except noise and a fear of accidents.

CONCLUSION

The sheer complexity of many industrialised societies especially makes the parameters of civil-military relations difficult to discern. However, from the above, we can readily pick out several spheres of activity which centre on air power: its acquisition, its preparation, its maintenance and its use. So far as the first three are concerned, politicians have a crucial role in finding sufficient resources and justifying their allocation to the creation and upkeep of this particular form of military power, particularly at times when there is no discernible threat to national security and spending on defence commands less voter-appeal than that on welfare programmes. It must never be forgotten that the cardinal *raison d'être* of armed forces in peacetime is deterrence: they exist to persuade any would-be opponent that a recourse to violence as an instrument of policy, including defence policy, would prove counterproductive; an adversary would lose any conflict, or the costs involved in winning it would exceed any likely gains. Whilst the absence of a palpable military threat at a given moment in time has often been used by some policy-makers to justify cuts in their state's military power, the existence of that armed strength is frequently the very reason why there is no obvious menace to their state's security. Moreover, as any military forces can only be expected to fulfil tasks for which they are adequately equipped and prepared, statesmen and women must endeavour to envisage the sort of missions that they will call upon air power to perform, if only because this will have tremendous ramifications for procurement policy. Aerospace capabilities are expensive and have a lengthy gestation period. It is therefore essential that the requisite capabilities be identified, a commitment to their development be secured over the longer term, and the necessary adjustments to national scientific and industrial policies be made. This can only be carried out with the support of society as a whole.

With regard to the actual use of air power, politicians must, to begin with, acknowledge that there is no point in possessing military muscle unless one has a willingness to use it when circumstances warrant it. They must also continue to regard aerospace assets as part of a balanced range of capabilities; even if it proves to be the case that we now stand on the cusp of a period in which we wage wars of choice more often than wars of necessity, planning must focus on the latter, not the former. Either type of conflict will inevitably bring power-struggles between the military and their political overlords, but the more choice there is concerning the prosecution of the war, the more intense these disputes are likely to prove. For whereas in Moltke's time the distribution of authority and responsibility within the state was so much simpler, today it is far less obvious who ultimately determines strategy and, in many instances, targeting policy. Is it the civil power in the form of politicians? Is it the international lawyers and other civil servants who advise them? Is it the military? Is it public opinion, channelled by the 'CNN Factor'? Or is it the 'smart' machinery to which we have entrusted so much of the running of our lives, including our battles? As war should be the continuation of policy by other means, the decision to initiate hostilities should always be the prerogative of the political authorities. However, once fighting commences, politicians should recognise that they, like everybody else involved in a war, will at best enjoy only imperfect control in what is, after all, a revolutionary process.

CHAPTER 3

COALITION AIR OPERATIONS
Group Captain Stuart Peach

"We have got to be of one family and it is more important today than it has ever been."

General Eisenhower, 1950

INTRODUCTION

THE CENTRAL THEME OF THIS BOOK is to place air power in context for the new Millennium. The thesis of this chapter is that working with allies is a central and vital tenet for the current and future employment of air power. Since the inception of manned aircraft to the present day, air forces have operated in coalition. As we enter the new Millennium and the post-Cold War era of uncertainty, air forces will continue to do so. This chapter postulates that it is not the nature of conflict that is changing, rather the way we plan to conduct that conflict. Therefore, as air power technology matures, the utility of air power across the spectrum of conflict – working in coalition to create synergy – appears to lend itself to the diverse and multifaceted battle space of the future.[1]

Throughout the history of conflict, groups of state or sub-state actors have sought comparative advantage or victory for their way of life over competing nations, groups or tribes. This has involved the creation of coalitions of the willing or, in the days of empire, the subordination of other groups in common cause in pursuit of perceived vital interest. Looking at the history of conflict, that interest has varied from extending or defending territory maintaining religious freedom or exercising the right of self-determination, to pursuing economic or trade advantage – the themes are enduring and independent of technology or the means and medium of waging war.[2] Coalitions, whether an *ad hoc* informal grouping or a formal alliance, remain part of that central theme of warfare to this day. Some coalitions develop an institutional framework and a bureaucratic momentum of their own and mature into robust alliances, whilst others founder

---

1. US commentators suggest air power may become the dominant military instrument of choice. See B.S. Lambeth, 'The Technology Revolution in Air Warfare', *Survival*, 39, 1, (1997), 65-83 for a contemporary view of those changes or Professor Mason's summary of the impact of technology on air power in Chapter 4.

2. M.Walzer, *Just and Unjust Wars*, Harper Collins, 1977, offers an excellent summary of the theory of conflict.

when the purpose for which they were established has been achieved. Regardless of the pattern of change to conflict, this chapter postulates that sovereign nations and sub-state groups will continue to seek friends and allies to build comparative advantage around the spectrum of conflict.

There is a significant distinction between coalitions and alliances. The OED defines an alliance as "the combination [of nations] for a specific object between sovereign states"[3]. Alliances are formal, can be bound into the rubric of international law by treaty and can be enduring. Coalitions, on the other hand, are less formal and can be less enduring. The OED definition of a coalition is "a temporary alliance of distinct parties for a limited purpose"[4]. Other definitions which are germane to the subject, are joint, combined and multinational. Joint operations are operations conducted by armies, navies and air forces of the same nation. NATO defines combined operations as: NATO allies working together operating to NATO doctrine and procedures,[5] whereas multinational operations represent an *ad hoc* coalition of nations or groups working together for a perceived common cause. Given the broad sweep of this Book, this Chapter will employ the term air coalition warfare.

The latter day nation state with its inherent right to maintain standing forces, was born out of the Peace of Westphalia in 1648; a benchmark both in international relations and international law. The larger mass army coalitions of the Napoleonic era heralded the age of large scale warfare.[6] Much of our military strategic thinking and concepts such as the principles of war were born during this period. Indeed, the influence of writers and thinkers such as Jomini and Clausewitz remains profound to this day.[7] The military context for both was the study of war and warfare in coalition. Many of the Clausewitzian dictums which abound in the military lexicon to this day, such as 'Decisive Points', 'Lines of Operation', 'Centres of Gravity' and 'Culminating Point', not to mention *Schwerpunkt* or *Auftragtaktik*, were developed from the study of coalition warfare.[8]

---

3. Shorter OED, Oxford, 1985.

4. Shorter OED, Oxford, 1985.

5. See NATO Information Handbook, NATO Information Service, Brussels, 1997 for details of NATO C2 and planning procedures for complex emergencies.

6. See D.Gates, *The Napoleonic Wars*, Macmillan, 1997 for an excellent survey of the impact of the Napoleonic Wars.

7. See P.Paret, *The Makers of Modern Strategy*, Princeton 1976, for a masterly reader on the development of strategic thought in its historical context.

8. M.Howard, *Clausewitz*, OUP, 1983 and *War in European History*, OUP,1976 provides a comprehensive introduction into Clausewitz's thinking and warfare in the context of the mid nineteenth century.

Whilst they remain relevant as concepts, this chapter postulates that the context in which they are applied has changed.

This Chapter will examine recent conceptual thinking on air power and air power doctrine. The historical experience of air power in coalition from the WWI and the Grand Coalition of WWII, through major regional conflicts in Korea, Vietnam and the Gulf to the NATO alliance test over Bosnia is considered from a coalition warfare perspective. Campaign study of coalition warfare offers valuable themes and lessons for the future, whilst highlighting the potential disharmonies which coalitions may confer. The remainder of the chapter develops a paradigm for coalition warfare built on sound sensible and simple command and control, interoperability in its broadest interpretation, sustainability and supportability issues before offering thoughts for the future.

AIR POWER CONCEPTUAL THINKING – DISCARDING THE HISTORICAL BAGGAGE?

Air Power is an unusually seductive form of military strength because, like modern courtship, it appears to offer gratification without commitment. Eliot Cohen, 1996.

It is not the place of this chapter to explore the legacy of exaggerated claims made by early air power theoreticians, nor the post-Gulf War evangelism of air power 'first, middle and last' exponents, but the characteristics of air power have enduring relevance in future planning for air coalition warfare. What is worth emphasising is that air power philosophy and theory were thrust into the public, political and strategic imagination before the technical means had been developed to deliver that promise. Douhet in his seminal work, *Command of the Air*, published in 1921 postulated that air power would enormously enhance the combat power available to states with little possibility of defensive measures against an offensive aerial strategy. In the UK, Trenchard saw his fledgling RAF as a war-winning weapon; indeed, in the context of the 1930s, even the British Prime Minister contended 'the bomber will always get through'.[9] WWII put such theories to the test with results that remain controversial to this day. Nevertheless, the air bombardment and its counters of WWII defined the characteristics of air power which have endured and remain relevant for the Millennium.

---

9. Sir Stanley Baldwin speaking in 1935.

Air power's comparative advantages such as speed of response, global reach, flexibility, versatility, interoperability and the ability to switch tempo and pace allow air power to operate free from the zonal and territorial constraints that may limit maritime or land forces. All have their enduring place in air coalition warfare. Indeed, some such as flexibility and versatility can operate in cadence in complex, fast-changing conflict scenarios to create the very synergy that intervention forces seek to build decisive advantage. On the other hand, the relative limitations of air power such as impermanence, complexity, fragility and host nation basing constraints may have equally enduring relevance. They can be mitigated and may be relative, but can not be ignored during the planning for and conduct of air coalition operations. Similarly, factors which affect any type of military intervention operations, which we might call pervasive factors, such as night, weather, terrain, collateral damage and differential casualty sensitivities, may represent new and important planning factors. All such factors need to be incorporated in any conceptual model for future air coalition operations.

Moreover, if we accept that the characteristics of air power have enduring relevance, so do the factors that define and bound the employment of land and maritime environments. Land forces need to be deployed, protected and supplied before and during their exploitation of land manoeuvre to resolve conflict, restore territorial integrity or, to hold ground.[10] Similarly, maritime forces can deploy intervention forces through international waters free from host nation restraint, poise in a crisis area and, if required, project force from afloat into the littoral to achieve the political end-state.[11] But, although many potential flashpoints for conflict are located in the littoral, many are not. Dealing with crises in land-locked terrain deep inside a continental land mass will continue to provide a searching challenge for any intervention force.

Therefore, just as air power exponents can exaggerate the overwhelming aspects of air power, so the evangelists of the other environments can have their blind spots. As the nature of conflict becomes more multidimensional and multi-faceted, the Clausewitzian view of mass v mass warfare is increasingly being modified to encompass many new concepts. The ubiquitous presence and exploitation of space-based assets, the advantages offered by miniaturisation and digitisation and the development of information warfare concepts all help to build the critical advantage for western coalition forces of information management.

---

10. Both *British Defence Doctrine* (BDD), HMSO, 1997 and *British Military Doctrine* (BMD), HMSO 1996, offer excellent summaries of the basic characteristics and principles for land manoeuvre warfare.
11. The Fundamentals of British Maritime Doctrine (BR 1806) is being revised and should be published in the summer of 1998.

When the need to operate in coalition because of the need to spread political legitimacy is added, there is a pressing need to encompass all force elements within the rubric of defence diplomacy, conflict prevention and, if necessary, military intervention.

Given the potential complexity of the future conflict model, how can we begin to develop a paradigm for air coalition operations?

DOCTRINE FOR COALITION OPERATIONS

"Doctrine provides a military organisation with a common philosophy, a common language, a common purpose, and a unity of effort." General George Decker, 1962.

During the Cold War, doctrine for NATO Alliance coalition air operations was relatively straightforward. NATO procedures were honed to apparent perfection during the annual military manoeuvres cycle. Now, as the spectrum of conflict becomes less linear and more multifaceted, the doctrine gearbox needs to be switched from automatic into manual mode with gearing ratios set from 'two wheel drive low ratio' for routine patrols and deterrence postures, through active peacekeeping and peace enforcement to 'four wheel drive high ratio' for high tempo warfighting. But, even after warfighting has achieved its aim, post-conflict activity such as peace inducement and peace building or even a return to peacekeeping complete what could be described as the circular spectrum of conflict, illustrated below:

Figure 3.1
The Non-linear Spectrum of Conflict.

Although this model is intended to be purely illustrative, its utility in helping to review and develop current air doctrine for air coalition operations could be helpful in clarifying how we might plan to conduct future air coalition warfare. But, doctrine itself is a loaded term meaning different things to different organisations.[12] Whilst air forces have adapted their national doctrine to the post-Cold War world, with the exception of NATO organisational doctrine, universal doctrine for coalition warfare has – thus far – proved elusive. If we accept the premise that, increasingly, all military operations will involve more than one nation or air force, the need for precision in military terminology is critical. Given this divergence in views, it is worth examining the doctrine position for likely air coalition partners.

US STRATEGIC THINKING AND AIR DOCTRINE

"Our goal is to make air power the instrument of choice for the National Command Authority". General R.R.Fogleman, Chief of Staff USAF, University of Birmingham, 4 April 1997.

The US term in common use around much of the spectrum of conflict is 'Military Operations Other Than War (MOOTW), what the UK calls Peace Support Operations (PSO). And yet, US doctrine for air power remains largely focused upon air campaign planning on the Gulf War model, which has grown to develop the component command model, which has led to the Joint Force Air Component Command (JFACC) model being adopted by the US, NATO and the UK.[13]

US doctrine provides guidance for the employment of US forces with a nod to allies. That said, given the experience in environments as diverse as Somalia and Bosnia and the growing squeeze on the US Defence Budget, renewed interest in coalition warfare and doctrine for it has surfaced in the US. The National Security Strategy, the National Military Strategy, the 1997 Strategic Assessment and elements of the Quadrennial Defence Review (QDR) all focus upon coalition operations to a greater extent than has previously been the case. The US National Security Strategy postulates several circumstances which favour the military use of coalitions, "we will act with allies whenever we can, in alliance and partnership

---

12. The OED defines doctrine as: 'that which is taught' (Shorter OED, Oxford, 1985, 589).
13. P.Sabin, Modern Air Power Theory some neglected issues, Air Clues, September 1994 encapsulates the post-Gulf War problems with Air Power theory.

when our interests are shared by others to enhance the effectiveness of coalition operations with an overseas presence to improve our ability to operate with other nations".[14] The National Military Strategy states: "our armed forces will most often fight in concert with regional allies and friends, as coalitions can decisively increase combat power and lead to a more favourable outcome to the conflict."[15] The 1997 Strategic Assessment confirms this central theme and is even more specific: "political imperatives will drive the US to co-operate with others even when US forces alone are adequate militarily. This co-operation is relatively straight forward when working with traditional allies, but increasingly US forces may work with coalition partners with different doctrine, technological sophistication and equipment from the US". The Strategic Assessment concludes that two approaches may be useful in addressing this problem: "ensure that the US retains a cadre of forces well trained to act as liaison officers with coalition partners and operate in vertical coalitions where the US have advanced military capabilities such as airlift, logistics, deployable communications and surveillance equipment to share information with coalition partners to enhance the capability of the coalition as a whole."[16]

This strategic guidance is now reflected in doctrine which is emerging in a myriad of US official and semi-official publications; doctrine which incorporates lessons learned both from the Gulf War and subsequent operations including Deliberate Force over Bosnia in 1995. The vision of 'Joint Vision 2010' has cascaded into revised basic USAF Air Power Doctrine, AFDD 1, published in November 1997, but this document does not specifically focus upon the likely needs and shortfalls of coalition partners nor the fundamental difficulties with interoperability as US technology outstrips likely partner's ability to keep up. Therefore, a generic paradigm for air coalition operations would appear to be an appropriate step in the right direction. But, what of NATO ? Surely NATO CJTFs are the answer for air coalition doctrine ?

---

14. Jt Pub 1, Ibid, Pages 45-48.

15. Quoted in "A.J.Rice, Command and Control, The Essence of Coalition Warfare", Parameters Spring 1997, Page 153.

16. 1997 Strategic Assessment, NDU Press Washington, Pages 252-253.

THE NATO POSITION

"NATO will become the military coalition that contains so many former adversaries that no serious student of history would have predicted it". Madeline Albright, US Secretary of State writing in the Economist, 15th February 1997.

One of the great successes of NATO, as acknowledged by leading US and UK strategists, has been to formulate and codify political processes and standard procedures for multilateral and multinational operations. It is widely acknowledged that NATO procedures lay behind the successful organisation of the air campaign during the Gulf War.[17]. At all levels, NATO publications reach and are understood by an international audience. NATO strategy is enshrined in Military Committee endorsed documents, translated into formal guidance by operational level commanders and developed by NATO staff officers into tactical procedures and doctrine.[18] The emerging NATO CJTF model provides an example of how far that Cold War organisational model has come. NATO governments agreed at the NATO summit of January 1994 "to adapt further the Alliance's political and military structures to reflect the development of European Security and Defence Identity (ESDI) and endorse the concept of CJTFs."[19] This was followed by the "Political-Military Framework of the CJTF HQ Concept" (PO 63) of May 1996 subsumed into MC 389, the "MC Directive for CJTF Implementation".

The resultant NATO CJTF HQ Organisational Doctrine has been issued to headquarters and will undoubtedly assist the process of integrating the new members of the Czech Republic, Hungary and Poland who will accede in 1999. It offers a detailed model for the formation of a multinational Headquarters to deal with both Article 5 and non-Article 5 contingency operations. Below this joint level, NATO continues to refine and develop tactical doctrine for the employment of air power. In particular, NATO has developed Standard Procedures for Composite Air Operations (COMAOs), air to air refuelling (AAR) and Supplementary Plans (SUPPLANs) for airspace management, the suppression of enemy air defences (SEAD) and co-ordination with land and maritime forces. A particular nugget for the subsequent development of NATO tactical concepts is the NATO Tactical Leadership Programme based at Florennes in Belgium. Under this academic and live exercise programme, aircrews from

---

17. R.P Hallion, *Storm over Iraq*, Smithsonian, 1992 gives a detailed overview into the thinking and principles of organisation that led to the Gulf War Air Campaign.
18. NATO Handbook, Part II, NATO 1995, gives a clear account of how the NATO 'process' works.
19. S.R.Sloan, NATO's Future, *Beyond Collective Defence*, NDU, INSS, 1996.

NATO and partnership nations fly together for a consolidated period to validate tactics and share and exchange information. But, despite the shift in emphasis away from Article V, in the alphabet soup of competing security organisations, NATO doctrine remains very focused upon Headquarters and 'Standard Operating Procedures' for Alliance partners. For air coalition operations, the lacuna remains. The UK, however, conscious of its need to rely on allies has recently led the charge in the development of doctrine for PSO-type operations. Doctrine which may have a wider applicability for air coalition warfare.

THE UK POSITION

"The UK has interests and responsibilities across the globe. Successive British Governments since the Second World War have concluded the UK's security can best be guaranteed through collective defence." Statement of the Defence Estimates 1996.

Although the UK is undergoing a Strategic Defence Review (SDR), the UK Secretary of State, George Robertson has confirmed that, in defence policy terms, the UK will continue – wherever possible – to work with friends and allies in coalition.[20] Moreover, the UK is leading many allies in putting real meaning into the term 'jointery' with the formation of the Permanent Joint Headquarters (PJHQ) at Northwood in 1996 and the Joint Services Command and Staff College in 1997. The PJHQ concept in particular has enormous utility for future coalition operations as it attempts predict and plan for joint and combined military operations. In addition to its planning and troubleshooting role, the PJHQ has established strong bilateral links with the operational headquarters of potential military partners and has become the natural UK focus for participation in both formal and informal international coalitions through the mechanism of the UK Joint Rapid Deployment Force (JRDF).[21] The PJHQ, therefore, has an important role to play in developing joint warfare doctrine and procedures,[22] a role recognised within "British Defence Doctrine" a capstone UK document published late in 1996, which has been issued to all senior serving officers and

---

20. See, G.Robertson, The Strategic Defence Review, RUSI Journal, 142,5, October 1997, 1-6, for an overview of the SDR process and the importance to the UK, in defence policy terms, of working with allies and coalition partners..

21. RUSI Newsbrief, September 1996, Pages 65-66.

22. RUSI Newsbrief, March 1997, Page 17.

offers clear guidance for the employment of British forces in a coalition context.[23] Within the overall defence doctrine context, generic UK air power doctrine is defined by 'Air Power Doctrine', AP 3000, which focuses on characteristics, capabilities and process of air power, identifies roles and describes the factors required to wage successful generic air operations. The current edition of AP 3000 does not offer guidance *per se* for air coalition operations,[24] but AP 3000 is in the process of revision and the 3rd Edition, to be published in 1998, will include revised conceptual and basic air doctrine to reflect utility in coalition around the spectrum of conflict.

Basic air power doctrine focuses upon control of the air, concurrent or parallel air operations which may be mounted, in coalition, independently from the joint campaign and combat air operations in indirect or direct support of the joint campaign. Due emphasis is given to interoperability in its widest interpretation and to force protection issues for deployed forces. In addition to BDD, therefore, AP 3000, 3rd Edition, may of benefit to air coalition partners. The doctrine family tree for UK and coalition air operations is completed by the Joint Operations Doctrine Manual published by the PJHQ and the Royal Air Force 'Air Operations Manual', published by the Air Warfare Centre. All volumes emphasise the need to take allies and coalition partners views and capabilities into account at all levels. The UK, therefore, is in a strong position to influence NATO partners and others.

But, definitions, concepts and doctrine can only take us so far in understanding coalition air operations. In the increasingly complex world of future conflict, our responses will continue to be shaped by our experiences of the past. But, airmen can be equally guilty of 're-fighting the last campaign' as the focus on the historical study of coalition air campaigns will now demonstrate.

AIR CAMPAIGN STUDY

WORLD WAR ONE

"Dealing with the enemy is a simple matter when contrasted with securing the close co-operation of an ally". Major General Fox Connor, 1918.

---

23. Jt Publication 1, Ibid, Para 7.7, Annexes C & D.
24. AP 3000, 2nd Edition, HMSO, 1993.

WWI was essentially waged between two coalitions: the Central Powers of Germany, Austro-Hungary and Turkey; and Britain, France, Italy, Russia and the USA. Co-ordination between nations was extremely loose with parallel command and autonomous control. Although Anglo-French military staff talks had taken place as early as 1906, the talks were not a great success and mutual distrust and suspicion remained high.[25]

In 1914 flying was a hazardous, haphazard affair of questionable military utility. By 1918, aircraft had developed into a strategic asset of growing military potency which was attracting the interest of politicians and generals alike. That said, for much of WWI, aircraft were employed as 'long range artillery' with command and control firmly exercised at local level. Indeed, until 1918 aircraft were not generally concentrated in time and space except for fighter sweep operations.[26] In the spring of 1918, however, 27 Air Squadrons were concentrated in time and space, tilting the balance of the ground offensive and helping to achieve tactical breakthrough.[27] Furthermore, although something of a side-show compared to the cauldron of the Western Front, the 'strategic' bombing by German Gotha Bombers and Zeppelins of London in 1917 and the actions of the newly-formed RAF's 'Independent' Force against the Ruhr in 1918, created a lasting psychological impact upon politicians and the populace alike and helped to create air forces independent from the organic air arms of the Navy and the Army.

At the grand strategic level, as the total war expanded to include the US as well as Britain and France in coalition, no serious co-ordination of air support was undertaken. US political leaders remained reluctant to commit any US forces under any form of British or French command. US politicians and commanders insisted on equal treatment at the general officer level, despite clearly unequal force numbers in the field. This failure to agree to any form of 'partner' status between coalition partners, despite huge discrepancies in the number of committed forces, was to have lasting consequences for armies and fledgling air forces alike.

In coalition terms, the legacy of WWI was that unity of effort would only emerge from unity of command – a unity that proved elusive in the bickering and recriminations between erstwhile allies and coalition partners throughout the war. After the armistice of 1918, the 'Great Powers' returned to the 'Great Game' for power, wealth and influence. Apart from the idealistic and woolly arrangements

---

25. D.Kagan, *On the Origins of War*, Hutchinson 1995, Page 210.
26. A Short History of the RAF, MOD, 1994, Page 22.
27. See P.Daybell, 'The March Offensive', to be published in *RAF Air Power Review* in 1998.

which established the League of Nations, military coalitions and alliances were all but forgotten. But, air power had made its mark. It had entered the experience of some and the imagination of many. In WWII, however, it would be very different – eventually.

COALITIONS IN WORLD WAR TWO

"The greatest lesson of this war has been the extent to which air, land and sea operations can and must be co-ordinated by joint planning and unified command". General Hap Arnold, 1946.

At first glance, the Second World War marked the greatest level of coalition integration and sophistication in history. In 1939, however, the beginnings were not auspicious. Anglo-French distrust ran deep. Disagreements between the British and the French quickly surfaced over strategy and subordination of command and control arrangements for British expeditionary forces. As the phoney war progressed, Anglo-French command arrangements became ever more convoluted and controversial. On the air side it was little better, with Dowding as Commander-in-Chief of RAF Fighter Command, insisting that his precious modern squadrons of Spitfires and Hurricanes be preserved for the Battle of Britain which he felt was bound to follow. As the battle for France became reality, divisions widened. Older aircraft such as early Marks of Blenheim or the Fairey Battle experienced heavy losses in France, as did the outclassed biplanes of the French Air Force. The battles between Dowding, Portal and the Prime Minister to prevent the strength of the RAF being leached out in France need not detain us, but perceptions of *Schwerpunkt* depended upon nationality. This was hardly unity of effort and common cause.

Churchill, upon taking office, knew that liaison needed to be enhanced and he appointed Major General Sir Edward Spears, a veteran liaison officer of WWI and confidant of Churchill in his wilderness years, as the Minister responsible for military liaison with the French. Spears proved to be a poor choice. His memoirs were titled 'Assignment to Catastrophe' which suggests how bad relations had become.[28] This is not the place to enter the debate over the objectivity of memoirs, simply to suggest that, until the US entered the European War at the end of 1941,

---

28. See Spears, Sir Edward, Assignment to Catastrophe, London, Collins, 1954 for a compelling account of the nadir of recent Anglo-French relations.

European divisions and disharmonies predominated and coalition arrangements were scant and dominated by mistrust.

The first real example of serious allied co-operation was in the Pacific, and that was short-lived. As the reality of the strategic situation for the 'Imperial Powers' in the Pacific became clear in the rapidly changing and deteriorating situation after Pearl Harbour, a theatre-wide US, British, Dutch and Australian Command (ABDACOM) was established under General Wavell[29]. The interlocutor in Washington was General Marshall who, as Chief of Staff to General Pershing from 1917-24, well remembered the squabbling of the earlier war. But, again this command arrangement foundered as western Imperial possessions in the Pacific fell like dominoes to the Japanese.

Meanwhile as the air war over Europe gathered momentum, co-operation began to improve but it was a slow process. At the Casablanca Conference the agreement to prosecute a joint USAAF/RAF bomber offensive against Germany led to tentative steps in real co-operation, but again rivalry between key personalities in command placed a brake on progress.[30] Nevertheless by 1944, given the availability of resources the tide began to turn and the Grand Coalition created a coalition air strategic striking force of a size and dimension unparalleled in history.

Key to understanding the success of the Grand Coalition is the relationship established within the Joint Chiefs and their representatives in Washington. General Sir John Dill and General Marshall and their respective staffs appeared to be the apogee of common cause. Of course this public harmony was only achieved by a great deal of hard work.[31] Despite the apparent harmony, there were significant differences between the British and American approach to the strategic level and theatre level. Britain agreed to the establishment of the Combined Chiefs of Staff in Washington, but remained reluctant to accept the freedom of action granted by the US to Theatre Commanders.

At the operational level, the split between the 'independent war winners' and the 'tactical air support' generals and air marshals widened. In the western desert, RAF commanders such as Coningham, Broadhurst and Tedder, proved that air power – when focused – could be decisive in support of the joint campaign. As

---

29. Rice, Ibid, Page 157.
30. Much has been written on RAF/USAAF disagreements over strategy and tactics. See Max Hastings account in Bomber Command, Pan 1987, or John Terraine in the 'Right of the Line', Macmillan, 1985, 468, for a more detailed account of the targeting controversy.
31. See, J.Keegan (Ed), *Churchill's Generals*, Warner, London, 1991, 51-69, for an outstanding monograph on the crucial role of Coalition interlocutor played by Sir John Dill.

Tedder himself remarked: "the four years of the Mediterranean campaign provided us with a clear step-by-step demonstration of the development of air power, and introduced in rather brutal terms the new factor of air superiority and its effect on the operations of the land and sea forces."[32] The lessons were not lost on commanders such as General Eisenhower who created a fully integrated combined staff.[33] The realisation that air power needed to be integrated into the whole plan was a key facet in the success of Operation Overlord and the war in Europe, but was over-shadowed in the years immediately after the WWII by the long controversy over strategic bombing.[34].

Looking for enduring lessons, we need look no further than General Eisenhower. His key characteristics for success in coalition remain as true today as when framed in 1944: "for commanders: patience, tolerance, frankness, absolute honesty are absolutely essential, as are the characteristics for good staff officers: confidence, logic and loyalty."[35] WWII saw the principle of unity of purpose translated into unity of command within widely different operating environments, leading to a unity of effort unsurpassed in military history. This legacy of co-operation and mutual understanding created in the wartime alliance – especially of air forces – was carried forward by junior and middle ranking commanders and staff officers into the embryonic military structure of NATO in the 1950s.[36]

WWII had united all allies in common cause with a common purpose. In a war of national survival, command and control compromises could be tolerated and worked around. As the immediate memories faded, however, air coalition procedures were soon to be put to the test under the auspices of the United Nations in Korea with very different results.

---

32. See A.Tedder, 'With Prejudice', Hodder & Stoughton, London ,1966.
33. N.Gelb, Ike and Monty, Morrow, New York, 1994, provides a comprehensive account into the UK/US command relationship.
34. Recent works such as R.Overy, Why the Allies Won, London, Pimlico, 1995, attempt to lay the ghosts of the controversy.
35. Quoted in Rice, Ibid, Page 159.
36. NATO, Facts and Figures, NATO, 1989, Page 23.

THE KOREAN WAR – A DIFFICULT COALITION

"Korea does not matter. I'd never heard of the place until I was 74. Its importance lies in the fact that it has led to the rearming of America". Winston Churchill, 1950.

Sixteen nations responded to the UN's request for assistance in Korea, seven of which contributed air forces. Canada, Greece and Thailand offered transport aircraft and the US, Britain, Australia and South Africa offered air to air and air to ground forces. The RAF played little part in unit strength although several individual pilots flew with the USAF and RAAF, and Army Austers and RAF Sunderlands played an important role filling gaps in the US inventory. Britain was over-stretched with imperial air policing and control operations in Malaya. Indeed, it was a source of irritation between Britain and the US that Britain continued to apply pressure to the RAAF to divert assets from Korea to Malaya[37]. Similarly, South Africa decided to send fighter squadrons to Korea as part of its commitment to the UN, not in response to any request from Britain.

Although Britain's contribution to the air power campaign was small, differences emerged between Britain and the US on a number of occasions from the grand strategic down to the tactical level. Although nominally a UN-led operation, the US called the shots. British Prime Minister Attlee engaged in shuttle diplomacy at the end of 1950 in an attempt to persuade President Truman to change his strategy of attempting to exploit nuclear coercion. He failed. At the strategic level, Britain would not support General MacArthur's plans to cross into China either in hot pursuit or to bomb targets across the Yalu River. Attacks which took place, despite British objections, in June 1951.[38] At the operational level, although not represented at unit level, the RAF were represented in some strength in all operational level headquarters. This created resentment amongst Commonwealth pilots who, despite commitment in unit strength, were under direct command of the US and had no representation in HQs. This was an important and enduring lesson. Although it may not be neat in textbook or doctrine terms, nations need a seat at the decision-making table. Complete subjugation of command causes problems – particularly when things go wrong.

Moreover, divisions deepened between US air arms. The newly independent USAF carried out a short B-29 strategic bombing campaign in an attempt to

---

37. D.Lee, Eastward, A History of NEAF, HMSO, 1984, Pages 107-120.
38. H.Probert, High Commanders of the RAF, HMSO, 1991, Page 44 reveals that ACM Slessor, Chief of Air Staff was despatched to Washington in an attempt to soften the US line; he failed

expel North Korean forces from the area around Pusan in 1950. This campaign was stopped when they ran out of targets. As the war dragged on, the amount of forces committed into Korea and the logistics effort to sustain them mounted.[39] Although air power historians can point to many firsts such as the advent of jet air to air combat and the tactical success of the Sabre against the Mig-15, at all levels air power was poorly co-ordinated and employed.[40] The USAF, USN and USMC clashed over strategy, doctrine and the conduct of operations with several avoidable fratricide incidents. The disharmonies between US air arms and allies appeared to outweigh any advantage of extra forces but the abundant lessons of WWII were ignored in the scrabble for command posts and influence.[41] Even after the conflict ended, the lessons for the employment of air power in joint and combined operations were ignored as 1950s air forces settled into an increasing reliance upon nuclear weapons even for tactical aircraft.[42] A reliance which dominated thinking and doctrine; a reliance that was to be shattered in Vietnam.

THE VIETNAM WAR

"In Vietnam, The US lacked an appreciation of strategy. They ignored Clausewitz at their peril, won on the battlefield, enjoyed overwhelming logistical superiority – but lost the war". Harry Summers, 1981.

Although not strictly viewed as a coalition operation, a number of air forces (the RAAF, RNZAF and South Vietnamese Air Force) participated in the conflict in Vietnam alongside US air army. Moreover, significant differences in doctrine and *modus operandi* emerged between US air arms, particularly between the USAF and USN. The lessons of Korea had gone unheeded. With regard to allies, Australian and New Zealand air power was placed directly under operational control of the

---

39. Operation STRANGLE, an interdiction campaign designed to 'break' North Korean supply lines makes the point. 350 Allied aircraft were lost and over 300 damaged. Damage to the enemy was negligible. Using WWII platforms and technology, if the pilots flew low enough to hit interdiction targets they were hit by ground fire. If they flew high enough to avoid the ground fire, they missed their targets.

40. See M.Hastings, *The Korean War*, London, 1987, 312-320, for an excellent survey of the 'Air War' in Korea.

41. J.A.Winnefeld & D.A Johnson, *Joint Air Operations*, Santa Monica, 1993, 61, offer a highly critical account of US air leadership and co-ordination during the Korean War.

42. Mason, *Air Power, A Centennial Appraisal*, Brasseys 1994, Page 92.

USAF with little direct liaison.[43] South Vietnamese's air forces, on the other hand, operated on a classic WWI parallel command model. This may have been a decent political compromise, but was a strategic, operational and tactical disaster.

Just as in Korea, serious squabbling took place for the command and control of US air assets[44]. The local commander did not have full command and control of participating aircraft, the air campaign was severely constrained by politically-influenced target selection and much Cold War designed equipment was found lacking in a lower intensity environment against an enemy who fought unconventionally The focus upon existential deterrence and preparation for nuclear war with the Soviet Union had left tactical aircraft and systems neglected.[45] The overall consequence was that any synergy of sea and land-based air power was wasted, as in Korea, in disharmony both within and without the US forces.

That said, at the tactical level, US air arms learned the lessons quickly, developed new doctrine in the single manager concept, tested new procedures, modified weapon systems and developed existing platforms to be much more effective. Attack assets were packaged with electronic jamming aircraft and early anti-radiation missiles were employed in the *Wild Weasel* concept using the F-105G to tackle the threat posed by North Vietnamese Surface to Air Missiles (SAM).[46] Towards the end of the conflict, early precision guided munitions (PGM) were employed and rapidly demonstrated that a few PGM could replace a great number of free fall bombs from the B-52.

At the strategic level, the bomb-pause-bomb-pause approach proved inconclusive to the chagrin of the social science 'coercion' theorists.[47] Clodfelter in his 1989 book, *"The limitations of air power"* suggests the air war could not have been won until conditions changed. In 1972, the campaign required 'normal' military logistics which could be attacked by aircraft flying air interdiction missions. Nevertheless, North Vietnam continued to adopt an asymmetric strategy and overall results from extensive air operations were inconclusive. To this day, the air war waged by the US-led coalition in Vietnam was perceived to have failed. As we approach the Millennium, the legacy is still with us. The young lieutenants and captains of the late 1960s who participated in the mistakes of Vietnam are

---

43. Rice, Ibid, Page 161.
44. W.J.Webb, *The Single Manager for Air in Vietnam*, NDU JFQ Washington, Winter 93/4, Page 89.
45. *The Vietnam War*, Salamander, 1979, Page 88-96 covers command and control problems.
46. J.Broughton, *Thud Ridge,* Friendswood Houston, 1996, gives an excellent account of Wild Weasel operations.
47. See Andrew Lambert's Chapter on Coercion in Chapter 10 for an up to date treatment of the psychology associated with air attack.

running the US air arms now. Their memories and experiences continue to influence the planning and conduct of air coalition operations.

But, the apparent failure of air power in Vietnam did, at least, have a profound impact on air power thinking and doctrine in the US forces. The legacy in terms of training, weapons development and professional military education led to the development of air campaign strategies and an air power ethos that was to prove decisive in a different theatre – the Middle East.

THE GULF WAR

"In the Gulf War, coalition airmen and air power had the 'right stuff'. Because of the confluence of political, geographical and military factors, air forces were able to exploit the full range of their capabilities". General M.J.Dugan, USAF, 1992.

During the Gulf War, air power appeared to have come of age. Pundits and practitioners alike wove tales of new dawns and promises fulfilled. Air power was employed in a US-led and US dominated coalition. During the six weeks of combat, ten coalition air forces flew together in common cause. This *ad hoc* coalition was legitimised in a series of UN Security Council Resolutions (UNSCR), culminating in UNSCR 678, which permitted 'all necessary means' to be employed to evict Iraqi forces from Kuwait. In a rare demonstration of diplomatic solidarity, Russia – for reasons of her own – offered robust support for the UN line. But, cohesion within the coalition was not achieved overnight. President Bush spent a great deal of effort in creating unity of purpose within the disparate group of nations. Motives varied from perceptions of national survival to more complex Arabic notions of the future of the Middle East.[48]

On the 'values' front, determining common cause was made easier by the instantaneous portrayal of Iraqi intransigence on the global media. Public support for military intervention in western nations remained firm during the build up phase as international condemnation of Iraq grew. On the national interest front, however, motivation to justify involvement was more diverse. Some Gulf nations, notably Saudi Arabia, Bahrain and United Arab Emirates (UAE) saw the potential domino effect – they could be next. In this context, the struggle

---

48. See W.L.Cleveland, *A History of the Modern Middle East*, Westview, 1994, 422-428, for a more detailed account of the political complexities which underpinned the apparently 'seamless' coalition.

to liberate Kuwait was portrayed as a struggle for 'national' survival with a complex element of pan-Arabic solidarity thrown in.[49] Egypt and Syria, although not directly threatened, had their own reasons for joining the coalition and were rewarded handsomely for their support. Egypt had many outstanding loans cancelled and Syria's international pariah status was removed.[50] Maintaining the Gulf coalition became ever more tricky for politicians and senior military commanders alike, particularly as the military build-up changed gear into decisive military action.

Air power planning was conducted both to defend Saudi Arabia and to identify centres of gravity at all levels within Iraq. The USAF-dominated planning team assembled in Washington were heavily influenced by the ideas of Colonel John Warden. His seminal work, 'The Air Campaign' had been first published in 1989 and undoubtedly influenced USAF thinking.[51] On the coalition front, despite the inherent requirement to share information within a coalition, details of the offensive plan were formulated by an exclusive US team.[52] Under high level pressure, this was widened in September 1990 to involve the RAF and the RSAF were added to the list in November.[53] The French were excluded; an exclusion which rankled. This split in the coalition widened with the French government requirement that French air power should only be employed in support of French troops. General Horner, the air commander, managed to accommodate French requests in the interests of coalition cohesion.

One event which clearly highlighted the fragility inherent within such a diverse coalition was Saddam Hussein's Scud attacks against Israel. The attacks very nearly unhinged the whole coalition. It was only pressure from the very highest level that prevented Israeli retaliation. If the Israelis had retaliated, it is quite possible that the coalition could have fractured. The requirement to mount the 'Great Scud Hunt' eventually accounted for over 25% of total air attack missions into Iraq, undoubtedly lengthened the air campaign and provides an excellent

---

49. The comparative policies of the Gulf states remain opaque, but there is little doubt from contemporary accounts and memoirs that the Gulf states saw the conflict ñ despite the intrinsic difficulty of accepting western forces on Arab soil ñ as a conflict for their survival. Of course opposition groups within those states sensed a different opportunity. See Cleveland, Ibid, 431.

50. The US cancelled $7Billion of Egypt's international debts and Syria received a number of soft loans from Saudi Arabia, brokered by EU banks.

51. Warden's Air Campaign ideas were developed into the '5 Rings' model, based upon the idea that attacks against the leadership would lead to strategic collapse.

52. Hunt, Ibid, Page 43.

53. Hunt, Ibid, Page 41.

example of how, in the era of complex emergencies, tactical aircraft fly missions which can have grand strategic impact.[54]

Execution of the air campaign benefited from two aspects: NATO standard operating procedures and experience and interoperability of US/Arab aircraft supplied under Foreign Military Sales (FMS) programmes. Furthermore, air coalition planners played to coalition strengths within the nations. A good example is the RAF and JP 233, a complex and highly specialised airfield denial weapon, which had to be delivered at low level. The role of Tornado in delivering JP 233 was criticised in the UK media immediately after the campaign but undoubtedly played a significant role in successful counter-air operations against Iraqi airfields, and was highly praised by the US air commanders.[55] In similar vein, RAF Tornado GR1A reconnaissance aircraft gave the coalition its only night low level reconnaissance capability – invaluable in the much-publicised Scud hunt. French AS 30 missiles gave the coalition a much-needed HAS busting capability although integration of French Air Force assets remained difficult because of their lack of familiarity with NATO procedures.

The Air Commander, General Horner, grounded French and Qatari Mirage F-1 aircraft because they might be mistaken for Iraqi Mirage F-1s, a sensible command decision but one which caused coalition difficulties. Similarly, the Italian Tornado detachment did not integrate well into the coalition despite the bravery of their crews, largely as a result of incompatible logistics, a lack of a Precision Guided Munition (PGM) capability, outdated electronic warfare equipment and a lack of familiarity with night Air to Air Refuelling (AAR).[56] The availability of secure and jam-resistant US-compatible communications was a major lesson learned for tactical air power, since without the 'right' communications fit, tactical aircraft could not integrate with US Electronic Warfare and SEAD support assets. This remains a significant and growing issue for many smaller air forces as they study the costs and implications of maintaining a minimum entry standard for future coalition warfare.

Command and control of air assets during the Gulf War worked well. NATO procedures came to the fore, particularly for the airspace management and choreography of large strike packages. For tasking purposes, the US daily Air Tasking Order (ATO) was adopted across the coalition and, where necessary, translated into mission specifics by over 100 US liaison officers. With regard to space, US

---

54. Taylor, Ibid, offers details of the Scud Hunt.

55. See Sir Peter de la Billiere's memoirs, '*Storm Command*', 33 for praise for Tornado and its weapon system.

56. Hunt, Ibid, Page 43.

assets dominated the use of space for surveillance, monitoring and navigation. Indeed, the space-based Rockwell Global Positioning System (GPS), became a pre-requisite for the delivery of PGMs, when most non-US allies did not have the equipment in their aircraft. General Horner allowed coalition forces to perform the missions they desired to satisfy national requirements, a feature of air coalition warfare which may not be repeated in an asset scarce environment. At times, the sharing of information could have been better and again the French felt isolated and frustrated by the use of the 'NOFORN'[57] caveat to protect US intelligence and targeting information. Similarly, the role of coalition media and its interplay with the emerging satellite news networks could have been better handled.

That said, personal relations between senior commanders were excellent. Relationships made early in selected officer's careers through the shared experience of multinational exercises, clearly paid off.[58] This was and remains particularly true if the coalition experience is bolstered by career-long bilateral contacts between air forces, as in the case of the USAF/RAF and USAF/RSAF; again this point was not lost on the French who have subsequently joined the RAF in the Franco-British Euro Air Group. Thus, in addition to the detailed co-ordination requirement for the whole panoply of combat support for composite air operations, a major lesson from the Gulf War was that the employment of air power requires more than good aircraft and crews, it is the overall system that counts. This lesson has not been lost on US planners, shaping 'system of systems' and RMA concepts. Other lessons need to be applied with caution. It is most unlikely that future adversaries of western intervention will allow a six month build up of forces, a nine week air campaign and allow forces deployed in static positions to be attacked by the full weight of western military technology. It is much more likely that future opponents will adopt an asymmetric strategy, which will not follow Saddam Hussein's pattern of strategy, deployment or tactics.[59]

Arguably, however, the most important lesson of the Gulf air campaign was the outstanding unity of effort compared to the earlier coalitions of Korea and Vietnam; a common purpose which led directly to a unity of control albeit for limited aims in a limited conflict. The ghosts of Vietnam had been exorcised, but unfortunately they had moved west to the Balkans.

---

57. A US security marking meaning, 'No Foreign Eyes' or US Eyes only.

58. Taylor, Ibid, page 50 offers a personal view from General Glosson.

59. See C.Bellamy, *Knights in White Armour,* Hutchinson, 1997, 177-181, for an excellent survey of the consequences of the Gulf war in the context of a paradigm for future conflict.

RAF Tornado GR1s of IX Sqn RAF tanking from a French C135 tanker
under the auspices of the Franco/British Euro Air Group

Coalition Commanders at the Military Co-ordination Centre Zakho,
Northern Iraq August 1993

DENY FLIGHT AND DELIBERATE FORCE

"Cease-fire imminent. Heavy fighting continues." Christopher Bellamy, 1996.

The air campaign over the Balkans represented an acid test for NATO air power. It survived, but the lessons are worthy of study. NATO began to monitor operations over former Yugoslavia in October 1992 under the auspices of United Nations Security Council Resolution 816 known as Operation DENY FLIGHT. This was NATO's first air combat operation. During 1993 and 1994, missions primarily fell into the Combat Air Patrol category to exercise air denial to prevent the former Yugoslav Air Force from flying and to protect UN peacekeepers in the UN Protection Force, (UNPROFOR). Aerial coercion was attempted by bombing attacks against mainly Serbian ground targets, authorised nine times over two years through a complex UN and NATO command and control matrix. With the political and time lapse constraints applied, however, the attacks were largely ineffective.[60]

After NATO air attacks against Serbian ammunition dumps in Pale in May 1995, UNPROFOR peacekeepers were taken hostage, chained to military installations and 'exposed' on the world's media. Following this humiliation, throughout the summer of 1995, General Rupert Smith re-brigaded his ground forces inside the Theatre of Operations, whilst General Mike Ryan, USAF, the NATO air commander planned a detailed escalatory air campaign. After the clear political support of the London Declaration of July 1995 and the solid resolve of NATO's North Atlantic Council (NAC), NATO – acting in concert with the UN – launched Operation DELIBERATE FORCE in August 1995. This Operation represented a significant escalation with target sets carefully planned to deny Serbian forces communications and logistic support. NATO flew over 3000 sorties, flown in 3 weeks with excellent precision, discipline and co-ordination.[61] Within the NATO nations represented, the non-US contribution was some 35% of the total, with the RAF participation 10% of the whole.

NATO air forces were well used to working together and could draw on standard NATO doctrine and procedures; therefore air coalition friction was reduced. The stated objective of Deliberate Force was, within the political context of the operation, carefully limited to protect safe havens using force if necessary. In terms of employment of air power, political considerations, especially in target

---

60. C.Bellamy, *Knights in White Armour*, Hutchinson, 1996, page 117.
61. Kramlinger, Ibid, page 68.

selection, impacted significantly on the campaign. Each target was personally approved by the air commander, General Ryan. 'Reach-back' of targeting data to capitals to secure national political clearance became a routine.

In coalition terms burden-sharing was undertaken even at the expense of military effectiveness. Despite the tightest control over target selection and the avoidance of collateral damage, nations which did not 'own' PGMs were allowed to drop 'dumb' bombs to preserve coalition cohesion.[62] The tightest political and military control of all was exercised over the Luftwaffe. After a lengthy debate in Germany over the 'Constitutionality' of participation, the deployment of German Electronic Combat Reconnaissance Tornados to Italy in the summer of 1995 was the first military deployment of the Luftwaffe since WWII. They flew reconnaissance and very limited SEAD support missions with 'HARM' Anti-Radiation Missiles (ARM) and a senior German officer was present in the CAOC to observe each individual flight.[63]

Despite the apparent solidarity it was not all plain sailing for host nation support. Although Italy provided a number of bases for NATO aircraft, basing rights for the F-117 were denied. Some commentators have suggested this action was as a result of a perceived Italian slight over exclusion from the Contact Group or, within the military, reaction to the perceived take-over of the Italian-commanded Five Allied Tactical Air Force (5ATAF) and the NATO Vicenza Combined Air Operations Centre (CAOC) by the USAF in summer 1995.[64] Fortunately, however, NATO political resolve was firm and cohesion was high; this harmony reached and reinforced NATO's commanders on the ground.

NATO commanders were determined that the complex 'Dual key' UN/NATO C2 arrangements should be simplified and one of the key features, therefore, of the London Conference of June 1995 was the insistence by the military for a clear mission statement – which was given. Both the UN and NATO C2 keys were 'turned' at the strategic level in advance of DELIBERATE FORCE.[65] The Theatre NATO 'Air C2' system was employed, but target selection and air tasking was, in fact, dominated by the USAF with the deployment of the 'Checkmate Group' from Washington and the support of the US Contingency Theatre Automated Planning System (CTAPs), to build the Air Tasking Order. As in the Gulf, air coalition partners were represented by liaison officers to spread

---

62. The lesson was not lost and most European air forces are now procuring PGMs.
63. RH. Dorff, Germany and Peace Support Operations, Parameters Spring 1996, Pages 73-87 highlights the convoluted tale of the involvement of the Luftwaffe over the Balkans.
64. Interview with Col Owen SAAS, Maxwell AFB ALA, 27 Mar 97.
65. Ripley, Ibid, Page 108.

support and keep in touch with capitals. In Bosnia, however, support from European air forces was more extensive. British, French and Dutch aircraft were able to offer tactical reconnaissance capabilities which added to the capabilities of the coalition. The lesson learned of the need for interoperability with allies has not been lost on US planners, but as new US 'stealthy' weapons platforms and 'uninhabited' weapon systems are deployed, this degree of interoperability could dissipate rapidly. In Bosnia, the US and Europeans could package and fly together. As US technology advances and 'information dominance' becomes reality, this degree of interoperability may be hard to repeat. But, politically, a campaign such as DELIBERATE FORCE, demonstrated that in NATO operations, national sensitivities must be observed.[66]

The results of DELIBERATE FORCE were impressive. NATO air power demonstrated the precision with which carefully selected targets could be struck by tactical air power operating in a multinational coalition[67]. Control was exercised virtually up to the last second prior to weapon release, but it was the ability of junior air crews to exercise discretion in targeting to 'guarantee' the avoidance of collateral damage and bring bombs back which has drawn particular praise from the air commander. This demonstrates the ability of 'tactical' air power to operate flexibly and switch from the tactical to the operational or, even, to the strategic level.[68]

As we look to the future, air coalitions have to evolve and adapt to the demands of messy complex emergencies and advancing technology. The US has led or dominated all air coalitions since WWI so it is, perhaps, inevitable that US Command authorities should assume a continuing leadership role for future air coalitions. But the needs and views of allies must be taken into account. As a recent USAF Commander in Saudi Arabia has observed: "Coalition partners need to be involved in more training with us – they will be with us in contingencies and war and need to train with us at all levels".[69] Although the context for each campaign will be unique, as this brief survey has suggested, certain trends in air coalition warfare emerge. This chapter will now attempt to draw those trends together to advance a paradigm for future air coalition operations.

---

66. Hunt, Ibid, Page 64.
67. NATO Declares war on the Bosnian Serbs, The Economist, September 2 1995, Page 35.
68. Interview, General Ryan, May 1997.
69. Lt Gen C.Franklin USAF, JFQ, 3/95, 7.

A PARADIGM FOR AIR COALITION OPERATIONS?

KEEP IT SIMPLE! – COMMAND AND CONTROL

"We must design our military forces in terms of their political purpose ... we must build an intellectual framework that links forces to policy." Admiral William Owens.

In campaigns where there has been clear unity of purpose between coalition partners, unity of effort has followed. If that unity of purpose is lacking and nations are pursuing separate agendas, unity of effort cannot be maintained and the coalition will falter or fracture. Coalitions will invariably continue to require some form of compromise, but learning to share information and intelligence to build information dominance may be hard to do. In NATO, information sharing and targeting regimes should emerge from existing arrangements without extensive remodelling, even allowing for new members. The UN now has a successful information and reporting department in New York which performs the 'soft' intelligence function for international crisis monitoring.[70] As the spread of 'soft' security information grows through the information revolution and the Internet, the fusion of information to offer commanders the right information at the right time may become a key determinant of success for future coalitions. To take an optimistic cut, this culture of sharing will succeed with top-down support from political leaders and bottom-up training to engender mutual trust and respect. To take a pessimistic cut, information dominance will remain the key coalition aspiration, but could prove the most elusive; perhaps information management might be a more appropriate term.

Turning to models for air C2, despite the apparent preponderance of US air power, the parallel command model, with the US in overall command, should not be regarded as the model of choice. Since the Gulf War, western military concepts and doctrine staff have developed the Component Command Model with a Joint (deployed) Force Commander and a separate Component Commander for each 'environment' land, sea and air. NATO's Combined Joint Task Force (CJTF) concept develops this into a Combined Model and ongoing air operations over Iraq and Bosnia suggest this amalgam of standing NATO and component C2 procedures works well. The question of who commands, however, may prove more difficult. In coalitions of the willing, imperfect C2 solutions may

---

70. Interview with Brigadier General Bhavat, UN Department of Peacekeeping, New York, 24 March 1997.

have to be accepted to preserve political legitimacy. US forces served under over-all Turkish Command in Somalia, although some in the US question the military efficiency of this arrangement.[71] A way out of the difficulty may be to recognise the inherent dangers in creating military organisations and procedures based upon a coalition operation that has gone well. The key issue is the abrogation of national command. The requirement for all participating nations to be repre-sented at a senior level within a coalition will remain paramount. Despite the apparent acceptance by nations of 'command' subordination implicit in NATO Cold War C2 arrangements, the reality of the world of complex emergencies suggests the most acceptable arrangement is for coalitions to exercise control with command retained at the national level through national representatives or liai-son officers. This is precisely the arrangement that has proved so successful for IFOR and SFOR in Bosnia and arrangements to acknowledge this political real-ity should be worked into component command models.

Another key conceptual lesson, is the requirement for the integration of coali-tion staffs to avoid national stovepipes or dominance by the senior partner. If this does not happen, 'bottom-up' friction within a coalition can quickly emerge. Again, NATO doctrine to support the CJTF concept may prove a successful start point for staffs charged with putting together an *ad hoc* coalition. In areas where NATO may not be the selected UN Chapter VIII regional security organisation, other security organisations such as the WEU or OSCE in Europe may fill the void. Recent agreements to nominate NATO's Deputy SACEUR, a British General, as the nominated NATO point of contact for WEU planning is a step in the right direction.[72] For air forces, the trick for the future will be to expose poten-tial air coalition commanders to sufficiently broad training, so they can operate efficiently and effectively in a multinational operation. Recent UK initiatives to focus a Higher Command and Staff Course (HCSC) and a JFACC Course at this military strategic/operational coalition level work well and may be expanded to include NATO partners. But, as David Gates points out in Chapter Two of this Volume, in an expeditionary era of interventions of choice, it may be equally important to ensure that diplomats, officials and politicians understand the complexities of coalition warfare C2 arrangements.

We can, therefore, be optimistic that C2 planning for air coalitions is well advanced. NATO's success in providing a matrix of standing combined C2

---

71. See, K.Allard, *Somalia Operations Lessons Learned*, NDU press, Washington, 1995, for an excellent summary of the problems associated with the US deployment in Somalia.

72. See E.Foster & G.Wilson (Ed), *'CJTF – A Lifeline for European Defence Policy'*, RUSI, London, 1997 for a fuller account of the wider utility of the CJTF concept.

arrangements provides a model built upon unity of control with common operating procedures, regular experience of combined training and integrated staffs. Such procedures are permeating to new and supplicant members in what, Jonathan Eyal has called the Radiator Effect.[73] With the comparative advantage of the English language as the *Lingua Franca* of the air, air coalitions can create efficient and flexible C2 arrangements which can build synergy in the application of air power. But, as Professor Mason has made clear in Chapter Five, air power relies implicitly upon technological advances and here the differential impact of technology can create disharmonies for any air coalition.

POTENTIAL DISHARMONIES – TECHNOLOGY AND INTEROPERABILITY

"Present equipment is but a step in progress". General H. Arnold

As the US develops the 'systems of systems' concepts and the Revolution in Military Affairs becomes more than a chimera, clear blue water is emerging between the air power technology available to the US air arms and the rest of the world's air forces. Clearly, there is a real risk that some nations will be left behind and will be unable to participate in coalitions of the willing. US authorities recognise that their technological lead could, in the coalition context, be counter-productive and are encouraging bilateral and multilateral links to address the issue.[74] Nevertheless, problems with technology transfer regimes, resource limitations and demands for a peace dividend, not to mention national pride all have a potentially negative role to play. But, not every campaign will require the deployment of the most expensive systems such as B2 Spirit, F-117 and JSTARs; indeed, the potential risk of loss of such high value platforms in peace support environments may militate against their deployment.

The hard question that NATO nations and others have dodged for many years is the question of role sharing or specialisation. If coalitions are a given for the future, why not specialise by nation, say, within Europe ? If we are only going to operate with allies, why not let Nation A specialise in, say, reconnaissance, Nation

---

73. J.Eyal, Director of Studies, RUSI speaking at NATO seminar University of Cambridge, December 1996.

74. General R.R.Fogleman in reply to a question following an address at the University of Birmingham, 4 April 1997 made clear the emphasis given to working with allies at all levels in the US forces.

B in air superiority platforms, Nation C in surface to air missiles and so on. Intellectually, this is logical and has great attractions for planners and treasury officials as other capabilities can be discarded. But, mindful of the planning fact that a capability once given up cannot be easily regenerated, most medium size air forces and air arms are attempting to maintain a balanced force approach with small numbers of multirole platforms. But, those platforms are ageing fast. Many air forces and air arms are struggling with, at best, aircraft and weapons systems designed 30-40 years ago for a specific Cold War purpose. Aircraft such as the Mig 21 and F-4 Phantom designed in the aftermath of the Korean War in the 1950s, will be flying well into the next century. Of course such systems can be modified with new avionics and equipment[75], but such programmes are expensive and do not alter inherently fuel hungry, maintenance intensive or, non-stealthy designs.

So, what can be done ? Post-Cold War operations have demonstrated that precision, discretion and the avoidance of collateral damage is of enduring importance for any application of air power. For most smaller air forces, the short term answer is the acquisition of a PGM capability. Rapid progress is being made in NATO European air forces, but the integration and interoperability of PGM capabilities with new NATO members could be more problematic. Other investments in interoperability need to focus upon communications and electronic warfare and self-protection systems which need to be interoperable with US systems. A classic case is the increasing requirement for datalinks. Systems such as the 'Joint Targeting Information Distribution System' (JTIDS) may become a pre-requisite for participation in air coalitions with US air arms. But, such systems are expensive and some defence analysts have already warned that the minimum entry standard for air coalitions with the US may be reaching, for many, unaffordable levels.[76]

Moreover, interoperability is more than platforms and weapons systems. It is the interoperability of the whole 'system' that matters. If the subject of maintaining a credible minimum entry standard of capability and interoperability for potential coalition partners is not addressed soon, the military disharmonies that might ensue in the next air coalition could erode or even negate the very decisive edge of information dominance that 'new' principles and doctrine seek to create. Without a wider spread of multinational interoperable capabilities, coalitions of the willing may well become, in reality, a single nation effort without the burden-

---

75. The Israeli aircraft industry is amongst the leaders in this field of re-engineering with recent update programmes for Romanian Mig 21 and Turkish F-4 Phantom aircraft.
76. P.Dibb, 'Asia and the RMA'. IISS, London, 1997.

Opponents now partners. RAF Tornado F3 flying with Russian Air Force

sharing benefits of political legitimacy and shared interest implicit in a coalition. Furthermore, even in the US the resource pot is not limitless. As defence spending is driven remorselessly down by conflicting priorities for the same money, working with allies may make as much economic sense as political sense.

Training and exercises can help to expose comparative strengths and weaknesses to allow air planners to build a realistic data base for potential coalition partners. Here again NATO may have an important role to play in training aircrews, taskers and staff officers to recognise the realities of air coalition warfare. The NATO Tactical Leadership Programme (TLP) will continue to act as a bridge to new members and a lead and introduction to new partners. TLP is a success story and has assisted greatly a wider understanding of the true meaning of interoperability leading to the development of credible and achievable NATO COMAO procedures. Another vital element for the synergistic employment of air power is the mutual understanding and interoperability of tasking systems. Potential NATO air commanders and staff officers will need to stay abreast of a bewildering number of national and NATO C4I systems. Computer assisted war games, command post exercises, military education programmes and military exchanges will all have an increasingly important role to play.

The thesis for a paradigm for air coalition warfare, is that interoperability is more than a black box concept. It means interoperability in a much wider sense: in military culture, training, doctrine, equipment, procedures and command and control. But, even if we manage to embrace and develop all that, as Wing Commander David Foster makes very clear in Chapter Eight, air coalitions will founder without the right level of logistic support.

SUSTAINABILITY AND SUPPORTABILITY OF COALITIONS

"Strategy decides where to act; logistics brings the troops to this point". Jomini.

As defence budgets reduce, expensive weaponry and consumables become harder to justify and retain. Missiles do not have an unlimited shelf life. US sources estimate 15-20% of air to air missile stocks should be expended every year in practice camps to guarantee aircraft integration, weapon system effectiveness and ensure a rotation of missile stocks, so that the latest model is available for combat.[77] In some nations, such expensive annual training is the first victim of budget cuts. Similar problems apply when the providing nation offers a mid-life update to an existing aircraft or missile system but some initial customers cannot afford the upgrade. Therefore, what may appear to planners to be equally capable air forces, in reality are not.[78]

Equal problems apply to flying training. Routine activity often suffers as a result of sudden budget cuts. Eastern European air forces have suffered from a lack of aviation fuel for routine training since the end of the Cold War.[79] It is the cumulative effect of such reductions that bite into military capability and sustainability in terms of aviation fuel and weapons stocks. It is unrealistic to expect 'force goals' redolent of the Central Region of NATO of the 1970s to re-appear. As readers will note from Chapter Eight, the stuff we need to apply air power effectively cannot be ignored; logistics can be the Achilles heel of air power.[80] Although many air forces share the same aircraft types, the sharing of logistics on anything more than an occasional basis, remains something of a pipedream.

---

77. Pentagon staff briefing 20 March 97.
78. The F-16 programme highlights this dilemma. There is a large difference in capability between an unmodified mid-70s F-16A and an F-16C Block 50 Dash.
79. B.S.Lambeth, *Russia's Air Power at the Cross-roads*, RAND,1996,Page 38.
80. Mason, Ibid, Page 143 highlights the essential problem of logistics in the Gulf War.

With regard to supportability, again a process of education can enable coalitions to play to strengths. The military infrastructure in Saudi Arabia in 1990 greatly assisted the build-up of air power prior to the Gulf War. Similarly, Italian air bases tested by NATO tactical evaluations provided the forward base for operations in Bosnia. In future, new NATO members may be able to offer well found bases with suitable support infrastructure. In the UK context of the Strategic Defence Review, much has been made of the potentially restrictive nature of Host Nation Support (HNS) for air coalition operations, as nations such as Saudi Arabia set the conditions for the employment of coalition air forces.[81] Therefore, an alternative may be to place greater emphasis on carrier-borne air power. Although carriers can increase flexibility and poise free from basing constraints, naval aircraft generally operate at relatively short ranges and rely on land-based aircraft for many combat support functions. Long range AI and precision attack operations will remain the domain of land-based aircraft such as Tornado and F-15E for some time to come and air coalition planners need to take a realistic look at HNS depending on context and scenario and shape the air package accordingly.

A similar constraint could be airlift. Transport aircraft can demonstrate resolve and deploy light forces into a crisis region rapidly. Other roles and missions include intra-Theatre mobility and humanitarian operations. All air forces – even the US – are short of airlift for the large scale support of intervention operations. This shortfall has been recognised in the UK and more resources may be devoted to strategic lift. A holistic approach to deployment is needed to carry out extensive reconnaissance of potential crisis deployment areas to evaluate and if necessary negotiate potential HNS and identify potential choke points for the deployment of forces. New NATO members may be able to offer short range tactical airlift and mobility with support helicopters – capabilities which could be offered by Poland, The Czech Republic and Hungary, in a similar way to the airlift support offered by Russia and the Ukraine – often on a contractual basis – to support operations in Bosnia. In the medium term, NATO could develop the undoubted success of the AWACs concept into a NATO/European airlift force and aerial tanker force possibly with surplus civilian aircraft converted by the European industrial base. Such a fleet need not be excessively expensive, would act as a force multiplier and could offer an important and specialist role for smaller nations marginalised by the expense of keeping up with the US.

---

81. See Arthur Williamson's survey in Chapter Twelve for a fuller explanation.

The paradigm for air coalitions, therefore, suggests we take a much wider approach to interoperability and develop 'smart' deployable C2 systems to build the information dominance we seek. Existing platforms need to be modified to allow COMAO interoperability with US assets and platforms and the US may have to give a little to coalition partners in ensuring their views are heard and acknowledged. Air coalitions can play to multinational strengths. With good contingency planning and sound negotiations in the stages before deployment, the inherent compatibility of air power platforms to build on that key character-istic of air power – flexibility – should be an achievable goal. But, the key to success for any air coalition is mutual trust built through shared experience, exer-cises and training.

CONCLUSION

"More than any other form of military power, politicians find air power easy to manipulate, to employ or to withhold in the hope of achieving a nicely measured political effect". Eliot Cohen.

Air Power has been employed in coalition since its inception. The characteristics of air power remain extant. The speed of response, reach, flexibility, precision and versatility of air power lends itself to multinationality to increase combat power and military effectiveness. As we approach the next Millennium, the utility of air power around the spectrum of conflict is a reality. Air power is free from zones and boundaries. Recent air campaigns in the Gulf and the Balkans have demonstrated the ability of air power to deliver force with great precision. Questions, however, remain. The US stands apart in terms of air power capabil-ity. Likely coalition partners are saddled with increasingly obsolescent legacy systems. Air doctrine continues to focus upon the generic air campaign with a bias towards high intensity conflict, rather than complex emergencies. Despite the rich seam of history, specific doctrine for coalition operations and models for the future are singularly lacking.

We can learn from history to prepare for future air coalitions. In WWI although air power appeared to have marginal impact, it found its way into conceptual thinking. Sadly, the coalition lessons were ignored. In WWII, with a clear objective, a true unity of effort was achieved. In Korea and Vietnam, that unity of purpose was missing and the coalition suffered. In the Gulf War, air operations succeeded in shaping whole campaign, but their impact should not be exaggerated. In the Balkans, although air power was subject to the increasingly familiar constraints of casualty sensitivity and limitations on targeting to avoid collateral damage, when the discredited NATO/UN dual key command arrangements were refined and cohesion improved, air power responded to the challenge, met the objective and helped to shape the political environment. Campaign study clearly demonstrates the synergy of air power in coalition, but to develop a paradigm we need to put as much emphasis on previous failures as on success.

In the future, air power will continue to be employed in a complex and messy environment. Traditional labels and models may have diminishing utility. Air power may not always be the preferred option, but it is flexible, can surge, ebb and flow to match a given scenario and, given the overriding political quest for solutions at minimum price with minimum risk and minimum casualties, the utility of air power for any intervention operation cannot be ignored. With simple C2 arrangements which retain national command but delegate control, air power can be concentrated to decisive effect. The gap between the US and its allies in air power capability needs to be recognised and addressed. Limited defence spending needs to be focused upon the retention of interoperability of platforms, weapons and systems. But, regardless of concepts, doctrine, and technology, the essential requirement for success in coalition is trust. There is no place for internecine disputes; international coalition harmony must extend between forces. Interoperability should be seen as a wider concept than tactical interaction; it is the lifeblood of coalitions.

The challenges for air power will remain unpredictable and, despite the best efforts of international organisations, the next crisis will probably be unforeseen. What is predictable is that we who employ air power will have to work together in common cause; that is our heritage and our destiny.

CHAPTER 4

AIR POWER AND INTERNATIONAL AIR LAW
Dr. K. A. Kyriakides

INTRODUCTION

THE BRITISH GOVERNMENT attaches great importance to international law. In times of both peace and conflict, international law therefore affects all classes of British forces, all levels of the chain of command, every category of operation and all types of air movements. No less significantly, legal considerations exert a tangible influence upon the formulation of British Rules of Engagement – the principal means of codifying instructions from central government to individual commanders, and from those commanders to individual units and sub-units.[1]

It is of course true that some states and non-state actors have used military force and managed to achieve their immediate objectives with negligible regard for the basic norms of international law. However, a concrete lesson of twentieth century history is that any violation of international law can prove costly and counter-productive. In the short term, any state perpetrating such a violation runs the risk of sparking or escalating a crisis, estranging allies or neutrals, inviting the unwelcome attention of the world's media, and giving rise to untold domestic and international complications. In the longer term, any violation of international law may tarnish the reputation of the culpable state, undermine public faith in its armed forces and result in legal proceedings against individual personnel or the state itself.[2]

This chapter focuses on just some of the areas of international law which have affected – and will continue to affect – air power. The bulk of the chapter dwells on international air law, with particular emphasis given to its aspects relating to airspace and military overflights. Perhaps surprisingly, these aspects have

---

1. ROE are considered in Lt. Col. John G. Humphries USAF, 'Operations Law and Rules of Engagement in Operations DESERT SHIELD and DESERT STORM', *Air Power Journal*, Fall 1992, pp. 25-41.
2. Christopher Greenwood, *Command and the Laws of Armed Conflict*, Strategic and Combat Studies Institute Occasional Paper No. 4, Staff College, Camberley, 1993, pp. 1, 33 and 34.

attracted comparatively little scholarly attention in the UK but, for reasons detailed below, they remain of undeniable importance to day-to-day air movements and military planning. The chapter then goes on to summarise the area of international law concerning the inherent right of self-defence, particularly with respect to intruding military and civil aircraft. The Laws of Armed Conflict are just as crucial to air power but as they are already the subject of numerous academic studies they are not considered in this chapter except in so far as they affect the law of airspace.[3] Neither does this chapter examine the impact of international law upon aircraft carriers *per se*, although it must not be overlooked that the cardinal legal principles considered below apply as much to navy (and army) aviation as they do to air force aviation.

INTERNATIONAL AIR LAW

STATE SOVEREIGNTY OVER NATIONAL AIRSPACE[4]

According to a leading authority on public international air law, 'sovereign states have since Roman times created, recognised, regulated and protected certain exclusive private rights of the surface owner in usable airspace above his lands ... [I]t follows that states claimed, held and in fact exercised sovereignty in the airspace above their national territory long prior to the age of flight'.[5] Even so, the concept of state sovereignty over airspace only burst to prominence with the genesis of aviation at the turn of the twentieth century. Quite suddenly, this dramatic development compelled states to contemplate the potential of aviation as a threat to both national security and public order. One of the first states to

---

3. The Laws of Armed Conflict are considered in numerous studies, including the following: Dieter Fleck (ed.), *The Handbook of Humanitarian Law in Armed Conflicts*, Oxford, Oxford University Press, 1995; Greenwood, *Command and the Laws of Armed Conflict*; Michael A. Meyer (ed.), *Armed Conflict and the New Law: Aspects of the 1977 Geneva Protocols and the 1981 Weapons Convention*, London, British Institute of International and Comparative Law, 1989; W. Hays Parks, 'Air War and the Law of War', *The Air Force Law Review*, 1990, pp. 1-225; and the *Tri-Service Law of Armed Conflict Manual*, (Current Draft).

4. The Chicago Convention 1944 spells 'airspace' as one word, unlike the Paris Convention 1919, UNCLOS 1982 and the ICJ (in *Nicaragua v USA*) which refer to 'air space'. Except in places where the Paris Convention, UNCLOS and the ICJ are quoted directly, this chapter adopts the practice of the Chicago Convention and consistently refers to 'airspace' as one word.

5. John Cobb Cooper, *Roman Law and the Maxim "Cujus Est Solum" in International Air Law*, Montreal, Institute of International Air Law, McGill University, 1952, p. 43.

grasp that potential was the UK which led the way in enacting legislation asserting national air sovereignty. Tellingly, its Aerial Navigation Act was passed in 1911, a year in which an airplane was first used to drop a bomb and to conduct reconnaissance.[6] By the time of the outbreak of the Great War, France, Germany and other states followed the example of the UK by asserting national air sovereignty,[7] as did a number of others during the Great War itself.[8] In the inter-war years, the principle of national air sovereignty was incorporated into the domestic legislation of many more states[9] as well as into a succession of international conventions beginning with the Paris Convention for the Regulation of Aerial Navigation (which was concluded in 1919 and came into force in 1922). Under the Paris Convention: 'The High Contracting Parties recognise that every Power has complete and exclusive sovereignty over the air space above its territory.'[10] As one scholar comments, the drafting of the Paris Convention was a 'triumph of the sovereignty principle', while the use of the words 'complete' and 'exclusive' clarified that military aircraft are not given a right of innocent passage through foreign national airspace;[11] by distinct contrast, warships generally enjoy a right of innocent passage in the territorial seas of other coastal states. The principle of state sovereignty over national airspace was subsequently reiterated in other international conventions, notably the Ibero-American Convention 1926,[12] the Pan-American Convention 1928,[13] and the Chicago Convention on International Civil Aviation 1944.[14]

---

6. Aerial Navigation Act, 2 June 1911, *Halisbury's Statutes of England* 53 (2nd Edition). Quoted in Jacob M. Denaro, 'State's Jurisdiction in Aerospace Under International Law', *Journal of Air Law and Commerce*, Vol. 36, No. 4, Autumn 1970, pp. 688-728.
7. Nicolas Mateesco Matte, *Treatise on Air-Aeronautical Law*, Montreal, Institute and Centre of Air and Space Law, McGill University, 1981, pp. 84-87.
8. Examples include Denmark, Greece, The Netherlands, Norway, Sweden and Switzerland. Matte, *Treatise on Air-Aeronautical Law*, p. 86.
9. Examples include Canada and the USA. Matte, *Treatise on Air-Aeronautical Law*, p. 86.
10. Article 1, Convention for the Regulation of Aerial Navigation, signed in Paris, 13 October 1919, with an additional protocol signed at Paris, 1 May 1920. *Air Laws and Treaties of the World*, Vol. III, Washington D.C., US Government Printing Office, 1965, pp. 30933095.
11. Matte, *Treatise on Air-Aeronautical Law*, pp. 105 and 132.
12. Ibero-American Convention Relating to Air Navigation 1926.
13. Pan-American Convention on Commercial Aviation 1928.
14. Chicago Convention on International Civil Aviation 1944. The above mentioned Conventions are considered in several studies including: I.H. Ph. Diedriks-Verschoor, *An Introduction to Air Law*, Sixth Revised Edition, The Hague, Kluwer Law International, 1997; Matte, *Treatise on Air-Aeronautical Law;* and Marek Zylicz, *International Air Transport Law*, Dordrecht, Martinus Nijhoff Publishers, 1992.

The Chicago Convention of 1944 superseded the earlier conventions. Described as 'the final chapter on the regime of airspace lateral to national territories',[15] it remains in force today and 186 states had become parties to it by January 1996.[16] Among these are the UK and the other four permanent members of the UNSC.[17] Although the Chicago Convention is principally concerned with civil aviation and does not accord military aircraft with the rights given to civil aircraft, it still has a significant bearing upon air power.

Under Article 1 of the Chicago Convention: 'The Contracting States recognise that every state has complete and exclusive sovereignty over the airspace above its territory'. Under Article 2 of the Convention, the 'territory' of a state 'shall be deemed to be the land areas and territorial waters adjacent thereto under the sovereignty, suzerainty, protection or mandate of such State.'[18] These fundamental legal principles have been restated in both the Geneva Convention on the Territorial Sea 1958 and the UN Convention on the Law of the Sea 1982. Moreover, they have been described by the International Court of Justice as 'respond[ing] to firmly established and long-standing tenets of customary international law.'[19] In view of the implications of these principles for air defence, airspace control, air navigation and all types of air operations, it is essential to consider the extent to which national airspace extends both horizontally and vertically.

---

15. Denaro, 'State's Jurisdiction in Aerospace Under International Law', p. 695.

16. Martin Dixon, *Textbook on International Law,* Third Edition, London, Blackstone, 1996, p. 153.

17. *Shawcross and Beaumont on Air Law,* (Third Edition by Peter B. Keenan, Anthony Lester and Peter Martin), Vol. 2, 'Appendices, Tables, Index, Service', London, Butterworths, Appendix [A8], 'The Chicago Agreements'; and W.V. Jianduan, 'A Milestone of Air Legislation in China – Some Thoughts on the Civil Aviation Law of the PRC', *Journal of Air Law and Commerce,* Vol. 62, No. 3, February-March 1997, pp. 823-840.

18. Chicago Convention on International Civil Aviation, 1944, Articles 1-2.

19. *Military and Paramilitary Activities in and against Nicaragua (Nicaragua v USA) (Merits),* 1986 ICJ Rep 14.

THE HORIZONTAL DELIMITATION OF NATIONAL AIRSPACE

THE UN CONVENTION ON THE LAW OF THE SEA 1982 [UNCLOS 1982][20]

The Chicago Convention 1944 affirms that the national airspace of a state extends to the superjacent airspace above its land and territorial sea, the term 'territorial sea' having the same meaning as 'territorial waters'.[21] For most of the twentieth century, there was much international debate over the permissible breadth of the territorial sea with some states, notably the UK and the USA, advocating that states should only claim a territorial sea with a breadth of three miles, and others advocating that they could claim a territorial sea with a much greater breadth. This international disagreement explains why the Geneva Convention on the Territorial Sea 1958 was silent over the permissible breadth of the territorial sea. It is instructive to record that by 1958 senior British military officials believed that any extension of the 3 mile limit for territorial seas would have generated damaging military ramifications. In large part, they feared that any extension of the breadth of the territorial sea would have 'restrict[ed] sea and air movements' across the world[22] and allowed the Straits of Gibraltar to 'become the territorial seas of either Spain or Morocco', thus limiting the ability of the UK to operate military aircraft from Gibraltar.[23]

Eventually, the issue of the breadth of the territorial sea was largely settled by UNCLOS 1982, a multilateral treaty which eventually came into effect in November 1994. As of July 1997, over 100 states were parties to UNCLOS 1982. For its part, the UK originally abstained in the 1982 vote on UNCLOS but, in

---

20. Some implications of UNCLOS 1982 upon aircraft are considered in: Kay Hailbronner, 'Freedom of the Air and the Convention on the Law of the Sea', *American Journal of International Law 1983*, Vol. 77, pp. 490-588; and John Mordike and Wing Commander E.E. Casagrande, *The Law of the Sea Convention: Some Implications for Air Operations*, Air Power Studies Centre Paper Number 51, RAAF Base Fairbairn, Air Power Studies Centre, 1997.

21. Remark by Baroness Young, Minister of State, FCO, during the Second Reading of the Territorial Sea Bill in the House of Lords, Hansard, *House of Lords Debates*, 5 February 1987, cols. 382-383. Excerpt reproduced in Geoffrey Marston (ed.), 'UK Materials on International Law 1987', *British Year Book of International Law 1987*, Vol. LVIII, Oxford, Oxford University Press, 1988, pp. 497-649.

22. AIR 8/2182. Formerly 'secret' (now declassified) note by the Air Ministry to the Chiefs of Staff Committee entitled 'Limits of the Territorial Sea and Air Space' recording the views of the Chiefs of Staff at their meeting of 23 January 1958 (COS (58) 8th meeting), Public Record Office, Kew Gardens, Surrey, (hereinafter referred to as 'PRO').

23. AIR 8/2182. Formerly 'confidential' (now declassified) brief from the Air Ministry to the Vice Chief of the Defence Staff entitled 'Limits of the Territorial Sea and Air Space', 7 March 1958, PRO.

July 1997, Robin Cook, the Foreign Secretary, disclosed that the British govern-ment would accede to the Convention forthwith.[24] As a result, UNCLOS 1982 has taken on a deeper significance for the UK, including its maritime forces and, for reasons outlined below, its air power.

Above all else, UNCLOS 1982 impinges upon air power by virtue of its provi-sions concerning the territorial sea and national airspace of coastal states. Article 2 provides:

> The sovereignty of a coastal State extends, beyond its land territory and internal waters and, in the case of an archipelagic State, its archipelagic waters, to an adjacent belt of sea, described as the territorial sea.
>
> The sovereignty extends to the air space over the territorial sea as well as to its bed and subsoil ...

Article 3 of UNCLOS 1982 provides:

> Every State has the right to establish the breadth of its territorial sea up to a limit not exceeding 12 nautical miles, measured from baselines determined in accordance with this Convention.

Article 4 of UNCLOS 1982 provides:

> The outer limit of the territorial sea is the line every point of which is at a distance from the nearest point of the baseline equal to the breadth of the territorial sea.[25]

Although the UK acceded to UNCLOS as late as 1997, a decade earlier Parliament had passed legislation extending the breadth of the UK's territorial sea from three to twelve nautical miles. Under Section 1 of the Territorial Sea Act 1987:

> the breadth of the territorial sea adjacent to the UK shall for all purposes be 12 nautical miles; and
>
> the baselines from which the breadth of that territorial sea is to be measured shall for all purposes be those established by Her Majesty by Order in Council.[26]

In passing the Territorial Sea Act, the UK not only extended its own territorial sea, but effectively abandoned its long-held support for the notion that coastal states could only extend the breadth of their territorial sea to a maximum of three miles.

---

24. Hansard, *House of Commons Debates*, Written Answer by Robin Cook, the Foreign Secretary, to Ronnie Campbell, 21 July 1997, columns WA 397-398.
25. Articles 2, 3 and 4, UN Convention on the Law of the Sea 1982.
26. Sections 1 (1) (a) and (b), Territorial Sea Act 1987.

Significantly, several states which have not ratified UNCLOS 1982 have nonetheless adopted legislation extending the breadth of their territorial sea to 12 miles, a fact which underlines that customary international law generally recognises the 12-mile maximum. Statistics bear this out. As of January 1996: 124 states claimed a territorial sea of 12 miles;[27] 6 states claimed a territorial sea of less than 12 miles,[28] as do some of the Dependent Territories of the UK;[29] while only 15 states continued to claim a territorial sea in excess of 12 miles[30] (although the UK, in common with many other states, does not recognise such claims).

By extending the breadth of their territorial sea to 12 miles, coastal states such as the UK consequently expanded their national airspace to encompass what had previously been international airspace.[31] Air power has been materially affected by this development, not least because of three factors:

- The widely shared tradition that the high seas, in contrast to the territorial seas and archipelagic waters of neutrals, 'belong to the areas of naval warfare'.[32]
- The established legal principle that aircraft possess freedom of overflight above waters which are beyond the territorial seas of states.[33]
- The established legal principle that the military aircraft of one state cannot enjoy a right of innocent passage above the territorial seas of other states.

---

27. In addition to the UK, these states include the other four permanent members of the UNSC: France, the People's Republic of China, Russia and the USA. 'Admiralty Notices to Mariners: National Claims to Maritime Jurisdiction', *Annual Summary of Admiralty Notices to Mariners in Force on 1 January 1996*. Excerpt reproduced in Geoffrey Marston (ed.), 'United Kingdom Materials on International Law 1995', *British Year Book of International Law 1995*, Vol. LXVI, Oxford, Oxford University Press, 1996, pp. 571-717.

28. The six are: Denmark (which claims a territorial sea of 3 nautical miles), the Dominican Republic (6 nautical miles); Greece (6 nautical miles), Jordan (3 nautical miles), Norway (4 nautical miles) and Singapore (3 nautical miles). 'Admiralty Notices to Mariners: National Claims to Maritime Jurisdiction'.

29. 'Admiralty Notices to Mariners: National Claims to Maritime Jurisdiction'.

30. Benin, Congo, Ecuador, El Salvador, Liberia, Nicaragua, Panama, Peru, Sierra Leone, Somalia and Uruguay all claim a territorial sea of 200 nautical miles, while Cameroon claims one of 50 nautical miles, Syria claims a territorial sea of 35 nautical miles and both Nigeria and Togo claim one of 30 nautical miles. 'Admiralty Notices to Mariners: National Claims to Maritime Jurisdiction'.

31. See the remarks by Baroness Young, Hansard, *House of Lords Debates*, 19 February 1987, Vol. 484, columns 1218-1219. Excerpt reproduced in Marston (ed.), 'UK Materials on International Law 1987', p. 596.

32. Wolff Heintschel von Heinegg, 'The Law of Armed Conflict At Sea', Chapter 10, Fleck (ed.), *The Handbook of Humanitarian Law in Armed Conflicts*, pp. 405-483.

33. The customary legal principle that aircraft are free to overfly the high seas is recognised in Article 2 of the Geneva Convention on the High Seas 1958 and UNCLOS 1982.

Most immediately, UNCLOS 1982 has placed an extra burden upon the air defence forces of those states which have elected to extend their territorial sea and their national airspace. Furthermore, the extension has had a pronounced effect upon military aircraft flying beyond their home state's frontiers. Among the military aircraft affected most of all are those intending to pass through some of the world's most used international straits. In some of these straits (such as the Strait of Malacca which lies between Sumatra and the Malay Peninsula) stretches of high seas and, more to the point, stretches of international airspace have narrowed considerably. In some other straits, meanwhile, stretches of high seas and international airspace have been eradicated completely. Conspicuous examples of the latter include the Strait of Dover (which narrows to 18 miles in width at its narrowest points and connects the Channel with the North Sea), the Strait of Gibraltar (which narrows to 8 miles in width at its narrowest points and connects the Atlantic Ocean with the Mediterranean Sea), and the western channel of the Strait of Mandeb (which narrows to 16 miles in width at its narrowest points and connects the Red Sea with the Gulf of Aden and the Indian Ocean).[34] Parts of these straits now fall under the sovereignty of coastal states.

The impact of this development upon military aircraft has been eased by Article 38 of UNCLOS 1982. Crucially, this Article introduces a special regime of transit passage through straits:

> In straits [which are used for international navigation between one part of the high seas or an exclusive economic zone and another part of the high seas or exclusive economic zone, a stipulation that excludes straits between an island and the mainland, and there is a convenient alternative route outside the island] ... all ships and aircraft enjoy the right of transit passage, which shall not be impeded ... .[35]

As the US Department of Defence observes, the significance of the right of transit passage above straits can be measured as follows: 'if the Law of the Sea Convention had not made special provision for the transit passage of straits then no fewer than 135 straits throughout the world would have been subject to severely restricted passage rights because they would have effectively been closed by the territorial seas of bordering states.'[36] In effect, Article 38 has prevented this from happening and so has the domestic legislation of many states, including the UK.[37]

---

34. The figures are drawn from *The New Encyclopaedia Britannica, Micropaedia*, Vols. 4, 5 and 7.
35. Article 38, UNCLOS 1982. Also see Articles 44 and 54 of UNCLOS 1982, together with the statement by Baroness Young, Minister of State, FCO, in moving the Second Reading of the Territorial Sea Bill, Hansard, *House of Lords Debates*, col. 382. Excerpt reproduced in Marston (ed.), 'UK Materials on International Law 1987', pp. 599-600.

UNCLOS 1982 does, however, qualify the right of transit passage through straits. Firstly, Article 38 (2) stipulates that:

> Transit passage means the exercise ... of the freedom of navigation and overflight solely for the purposes of continuous and expeditious transit of the strait ... However the requirement of continuous and expeditious transit does not preclude passage through the strait for the purpose of entering, leaving or returning from a State bordering the strait, subject to the conditions of entry of that state.[38]

Secondly, Article 39 of UNCLOS 1982 places a number of obligations on any aircraft exercising the right of transit passage through straits. Under Article 39 (1):

> Ships and aircraft, while exercising the right of transit passage, shall:
>
> (a) proceed without delay through or over the strait;
>
> (b) refrain from any threat or use of force against the sovereignty, territorial integrity or political independence of States bordering the strait, or in any other manner in violation of the principles of international law embodied in the Charter of the UN;
>
> (c) refrain from any activities other than those incident to their normal modes of continuous and expeditious transit unless rendered necessary by *force majeure* or by distress;
>
> (d) comply with other relevant provisions of this Part [VII].[39]

The wording of UNCLOS 1982 does, however, leave a number of questions open to debate. Before exercising the right of transit passage across a strait, is it necessary for the pilot of a foreign military aircraft to secure overflight clearance from the coastal state through whose airspace he or she wishes to pass? Is it permissible under international law for a coastal state to enact domestic legislation regulating the transit passage of foreign military aircraft? And can the coastal state lawfully interfere with foreign military aircraft in transit which are not complying with its domestic legislation?[40] As UNCLOS 1982 does not address these questions directly, international opinions continue to differ.

---

36. Mordike and Casagrande, *The Law of the Sea Convention: Some Implications for Air Operations*, p. 12, citing *National Security and the Convention of the Law of the Sea*, US Department of Defense, 2nd edition, January 1996, p. 5.

37. See the remark by Baroness Young, Hansard, House of Lords Debates, 2 March 1987, cols. 445-446. Excerpt reproduced in Marston (ed.), 'UK Materials on International Law 1987', pp. 600-601.

38. Article 38 (2), UNCLOS 1982.

39. Article 39, UNCLOS 1982.

40. These points are discussed in Hailbronner, 'Freedom of the Air and the Convention on the Law of the Sea'.

In addition to recognising the right of states to extend the breadth of their territorial sea to 12 miles, UNCLOS 1982 clarified the circumstances and the extent to which states may extend: their contiguous zone (for a further 12 nautical miles beyond the outer limit of the territorial sea); their Exclusive Economic Zone (up to a distance of 200 nautical miles from the baseline); and their Continental Shelf (up to a maximum distance of 350 nautical miles from the baseline or 100 nautical miles from the 2,500 metre isobath). However, as these zones extend beyond the boundary of the territorial sea – and hence beyond national airspace – all military aircraft enjoy, subject to the relevant provisions of UNCLOS 1982, the right to overfly them.[41] For like the high seas and the Arctic, these zones are not subject to territorial sovereignty.[42]

Of much greater concern to military aviation are the complex provisions in Part IV of UNCLOS 1982 which stipulate the rights and duties of the world's archipelagic states, such as Fiji, Indonesia, Papua-New Guinea and the Philippines, which are 'constituted wholly by one or more archipelagos'.[43] Most importantly, Article 47 (of Part IV) ascertains the means by which archipelagic states can 'draw straight baselines joining the outermost points of the outermost islands and drying reefs of the archipelago around the outermost points of their outermost islands'.[44] In places where archipelagic states have legitimately exercised their right under Article 47, corridors of international airspace have consequently been transformed into national airspace. Military air movements have been complicated accordingly.[45] It must be stressed, however, that the provisions of Article 47 are balanced by a set of detailed rules contained in Article 53 (1) and (2) of UNCLOS 1982[46] laying down *inter alia* that:

---

41. Regarding the exclusive economic zone, see Article 58 (1) of UNCLOS 1982. Regarding the continental shelf, see Article 78 of UNCLOS 1982.

42. Operations *Law for Royal Australian Air Force Commanders*, par. 2.13.

43. Article 46 (a), UNCLOS 1982. Article 49 provides that the sovereignty of a state 'extends to the air space over the archipelagic waters … '.

44. Article 47, UNCLOS 1982. Also see *Operations Law for Royal Australian Air Force Commanders*, DI (AF) AAP 1003, Compiled and Edited by the Air Power Studies Centre, RAAF, RAAF Base Fairbairn, 1994, par. 1.18.

45. Mordike and Casagrande, *The Law of the Sea Convention*, p. 11.

46. In turn, Article 53 (1) and (2) must be viewed together with certain specific duties and conditions laid down elsewhere in UNCLOS 1982. Article 39 (which applies *mutatis mutandis* to archipelagic sea lanes passage) and Article 54 of UNCLOS 1982 contain the duties of ships and aircraft during transit passage.

All ships and aircraft enjoy the right of archipelagic sea lanes passage in such sea lanes and air routes [designated by the archipelagic state] ... Archipelagic sea lanes passage means the exercise in accordance with this Convention of the rights of navigation and overflight in the normal mode solely for the purpose of continuous, expeditious and unobstructed transit between one part of the high seas or an exclusive economic zone and another part of the high seas or an exclusive economic zone.[47]

Since 1945, air power has had to cope with another serious development concerning the horizontal limit of national airspace: the unilateral establishment of various designated regions or zones which extend seaward to the airspace above the high seas adjacent to the territorial sea of coastal states. Since 1945, several categories have come into existence. The following stand out.

AIR DEFENCE REGIONS

Air Defence Regions (as distinct from Flight Information Regions) fall into one category. A prime example is the UK Air Defence Region. In the words of the British government, the UK Air Defence Region is 'a nationally defined area which has no status in international law' and can be flown into without violating British sovereignty, although any aircraft doing so may be intercepted by the RAF.[48]

EXTERIOR AIR DEFENCE IDENTIFICATION ZONES (ADIZS)

Exterior ADIZs fall into a second category. By virtue of the fact that they extend *beyond* the internationally recognised frontiers of a country, exterior ADIZs should not be confused with interior ADIZs. For the most part, interior ADIZs are declared lawfully with reference to Article 9 of the Chicago Convention 1944 (quoted below in the section on 'International and Overflights'). Interior ADIZs have been established by Burma (within its borders adjacent to both the PRC and Thailand), Canada (within its borders adjacent to the USA), India (within its

---

47. Article 53 (1) and (2), UNCLOS 1982.
48. Written ministerial answer, Hansard, *House of Lords Debates*, 4 November 1980, Vol. 414, column 1040. Excerpt reproduced in Geoffrey Marston (ed.), 'United Kingdom Materials on International Law 1980', *British Year Book of International Law 1980*, Vol. LI, Oxford, Oxford University Press, 1982, pp. 355-496.

borders adjacent to Pakistan) and Thailand (within its borders adjacent to Vietnam).[49]

In 1950, the USA became the first state to establish exterior ADIZs extending seaward in the airspace adjacent to its territorial sea above the high seas.[50] Since then, around twenty other states have likewise established exterior ADIZs; these include Burma, Canada, Iceland, India, Italy, Japan, Korea, Malaysia, Oman, the Philippines, Sweden, Thailand and Vietnam (plus Taiwan).[51] A few others, such as Australia, have occasionally declared temporary ADIZs for military exercise purposes.[52]

Exterior ADIZs primarily concern civil aviation, but they have also affected military aviation. By way of illustration, it is worth citing the rules of the American ADIZ. Under these rules, military aircraft on course to penetrate American national airspace may be requested to identify themselves and, failing voluntary identification, may be intercepted.[53] Military aircraft are not obliged to comply with the identification procedures of the ADIZ if they are not intending to enter US airspace although the USAF encourages them to comply with the procedures at all times.[54] The ADIZ procedures of Taiwan, Thailand and Vietnam go further. As one investigation reveals, the published procedures for flights within their ADIZs announce that any aircraft which disregards the ADIZ procedures and compounds this by failing to follow the (radio or visual signals) instructions of the interceptor aircraft will end up 'being attacked by the interceptor aircraft.'[55]

---

49. Elizabeth Cuadra, 'Air Defence Identification Zones: Creeping Jurisdiction in the Airspace', *Virginia Journal of International Law*, Vol. 18, No. 3, Spring 1978, pp. 485-512.

50. The USA has established seven ADIZs: on the Atlantic coast, the Pacific coast, the Gulf of Mexico, Alaska, Hawaii, Guam and the Panama Canal Zone. Cuadra, 'Air Defence Identification Zones: Creeping Jurisdiction in the Airspace', Appendix, Table 1, 'Current Extent of Air Defence Identification Zones', p. 509.

51. Cuadra, 'Air Defence Identification Zones: Creeping Jurisdiction in the Airspace', pp. 484-512; *Operations Law for Royal Australian Air Force Commanders*, par. 2.18; *Shawcross and Beaumont on Air Law*, (by Peter Martin, J.D. McClean and Elizabeth de Montlaur Martin), Fourth Edition, Vol. IV, Issue 48, London, Butterworths, 1996, p. 2, par. 204 (a); and Nicholas Grief, *Public International Law in the Airspace of the High Seas*, Dordrecht, Martinus Nijhoff Publishers, 1994, p. 147. Under the 1951 US-Iceland Defence Agreement, the Icelandic ADIZ is patrolled by the USAF.

52. *Operations Law for Royal Australian Air Force Commanders*, par. 2.18.

53. USAF Pamphlet AFP 110-31. Cited in Grief, *Public International Law in the Airspace of the High Seas*, pp. 147-149.

54. Group Captain G.W. Carleton RAF, Directorate of Legal Services (RAF), 'Civil and Military Intrusion into Airspace', *The Hawk*, March 1985, pp. 95-101.

55. Cuadra, 'Air Defence Identification Zones: Creeping Jurisdiction in the Airspace', p. 495.

Several studies have cast doubt on the legality of exterior ADIZs and their rules. According to one study, exterior ADIZs have 'clouded' the issue of horizontal sovereignty and are 'questionable under international law'.[56] According to another, it is hard to reconcile exterior ADIZs with Article 89 of UNCLOS 1982 which provides that: 'No state may validly purport to subject any part of the high seas to its sovereignty.'[57] A counter-argument is offered by the UK's *Tri-Service Law of Armed Conflict Manual*. With specific reference to the US ADIZ, it contends that 'ADIZs do not constitute an extension of national sovereignty; their primary purpose is identification and they are, in practical terms, a means of early warning of suspicious activity.'[58] Irrespective of whether exterior ADIZs are legitimate or not, the fact remains that they have become a factor in the conduct of military air movements.

'PROHIBITED' AREAS AND 'PROHIBITED' ZONES

'Prohibited' areas beyond the horizontal limit of the territorial sea closely resemble exterior ADIZs. Nonetheless, 'prohibited' areas are clearly distinguishable by dint of the added danger that they present to aviation. As such, 'prohibited' areas fall into another, much more controversial, category. Examples include:

- The French 'zone of special responsibility' extending some 80 nautical miles off the coast of Algeria which lasted from 1956 until Algerian independence in 1962.[59]
- The 'prohibited area' established to the north and east of Indonesia's territorial sea at the time of the 'Confrontation' between Indonesia and Malaysia (1963-66).
- The Spanish 'prohibited zone' in the immediate vicinity of Gibraltar airport which was established in May 1967.[60]

---

56. *Shawcross and Beaumont on Air Law*, Fourth Edition, Vol. IV, Issue 48, p. 2. Other studies which have questioned the legality of exterior ADIZs include: Cuadra, 'Air Defence Identification Zones: Creeping Jurisdiction in the Airspace'; and Hailbronner, 'Freedom of the Air and the Convention on the Law of the Sea'.
57. Hailbronner, 'Freedom of the Air and the Convention on the Law of the Sea', p. 517.
58. *Tri-Service Law of Armed Conflict Manual*, (Current Draft), Section II – 'Air Operations', Chapter 12, par. 12.013.
59. Zone réglementée No. 230. Cited in Hailbronner, 'Freedom of the Air and the Convention on the Law of the Sea', p. 516. Also see Cuadra, 'Air Defence Identification Zones: Creeping Jurisdiction in the Airspace', pp. 494-495.
60. Matte, *Treatise on Air-Aeronautical Law*, pp. 173-174.

- The Libyan 'prohibited zone' which extends 100 nautical miles seawards from Tripoli into the Gulf of Sirte.[61]

Various arguments have been forwarded to try to justify the creation of 'prohibited' areas or zones. It has, for example, been suggested that they are necessary to identify and control foreign aircraft in order to prevent surprise attacks or infringements upon essential security interests.[62] Many states have nonetheless taken serious exception to these unilaterally created zones. They have thus contended that the zones are at variance with generally recognised principles of international law and that they amount to little more than artful attempts to extend sovereign rights beyond internationally recognised limits.[63]

To a far greater degree than both Air Defence Regions and exterior ADIZs, 'prohibited zones' are designed to impede the movements of foreign military aircraft irrespective of whether they are on a course to penetrate national airspace. Nonetheless, some states have actually taken practical steps to register their disapproval. For example, during the early phase of the Confrontation in 1963, the British Air Ministry agreed 'to test Indonesian reactions' by openly flying RAF aircraft 'over their so-called prohibited area, but keeping twelve miles from land.'[64] This actually happened when 'the Valiant and Vulcan flights from Darwin to Butterworth on the night of 19/20 September [1963] were flown without incident'.[65] More recently, ships and aircraft of the US Sixth Fleet have occasionally entered and exercised in the Gulf of Sirte, which Libya claims to be part of its territorial waters, resulting in armed clashes, notably in August 1981 and in March 1986 (a month before the prosecution of Operation EL DORADO CANYON).[66]

Exclusion Zones (EZ is a term that encompasses Total Exclusion Zones, Maritime Exclusion Zones and Air Exclusion Zones)

EZs fall into yet another, quite separate, category. As the RAAF notes:

---

61. *Keesing's Contemporary Archives*, Vol. XXVII, 13 November 1981, p. 31181.
62. See Hailbronner, 'Freedom of the Air and the Convention on the Law of the Sea', p. 516.
63. This, for example, has been the view of the USA in regard to the Libyan area. See Hailbronner, 'Freedom of the Air and the Convention on the Law of the Sea', pp. 516-517.
64. DEFE 7/1560. Formerly 'confidential' (now declassified) memorandum from Julian Risdale, Under Secretary of State for Air, to Peter Thorneycroft, the Minister of Defence, 17 September 1963, PRO.
65. DEFE 7/1560. Formerly 'secret' (now declassified) memorandum from R.F. Havell, Head of S.6, Air Ministry, to D.F. Lomax, Foreign Office, 23 September 1963, PRO.
66. *See the Yearbook of the UN 1986*, Vol. 40, New York, UN Department of Public Information, 1990, pp. 248-249.

On many occasions this century, nations [such as the UK during the South Atlantic Conflict of 1982] have declared an EZ in areas adjacent to national territory invoking the principle of individual or collective self-defence ... An EZ is an area declared by a nation, or military force, into which entry by designated forces is prohibited. An EZ may be stationary or moving. Neutral aircraft and ships should avoid such zones; those that enter may navigate at their own risk. The use of EZs is expected to increase, as not only nations but also the UN, seek ways to localise conflicts. Because assessment of the acceptability of EZs will depend on a number of factors, clear guidance on the legal acceptability of an EZ is difficult, as each occasion is unique.[67]

Opinion will remain divided over the legality or otherwise of all the air zones that have in recent years arisen beyond internationally recognised boundaries. Even so, they have undoubtedly become an obtrusive and enduring feature of contemporary international relations with perceptible implications for air power.

THE VERTICAL DELIMITATION OF NATIONAL/TERRESTRIAL AIRSPACE

The advances in aviation during the first years of the twentieth century under-lined that the old maxim *cujus est solum ejus est usque ad coelum et ad inferos* – i.e. 'to whom belongs the soil, his it is, even to heaven, and to the middle of the earth'[68] – still applied to the superjacent airspace of states.[69] Nonetheless, just as the development of aviation had the effect of qualifying the application of the maxim in domestic law,[70] the genesis of the space age in 1957 suddenly undermined the application of the maxim in international air law. After all, the launch of the Sputnik I satellite by the USSR in that year highlighted what the MoD Scientific Adviser described as 'the difficulty arising from the fact that there is no clear-cut neutral boundary which divides outer space from the earth's atmosphere'.[71]

---

67. *Operations Law for Royal Australian Air Force Commanders*, col. 2.23.
68. For a detailed analysis of the origins and development of the maxim in international air law, see Cooper, *Roman Law and the Maxim "Cujus Est Solum" in International Air Law.*
69. Ian Brownlie, *Principles of Public International Law*, Fourth Edition, Oxford, Oxford University Press, 1990, p. 119.
70. In the UK, section 76 (1) of the Civil Aviation Act 1982 provides that no action lies in respect of trespass or nuisance by reason only of the flight of an aircraft over property at a reasonable height.
71. AIR 8/2254. Formerly 'confidential' (now declassified) copy of a minute from Sir Frederick Brundrett, Scientific Adviser to the MoD, to the Secretary of the Chiefs of Staff Committee, 23 April 1958, par. 3, PRO.

Shortly thereafter, an *Ad Hoc* Committee of the UN suggested that the establishment of a boundary did 'not present a legal problem for priority consideration at this moment'.[72] Even so, there remained a degree of international support for the idea that the matter had to be considered on an inter-governmental basis with the aim of adopting an amendment to the Chicago Convention 1944 delineating a boundary.[73]

The idea met with a cold response in Washington. During the 1960s, the decade in which space law took proper shape, the possibility of agreement was therefore thwarted and the boundary issue side-stepped. So much so that the Outer Space Treaty of 1967 – the 'Magna Carta' of space law[74] to which the UK, the USA, the Russian Federation and others are parties – is silent on the matter.[75] Subsequent treaties have also been silent, while three Soviet proposals (of 1979, 1983 and 1987) to set an arbitrary boundary at an altitude not higher than 100 to 110 km above sea level[76] failed to gather sufficient support. In consequence, the vertical extent of airspace has remained unsettled.[77] As the FCO pronounced in 1993: 'There is no universally agreed precise legal, technical or political definition of either the boundaries separating airspace from outer space or of the term outer space itself.' [78]

In the late 1950s and 1960s, the stance of the USA, as endorsed by the UK, successfully precluded the negotiation of a workable agreement identifying the upward extent of national/terrestrial sovereignty. Given this, it is helpful to

---

72. 1959 Report of the *Ad Hoc* Committee of the UN, UNGA, 14 July 1959, A 4141, p. 68. Excerpt quoted in Alex Meyer, 'Legal Problems of Outer Space', *Journal of Air Law and Commerce*, Vol. XXVIII, 1961-62, pp. 339-346.

73. A useful survey of the various suggestions which were being advanced in the late 1950s and early 1960s is furnished in: Albert I. Moon, 'A Look At Airspace Sovereignty', *Journal of Air Law and Commerce*, Vol. XXIX, 1963, pp. 328-345.

74. Peter Jankowitsch, 'Legal Aspects of Military Space Activities', Chapter 11, Nandasiri Jasentuliyana (ed.), *Space Law: Development and Scope*, London, Praeger, pp. 143-157.

75. D. J. Harris, *Cases and Materials on International Law*, Fourth Edition, London, Sweet & Maxwell, 1991, p. 231.

76. Andrei D. Terekhov, 'Passage of Space Objects Through Foreign Airspace: International Custom?', *Journal of Space Law*, Vol. 25., No. 1, 1997, pp. 1-16. Also see the *Yearbook of the UN 1981*, Vol. 35, UN Department of Public Information, New York, UN, 1985, p. 123.

77. *Tri-Service Law of Armed Conflict Manual*, (Current Draft), Section II – Air Operations, Chapter 12, par. 12.011.

78. Written answer by the Minister of State, FCO, 23 July 1993, Hansard, House of Lords Debates, Vol. 548, written answer 66. Excerpt reproduced in Geoffrey Marston (ed.), 'United Kingdom Materials on International Law 1993', *British Year Book of International Law 1993*, Vol. LXIV, Oxford, Oxford University Press, 1994, pp. 579-758.

consider why the two allies adopted such a position. There is no simple explanation. However, recently declassified official documents confirm that strategic
factors lay at the heart of Anglo-American calculations. Just as clearly, policy-
making in both Washington and Whitehall was consistently influenced by the US
Joint Chiefs of Staff[79] and the UK Chiefs of Staff respectively. They and their
advisers plainly recoiled at the prospect of a boundary, fearing that it might limit
their future ability to use outer space for military purposes.[80] Although in 1961 the
UK Chiefs of Staff did momentarily feel the need to consider the idea of fixing a
boundary at 13 nautical miles above sea level – 'to allow flights over the Middle
East air barrier' – the Chiefs of Staff readily 'accepted that this was politically out
of the question',[81] and therefore readopted their earlier position.

As the *Tri-Service Law of Armed Conflict Manual* remarks: 'For practical purposes,
it can be said that the upper limit to a state's rights in airspace is above the highest altitude at which an aircraft can fly and below the lowest possible perigee of an
earth satellite in orbit.'[82] Nevertheless, the silence of the Outer Space Treaty over
the vexed question of the boundary, coupled with the continuing absence of any

---

79. For example, see AIR 8/2255. Formerly 'secret' (now declassified) memo from the Air Ministry to
the Vice Chief of the Air Staff, 26 October 1960, PRO.

80. In June 1958, the ACAS (Ops.) advised the CAS that there were 'dangers' associated with 'trying
to legislate in fields where so little is known.' He added that: 'We could very well come to regret
'dabbling in the dark'.' AIR 8/2254. Formerly 'secret' now declassified brief from the Assistant
Chief of the Air Staff (Operations) to the Chief of the Air Staff, 30 June 1958, PRO. Interestingly,
by 1960, the Air Ministry had identified space as being of 'military interest' and '*prima facie* worth
examining' in at least eight 'principal fields'. The eight were: 'early warning; reconnaissance;
communications; defence against ballistic missiles; navigation; meteorology; bombardment; and
interception of enemy satellites.' AIR 8/2255. Formerly 'secret' now declassified report (third
draft) by the Air Ministry Strategic Scientific Policy Committee, 28 October 1960, PRO. It is also
interesting to note that in anticipation of a possible inter-governmental initiative to delineate the
boundary between airspace and outer space, the Chiefs of the Staff urged the Foreign Office to
accept their advice that if the question was ever opened the British government should seek the
establishment of the boundary at 'about 20,000 nm, which would accommodate all foreseeable
vehicles of military use or, alternately, a limit as low as 2,500 nm provided that meteorological and
communications satellites were classified as 'peaceful'.' DEFE 5/113. Declassified Annex to
COS(61)165, 'Defence Implications of Defining the Limits and Uses of Outer Space', p. 3,
paragraph 7, PRO. (This report referred to a meeting of the Chiefs of Staff Committee on 21
April 1960 where the question of the military implications of defining limits in space was
discussed.)

81. FO 371/157326. Formerly 'confidential' (now declassified) hand-written minute by D.J. Gibson,
Foreign Office, 2 August 1961, PRO.

82. *Tri-Service Law of Armed Conflict Manual*, (Current Draft), Section II – Air Operations, Chapter 12,
par. 12.011.

international consensus, generates uncertainty and raises a number of problematical questions:

- Are certain platforms or vehicles poised in or passing through the stratosphere and mesosphere[83] to be regarded as located in national/terrestrial airspace or in outer space?[84]
- At what altitude do aerospace or space objects leave national/terrestrial airspace and enter outer space? Or put another way, at what altitude does it cease to be necessary for a state to seek and obtain overflight clearance from another state before one of its aerospace or space objects can pass above the territory of the other state en route to outer space?
- Related to the above, does customary international law permit the unauthorised passage of an aerospace or space object of one state through the airspace of another state after it has re-entered the Earth's atmosphere from outer space?[85]
- Lastly, at which upward point does Article 4 (together with the other Articles) of the 1967 Outer Space Treaty begin to apply? For under Article 4, 'State Parties to the Treaty undertake not to place in orbit around the Earth any object carrying nuclear

---

83. The stratosphere extends from approximately 20 km to approximately 50 km. The mesosphere extends from approximately 50 km to approximately 80 km. *Upper Atmosphere Research Satellite*, NASA brochure, 1989. Extract reproduced in Caesar Voûte, 'Boundaries in Space', Chapter 2, Bhupendra Jasani (ed.), *Peaceful and Non-Peaceful Uses of Space: Problems of Definition for the Prevention of an Arms Race*, United Nations Institute for Disarmament Research, London, Taylor & Francis, 1991, pp. 19-35.

84. According to one analysis of the stratosphere, 'the stratosphere is not part of airspace as legally defined today because there is no legal boundary for airspace ... [The stratosphere] is far above the altitude at which countries seek and obtain overflight permission.' M. Rothblatt, 'Are Stratospheric Platforms in Airspace or Outer Space?', *Journal of Space Law*, Vol. 24, No. 2, 1996, pp. 107-111.

85. The UN Committee on the Peaceful Uses of Outer Space has recently considered this question and in 1996 it despatched an official Questionnaire to its membership of 61 states. For its part, the British government replied as follows:

   [HMG] acknowledges the importance of this subject area and the future possible implications of considering legal issues in this area of aerospace objects, but regrets to inform the Secretary-General that the questionnaire is still under active consideration in both national and European contexts. The matter will be kept under close review and an agreed response to the questionnaire will be forwarded to the UNCOPUS in due course.

   UN document A/AC.105/635/Add.3 of 1 December 1996, p. 11. Excerpt reproduced in Terekhov, 'Passage of Space Objects Through Foreign Airspace: International Custom?', p. 8, footnote 29. This article provides a very useful summary of the contrasting positions of numerous international lawyers and those 14 states which have issued substantive responses to the 1996 UN questionnaire. Terekhov, 'Passage of Space Objects Through Foreign Airspace: International Custom?', pp. 9-10.

weapons or any other kind of weapons of mass destruction ... or station such weapons in outer space in any other manner.'[86]

Quite palpably, these unresolved issues bear upon the sovereign rights and air defence tasks of all states, including neutral states which, as outlined below, have certain rights and duties under the laws of armed conflict. They also bear upon NATO, partly because of the reference in the North Atlantic Treaty to armed attacks 'in or over' the applicable territories of NATO states.[87]

In years to come, these issues are likely to magnify in importance. The main reason springs from the growing emphasis placed on space flights by the USA. Take the anticipated deployment of pilotless Space Manoeuvring Vehicles. According to recent reports, the SMVs currently under development should be capable of operating 'within or outside the atmosphere'. However, in contrast to the Space Shuttles, SMVs will possess an overwhelmingly military function. As such, they will be controlled by the USAF rather than by NASA. Moreover, SMVs are expected to perform 'surveillance missions' and to act as 'highly manoeuvrable' and 'reusable' satellites 'capable of remaining in orbit for between 3 and 12 months.'[88] No doubt the projected ability of SMVs to operate 'within or outside the atmosphere' will fuel the debate over the location of the boundary with Outer Space and open the question of whether SMVs require overflight clearance before passing over foreign territory.

The issue of the boundary has been a live one since 1957. Since then, three schools of thought have emerged. One school of thought espouses the spatial or perigee approach.[89] Under this view, a delimitation between airspace and outer space is required in order to establish which activities would be governed under the sovereignty of States and which under the generally recognised principles of the Outer Space Treaty 1967, namely that the 'exploration' of outer space is open 'for the benefit and in the interests of all countries', and that 'outer space,

---

86. Article 1, Treaty on Principles Governing the Activities of States in the Exploration and Use of Outer Space, Including the Moon and Other Celestial Bodies, (London, Moscow and Washington), 27 January 1967.

87. In particular, see Article 2, Protocol to the North Atlantic Treaty on the Accession of Greece and Turkey, London, 22 October 1951.

88. David Windle, 'Fighter planes move into space', *Sunday Times*, 17 August 1997, section 2, p. 17; and 'US Air Force prepares for new space invasion', *The Times*, 5 September 1997, p. 12.

89. The perigee is the 'the point in the orbit of an earth satellite that is closest to the earth.' Jasani (ed.), *Peaceful and Non-Peaceful Uses of Space*, Glossary, pp. 173-176. The perigee approach specifically points to the minimum altitude at which satellites are able to orbit and holds that outer space should therefore begin there.

including the Moon and other celestial bodies, is not subject to national appropriation by claim of sovereignty'.[90] Various suggestions have been made as to where the boundary should be drawn. It has been proposed that it would be appropriate to establish the boundary: at 12 miles above sea level, the point at which an exposed human body begins to boil; at 100-110 kilometres, as the USSR has proposed;[91] and at 600 miles, the point described by space scientists as the 'exosphere' or the 'astronomical material frontier' where 'collisions between air particles are extremely rare.'[92] Advocates of this approach also seek a proper definition of outer space.[93]

A second school of thought contends that 'the legal regime governing outer space should be based primarily on the nature and type of particular space activities.' Proponents of this approach have pressed for a formal distinction to be drawn between 'aeronautical and astronautical activities wherein the latter should be subject to space law, irrespective of the altitude at which they are carried out.'[94]

A third school of thought cautions against any change at all.[95] Advocates of this pragmatic approach, particularly the USA, suggest that the establishment of a boundary would be unnecessary and would 'impede progress in the peaceful exploration and use of outer space.'[96] Crucially, the US administration has consistently advocated the pragmatic approach.[97]

---

90. Articles 1 and 2, Treaty on Principles Governing the Activities of States in the Exploration and Use of Outer Space, Including the Moon and Other Celestial Bodies 1967. This view was reported in the 'Report of the Committee on the Peaceful Uses of Outer Space', *General Assembly Official Records 1996*, 51st Session, Supplement no. 20 (A/51/20), New York, UN Publication, 1996, p. 21.

91. The USSR also proposed that space objects should be given passage, at lower altitudes, through the airspace of another state in order to reach orbit or return to Earth, on condition that the passage did not create any adverse effect to the other state. See Stephen Gorove, *Developments in Space Law: Issues and Policies*, Dordrecht, Martinus Nijhoff Publishers, 1991, p. 22.

92. Rothblatt, 'Are Stratospheric Platforms in Airspace or Outer Space?', p. 111.

93. See, for example, G.C.M. Reijnen and W. de Graaff, *The Pollution of Outer Space, in Particular of the Outer Orbit: Scientific, Policy and Legal Aspects*, Dordrecht, Martinus Nijhoff Publishers, 1989, p. 3.

94. Voûte, 'Boundaries in Space', p. 28. Another advocate of the approach varies this suggestion by asserting that 'even vehicles designed to reach outer space, but not in fact reaching outer space, are not space objects ... [S]uch activities do not (should not) come under international space law.' Henri A. Wassenbergh, 'A Launch and a Space Transportation Law, separate from Outer Space Law?', *Air and Space Law*, Vol. XXI, No. 1, February 1996, pp. 28-32.

95. Gorove, for example, argues that 'a delimitation between airspace and outer space would serve no practical purpose and could have unforeseen adverse effects on the future development of space activities and space law.' Gorove, *Developments in Space Law*, p. 23.

96. This view was reported in 'Report of the Committee on the Peaceful Uses of Outer Space', *General Assembly Official Records 1996*, p. 21.

97. Bhupendra Jasani, 'Introduction', Chapter 1, Jasani (ed.), *Peaceful and Non-Peaceful Uses of Space*, pp.1-18.

The perigee approach (referred to above) has been depicted as the one 'most likely to be accepted' by states in the event of a breakthrough.[98] This is debatable. For as long as the USA maintains its long-standing policy, it is unlikely that an internationally agreed boundary will be forthcoming in the foreseeable future.

Another question stemming from the absence of any generally accepted boundary between airspace and outer space concerns the status of satellites in orbit. On this score, at least, there is a tangible degree of international consensus. In the phrase of the Director of the UN Office for Outer Space Affairs, 'space activities have proceeded on the general assumption that anything in orbit or beyond is in outer space.'[99] During the formative years of the modern space age, states did not object to the deployment and use of satellites in orbit above their territory, there being none of the protests of the kind which accompanied aviation's first intrusions into national airspace. As MoD officials acknowledged privately as far back as 1958: 'by customary usage, the lower limit of outer space is coming to be defined as including the orbits of the lowest satellites'.[100] Over the years, the sustained absence of any formal protest has spawned what has been termed 'the emergence of a new customary rule of international law to the effect that such satellites moved in an area which was outside of the national jurisdiction of the underlying state.'[101] While there is still no consensus over where this area begins, most states have accepted that, subject to rules contained in the relevant treaties,[102] states are free to station satellites in this area.

As already noted, the Outer Space Treaty 1967 prohibits states from claiming sovereign rights beyond their national airspace and into outer space. However, some states have effectively challenged this principle in the context of the legal status of the geostationary orbit. Located at a height of 35,786.56 km above the Earth's equator,[103] the geostationary orbit can be defined as 'a circular equatorial orbit in which a spacecraft has an orbital period precisely equal to the period of

---

98. Harris, *Cases and Materials on International Law*, p. 232.

99. Nandasiri Jasentuliyana, 'The Lawmaking Process in the United Nations', Chapter 3, Jasentuliyana (ed.), *Space Law*, Chapter 3, pp. 33-44.

100. DEFE 5/113, Annex to COS(61)165, 'Defence Implications of Defining the Limits and Uses of Outer Space'. Formerly 'secret' (now declassified) Ministry of Defence Report, 15 May 1961, (approved by the Chiefs of Staff at their meeting of 11 May 1961), p. 4, par. 33, PRO.

101. Gorove, *Developments in Space Law*, p. 21.

102. Among the most notable is the Convention on Registration of Objects Launched into Outer Space, New York, 14 January 1975.

103. Reijnen and de Graaff, *The Pollution of Outer Space, in Particular of the Outer Orbit*, p. 3.

rotation of the Earth, that is, 23 hours 56 minutes.'[104] In 1975, Columbia first raised the issue of its status at the UNGA in 1975 by actually staking a claim to sovereignty over a 5.5° segment of the geostationary orbit above its territory. Seven other equatorial states rallied round Columbia and in 1976 they took the step of signing the Bogotá Declaration. Under its terms, these states claimed that 'the segments of the geostationary synchronous orbit are an integral part of the territory over which Equatorial states exercise their national sovereignty.'[105] Furthermore, they declared that any devices placed permanently on the geostationary orbit of an equatorial state require 'previous and express authorisation on the part of the concerned state'; they did not condone existing satellites on the geostationary orbit,[106] although they did not object to satellites authorised by the International Telecommunication Convention.

It has been assumed that claiming rights of sovereignty into the geostationary orbit 'clearly goes against' the wording of Article II of the Outer Space Treaty,[107] an opinion that has been consistently held by an overwhelming majority in the UN.[108] Indeed, the developed states continue to assert that the geostationary orbit is an integral part of outer space and is adequately regulated by the regime established by the Outer Space Treaty.[109] That said, some states have insisted that in view of the needs of developing states and the particular characteristics of the geostationary orbit, a special *sui generis* legal regime is necessary to regulate both

---

104. Lubos Perek, 'The scientific and technological basis of Space Law', Chapter 13, Jasentuliyana, *Space Law*, pp. 175-190.
105. Section 1, Declaration of the First Meeting of Equatorial Countries, Bogotá, Columbia, 2 December 1976, by Brazil, Colombia, Congo, Ecuador, Indonesia, Kenya, Uganda and Zaire. See Gorove, *Developments in Space Law*, p. 41; and Jasentuliyana, *Space Law*, especially chapter 1, Hamilton DeSaussure, 'The Freedoms of Outer Space and Their Maritime Antecedents', pp. 1-15; and Chapter 13, Lubos Perek, 'The Scientific and Technological Basis of Space Law', pp. 175-190.
106. Sections 3 (c) and 3 (e), Declaration of the First Meeting of Equatorial Countries, Bogotá, Columbia, 2 December 1976.
107. I.H. Ph. Diedriks-Verschoor, *An Introduction to Space Law*, Deventer (The Netherlands), Kluwer Law and Taxation Publishers, 1993, p. 19. Interestingly, this study adds that Indonesia has 'conceded as much' in discussions held in the UN Committee on the Peaceful Uses of Outer Space.
108. These states included the USSR, France, the USA and the UK. The UK has argued that 'the use of the geostationary orbit is subject to the legal regime of the Outer Space Treaty', and that 'the best solution was to have all states equitably share the benefits of the geostationary orbit'. Gorove, *Developments in Space Law*, pp. 43, 46, 54 and 55.
109. Jitendra S. Thaker, 'UN Legal Subcommittee on Space Makes Progress on Definition/Delimitation Issue', *Journal of Space Law*, Vol. 23, No. 2, 1995, pp. 149-156.

access to it and the utilisation of it.[110] The UN Committee on the Peaceful Uses of Outer Space is thus considering 'matters relating to the definition and delimitation of outer space and to the character and utilisation of the geostationary orbit.' However, the continuing international divisions were again laid bare during the Committee's latest session held in June 1996.[111]

INTERNATIONAL LAW AND OVERFLIGHTS

This chapter has already referred to the Chicago Convention on International Civil Aviation 1944 in respect of its reiteration of the principle of state sovereignty over national airspace. By extension, the Chicago Convention is also of central importance in relation to the rights of sovereign states within their national airspace:

- Under Article 9 (a) of the Chicago Convention: 'Each contracting State may, for reasons of military necessity or public safety, restrict or prohibit uniformly the aircraft of other States from flying over certain areas of its territory ... '.
- Under Article 9 (b): 'Each contracting State reserves also the right, in exceptional circumstances or during a period of emergency, or in the interest of public safety, and with immediate effect, temporarily to restrict or prohibit flying over the whole or any part of its territory ... '.
- Under Article 9 (c): 'Each contracting State, under such regulations as it may prescribe, may require any aircraft entering the areas contemplated in subparagraphs (a) or (b) above to effect a landing as soon as practicable thereafter at some designated airport within its territory.'[112]
- Under Article 13: 'The laws and regulations of a contracting State as to the admission to or departure from its territory of passengers ... shall be complied with by or on behalf of such passengers, crew or cargo upon entrance into or departure from, or while within the territory of that State.' As interpreted by several states, including the UK and the USA, Article 13 grants states a right to refuse to permit the carriage

---

110. Matthew W. Sanidas and Jitendra S. Thaker (UN Office for Outer Space Affairs), 'Third UNISPACE Conference Possible by Turn of Century: Agreement At 38th Session of UN Committee on Space', *Journal of Space Law*, Vol. 23, No. 2, 1995, pp. 157-164; and Thaker, 'UN Legal Subcommittee on Space Makes Progress on Definition/Delimitation Issue', p. 153.

111. 'Report of the Committee on the Peaceful Uses of Outer Space', *General Assembly Official Records 1996*.

112. See John Kish (edited by David Turns), *International Law and Espionage*, The Hague, Martinus Nijhoff Publishers, 1995, p. 99.

by foreign aircraft through their sovereign airspace of personnel in military uniform, even if the personnel are travelling in 'civil aircraft'. Article 13 has long inhibited air movements, but it will continue to do so as long as air forces continue to employ civil aircraft.[113]

- Under Article 35: '(a) No munitions of war or implements or war may be carried in or above the territory of a State in aircraft engaged in international navigation, except by permission of such State ... (b) Each contracting State reserves the right, for reasons of public order and safety, to regulate or prohibit the carriage in or above its territory of articles other than those enumerated in paragraph (a) ... '.
- Under Article 36: 'Each contracting State may prohibit or regulate the use of photographic apparatus in aircraft over its territory.'

States have jealously protected and, whenever they have felt it necessary, exercised all the above rights. But it has been the exercise of another legal right which has had – and will continue to have – the deepest impact upon air power: the denial of overflight clearance. This right is well established in customary international law and is enshrined in the Chicago Convention.

Under Article 3 (c) of the Chicago Convention, which should be read in conjunction with Articles 1 and 2 (quoted earlier):

> no state aircraft [defined by Article 3 (b) of the Convention as aircraft 'used in military, customs and police service' irrespective of whether they are armed or not] shall fly over the territory of another state or land thereon without authorisation by special agreement or otherwise.[114]

Generally, this means that in the absence of a 'special agreement' or circumstance of the type included in the enclosed examples [see Tables I and II], prior permission is required for every overflight. For these reasons, a state must comply with two conditions before each of its military aircraft may lawfully overfly (or land in) the territory of any foreign state. Firstly, it must submit an overflight request to the relevant authorities of the host government concerned; clearly, if the request is submitted at the start of an operation, it may possibly reveal a state's intentions, mitigate the element of surprise and induce the host state to demand concessions.[115] Secondly, the state must receive the necessary clearance from the

---

113. See Group Captain Gordon Woolley, 'Air Transport in Peace Support Operations', Chapter 10, Group Captain Andrew Lambert and Arthur C. Williamson (eds.), *The Dynamics of Air Power*, Bracknell, MoD, RAF Staff College, 1996, pp. 146-156.

114. Chicago Convention 1944, Article 3 (c).

115. Philip Towle, 'The Distinctive Characteristics of Air Power', Chapter 1, Lambert and Williamson (eds.), *The Dynamics of Air Power*, pp. 3-17.

host government and, in the absence of a 'special agreement or otherwise', that government is under no legal obligation to consent. Moreover, the host state is under no legal obligation to grant immediate clearance, a factor which may further mitigate the element of surprise.

In the absence of any applicable treaty or agreement, every state is thus entitled to grant (either conditionally or unconditionally), deny, suspend, or rescind overflight (or landing) clearance for military aircraft. Quite purposefully, many states have elected to exercise these rights:

- In 1958, Israel temporarily refused to grant overflight clearance to RAF aircraft stationed in Cyprus at the start of the British airlift to Jordan.[116]
- In 1961, Sudan and Turkey initially prohibited, then conditionally allowed, RAF aircraft to overfly their territory during the course of the tri-service British operation to defend Kuwait against a perceived threat from Iraq (Operation VANTAGE).[117]
- In 1973, Spain alongside all of the USA's NATO allies 'except Portugal, the Netherlands and the Federal Republic of Germany (for a time) either directly or indirectly dissociated' from the American airlift to Israel (Operation NICKEL GRASS) and 'banned' American military overflights of their territory;[118] for its part, the British government also turned down a request for American military aircraft to stage through the British bases in Cyprus.[119]
- In 1986, the French government turned down a request to permit US aircraft to fly across France to facilitate their mission to reach Libya from the UK and, according to Margaret Thatcher, the Spanish government would only allow US aircraft to overfly Spain on condition that 'it was done in a way which would not be noticed',

---

116. For details, see the relevant documents in: *Foreign Relations of the United States, 1958-1960*, Vol. XI, Washington DC, US Government Printing Office (Department of State Publication). More generally, see Air Chief Marshal Sir David Lee, *Wings in the Sun: A History of the RAF in the Mediterranean 1945-1986*, London, HMSO, 1989, Chapter 10, pp. 132-146; and Orna Almog, 'An End of an Era – The Crisis of 1958 and the Anglo-Israeli Relationship', *Contemporary Record*, Vol. 8, Number 1, Summer 1994, pp. 49-76.

117. Air Chief Marshal Sir David Lee, *Flight from the Middle East*, London, HMSO, Chapter 9; and K.A. Kyriakides, 'The RAF and Power Projection: Overflight Constraints, 1958-61', *Air Clues: The RAF Magazine*, November 1995, pp. 404-410.

118. Henry Kissinger, *Years of Upheaval, London*, Wiedenfeld and Nicolson and Michael Joseph, pp. 708-709.

119. Edward Heath, the British Prime Minister from 1970-74, made this disclosure in the House of Commons in the context of the debate on the American bombing of Libya in April 1986. See: Parliamentary Report, 'A No from Heath and Callaghan', *The Times*, 17 April 1986, p. 4; and Richard Norton-Taylor, 'Heath insists on veto', *The Guardian*, 17 April 1986, p. 1.

a condition unacceptable to the USA.[120] This compelled 18 F-111s and 4 EF-111s, based in the UK, supported by tankers, to reach Libya by conducting a circuitous 13 hour round trip of 6,000 miles across the Bay of Biscay, around the Iberian Peninsula, and then through the Strait of Gibraltar.[121]

• In 1990-91, India refused to grant overflying rights to USAF aircraft.[122]

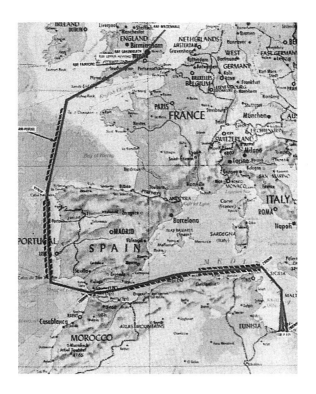

The F-111 route to Libya, 1986

120. Margaret Thatcher, *The Downing Street Years*, London, HarperCollins, 1993, p. 446. Also see Diana Geddes, 'Airspace denial confirmed', *The Times*, 16 April 1986, p.6; and Richard Wigg, 'Spain', *The Times*, 16 April 1986, p. 6.

121. 'How the blows went in', *The Economist*, 19 April 1986, p. 20.

122. *Department of Defense Final Report to Congress on the Conduct of the Persian Gulf War*, Appendix O, 'The Role of the Law of War', (an unclassified chapter of the report), Washington D.C., 1992, pp. O-30-O-31.

Given the sanctity of national airspace and the customary nature of Article 3 (c) of the Chicago Convention, it is *prima facie* unlawful for military aircraft to engage in unauthorised overflights within the airspace of another state. When, in March 1950, Clement Attlee, the Labour Prime Minister, sought a legal opinion on the question of whether the RAF could lawfully conduct aerial reconnaissance on the coast of Albania to ascertain whether any Soviet submarines were positioned there, Hartley Shawcross, the Attorney-General, explained that 'the importance of obtaining accurate information ... has to be set against the undoubted illegality of an aerial reconnaissance over the territorial waters of another country.'[123] As it happened, Attlee authorised the reconnaissance to take place,[124] but his Attorney-General's remark captured the essence of a conundrum that governments still face today.

Significantly, the practice of unauthorised overflying for reconnaissance purposes was considered by the International Court of Justice in the case of *Nicaragua v United States 1986*. The case arose after Nicaragua had lodged a series of complaints against the USA, one of which charged that American military aircraft had infringed Nicaraguan airspace. This charge, together with numerous others, was subsequently brought before the ICJ, although the USA did not contest the case.[125] In one of several landmark rulings, the ICJ decided, by twelve votes to three, that 'the USA, by directing or authorising overflights of Nicaraguan territory ... has acted against the Republic of Nicaragua, in breach of its obligation under customary international law not to violate the sovereignty of another state;'[126] three judges, who were from Japan, the UK and the USA, dissented by reference to the right of self-defence.[127] In its judgement, the ICJ found that 'the only violations of air space imputable to the United States on the basis of the evidence are high altitude reconnaissance flights and low altitude

---

123. AIR 19/1107. Formerly 'top secret' (now declassified) memorandum from Hartley Shawcross, the Attorney-General, to Clement Attlee, the Prime Minister, 20 March 1950, a copy of which was also sent to the Secretary of State for Air, PRO.

124. AIR 19/1107. Formerly 'top secret' (now declassified) memorandum from Laurie Pumphrey, Prime Minister's Office, 10 Downing Street, to A.L.M. Cary, Air Ministry, 20 March 1950, PRO.

125. The Americans did not contest the case in court, arguing that the Court lacked the necessary jurisdiction to rule upon an 'ongoing conflict'. Even so, the ICJ rejected this plea by a vote of 15 to 1 and decided to consider the complaints anyway.

126. *Case Concerning Military and Paramilitary Activities In and Against Nicaragua (Nicaragua v USA)*, ICJ Reports 1986, *Operative Part of the Court's Judgement*, subparagraph (5). Reproduced in the *American Journal of International Law*, Vol. 80, 1986, pp. 785-807.

127. Kish, *International Law and Espionage*, p. 100.

flights on 7-11 November 1984 causing 'sonic booms'.' [128] Furthermore, the ICJ recalled that 'the concept of sovereignty, both in treaty-law and in customary international law, extends to the internal waters and territorial sea of every State and to the air space above its territory' and pronounced that the principle of respect for territorial sovereignty is 'directly infringed by the unauthorised overflight of Nicaragua's territory.' [129] (The question of whether unauthorised overflights can be met with any use of force is discussed below.)

An associated question is whether the customary prohibition on unauthorised overflights by aircraft applies to overflights by missiles and to other aerospace aviation vehicles. In this regard, any analysis must begin with Article 8 of the Chicago Convention 1944 [130] under which:

> No aircraft capable of being flown without a pilot shall be flown without a pilot over the territory of a contracting State without special authorisation by that State and in accordance with the terms of such authorisation. [131]

In recent years, Article 8 has gained added prominence, not least because of the ongoing development [132] and increasing military use of UAVs (for instance by Israel over Lebanon in 1982, by the USA over the Gulf in 1991, and by France and the USA over Bosnia-Herzegovina in the 1990s). [133] To all intents and purposes, UAVs fall under the definition of aircraft 'capable of being flown without a pilot', but do missiles or other aerospace aviation vehicles? Much turns on the legal definition of the word 'aircraft'. The Chicago Convention does not include a generic definition of the word, although Annex 7 of the Convention refers to 'all machines which can derive support in the atmosphere from the reactions of the air', while Article 3 (b) supplies a definition of 'State Aircraft' (as

---

128. *Nicaragua v USA*, 'Summary of the Judgement', paragraphs 75 to 125.

129. *Nicaragua v USA*, 'Summary of the Judgement', paragraphs 212-214 and 250-253.

130. Interestingly enough, Article 8 was drafted on the recommendation of the Indian delegation to the International Civil Aviation Conference of 1944. *Proceedings of the International Civil Aviation Conference, Chicago, Illinois, November 1-December 7, 1944*, Vol. II, Washington, US Government Printing Office, 1949, Appendix 2, 'Commentary on the Development of the Individual Articles of the Convention on International Civil Aviation', p. 1382.

131. Article 8, Chicago Convention 1944.

132. See: 'Predator, Darkstar and other cult classics', *The Economist*, 17 June 1995, pp. 111-112; Mark Prigg, 'Nowhere to hide from flying eye', *Sunday Times*, 2 March 1997, Section 5, p. 10; and Ian Brodie, 'Pentagon plans 'smart' substitute for landmines', *The Times*, 8 September 1997, p. 15. Also see Professor Tony Mason's chapter in this book.

133. See: 'Predator, Darkstar and other cult classics', *The Economist,* 17 June 1995, pp. 111-112; and Michael Evans, 'US spy plane keeps eye on Karadzic's hideout', *The Times*, 31 May 1997, p. 14.

quoted above). The wording of the Chicago Convention has led some authorities in the field of air law to conclude that missiles, rockets or artificial satellites are excluded from these definitions.[134] None of which is to say that missiles can evade the general prohibition on unauthorised overflights. There appears to be little state practice regarding missile overflights, although it is a matter of public record that Iran objected to alleged American missile overflights during DESERT STORM.[135] However, it is not unreasonable to argue that the customary prohibition on overflights does indeed apply to missiles and other aerospace aviation vehicles. At least three factors suggest this is the case.

Firstly, the *Proceedings of the International Civil Aviation Conference, Chicago, 1944* clearly demonstrate that the contracting states did not intend the Chicago Convention to confine the prohibition on unauthorised overflights solely to piloted aircraft. In 1944, rockets may have been in their infancy, but the *Proceedings* do suggest that the contracting states intended the prohibition on overflights to apply as widely as possible; hence the reference of Article 8 to aircraft 'capable of being flown without a pilot'.[136]

Secondly, since the invention of the missile, several states have expressed their opposition to the notion that the missiles or other aerospace aviation vehicles of other states possess a right to pass through their airspace. For example, in 1955, the government of Czechoslovakia invoked the provisions of Article 8 of the Chicago Convention to object to the passage of (apparently pilotless) balloons from which propaganda leaflets were descending over Czechoslovak territory; Hungary and Poland lodged similar complaints in 1956.[137]

Thirdly, one can point to the domestic law of several states to demonstrate that they effectively see no distinction between 'aircraft' and other air vehicles. A good example is the US Federal Aviation Act which defines an 'aircraft' as 'any contrivance known or hereafter invented, used, or designed for navigation of or flight in air.'[138]

---

134. *Shawcross and Beaumont on Air Law*, Fourth Edition, Vol. V, Issue 62, p. 1; and Matte, *Treatise on Air-Aeronautical Law*, p. 172.

135. See *Department of Defense Final Report to Congress on the Conduct of the Persian Gulf War*, Appendix O, 'The Role of the Law of War', (an unclassified chapter of the report), Washington D.C., 1992, pp. O-30-O-31.

136. See *Proceedings of the International Civil Aviation Conference, Chicago, Illinois, November 1-December 7, 1944*, Vol. II, (published in two volumes), Washington, US Government Printing Office, 1949.

137. Matte, *Treatise on Air-Aeronautical Law*, p. 172.

138. US Federal Aviation Act. Quoted in L.C. Green, *The Contemporary Law of Armed Conflict*, Manchester, Manchester University Press, 1993, p. 174.

To recap, the prohibition on unauthorised overflights of foreign national airspace applies generally to piloted military aircraft, to UAVs, and also, by custom, to a wide range of other aerospace aviation vehicles. One might presume that, in the years to come, the prohibition will apply to UCAVs as well as SMVs (if they are operating in terrestrial airspace, however that may be defined). Nonetheless, for reasons hereinbefore explained, the prohibition does not apply to satellites in orbit, even if they are being used for military reconnaissance or surveillance purposes.

Notwithstanding the aforementioned legal constraints, there are still many circumstances in which aerial overflights may occur legitimately. The following examples contained are not exhaustive, but they demonstrate the range of ways in which overflights might take place lawfully.

Some circumstances in which the military aircraft of one state might lawfully overfly the territory of another state:

- *With the express consent of the host state after the submission of an overflight request by the foreign state.*
- *At the express invitation of the host state.*[139]
- *When the host state indicates that it will deliberately turn a blind eye to any specified overflights that might take place by military aircraft of the foreign state.*[140]
- *Under treaty.* The best example is the 1960 Treaty of Establishment under which British military aircraft have the right 'to fly in the airspace over the territory of the Republic of Cyprus without restriction other than to have due regard for the safety of other aircraft and the safety of life and property in the Republic of Cyprus'.[141] Another example is the Open-Skies Agreement (Helsinki, 1992).[142]

---

139. For a detailed analysis of the relevant legal principles, see Louise Doswald-Beck, 'The Legal Validity of Military Intervention by Invitation of the Government', *British Year Book of International Law 1985*, Vol. LVI, Oxford, Oxford University Press, 1986, pp. 189-252.

140. For example, in the late 1950s, the British government was assured that whenever RAF aircraft overflew the Belgian Congo, the civil-military authorities there would, subject to certain conditions, 'shut their eyes'. See Kyriakides, 'The RAF and Power Projection: Overflight Constraints, 1958-61'.

141. Annex B, Part II, Section 4 (2), Treaty Concerning the Establishment of the Republic of Cyprus, 1960, (signed and ratified by the Republic of Cyprus, the UK, Greece and Turkey). Reproduced in Cmnd. 1093, *Cyprus*, London, HMSO, 1960.

142. For further details, see the analysis of the Open Skies Agreement in Marian Nash (Leigh), 'Contemporary Practice of the United States Relating to International Law', *American Journal of International Law 1994*, Vol. 88, pp. 89-104.

- *Under a Status of Forces Agreement, a Memorandum of Understanding or other legal instrument.* These are sometimes concluded to facilitate military air movements conducted in peacetime or during an operation under international auspices.[143]
- *By bilateral or multilateral arrangement short of the conclusion of a formal agreement.* For example, after the defeat of Germany in 1945, France, the UK, the USA and the USSR forged an arrangement whereby aircraft of the three western allies could reach West Berlin through three air corridors.

Some additional circumstances in which it has been argued that the military aircraft of one state may lawfully perform unauthorised overflights of another state. It must be stressed, however, that international opinion is divided over the legality of such unauthorised overflights:

- *Under the authority of a UNSC resolution.* For example, the USA, the UK and France have tried to justify the 'air exclusion zones' established in 1992 in northern and southern Iraq, together with the associated aerial reconnaissance missions within these zones, on two main grounds: (a) as coming within the scope of general principles of humanitarian international law,[144] and (b) as consistent with, if not directly the subject of, UNSC Resolution 688.[145] In addition to Iraq itself, some Arab states, namely Algeria, Jordan, Sudan, Syria and Jordan, strongly condemned the move.[146]
- *In preparation for and in connection with a mission mounted in line with the inherent right of individual or collective self-defence.* Most obviously, the unauthorised overflight of the target state might be permissible if it is carried out in order to mount a lawful action in self-defence. It is more difficult to determine the legality of unauthorised overflights of neutral states or third parties during the course of such an action. This argument has been used to justify the unauthorised Israeli overflights (of Sudan and Uganda) required to accomplish the rescue of Israeli and other nationals at Entebbe,

---

143. John Woodliffe, *The Peacetime Use of Foreign Military Installations under Modern International Law*, Dordrecht, Martinus Nijhoff Publishers, 1992.

144. *Keesing's Record of World Events*, Vol. 38, News Digest for August 1992, p. 39068.

145. Written answer by the Minister of State, FCO, Hansard, *House of Lords Debates*, Vol. 560, WA 5, 9 January 1995. Excerpt reproduced in Marston (ed.), 'United Kingdom materials on International Law 1994', p. 683. For an analysis which suggests that 'there must be serious doubt' about the legality of the 'no-fly zones' and hence the right of coalition aircraft to overfly Iraq, see: Christine Gray, 'After the Ceasefire: Iraq, the Security Council and the use of force', *British Year Book of International Law 1994*, Vol. LXV, Oxford, Oxford University Press, 1995, pp. 135-174.

146. *Keesing's Record of World Events*, Vol. 38, News Digest for August 1992, p. 39068.

Uganda, in July 1976.[147] However, there does not appear to be universal international support for the notion that military aircraft have a right to undertake unauthorised overflights in such circumstances. In 1991, for instance, King Hussein of Jordan reportedly 'vowed to repulse any intrusion' of Jordanian airspace by Israeli aircraft which were responding to Iraqi missile strikes upon Israel.[148]

- *If consent to overfly is implied.* This might be the case in the context of regional security pacts, although it has been argued cogently that the practice of individual NATO states would suggest otherwise.[149] Spain, for example, denies overflight clearance to any NATO aircraft (and civil aircraft) flying en route to or from Gibraltar.[150]

- *If an aircraft is in genuine distress.*

N.B. Aircraft flying in hot pursuit – i.e. 'in immediate and continuous pursuit when the intercepting aircraft has not lost contact with the aircraft or vessel being pursued' – can fly into international airspace but not into the national airspace of another state without the permission of that state. Detailed rules regarding the hot pursuit of ships by aircraft are contained in Article 111 of UNCLOS 1982 which affirms that 'the right of hot pursuit ceases as soon as the ship pursued enters the territorial sea of its own State or of a third State.[151] However, it is arguable that it may be permissible for hot pursuit to extend into the airspace belonging to the state of the pursued military vessel (or military aircraft) – but not the airspace of a neutral state – if it is undertaken in exercise of the inherent right of self-defence.

---

147. Wing Commander Ric Casagrande, 'An Introduction to Air Law and the Law of Armed Conflict as it Affects Air Operations', Chapter Nine, *Air Power Presentations 1993*, (Compiled by Gary Waters and Mark Kelton), RAAF Base Fairbairn, Air Power Studies Centre, 1993, pp. 115-120. Also see Yoram Dinstein, *War, Aggression and Self-Defence*, Second Edition, Cambridge, Cambridge University Press, 1994, pp 226-230.
148. Scott MacLeod, 'Jordan', *Time International*, 28 January 1991, pp. 32-33.
149. Woodliffe, *The Peacetime Use of Foreign Military Installations under Modern International Law*, 1992, p. 147. In this regard, Woodliffe points to the case of France when she withdrew from the NATO integrated command structure of NATO in 1966. France followed this up by replacing the year-to-year permission with a requirement of 30 days prior notice of military overflights.
150. See David White and David Buchan, 'UK takes firm line with Spain on Gibraltar', *Financial Times*, 9 July 1997, p. 2; Adela Gooch, 'Cook threatens to block Spain as row on Gibraltar erupts', *Guardian*, 9 July 1997, p. 14; and Christopher Lockwood, 'Spain faces veto threat over Gibraltar flights', *Daily Telegraph*, 9 July 1997, p. 15.
151. Article 111 (3) UNCLOS 1982.

THE RIGHTS AND DUTIES OF NEUTRAL STATES IN RESPECT OF OVERFLIGHTS DURING AN ARMED CONFLICT OR UN ENFORCEMENT ACTION

Several principles of the laws of armed conflict can have a direct bearing upon air movements during an armed conflict. A cardinal principle is that a conflict between two or more belligerents may take place on or above the high seas, the exclusive economic zone and 'the territories subject to the sovereignty of belligerent States'. These normally include: the land areas of the belligerents; their internal waters; their archipelagic waters; their territorial seas; the subsoil and submarine areas underneath these expanses of land and water; and the superjacent airspace above these areas and waters.[152] It follows that belligerents cannot lawfully conduct military operations in the territory, territorial sea and national airspace of neutral states. Under Articles 39 and 40 of the 1923 Hague Draft Rules of Aerial Warfare:

> Belligerent aircraft are bound to respect the rights of neutral Powers and to abstain within the jurisdiction of a neutral state from the commission of any act which it is the duty of that state to prevent.
>
> Belligerent military aircraft are forbidden to enter the jurisdiction of a neutral state.[153]

The Draft Rules were never adopted in a legally binding form. But the European neutrals acted in accordance with this principle during World War I, others have done likewise in more recent conflicts, and the principle is now regarded as part of customary international law.

All the same, it has been argued that there is an exception to this basic principle. In the wake of the Gulf crisis of 1990-91, the US administration suggested that:

> traditional concepts of neutral rights and duties are substantially modified when, as in this case, the UN authorises collective action against an aggressor nation. It was the US position during the Persian Gulf crisis that, regardless of assertions of neutrality, all nations were obligated to avoid hindrance of Coalition operations undertaken pursuant to, or in conjunction with, UNSC decisions, and to provide whatever assistance possible.

In presenting this argument, the US administration pointed to UNSC resolution 687 (of 29 November 1990) which called on states 'to provide appropriate support

---

152. Dinstein, War, *Aggression and Self-Defence*, pp. 20-25.
153. Articles 39 & 40, 1923 Hague Rules of Aerial Warfare. Reproduced in Adam Roberts and Richard Guelff, *Documents on the Laws of War*, Second Edition, Oxford, Oxford University Press, 1989.

for the actions undertaken' by the coalition and, more broadly, to Articles 2(5), 2(6), 25, and 49 of the UN Charter.[154] These provisions have been taken to mean that during an enforcement action, 'the military aircraft of those members enforcing the UN resolutions may call upon the subjacent state to permit overflying.'[155]

Perhaps more than any other recent episode, the 1990-91 Gulf crisis provided an insight into how neutral states respond to overflight requests during an armed conflict. To quote a US Department of Defense report on the legal issues arising in the Gulf:

> On several occasions, Iran protested [against the] alleged entry of its airspace by Coalition aircraft or missiles. The US expressed regret for any damage that may have occurred within Iranian territory by virtue of inadvertent entry into Iranian airspace. The US replies did not, however, address whether Iranian expectations of airspace inviolability were affected by UNSC Resolution 678.
>
> Although military aircraft must gain permission to enter another state's airspace (except in distress), both Switzerland and Austria routinely granted such clearance for US military transport aircraft prior to the Iraqi invasion of Kuwait [which occurred in August 1990]. Early in the Persian Gulf crisis, the US approached the Governments of Austria and Switzerland, seeking permission for overflight of US military transport aircraft carrying equipment to SWA. Despite initial misgivings, based upon their traditional neutrality, each nation assented ... Given their reluctance to permit pre-hostilities overflights [in the period between August 1990 and January 1991], it was natural to expect that Switzerland and Austria would weigh very carefully any requests for overflights once offensive actions began, which each did. In light of the UNSC request that all states support the efforts of those acting to uphold and implement UNSC resolutions, each government decided that overflights by US military transport aircraft would not be inconsistent with its neutral obligations. Accordingly, permission for overflights was granted, easing logistical support for combat operations.
>
> In contrast, overflight denial by the Government of India required [US] Marine combat aviation assets in the Western Pacific to fly across the Pacific, the continental US, the Atlantic, and through Europe to reach SWA, substantially increasing the transit route. Air Force transport aircraft delivering ammunition to [the] theater of operations also were denied overflight permission.[156]

---

154. See the Charter of the UN. Reproduced in Ian Brownlie (ed.), *Basic Documents in International Law*, Third Edition, Oxford, Oxford University Press, 1983, pp. 1-44.

155. I. A. Shearer, *Starke's International Law*, Eleventh Edition, London, Butterworths, p. 159.

156. *Department of Defense Final Report to Congress on the Conduct of the Persian Gulf War*, Appendix O, 'The Role of the Law of War', (an unclassified chapter of the report), Washington D.C., 1992, pp. O-30-O-31.

Interestingly, there is compelling evidence to show that neutrals are not alone in reserving a right to withhold overflight clearance to foreign military aircraft operating in support of operations conducted under the authority of the UN. Shortly after the Iraqi invasion of Kuwait in 1990, President Mubarak of Egypt, a supporter of the international coalition, responded to General Schwarzkopf's request to allow the USA use Egypt as a base for B-52s by claiming 'he was not ready to let US bombers operate from his soil'.[157] In 1994, the Hungarian government, which had until then permitted E-3 AWACS aircraft to operate from their country in support of Operation DENY FLIGHT, threatened to withdraw this permission if air attacks were launched in Bosnia-Herzegovina.[158]

A separate question concerning neutral states springs from Article 11 of the 1907 Hague Convention (V) as applied to aircraft by Article 42 of the Hague Draft Rules:

> A neutral government must use all the means at its disposal to prevent the entry within its jurisdiction of belligerent military aircraft and to compel them to alight if they have entered such jurisdiction. A neutral government shall use the means at its disposal to intern any belligerent military aircraft which is within its jurisdiction after having alighted for any reason whatsoever, together with its crew and the passengers, if any.[159]

With reference to the relevant provisions of the Hague Convention (V), the *Tri-Service Law of Armed Conflict Manual* asserts that:

> Military aircraft of belligerent states must not enter the airspace of a neutral state. The neutral state's right of territorial integrity is coupled with the duty to prevent, by force if necessary, violations of its neutrality such as intrusions into its airspace by belligerent aircraft. If the neutral state cannot or will not prevent violations or its airspace or territory by a belligerent, an opposing belligerent may take appropriate action.[160]

---

157. General H. Norman Schwarzkopf, (written with Peter Petre), *The Autobiography: It Doesn't Take A Hero*, London, Transworld, 1992, p. 307.

158. Air Vice-Marshal Tony Mason, 'Operations in Search of a Title: Air Power in Operations Other Than War', Chapter 6, Richard P. Hallion (ed.), *Air Power Confronts an Unstable World*, London, Brassey's, pp. 157-177.

159. Article 42, 1923 Hague Rules of Aerial Warfare.

160. *Tri-Service Law of Armed Conflict Manual*, (Current Draft), Section II – 'Air Operations', Chapter 12, par. 12. 021. A similar view is expressed in *Operations Law for Royal Australian Air Force Commanders*, DI (AF) AAP 1003, Compiled and Edited by the Air Power Studies Centre, RAAF Base Fairbairn, First Edition, May 1994, par. 12. 8.

Meanwhile, with reference to the Gulf Conflict of 1990-91 and Article 11 of the Hague Convention (V), the *Manual* adds that:

> Military aircraft brought down by a neutral state, or which, intentionally or inadvertently, whether as a result of distress or other circumstances, land in the territory of a neutral state must be detained by that state until the cessation of hostilities and military personnel aboard must be interned.[161]

These principles apply to virtually all types of military aircraft, not just combat aircraft.[162] It is nonetheless appropriate to add that a neutral state does not relinquish its neutral status if it uses force to defend its sovereignty in the face of an unauthorised aerial intrusion by a military aircraft belonging to one of the belligerents.[163]

Neutral states have usually acted in consonance with this long-standing principle. During World War II, for example, Switzerland and Sweden interned Allied and German aircraft and aircrews which had landed on their territory. Furthermore, as the US administration readily concedes, shortly after the outbreak of Operation DESERT STORM in 1991 Iran 'complied with the traditional obligations of a neutral' when it interned Iraqi tactical aircraft which had fled into its territory, although 'US forces nonetheless remained alert to the possibility of a flanking attack by Iraqi aircraft operating from Iran' and the administration still suspects that 'some civil (possibly some military) transport aircraft may have returned to Iraq.'[164]

---

161. *Tri-Service Law of Armed Conflict Manual*, (Current Draft), Section II – 'Air Operations', Chapter 12, par. 12. 022.

162. The rights and duties of states with regard to medical aircraft are separate and are included in Geneva Convention [I] for the Amelioration of the Condition of the Wounded and Sick in Armed Forces in the Field of August 12 1949. Reproduced in Roberts and Guelff, *Documents on the Laws of War*, pp. 171-192. For a detailed analysis of the laws regarding medical aircraft, see: *Tri-Service Law of Armed Conflict Manual*, (Current Draft), Section II – Air Operations, Chapter 12, Part VII, 'Medical Aircraft', paragraphs 12.065-12.081.

163. *Operations Law for Royal Australian Air Force Commanders*, par. 12.18.

164. *Department of Defense Final Report to Congress on the Conduct of the Persian Gulf War*, Appendix O, 'The Role of the Law of War', p. O-30.

INTERNATIONAL LAW AND THE INHERENT RIGHT
OF SELF-DEFENCE

THE UNITED NATIONS CHARTER AND THE PROHIBITION ON
THE USE OF INTER-STATE FORCE

Under Article 1 of the UN Charter, the purposes of the UN include the maintenance of 'international peace and security'.[165] Articles 2 (3) and (4) therefore provide that:

> All Members shall settle their international disputes by peaceful means in such manner that international peace and security, and justice, are not endangered.
>
> All members shall refrain in their international relations from the threat or use of force against the territorial integrity or political independence of any State, or in any other manner inconsistent with the purposes of the UN.[166]

As the ICJ observed in the case of *Nicaragua v USA*, the prohibition on the use of force is 'established in customary law'.[167] Nevertheless, there are exceptions to the rule. The Charter identifies two: enforcement action sanctioned by the UNSC and force used by states in self-defence. International opinion is divided over whether there are others. Above all, debate persists over whether it is permissible for states to use force in other circumstances including: military interventions in support a perceived right to self-determination (an argument employed to support the Indian operation in Goa); and humanitarian interventions in states where large-scale human rights violations have taken place.

Enforcement action under Chapter VII of the UN Charter is the first major exception to the general prohibition on the use of force. During the Cold War, superpower rivalry meant that the UNSC authorised enforcement actions under Chapter VII in only two instances – in respect of Korea in 1950 and Rhodesia in 1965. However, the 1990s have witnessed a succession of occasions in which the UNSC has seemingly authorised foreign powers to undertake Chapter VII

---

165. Article 1, Charter of the UN.
166. Articles 2 (3) and (4), Charter of the UN.
167. *Nicaragua v The USA*. The UNGA has also reaffirmed the prohibition in UNGA Resolution 2625 (XXV), 1965, 'Declaration on Principles of International Law Concerning Friendly Relations and Co-operation Among States in Accordance with the Charter of the UN'; UNGA Resolution 3314 (XXIX), 1974, 'Declaration on the Inadmissibility of Intervention in the Domestic Affairs of States, and the Definition of Aggression'.

enforcement action in line with UNSC resolutions. Operations in Kuwait, Somalia and Haiti have all been described as falling under Chapter VII, as has Operation DELIBERATE FORCE.[168]

ARTICLE 51 OF THE UN CHARTER AND THE INHERENT RIGHT OF SELF-DEFENCE

Aside from enforcement action, the UN Charter explicitly recognises only one other exception to the prohibition on the use of force: the inherent right of self-defence. Under Article 51:

> Nothing in the present Charter shall impair the inherent right of individual or collective self-defence if an armed attack occurs against a Member of the UN, until the Security Council has taken measures necessary to maintain international peace and security ... .[169]

The inherent right of individual self-defence has been invoked by many states. A classic example is the UK after the Argentine invasion and occupation of the Falkland Islands in 1982. On this occasion, the UK employed force in self-defence *after* an armed attack had occurred against the Islands. However, the wording of Article 51 has sown confusion over *when* and *how* the right may be invoked legitimately.

The first problem relates to the meaning of the phrase 'armed attack'. As the Charter does not elaborate on its meaning, the UNGA came to address the question in a resolution adopted in 1974. Its significance lies in that much of it is generally considered to reflect customary international law. The resolution defined aggression as 'the use of armed force by a State against the sovereignty, territorial integrity, or political independence of another State, or in any other manner inconsistent with the Charter of the UN ...'. The resolution provided a number of acts which, 'regardless of a declaration of war', qualified as acts of aggression. The acts listed include:

---

168. On 28 August 1995, the UN authorised NATO to use Air Power against the Bosnian Serbs in fulfilment of UNSC Resolution 836 (1993). Two days later, NATO forces therefore delivered a total of 256 air strikes during 812 sorties including cruise missile strikes. *UN Chronicle*, Vol. XXXII, No. 4, December 1995, pp. 4-11.
169. Article 51, Charter of the UN.

- An invasion or attack by the armed forces of a State of the territory of another state; a military occupation, 'however temporary'.
- An annexation of territory.
- Bombardment or the use of any weapons by a state against the territory of another state; the blockade of the ports or coasts by armed forces of another State.
- An attack by the armed forces of a State against the land, sea or air forces of another State.
- The use of armed forces of one State which are within the territory of another State with the agreement of the receiving State, in contravention of the conditions provided in the agreement.
- The action of a State in allowing its territory, which it has placed at the disposal of another State to be used by that other State for perpetrating an act of aggression against a third State.
- The sending by or on behalf of a State of armed band, groups, irregulars or mercenaries, which carry out acts of armed force against another State of such gravity as to amount to the acts listed above.[170]

The resolution stressed that its list was 'not exhaustive' and it is obvious that some of its provisions are themselves open to interpretation. While the Charter and the resolution are useful as far as they go, there remains uncertainty over the legality of certain activities. Examples include:

- Jamming or chaffing.
- Unauthorised hacking performed by the officials or agents of State A against the computers of either the government or armed forces of State B.
- The clandestine injection by officials or agents of State A of a damaging software virus into the computers of: the government and armed forces of State B; the police force, ports, air ports of State B; the electricity power generating stations, telecommunications system, water boards, or railway networks of State B; or the banks and businesses of State B.
- Interference by State A, partly disabling or rendering useless the outer space satellites, space objects or spacecraft of State B.
- The use of 'non-lethal' weapons (such as melting agents upon a runway) by State A against the armed forces of State B.

---

170. UNGA Resolution 3314 (XXIX), 1974, 'Declaration on the Inadmissibility of Intervention in the Domestic Affairs of States, and the Definition of Aggression'.

Further questions abound. How many of these actions would contravene Article 2(4)? If any do contravene Article 2(4), what methods can a state employ in exercising its right to self-defence against these activities? Can a state employ armed force in response to – or in pre-emption of – a virus 'attack' upon its computers? Assuming a state is entitled to use force in self-defence in response an 'attack' upon its satellites, space objects or space craft, must its actions be confined to earth, or can force be employed in outer space? In the absence of any substantial state practice or applicable treaty, it is not instantly clear what the answer to each of these questions should be.

A second problem arising from Article 51 is whether a state may use force in exercise of its right to self-defence in order to pre-empt an armed attack. Broadly speaking, there are two schools of thought on this question, a fact which reflects the divisions among states and jurists. The 'restrictive' school takes a narrow view. By reading Article 51 in conjunction with Article 2(4), this school holds that the Charter supersedes the old customary law and, *ipso facto*, Article 51 cannot be interpreted as permitting anticipatory self-defence. From this perspective, self-defence can only be invoked 'if' – not before – 'an armed attack occurs'.

On the other hand, many developed states (including the USA and the UK) and eminent international lawyers have countered the 'restrictive' approach. They have embraced what is known as the 'permissive' approach to self-defence which promotes a wider view of Article 51. This approach suggests that Article 51 merely reaffirmed, without qualifying or curtailing, the long-standing doctrine which was explicated by US Secretary of State Webster in *The Caroline* case: namely, that the use of force in self-defence should be confined to cases in which the 'necessity of that self-defence' is instant, overwhelming and leaving no choice of means and no moment for deliberation.[171]

Significantly, the International Military Tribunal at Nuremberg cited *The Caroline* dictum when considering – and rejecting – the argument that Germany had no choice but to invade Norway in 1941.[172] In the post-war era, many developed states have invoked a right of anticipatory self-defence. For instance, Israel did so in 1967, as did the USA when its naval forces were tasked with operating in the Gulf during the Iran-Iraq War. In addition, the UK, France and the USSR (as well as the UN itself, during the Congo crisis) have all invoked the perceived

---

171. *The Caroline*, 2 Moore, *Digest of International Law* 412 (1906). Reproduced in Louis Henkin, Richard Crawford Pugh, Oscar Schachter and Hans Smit, *International Law Cases and Materials*, Second Edition, St Paul, West Publishing, 1987, pp. 662-663.

172. International Military Tribunal (Nuremberg) Judgement (1946). Cited in Dinstein, *War, Aggression and Self-Defence*, p. 244.

right.[173] Under this view, it would thus be permissible for a state to resort to force in self-defence, for example, to repel an imminent armed attack or to intercept a ballistic missile which has just been launched from the territory of another state or indeed elsewhere.

Advances in technology have invariably raced ahead of developments in international law. So much so that some treaty provisions appear dated, while the legality of several military practices is far from clear. The legal picture has been confused still further by missile technology. With respect to the formidable challenges this technology presents to international law, one writer has remarked adroitly that:

> Advances in missile technology necessarily influence the response to this question, and in the light of modern weapons technology it can be difficult to assess whether action in self-defence is required in a given situation. According to one view, it can be argued that an armed attack does not occur until a missile has actually been fired. On the other hand, with missiles which are guided to their target by means of a radar beam, it could be said that an armed attack is under way when the target aircraft or ship perceives, through instruments on board, that the missile is 'locked on', even before it has been fired. However, radar targeting of a ship or aircraft is not unequivocal evidence of an imminent attack ... It is clearly important to take account of the overall political and military context in determining when and how to respond ... Realistically, international agreement on the conditions governing the use of force in self-defence is unlikely to be forthcoming.[174]

AIR POWER AS AN INSTRUMENT OF EXERCISING SELF-DEFENCE

Air power is expected to remain an indispensable instrument enabling the UK to exercise its inherent right to self-defence. Threats may appear in any number of different ways and not least in view of the emphasis western governments now place on adhering to international law. It is therefore important to understand how force may be used in lawful self-defence. Following on from the earlier analysis of airspace, the following sections consider the current state of the law in respect of the use of force against the military and civil aircraft of one state penetrating the national airspace of another state.

---

173. Christopher Greenwood, 'Historical Development and Legal Basis', Chapter 1, Fleck (ed.), *The Handbook of Humanitarian Law in Armed Conflicts*, pp. 1-38.
174. Grief, *Public International Law in the Airspace of the High Seas*, pp. 206-208.

ENGAGEMENT OF INTRUDING MILITARY AIRCRAFT DURING PEACETIME

The practice of unauthorised overflights throws up a number of ancillary legal questions. Firstly, when the military aircraft of one state unlawfully enters the national airspace of a foreign country, thereby violating its sovereignty, does it also violate Article 2 (4) of the UN Charter? Secondly, can the armed forces of the overflown state invoke Article 51 of the Charter to lawfully fire upon the intruding military aircraft in self-defence? In the case of Nicaragua v USA 1986, the ICJ ruled that unauthorised American military overflights of Nicaragua were unlawful as they violated the sovereignty of another state. However, the ICJ did not go as far as to refer to these specific overflights as a use of force against the territory of Nicaragua. The ICJ did little, therefore, to clarify the two questions mentioned above.[175]

The relevance of these questions to air power is highlighted by the regularity of peacetime incidents in which military aircraft have been fired upon and shot down.[176] The following are among the most tragic examples of the post-war era:

- On 8 November 1956, an RAF Canberra PR7 of 13 Squadron on a clandestine reconnaissance over Syria was brought down over the Lebanese border resulting in the death of its navigator.[177]
- On 2 September 1958, an American C130 was brought down near the Soviet-Iranian border resulting in four deaths and thirteen missing;[178]
- Towards the end of the Cuban Missile Crisis, on 30 October 1962, the Cubans destroyed an American U-2 over Cuba resulting in the death of its pilot.[179]

---

175. Hugh Thirlway, 'The Law and Procedure of the International Court of Justice 1960-1989: Part Seven: III. Points of Substantive Law, 1960-1989 (continued): III. Division B: State Sovereignty, Territory and Frontiers', *British Year Book of International Law 1995*, Vol. LXVI, Oxford, Oxford University Press, 1996, pp. 1-96.

176. For example, see 'Special Investigative Report: America's Top-Secret Spy War: Secrets of the Cold War', *US News and World Report*, 15 March 1993, pp. 30-55.

177. Roy Conyers Nesbit, *Eyes of the RAF: A History of Photo-Reconnaissance*, Stroud, Alan Sutton, 1996, p. 274.

178. 'Grim Tally', *US News and World Report*, 15 March 1993, pp. 32-33.

179. *Foreign Relations of the United States, 1961-1963, Vol. XI*, Document 96, Memorandum from Attorney General Kennedy to Secretary of State Rusk, Washington, 30 October 1962, pp. 270-271. (Source: Kennedy Library, President's Office Files, Cuba Missile Crisis, Khrushchev Correspondence.) The death is recorded in 'Grim Tally', *US News and World Report*, 15 March 1993, pp. 32-33.

Some incidents of this kind were not reported at all. A few incidents stirred little or no public discussion, while the debates over some of the others that did arouse discussion were largely overshadowed by disagreements over the facts, particularly over whether the downed aircraft had actually penetrated foreign airspace. In contrast, there was no dispute over the location of the ill-fated U2 when it was brought down in the USSR in 1960. For this reason, delegates of many states were able to participate in a series of seminal UNSC debates in which they could focus on a number of delicate questions of international law and clearly voice their legal opinions with regard to the issue of military over-flights and self-defence. The U2 incident therefore remains of fundamental legal importance and is worthy of a brief analysis.

In summary, the U2 incident arose after a US U2 plane, which had been previously based in Turkey, set off from Pakistan with a view to carrying out a reconnaissance mission over the USSR and landing in Norway. Having been spotted by Soviet forces in Soviet airspace, it was shot down near Sverdlovsk (now Ekaterinburg) and its pilot, Captain Gary Powers, was charged, convicted and imprisoned by a Soviet court.

On both sides of the Iron Curtain, there was, by 1960, widespread support for the notion that unauthorised military overflights were generally unlawful. Nevertheless, the U2 incident of that year prompted the USSR to raise the alto-gether separate legal question of whether an unauthorised overflight by a military aircraft represented an 'armed attack' or an 'act of aggression' which might activate a legitimate response under Article 51 of the UN Charter. On this point, states were divided, as the UNSC records attest. The USSR, for its part, referred to the U2 incursion as 'a high-handed invasion of the airspace of a sovereign state'[180] and therefore submitted a draft resolution 'noting that violations of the sovereignty of other states are incompatible with the principles and purposes of the Charter of the UN' and 'condemn[ing] the incursions by US aircraft into the territory of other states and regards them as aggressive acts.'[181] The USA, on the other hand, took a markedly different line. In the immediate aftermath of the incident, the US State Department admitted that U2s had been 'penetrating' Soviet airspace for four years and President Eisenhower took full responsibility for the ill-fated mission. However, the President initially appeared to justify the prac-tice of overflying the USSR by telling the media that 'no-one wants another Pearl

---

180. Statement by Andrei Gromyko, Foreign Minister of the USSR. *UNSC Official Records*, 857th meeting, 23 May 1960, p. 10, par. 53.
181. Draft Security Council Resolution. *UNSC Official Records*, 857th meeting, 23 May 1960, pp. 18-19.

Harbour'.[182] Later, he added that the flights 'had no aggressive intent but rather were to assure the safety of the US and the free world against [a] surprise attack by a power which boasts of its ability to devastate the US and other countries by missiles armed with atomic warheads.'[183] Developing the American argument in the UNSC, Ambassador Lodge of the USA explained that 'the difference between the US and the Soviet Union is that we shoot their aircraft with cameras; they shoot ours with guns and rockets and kill or imprison our crews – even though not one man, woman or child in Russia has ever been injured by any of our aircraft.'[184] These remarks appeared to suggest that unauthorised military oveflights might be carried out in line with a wide concept of self-defence, as long as they are conducted in a manner which does not involve any use of force or any infringement of territory. As so often before, the UK leapt to the defence of the USA. To this end, Sir Pierson Dixon, the British Ambassador to the UN, informed the UNSC that he was 'unconvinced' that the US action was aggressive and argued that the unauthorised U2 overflight involved neither a threat nor a use of force.[185]

By a vote of 7 to 2 with 2 abstentions the UNSC rejected the draft Soviet resolution.[186] Yet, as the *American Journal of International Law* noted in 1962, the episode carries considerable legal significance. For throughout the U2 affair, the US government did not actually make a formal protest against the shooting down of the U2, nor against the imprisonment, trial and conviction of Captain Powers. Neither did the USA deny that its aircraft had been engaging in the practice of unauthorised overflying. All of which suggests that 'in some circumstances no previous warning or order to land is required by international law before an

---

182. Quincy Wright, 'Legal Aspects of the U2 Incident', *American Journal of International Law 1960*, Vol. 54, Lancaster, The American Society of International Law, 1960, pp. 836-854. For a well-documented memoir of the first American reconnaissance flights of the USSR during the Cold War, see Donald E. Hill with R. Cargill Hall, 'Overflight: Strategic Reconnaissance of the USSR', *Air Power History*, Spring 1996, pp. 28-29. For a detailed legal analysis of the questions posed by the early post-war practice of unauthorised overlying, see Lissitzyn, 'The Treatment of Aerial Intruders in Recent Practice and International Law', pp. 559-589.

183. Wright, 'Legal Aspects of the U2 Incident', pp. 841-842.

184. Statement by Henry Cabot Lodge, Ambassador of the USA to the UN. *UNSC Official Records*, 883rd meeting, 26 July 1960, p. 34, par. 162.

185. Statement by Sir Pierson Dixon, Ambassador of the UK to the UN. *UNSC Official Records*, 858th meeting, 24 May 1960, p. 3, par. 10.

186. The only states in the UNSC supporting the draft resolution were the USSR and Poland. It was opposed by the USA, the UK, France, Italy, the Republic of China, Argentina and Ecuador, with Ceylon and Tunisia abstaining. Wright, 'Legal Aspects of the U2 Incident', pp. 841-843.

intruding foreign [military] aircraft is shot down, even if the intruding aircraft does not itself attack or is likely to attack', but that 'deliberate intrusions of single unarmed aircraft for reconnaissance purposes need not be regarded in all cases as aggressive acts.'[187]

There is no settled international consensus over whether or not an intruding military aircraft (or any aerospace aviation vehicle) can by its mere unauthorised presence in foreign airspace violate Article 2(4) of the UN Charter and thereby activate a lawful response in self-defence under Article 51. What can be said is that, whatever the nature of their mission or the precise contents of their ROE, the armed forces of every state retain an inherent right of self-defence,[188] which the UK has consistently interpreted in a wide sense. By extension, that inherent right of self-defence prevails 'regardless of whether or not it is explicitly stated in the ROE.'[189]

INTERNATIONAL LAW AND THE INTERCEPTION OF INTRUDING CIVIL AIRCRAFT

Under Article 6 of the Chicago Convention 1944:

No scheduled international air service may be operated over or into the territory of a contracting State, except with the special permission or other authorisation of that State, and in accordance with the terms of such permission or authorisation.'

As commonly interpreted, Article 6 prohibits foreign civilian passenger airlines from passing into the airspace of another state without its permission[190] or in the absence of an open-skies agreement with that state. The Chicago Convention identifies only one exception to this rule. Concerning civil aircraft in distress, Article 25 provides that:

---

187. Editorial Comment, 'Some Legal Implications of the U2 and RB47 incidents', *American Journal of International Law*, Vol. 56, 1962, pp. 135-142.

188. For example, speaking in the context of the involvement of British forces in the multinational force deployed in Lebanon in 1983, Malcolm Rifkind, then Minister of State at the FCO, voiced the British government's view that: ' ... the various forces in the multinational force have an inherent right of self-defence and that right is specifically mentioned in the mandate.' Remarks by Malcolm Rifkind, Hansard, *House of Commons Debates*, 5 December 1983, col. 25. Excerpt reproduced in Geoffrey Marston (ed.), 'UK Materials on International Law 1983', *British Year Book of International Law 1983*, Vol. LIV, Oxford, Oxford University Press, 1984, pp. 363-559.

189. *Operations Law for Royal Australian Air Force Commanders*, par. 5.16.

190. William J. Hughes, 'Aerial Intrusions by Civil Airliners and the Use of Force', *Journal of Air Law and Commerce*, Vol. 45, 1979-80, pp. 595-620.

Each contracting State undertakes to provide such measures of assistance to aircraft in distress in its territory as it may find practicable, and to permit, subject to control by its own authorities, the owners of the aircraft or authorities of the State in which the aircraft is registered to provide such measures of assistance as may be necessitated by the circumstances.[191]

Apropos of the rather separate question of whether states can lawfully fire upon a civil aircraft which strays into its national airspace, the Chicago Convention is silent, a fact which the UK and others have consistently interpreted as implying that there is no right to shoot down any intruding civil aircraft.[192] However, the post-war era has shown that civil aircraft are not immune from attack. On occasion, several states have found reason to attack civil aircraft, usually with reference to Article 51 of the UN Charter and the notion of military necessity. For example:

- In February 1973, Israel shot down a Libyan Airlines Boeing 707, killing 108 people, because it strayed over 50 miles into the airspace above the Israeli-occupied Sinai and had allegedly overflown military installations.
- In September 1983, a Soviet military aircraft fired upon Korean Airlines Flight 007, a Boeing 747, on a scheduled civil flight between New York and Seoul; the resulting clash claimed 269 lives.[193]
- In February 1996, Cuba shot down two US-registered civil aircraft.[194]

In the past, some states, such as the former USSR, publicly stated that *any* aircraft engaging in an unauthorised overflight – irrespective of whether it was state or civil – might be intercepted and be met by a threat or use of force. Others, notably the UK and the USA, objected to this notion.[195] Indeed, the UK is on record as stating that:

---

191. Article 25, Chicago Convention on Civil Aviation.
192. 'Memorial of the Government of the UK, 18 August 1958'. *Aerial Incident of July 27 1955 (Israel v Bulgaria) 1959 ICJ Pleadings 5.* Cited in Farooq Hassan, 'A Legal Analysis of the Shooting of Korean Airlines Flight 007 by the Soviet Union', *Journal of Air Law and Commerce,* Vol. 49, 1983-84, pp. 555-588.
193. *Keesing's Record of World Events,* Vol. 39, 'News Digest for June 1993', p. 39539, citing the ICAO report completed on 14 June 1993.
194. *Shawcross and Beaumont on Air Law,* Fourth Edition, Vol. IV, Issue 66, p. 5, footnote 12.
195. In the UNSC debate regarding Flight 007, the Soviets defended their actions by pointing to the 'sovereign right of every state to protect its borders including its airspace', while the Americans argued that 'sovereignty neither requires nor permits the shooting down of airlines in peacetime'. Martin Dixon and Robert McCorquodale, *Cases and Materials on International Law,* London, Blackstone Press, 1991, p.262.

there can be no justification in international law for the destruction, by a state using armed force, of a foreign civil aircraft, clearly identifiable as such, which is on a scheduled passenger flight, even if that aircraft enters without previous authorisation the airspace of the territory of that State.[196]

Similar views were expressed in the light the Korean Airlines incident and, in its aftermath, the ICAO revised its rules and procedures regarding the interception of civil aircraft.[197] What is more, the ICAO encouraged states to draft an amendment to the Chicago Convention. Under Article 3 *bis* (a) of the Convention which was adopted unanimously by states in the ICAO in May 1984 but has not yet come into force:

> The contracting parties recognise that every State must refrain from resorting to the use of weapons against civil aircraft in flight and that, in case of interception, the lives of persons on board and the safety of aircraft must not be endangered. This provision shall not be interpreted as modifying in any way the rights and obligations of States set forth in the Charter of the UN. ... The contracting parties recognise that every state, in exercise of its sovereignty, is entitled to require the landing ... of a civil aircraft flying above its territory without authority.[198]

All this appears to be in line with the long established position of the UK. Like the USA, the UK is not yet a party to Article 3 *bis*[199] but its provisions have effectively been incorporated into English domestic law.[200]

While the use of force against civil aircraft is not normally justifiable in international law, it might be justifiable if is used in the legitimate exercise of self-defence. It would appear that force might lawfully be used against civil aircraft in at least two circumstances. One circumstance might arise if, for example, a civil aircraft is out of control, heading for an oil refinery in a populated area

---

196. Memorial of the UK, p. 358, *Aerial Incident of July 1955, Israel v Bulgaria; US v Bulgaria; UK v Bulgaria, ICJ Pleadings.* Excerpt quoted in Hughes, 'Aerial Intrusions by Civil Airliners and the Use of Force', p. 605.

197. Grief, *Public International Law in the Airspace of the High Seas,* p. 217.

198. Article 3 *bis* (a) of the Chicago Convention. Quoted in Grief, *Public International Law in the Airspace of the High Seas,* p. 199. Writing in 1994, Grief notes that Article 3 *bis* will come into force 'with the deposit of the 102nd instrument of ratification or accession. To date, 68 instruments have been adopted.'

199. Rebecca Wallace, *International Law,* Second Edition, London, Sweet & Maxwell, 1992, p. 103, footnote 62.

200. Air Navigation Order 1989, SI 1989/2004, Article 93. Cited in *Shawcross and Beaumont* on Air Law, Fourth Edition, Vol. IV, Issue 66, p. 5, footnote 12.

and threatening to cause terrible loss of life on the ground. As a member of the RAF Directorate of Legal Services has indicated, the use of force to bring the civil aircraft down might therefore be justifiable on the ground of necessity if other methods to stop it have failed.[201] A second circumstance might arise if, by the nature of its mission, an aircraft forfeits its status as a 'civil aircraft' and in effect becomes a 'state aircraft' as defined by the Chicago Convention.[202] The transition from 'civil' to 'state' can occur in a number of ways. For example, as the Legal Adviser to the Foreign Office mooted in 1952, 'Article 3 (b) [of the Chicago Convention which is quoted earlier] is so worded that it is open to interpretation that civil aircraft chartered for the carriage of troops are 'state aircraft' for the purpose of the Convention.'[203] Whether this fact alone would make the aircraft a legitimate target for attack during the course of an exercise of self-defence would, of course, depend upon a number of factors such as those noted in earlier in this chapter. However, in 1984 the British representative to the ICAO provided a measure of guidance. He suggested that, in strict accordance with a state's inherent right to self-defence, force could be used legitimately against a nominally civil aircraft:

> if the aircraft is making, or is about to make, an attack, or is, for example, dropping paratroops. The aircraft would then, in effect, be operating as a military aircraft. Lives of persons not on board would be endangered. The State would be entitled to use force against it.[204]

---

201. Carleton, 'Civil and Military Intrusion into Airspace', p. 100.

202. Article 3 bis (d) of the Chicago Convention now prohibits the use of civil aircraft for purposes inconsistent with the aims of the Convention. Article 3 bis (d), Chicago Convention. Cited in Grief, *Public International Law in the Airspace of the High Seas*, p. 215.

203. AIR 2/10948. Opinion of the Legal Adviser of the Foreign Office as summarised in a formerly 'confidential' (now declassified) memorandum from P.F. de Zulueta, Foreign Office, to R.S. Kinsey, Ministry of Civil Aviation, 13 August 1952, PRO.

204. Address by Mr F.A. Neal, the representative of the UK, to the 25th (Extraordinary) Assembly of ICAO, 24 April 1984. Excerpt reproduced in Geoffrey Marston (ed.), 'United Kingdom Materials on International Law 1984', *British Year Book of International Law 1984*, Vol. LV, Oxford, Oxford University Press, 1985, pp. 405-604.

CONCLUSION

Air power possesses the formidable capacity to exploit the third dimension for military and, by extension, political purposes. Whatever the future holds, it seems certain that adherence to international law will continue to condition this capacity. By the same token, international law will continue to have a considerable bearing upon how states elect to deploy – and defend themselves against – air power.

As the twentieth century draws to a close, it is perhaps appropriate to conclude this chapter by quoting one scholarly analysis of the extent to which the diverse strands of international law had, by the 1950s, already impinged upon air movements:

> In the year 414 B.C., a play [The Birds] was produced in Athens in which Aristophanes described how the birds when building a free city in the air beat off the legislators who came to offer their services. If Aristophanes could look at the present situation in the air and see in what measure the legislators have prevented the birds of this day from unfolding their wings, he would have prided himself on his foresight.[205]

---

205. Goedhuis, 'The Air Sovereignty of Concept and United States Influence on its Future Development', *Journal of Air Law and Commerce*, Vol. 22, 1955. Quoted in Moon, 'A Look At Airspace Sovereignty', pp 340-341.

PART II

TECHNOLOGICAL CONTEXT

CHAPTER 5

THE TECHNOLOGY INTERACTION
Air Vice-Marshal Professor Tony Mason

INTRODUCTION

AIR POWER is the product of 20th Century technology. In the last three decades, the modern computer with its ever increasing capacity has reduced the volume, weight and power requirements of equipment, while increasing its effectiveness. This combination has an obvious value in an environment which has always called for finely judged compromise between size, payload, fuel and propulsion.

The microprocessor has enabled improvements in navigation, sensors, weapon accuracy, reach, communication speed, volume and connectivity. It has also enhanced the design and construction of lighter weight aircraft structures with improved aerodynamics and control and, most dramatically, stealth. Lastly, it has facilitated design, construction and maintenance of greatly improved engines and associated components.

The rate of accelerating enhancement and innovation across such a broad front justifies the appellation, "Technological Revolution". It has brought air power to the threshold of effectiveness foreseen by the early visionaries. The impact of technology has been amplified because it is enabling air power to adapt, albeit with new constraints, challenges and competition, to the demands of a rapidly changing post Cold War international environment.

This revolution confers an obvious advantage on states with relevant industrial base, research, wealth and political inclination. Whereas up to 1939, the air forces of several countries were roughly comparable in size and levels of technology, at the close of the century United States military aviation, after the demise of the USSR, has no peers, either numerically or in technology.

The scale of United States air power is unlikely to be matched for a very long time, but its technological advantage will be constrained in a number of ways as the products of the revolution spread across the globe.

Even the USA will be unable to place orders large enough to sustain its aerospace companies, stimulating even more intense international market searches. US exports may be restricted, but very sophisticated items, such as the Boeing

767 AWACS, and many advanced weapons are already on offer. Russia, despite her economic and political disruption, is giving high priority to exports of fighter aircraft, air-to-air and surface-to-air missiles of considerable sophistication, at greatly reduced prices. The proliferation of mobile, increasingly effective SAM will have a considerable impact on all air operations.

Some companies are offering avionics and weapon systems updates for older aircraft. Other countries are benefiting from the cascade of obsolescent combat aircraft, stimulated by the CFE agreements and NATO enlargement.

At the forefront of influential satellite sensor and communications technology, an increasing number of components can be bought "commercially off the shelf" (COTS) and adapted for inclusion in military systems. In an environment where airframe life can be expected to be extensive, military adoption of COTS equipment allows quick and cheap response to the expansion of commercial microprocessor capacity for battle management, communications, data acquisition and display systems. Such commercial exploitation however, raises the risk of computer hacking or virus infection and, as explained elsewhere in this volume, will prompt close examination of the problem of isolating and protecting sub systems while preserving essential connectivity between them.

Some aerospace technologies constrain others: air-to-air weapons are an obvious example. Even less sophisticated AWACS aircraft induce caution among all but the most stealthy. Meanwhile, on the surface, "industrial age" ballistic missiles with conventional or WMD warheads can threaten the bases of even the most stealthy aircraft at longer and longer range.

In previous generations, warfare has stimulated weapon innovation and evolution. Now, international commercial competition is a forceful influence on provision for the uncertainties of the post-Cold War era. Consequently, sophisticated weapons and systems will be encountered, albeit often in small numbers, in many theatres, in crises and confrontations at all levels of intensity.

Finally, whereas air power was, for the greater part of the Century, largely the preserve of the manned aircraft, albeit with frequent and punishing intervention from anti aircraft defences, technology now demands re-evaluation of the aircraft's relationship with uninhabited aerial vehicles (UAV), missiles and satellites.

Their interaction will be examined by reference to each of air power's traditional roles: defence, offence, reconnaissance, air mobility and maritime. A small number of systems will be described in detail as examples of the cumulative impact of the technology revolution.

DEFENCE

Since the end of the Cold War, air defence requirements for members and friends of the "Atlantic Community" have changed considerably.

First, the threat of traditional air attack on any homeland has virtually gone. In the foreseeable future, a threat from cruise (CM) or ballistic missiles (BM) will probably arise, but meanwhile, security of the home base, a cardinal principle of war, has slipped in air operations priority. As missile ranges increase and international interests become increasingly interdependent, provision for national aerospace defence in the longer term cannot, be ignored; nor can it be pursued in national isolation.

Second, protection of forces deployed beyond the home territory was previously focused on Central Europe. Now, with the expansion of UN operations, the despatch of expeditionary forces and the residual risk of regional conflict beyond Europe, provision of air cover to deployed forces will be needed in widely different circumstances.

The third traditional requirement for air defence arose from the need to protect air operations deep in hostile air space. It was classically represented by the P51 Mustang escort fighters of WWII and, more recently, by the "packages" of combat aircraft deployed by allied coalitions in the Gulf War and over Bosnia, which included aircraft such as F-15s and F-16s employed as air-to-air interceptors. The need and priority for deep protection are likely to remain unpredictable, but declared USAF policy is to extend air supremacy into an opponent's air space[1] and advanced technology is already being harnessed to it. Long range protection is likely to be accompanied by offensive counter air (OCA) and suppression of enemy air defences (SEAD) operations.

EARLY WARNING

Since WWII, air defence fighters have depended for their effectiveness on information about an enemy's whereabouts, derived in the first instance from an external source, such as ground based radar. Details were "fused" at a ground control centre and relayed to the fighter pilot to place him in a favourable attacking position.

---

1. " Global Engagement: A Vision for the 21st Century Air Force", Department of the Air Force Washington DC 1997, p.10.

In the early 1950s, both sides in the Cold War began to experiment with airborne early warning radars to extend warning time and to direct interceptors to within their own radar or visual identification range. The Boeing E-3 AWACS entered service in 1977 and immediately marked the arrival of the information age in air warfare. From the outset it could register 600 aircraft tracks in 32 surveillance sectors at distances up to 250 miles, from an operating height of 30,000 feet.

The subsequent impact of the microprocessor can be illustrated by a list of updates to E-3D systems[2]. Global Positioning System (GPS) satellite links give the aircraft's position to within less than ten feet. Twenty UHF radios have been replaced with one "Have Quick Net" system to provide, anti-jam communications with other AWACS, friendly aircraft and ground stations. Class 2 Joint Tactical Information Distributional System (JTIDS) are encrypted, use frequency hopping to counter jamming and transmit more information six times faster than its predecessor. Class 2 JTIDS also allocates priorities to incoming communications to reduce information overload.

A new electronic support system measure (ESM), known as "Quick Look", covers a large number of frequencies in two seconds, classifies received signals, compares them with a data base stored in the aircraft's computers and presents information about the emitter on to the operator's console. The ESM system can identify more than 100 non-co-operative targets in 10 seconds at distances of more than 300 nm, which is approximately six times the range of a typical interrogating signal from a fighter interceptor. This modernisation now renders E-3D virtually immune to hostile spoofing, code breaking or failure of a friendly aircraft's Identification Friend or Foe (IFF) transponder.

Even though the update programme was not complete during the Gulf War, and while E-3D had little early warning and interception activity, AWACS aircraft flew constantly during the Coalition air campaign. They controlled over 3,000 allied sorties per day, giving threat warnings, deconflicting routes, enhancing target acquisition, co-ordinating tanker rendezvous and networking communications between participants in the air, on land and at sea. As a result, as far as is known, no allied aircraft was lost in collision, friendly fire, failure to refuel in flight or air to air interception.

In the lower intensity environment of Bosnia, E-3D Sentries monitored the imposition of sanctions, air exclusion zones and activity on air bases operated by the warring factions. By disseminating early and distant detection of politically hostile or sanction breaking activity, AWACS allowed the requirement for stand-

---

2. "Aviation Week and Space Technology"(AWST), 10 Mar 97, pp 52-53.

ing combat air patrols to be reduced considerably, with lower alert states and swifter response on demand.

By 1996, the potential international market for AWACS was assessed at 34 countries[3]. Japan ordered four Boeing 767-27C AWACS at a cost of $400 million each, including support and ground systems. The original Boeing 707 E-3D Sentry had cost approximately $150 million. Its four engines had generated 21,000 lbs of thrust each; the E767's pair produced 56,500 lbs each representing an increase in powerplant effectiveness of 30%, giving a considerably extended range at 40,000 feet.

For states which did not need or could not afford an E767 there were several options on the market. Russia offered an A50 airframe and engines with Israeli Aircraft Industries radar and sub systems. The Ericsson FSR 90 surveillance radar will be married with five Brasilian Embraer 120 EWs to contribute to the Amazon Surveillance System which, in addition to anti-drug and border patrols, co-ordinates and supports protection, authorised exploitation and development of the Amazon region.

The Indonesian Air Force was one of several on the Pacific Rim expressing an interest in acquiring an AWACS capability. It would monitor peaceful traffic, give early warning of potentially hostile force intrusion and, in extremis, discharge full conflict AWACS tasks. The presence of such technology would have a significant impact on the outcome of any international disputes in the South China Sea, which would undoubtedly be determined by control of the skies above it.

The E-3 AWACS is no longer simply a link in a single chain, but a junction, or nodal point, in a US information web, popularly referred to as a "System of Systems", which is gradually including sensors, communications, decision makers and executors in the air and on the ground. AWACS aircraft are highly versatile force multipliers in either defence or offence, readily deployable into a theatre with sufficient range to remain outside most AD threats and self sufficient in early warning and evasion of air to air interception. Consequently, while manpower intensive and comparatively expensive, AWACS is unlikely to be replaced by satellites or UAVs for many years.

THE FIGHTER

The circumstances of the Cold War led to the evolution of two distinct kinds of fighter aircraft. One, still usually referred to as a "fighter", had comparatively

---

3. AWST, 4 Nov 96, p 98.

short range, was manoeuvrable and cast for the role of air superiority in traditional dog fights with opponents with similar characteristics – F-16 and Mig 29 aircraft were typical of the genre. Their weapons would be highly agile short range air to air missiles guided by infra red sensors, with the AIM 9 Sidewinder the most widely deployed in the West, with air-to-air cannon as back-up.

The second type was the "interceptor", designed primarily to operate at longer ranges against incoming bombers, using radar homing missiles launched "beyond visual range" (BVR). The British F3 variant of the Tornado and the Soviet Mig 25 or 31 were the last examples of such fighters which were not designed to "dogfight" with the F-16s and Mig 29s of this world.

The cumulative impact of new technology has been to close the gap between the "fighter" and the "interceptor". Over the last twenty years, manoeuvrability, acceleration, high rates of turn and climb with short and long range night/all weather avionics and weapon systems have become prerequisites for almost all fighters. At the same time, the lethality, speed and range of air-to-air missiles (AAM) has driven the need for integral early warning and passive defence equipment.

Although the F-15 and the SU 27 are untested in combat against each other, their fundamental statistics are very similar: both can carry eight to ten short and long range AAMs over combat radii in excess of 750 miles at heights up to 60,000 feet; both can accelerate up to Mach 2.5, both can track and engage multiple BVR targets. The SU 27's aerobatic performance is spectacular and, should any opponent allow it to get so close, would be a useful asset in a dogfight. But, like the F-15, it has one major disadvantage: it is not stealthy – both aircraft when hung with missiles using their search or interrogation radars, are readily detectable at long range by AWACS and other sensors.

Notwithstanding such handicaps, the Sukhoi bureau is producing several variants for export. The USAF, on the other hand is looking to the totally stealthy but hugely expensive F-22, as a more cost effective return on investment.

Three examples illustrate the impact of technology acceleration on the manned fighter. In 1996, the Romanian Air Force took back its first Mig 21, updated by Israeli Elbit Defence systems to carry pulse Doppler acquisition and tracking radar, digital avionics, multirole mission computer, data link communications, passive warning radar and the ability to deliver a variety of Russian, Israeli and Western AAMs.

Moving up the scale, the agility of the multinational Eurofighter is achieved from an airframe which is inherently aerodynamically unstable. Control is maintained by electrical signals generated by the control column to a computer which relays them to the appropriate control surface, hence the expression "fly by wire".

The computer's software supports a quadruple control system designed to sustain two major failures with no operational degradation while still keeping the aircraft safe to fly. It also prevents the pilot inadvertently exceeding the aircraft's tolerance limits.

The fighter's weapons radar can search and track multiple targets which are automatically placed in priority by the weapons system computer. A further system provides automated defensive threat assessment and responses. In pursuit of economies on the ground, priority was given to ease of maintenance and automatic defect identification. All avionics, communications, weapon and defensive system information is fused onto multi-function displays in the cockpit. The aircraft does not have a stealthy configuration, but incorporates stealthy features, including modified structural materials and engine intake masking. It will deliver a wide range of short and BVR air-to-air missiles. In December 1997 Eurofighter was reported to cost £37 million ($60 million)[4].

The third example, the USAF F-22 Raptor will be the benchmark for the 21st Century manned fighter. Raptor will have an unprecedented amount of integrated sensors. Data from radar, radar warning receiver, missile launch detector, communications, navigation and identification system will be merged into a single "situational awareness" display for the pilot. Information will include the location of friendly, unknown and hostile aircraft; threat identification; radar classification, missile launch detection, electronic counter measures and external data links.

The 'Future' of Air Superiority, the F-22 RAPTOR.

---

4. "Daily Telegraph", 23 Dec 97.

F-22 is also flown by wire and is aerodynamically unstable. Although its combat radius is, like that of Eurofighter, still classified, it is expected that deep penetration escort without refuelling will be one role assigned to it. It was designed to establish air superiority in an opponent's airspace without exposing supporting tankers to hostile air defences. Computerised engine control and a high thrust to weight ratio are designed to allow the aircraft high altitude super-sonic cruise without resort to afterburner. Short field operations and slow speed manoeuvrability are enhanced by thrust vectoring.

It is, however, F-22's stealth characteristics which set it apart from all known competitors. A very low radar cross section is achieved by overall shape and radar absorbent materials in which high frequency signals are absorbed in a surface layer and lower frequency by a deeper honeycomb structure. In addition, it carries an automated electronic combat suite which gives threat location from air and ground to enable either evasion or defensive manoeuvring to reduce direc-tional radar cross section.

The aircraft's weapons radar has 2,000 transmit/receive modules which ensure simultaneous engagement of several widely dispersed targets with multiple missiles, all of which will be carried in recessed bays and ejected for launching.

F-22 has pushed several technological frontiers at the same time, with predictable results for programme delays and increased costs. The US govern-ment's Quadrennial Review of 1997 stated a programme goal of $43 billion for 339 fighters[5] and estimates for individual aircraft range from $75 million to over $100 million. The USAF expects that price to buy an aircraft which can operate deep within hostile airspace and be adapted to other roles, including SEAD. F-22 will be "netted" with other systems, but will retain considerable operational autonomy.

THE MISSILES

The impact of the microprocessor on air-to-air missiles (AAM) has been to increase their sensitivity to targets, improve their agility, increase their speed and extend their range. Traditionally, early location of an opponent conferred consid-erable advantage in air to air combat. Now, survival may depend upon it.

While the usual caveats apply to manufacturers' marketing claims, there appears to be much closer international competition between AAMs than between combat aircraft. Russian families of short range heat seeking and radar

---

5. AWST, 12 May 97, p 22.

guided BVR AAM are held in high regard and priced attractively for smaller air forces. The Vympel R 73 is reported to have passive infra red (IR) seeker and laser or radar proximity fuzes, with a sensor field of 140-180 degrees against a target manoeuvring at up to 12g up to 18 miles away. If so, it is superior to existing models of AIM 9 Sidewinder.

Yet, despite extended warning and detection ranges, a large number of air to air encounters may still culminate in close combat. If so, the advantages conferred by AWACS and other reconnaissance systems noted below would be dissipated and air superiority would, as of old, depend upon pilot skill and manoeuvrability of the aircraft.

In 1996, Hughes Missile Systems won the contract for a new AIM 9X, harmonised with helmet mounted sights, with an acquisition field of more than 180 degrees, thrust vector control, cryogenic cooler to increase IR seeker sensitivity, IR counter measures and other improvements designed to regain superiority over competitors such as Vympel. AIM 9X is also the first AAM to be designed from the outset to be carried internally by a stealth fighter.

International access to short range, fire and forget AAMs with a very high kill probability raises the unwelcome prospect of mutual destruction. A Russian rearward firing missile is probably under development but, even with existing or imminent weapons possessing a 180 degree acquisition arc, a small manoeuvre by a "target" could bring the attacker within reciprocal engagement range.

In such a combat environment, information advantage based on superior detection and engagement range, becomes critical. At present, the most effective BVR AAM, the US – built AIM 120, has an effective range of about 30 miles, but its associated radar can "see" for over 50 miles[6] and, as noted above, AWACS can detect and identify at four times that distance. Not surprisingly, therefore, there is strong international competition to close the gap between detection range and BVR missile lethality.

The propulsion challenge is to increase the energy available after rocket motor burn out, when the missile gradually loses speed and hence the agility to attack at maximum theoretical range, an alerted, manoeuvring target. Several companies are combining the boost of a rocket motor with the sustained power of a ramjet to achieve 2-3 times the terminal energy of AIM 120 at a greatly increased range. The European future medium air-to-air missile (FMRAAM) is designed for carriage by Eurofighter, among others. Its main computer can be fed with target identities and priorities before launch and updated in flight by data link either

---

6. Brassey's "World Aircraft and Systems Directory 1996/97", p 630.

from the launch aircraft or from other sources. It uses an active radar seeker and will, therefore, have to penetrate a target's electronic defences before interception.

Meanwhile, the search for a multi mode AAM, combining IR and radar sensors will continue. In 1996, a USAF evaluation programme was funded for a dual range missile which could manoeuvre at 30g over 360 degrees at a range of 100 nm and at 9g within five seconds of launch against a target within 45 degrees either side of the missile's heading, to be in service by 2020. Unsurprisingly, the programme was designed to identify the problems to be overcome in technology, propulsion and flight controls.

Looking further ahead, the USAF Scientific Advisory Board in 1995 speculated in "New World Vistas" about the prospects of fighter uninhabited combat air vehicles (UCAV)[7]. In air-to-air combat, where awareness, responsiveness, reach, speed and agility are likely to be determining factors, the removal of the pilot from the cockpit offers several advantages. It would reduce airframe radar cross section (RCS), increase acceleration limits from +9/-3g to +/-20g, permit omni-directional acceleration and the execution of high g manoeuvres to present minimum RCS to a threat and to evade missiles. Information fusion and analysis could be retained at a ground control point which, with satellite communication (SATCOM) relay, could be hundreds of miles away from the combat area, reducing pilot vulnerability and overload.

Before then, however, virtual situational awareness will also need to be created, whether for a free-ranging autonomous pre-programmed UCAV or one under ground control, with attendant problems of operations in a dense and hostile electronic environment. Even then, unless the UCAV is given the combat radius of an F-22, it will have to deploy to potentially vulnerable in-theatre bases. Unsurprisingly, USAF response to the New World Vistas UCAV suggestions was cautious[8].

SURFACE TO AIR MISSILES (SAM)

The experience of the Soviet Air Force against Stinger in the Afghanistan War from 1986 onwards is likely to be repeated by any air force which chooses to fly at low level over territory affording protection to hand held or low profile mobile short range air defences (SHORAD).

---

7. "New World Vistas: Air and Space Power for the 21st Century", Washington DC, 1996 Summary Volume, p 34.
8. General R R Fogleman, "Jane's Defence Weekly"(JDW), 18 Sep 96, p 40.

In the Gulf War, Coalition air forces were reported to have been opposed by 11,000 SAM and 8,500 AA guns, integrated and controlled from hardened bunkers with multiple communication links[9]. That system was demolished within 48 hours, but the subsequent victorious air campaign was prosecuted from above 10,000 feet. Coalition air supremacy was restricted to heights above that by the residue of low level SAM and guns less dependent on co-ordinated command and control.

Since then, SAM have also benefited from the microprocessor to increase their responsiveness, range, sensitivity and lethality. A number of factors have coincided to encourage their proliferation.

Some countries might not wish to see an American-led expeditionary force in their region, but could not hope to compete with the USAF in the air. They will have noted US sensitivity to casualties after Mogadishu and the Bosnia F-16 loss of Captain Scott O'Grady and see in the deployment of mobile SAM a useful constraint, if not deterrent, to US or any other unwelcome intervention.

Countries participating in an expeditionary forces on the other hand, may wish to have integral protection against small numbers of potentially hostile, less sophisticated, combat aircraft in circumstances where friendly air cover may be intermittent.

In 1996, Pentagon sources acknowledged that several hundred Stingers were still unaccounted for, fetching between $50,000 and $80,000 on the underground market. A similar weapon, the BAe Matra Mistral, was priced at $60-$100,000 and continues to sell well. In addition, large numbers of ex Soviet SA 7, 14, 16 and 18 were internationally available[10].

The Russian competitor to Patriot, S 300V, was marketed in 1997 as intercepting six targets up to 150 km in range and from ten to twenty five thousand metres in altitude. In January 1997, the (Greek) Republic of Cyprus placed an order for an unspecified number of S 300s and both the United Arab Emirates (UAE) and South Korea have expressed interest in acquiring the weapon system.

Prices were not advertised but Raytheon helpfully published detailed cost comparisons on Patriot and S 300V, alleging $4.8 billion operating costs a year for the latter, which required 1,389 personnel and 476 equipment items against $1.8 billion for Patriot, with 197 personnel and 102 items[11]. France generously offered

---

9. "Conduct of the Gulf War, Final Report to Congress", US Department of Defence, Washington Apr 92, p 241.

10. AWST, 12 May 97, p 22.

11. JDW, 26 Mar 97, p 3.

to evaluate the two systems and to assist with reconfiguring S 300V to increase compatibility with western systems.

Despite proliferation and enhancement, traditional shortcomings of SAM remain. Short range systems can be outdistanced by stand-off weapons launched beyond the SAM's engagement zone. Fast, low flying aircraft approaching from any quadrant, especially if equipped with automated warning and chaff/flare dispensers, are still difficult to knock down. Medium and longer range SAM are susceptible to low level penetration. If they are widely dispersed, a gap can be opened and exploited by concentration of defence suppression attacks. Of particular significance to an expeditionary or peacekeeping force, the secure deployment of SAM depends on control of the territory surrounding each battery.

That said, competition between Western manufacturers, determined Russian attempts to hold and expand traditional markets, the widespread attraction of comparatively cheap and easily operated systems: to emerging states, warring factions, irregulars, terrorists and, ultimately, international criminals, will ensure that SAM continue to proliferate with increased effectiveness.

Consequently, in many lower intensity scenarios, air supremacy may be contested between Western combat aircraft and opposing SAM rather than in the air in the more traditional manner. SEAD should therefore be given equal priority to air-to-air combat in the establishment of air supremacy.

BALLISTIC MISSILE DEFENCE

Since the political impact of SCUDS in the Gulf War, and the US military casualties sustained in Dharan barracks during the war, defence against ballistic missiles has been given increasing attention in the west.

It was estimated that by 1997 approximately 50 countries had deployed 40 different types of ballistic missile. Many were SCUD derivatives with ranges of less than 740 km, but North Korea, Iraq and Iran have extended the missiles' range to an estimated 2,000 km with a payload of 770 kg[12]. The Missile Technology Control Regime (MTCR) was established in 1987 by a number of countries, largely western in origin, to place export restrictions on components and technology associated with the construction of ballistic missiles capable of carrying a nuclear payload of more than 500 kg over 300 kms. Russia and China

12. AWST, 24 Jan 97, pp44-48

are not signatories but in meetings with President Clinton in October 1997, Chinese President Jiang Zemin was reported to have agreed to abide by the Regime[13]. Already, however, equipment or assistance was widely believed to have been acquired by Iraq, Libya, Pakistan, Algeria, Egypt, Iran and Syria.

Ballistic missile guidance systems have not yet incorporated the products of the microprocessor revolution. Their CEPs (circular error probable: the area within which 50% of the weapons could be expected to land) are usually assumed to be several hundreds of yards. They are, therefore, unreliable when delivering a conventional unitary explosive warhead against a specific military target.

At least 25 countries, however, have access to nuclear, chemical or biological weapons of mass destruction (WMD). Several of those already deploy ballistic missiles and some have already used chemical weapons. Such missiles, armed with WMD warheads, could be highly effective against ports, airfields and any other installations essential for expeditionary force deployment into theatre. They are also cheap terror weapons whose possession by a potential opponent could introduce a complication into interventionist decision making.

Patriot's actual interception rate of incoming SCUDS in the Gulf War remains debatable, while the Russian S 300V remains unproved in combat. But however effective, interception of an incoming missile with a WMD warhead in its terminal phase, over friendly territory, is unlikely to be politically or militarily attractive. Yet, with total air supremacy in the Gulf, over terrain which provided comparatively little cover for missile launchers, no mobile SCUDS were killed before launch by air attack, or by any other method for that matter. It is probable that launches were restricted by the frequent presence of coalition aircraft, but if the SCUDS had been armed with WMD, that would have been little consolation for targets in Israel or Saudi Arabia.

A 500 km range missile may be under rocket power for only 36 seconds and a 1000 km missile for 55 seconds. Contemporary air-to-air missiles have speeds of Mach 2-3. Even if a missile launch was detected by satellite or other sensor platform, and the precise location relayed instantaneously to a missile carrying aircraft, a missile speed of Mach 10, or approximately 3.4 km per second, would be required to intercept. That would still depend upon the aircraft, or other platform, being within range and being able to bring a weapon to bear on the target at the precise moment.

Consequently, while investment in, and competition between, Patriot derivatives and S 300V continue in the search to provide a more effective anti-ballistic

---

13. "The Economist", 1 Nov 97, p 56.

missile defence, and while other theatre ABM systems are developed, a US airborne laser programme remains funded towards shooting tests in 2002. Its objective is to destroy ballistic missiles while still in their boost phase over their own territory.

The airborne system, comprising a chemical oxygen-iodine laser (COIL) mounted on a Boeing 747 airframe, has a projected range in excess of 300 km over a 360 degree radius. If the aircraft flew at 40,000 feet, it could detect a missile above cloud and have several seconds in which to destroy it. Three aircraft are programmed for USAF operation by 2006 and a further four by 2008 . The YAL 1A programme cost is $5.6 billion[14].

Long range narrow laser beam accuracy is achieved by "adaptive optics". Nine infra red search and track (IRST) sensors detect the initial missile plume, with or without external cueing from space-based sensors. The target is illuminated by a low power ranging laser, sensors on the aircraft measure distortion and the high energy beam is adjusted 500-1,000 times per second, to ensure it remains focused on the target.

Considerable engineering and manufacturing development lies ahead of YAL 1A, but the advent of an airborne laser weapon totally dependent on the micro-processor for its functioning to replace "industrial age" missiles, could be the most tangible step forward by aerospace power from one century to another.

The technological difficulties may however, prove easier to overcome than the operational demands. Initially, at least, with a detection range of 300 km, the aircraft will need to deploy into theatre and possibly enter hostile or antagonistic air space. A state capable of launching surface to surface missiles is unlikely to lack modern SAM. If so, YAL will require air to air and surface to air protection. For the foreseeable future, either Treaty adherence or pre-emptive strike are likely to prove the best of unsatisfactory options against elusive SSM.

CRUISE MISSILE DEFENCE

Cruise missiles are usually defined as stand-off weapons capable of mid-flight and terminal guidance with a range in excess of 50 km. In 1997, some 130 types were reported to be deployed by 90 countries, although not all were designed to attack targets on land. Chinese Hai Ying missiles, derived from the Soviet anti-shipping Styx, have been uprated by several states, including north Korea, Iran and Iraq.

---

14. AWST, 18 Nov 96, pp 22-23.

Their reported ranges and accuracy were well short of the US Tomahawk or USAF air-launched cruise missiles. Concern was, however, expressed[15] about international access to commercially available INS and GPS components which would give shorter range missiles the accuracy to attack, like their ballistic counterparts, ports, airfields and military installations. Adequate target information is readily available from commercial satellite imagery and maps.

Cruise missiles require lower levels of technology than their ballistic counterparts, are cheaper and at least as difficult to detect and intercept. States which sought to use them, either against expeditionary forces or to reach rear base areas in Europe or the Pacific Rim, would be unconcerned about low interim levels of terminal accuracy or small warhead size, especially if they were delivering WMD. There is a disconcerting asymmetry in the need for precision in attack by western/UN/coalition forces and its irrelevance to many potential opponents, who may have little concern about inflicting indiscriminate casualties or collateral damage. Indeed, such a perception enhances their deterrent effect.

For the foreseeable future, defence against cruise missiles is likely to depend heavily and unsatisfactorily on short range air defence and air to air intercept. Here also, the destabilising potential for pre-emptive strike is obvious.

Overall, the technology revolution has reinforced the need for air and missile defence of expeditionary forces, but at the same time considerably complicated its provision.

OFFENSIVE OPERATIONS

The search by less well endowed states and organisations to counter western aerospace power by alternative strategies and equipment is hardly surprising. The addition of information, precision and to a lesser extent stealth, to air power's intrinsic qualities of reach, speed, and responsiveness has transformed its offensive capacity and versatility, especially in smaller scale conflicts.

PRECISION GUIDED MUNITIONS (PGM)

The most highly visible product of the revolution is the contemporary precision guided munition (PGM). Guided air-launched munitions have been used effec-

---

15. AWST, 14 Jul 97, p 44.

tively since the Vietnam war, but their proportional contribution has increased rapidly in the last decade. In the Gulf War, only 9% of the total weapon tonnage dropped by the USAF were PGMs, but they were credited with 75% of the damage inflicted on major Iraqi targets[16]. In September 1995, in Operation Deliberate Force against Bosnian Serb positions, 98% of the munitions dropped by the USAF were PGMs[17].

The PGM has allowed air attacks to be made discriminatory at a time when civilian casualties and collateral damage can be self defeating. In WWII, a "precision" dive bomber could expect to place 50% of its bombs within a 1,000 feet radius from its target. To have a 96% chance of getting two bombs on to a German power station measuring 400 x 500 feet, 648 bombs were required from 108 B-17s over the target[18]. In the Gulf War, a single aircraft with two PGMs could achieve the same effect. As explained in greater detail in Chapter 11, the PGM can transform "strategic" bombing from a bludgeon into a rapier.

More than any other single advance in technology, the PGM has provided air power with a highly cost-effective entrée at all levels of conflict. The cost effectiveness is all pervasive. It begins with the reduced number of weapons required to achieve a given objective, then proportionately reduces numbers of aircraft, aircrew, ground crew, training hours, maintenance items, logistic support and basing requirements across the whole air force infrastructure.

Concentration of force can be achieved without mass, attacks can be simultaneous on widely spread targets and numbers exposed to hostile action are reduced. The perception of certain destruction with each munition has a strong psychological impact on the recipients as Group Captain Lambert describes in Chapter 10.

The corollary should not, however, be ignored. If ten B-17s were lost en route to a target, there was still a good prospect of mission success. If a single PGM carrier is intercepted, mission failure is total and the associated replacement costs of aircraft, weapons and crew are going to be very high.

Older established weapon guidance systems: inertial navigation (INS), IR, optical and anti radiation have all been enhanced by the microprocessor, by improved sensors and by the inclusion of memory circuits in "fire and forget" stand-off weapon systems. Additional all weather guidance is now provided from GPS-derived signals and synthetic aperture SAR and millimetric radar. The prin-

---

16. Richard Hallion, "Precision Guided Munitions and the New Era of Warfare", Royal Australian Air Force, Air Power Studies Centre paper No.53, April 1997, p 13.
17. Ibid p 17.
18. Ibid p 3.

ciple of "strap on" laser guidance units to free fall bombs has been extended to the new sensors. In 1997, sixteen 2000 lb "dumb" bombs, fitted with Joint Direct Attack Munition (JDAM) GPS/INS/SAR guidance kits were dropped in tests by the USAF from 39,000 feet through cloud. All were reported to have hit their targets[19] but later low level high speed trials disclosed problems of weapon instability which would slow the programme down[20]. The Lockheed Martin kits were reported to cost $18,000 each, but if an additional terminal sensor, to eliminate errors in initial target location and the tail guidance sequence, were to be included to reduce target accuracy to less than ten feet, the unit cost would rise to $40,000[21].

USAF experiments are taking place with wind corrected munitions dispensers, programmed by INS/GPS to compensate for wind and ballistic errors on bombs released at high altitude. The units were priced at $8,900 each in 1997[22] and could also be applied to non-lethal weapons, as well as to combined effects and anti-armour submunitions.

Stand-off air-launched munitions have usually been limited in range by either the weapons' own target acquisition sensors or those of the launching aircraft. Exceptions, such as various anti shipping missiles, required mid course up dates from other aircraft which could themselves be vulnerable. Now however, inclusion of INS/GPS guidance confers weapon accuracy to within very few feet at night and in all weather, at distances constrained only by the powerplant or kinetic energy of the missile.

The Texas Instruments Joint Stand Off Weapon (JSOW), well advanced in flight tests in 1998, will be the first of its generation to be widely deployed. It has an unpowered range of 15-40 nautical miles depending on the height and speed of the launch aircraft, homing onto co-ordinates by combined INS/GPS. Target information may be pre-programmed or loaded after launch. It will deliver submunitions or a 500 lb unitary warhead. The US Department of Defense has ordered 21,000 weapons at an approximate cost of $100,000 each. If an imaging IR and data link seeker is added, to allow visual guidance, the cost will rise to between $300-400,000. JSOW can be carried by all USAF, USN and USMC combat aircraft.

JDAM and JSOW represent two complementary, or alternative, approaches to PGM attack by manned aircraft. JDAM delivery requires an aircraft to fly over or

---

19. JDW, 25 Jun 97, p 12.
20. JDW, 5 Nov 97, p 6
21. JDW, 21 Aug 96, p 10
22. AWST, 3 Feb 97, p 34.

near the target, relying on accurate bomb release positioning followed by guided, gravity-induced energy. The cost of the individual weapon, with similar destructive effect, is much less than that of the stand-off missile but on many occasions additional costs will be incurred from the need to suppress or evade local air defences. For longer term cost effectiveness, stand-off lethality may be preferable. However, consideration to adding a further terminal sensor to both JDAM and JSOW suggests that INS/GPS guidance induces "near" precision rather than the spectacular products of laser guidance as seen on BBC and CNN during Desert Storm. If so, INS/GPS guidance remains more suitable for submunition or non-lethal weapon delivery.

One further consequence of delegating effectiveness to the weapon, enhanced by "strap on" equipment, is to facilitate multi role operations by aircraft designed initially for air-to-air combat. F-15, F-16, Mig 29, SU 27, Eurofighter, F-14 and almost certainly F-22 could benefit, without detriment to their original role. Implications for multirole air crew training and ground crew maintenance hours are, however, more debatable. Either the same amount of training must be shared between different roles, with possible implications for readiness or effectiveness, or training expanded to accommodate additional roles with associated increase in manpower and maintenance requirements.

THE MANNED AIRCRAFT

Parallel development of JDAM and JSOW fuels discussion about how much sophistication should be "delegated" to the weapon and how much remain in the aircraft, but a further, more fundamental question is how far the manned aircraft plus any weapon can be replaced cost effectively either by ballistic or cruise missile, or by a UCAV.

The B-2 bomber, is the best example of the virtually self-contained, comprehensively equipped combat aircraft. It is variously costed from $800 million to $2 billion a copy[23]. Until its image was slightly tarnished in September 1997 by reports that its stealthy structure was susceptible to moisture, its costs, rather than its potential operational effectiveness, were the target for critics.

Although conceived during the Cold War, the B-2 is, like the F-22, a product of the revolution in military technology. Like the fighter, it is designed structurally to reduce infra red, electro-optical, acoustic and radar signatures to a minimum. It

---

23. AWST, 10 Oct 97, p 8.

has an unrefuelled intercontinental range of 6,900 miles with a bomb load of 32,000 lbs. Its fully automated mission planning system may be programmed before departure from home base, or at a deployed location or at any time in flight. It can deliver a wide variety of free fall and guided bombs, sub-munitions, missiles and nuclear weapons, including a GPS guided bomb with a deep penetration warhead for use against bunkers and underground installations. Details of the aircraft's communications equipment remain classified but it may be assumed that it can receive in flight updates on threats, target position and alternates without compromising its stealth character.

Global Engagement, Global Attack. The B-2.

The USAF has given several examples of the cost effectiveness of the B-2 when compared with alternative methods of reaching deep into hostile air space. Even without specific figures, the comparisons are compelling. With a non-stealthy aircraft, an effective package would be required to provide air-to-air, ECM and SEAD protection. With the possible exception of F-22, the supporting aircraft would require forward deployment into theatre entailing considerable basing and logistic support. Response time would be extended proportionally and the political acceptability of the entire response would be questionable. The US attack on Libya in 1986, ELDORADO CANYON, required over 100 combat and support aircraft. The task could have been carried out by six B-2s and six tankers.

However, despite US House of Representatives' funding in 1997 for a further nine aircraft and a "cut price" offer from Northrop Grumman of $9.3 billion for them, it is likely that the USAF B-2 fleet will remain at twenty one. The debate will continue: the considerable operational quality of B-2 against its costs, the political implications of losing even one in combat, its relevance to lower intensity operations and its subsonic speed.

Meanwhile, the venerable B-52, already in USAF service for 40 years, may well be flying for another 40. Its huge airframe is a ready receptacle for digital weapon and navigational updates, new ECM suites, GPS, SATCOM and FLIR to enhance its bombload capacity of 50,000 lbs over a maximum range of 10,000 miles. It will however, continue to need protection against air and surface threats.

Only the USAF can afford to operate B-2, B-52 and B-1B in addition to the F117, F-15E and F-16. Britain and other medium powers have exploited technology to update earlier generation attack aircraft by all weather navigation and targeting systems, self protection, netted communications and, in particular, the capacity to launch PGMs.

Typical systems include the British Thermal Imaging Airborne Laser Designator (TIALD), forward looking infra red (FLIR) to enhance low level navigation and target acquisition at night, and the US Low Altitude Navigation and Targeting Infra Red for Night (LANTIRN). While TIALD and LANTIRN occupy weapon stations and increase an aircraft's radar signature, they confer a 24 hour precision attack capability essential for offensive operations at all levels of intensity.

JOINT STRIKE FIGHTER

The most ambitious and important multirole combat aircraft programme at the turn of the century adapts a very different approach to offensive operations. The US Joint Strike Fighter (JSF) will depend heavily on external sources to deliver timely and effective ordnance. It is intended to produce a family of stealthy aircraft for the USAF, USN, USMC, British Royal Navy and, possibly, the Royal Air Force. A four year demonstrator programme was begun in 1996 with two competitors: Boeing/Macdonnell Douglas and Lockheed Martin joined by British Aerospace.

The USAF gives priority to air-to-ground operations, while the USN specifies a strike fighter which can survive before air control has been won. Consequently, three variants were specified: conventional take off and landing (CTOL), short take off and vertical landing (STOVL) and aircraft carrier capable (CV). Potential orders could be as high as 3,000 and the US target prices for each type, in 1997, were stated to be $28 million, $30-35 million and $38 million respectively, in line with declared objectives of affordability, lethality, survivability and supportability[24]. Despite innovative production techniques and tight programme control these figures, like most of their predecessors in other projects may be revised upwards. The overall production programme could be worth more than $200 billion to the manufacturers.

Inevitably, the inclusion of a vertical lift engine increases weight, and both competitors have offered performance figures in which manoeuvrability has been traded for internal fuel load and extended combat radius up to 850 nm. Both aircraft will carry two AIM 120C AMRAAMs and two GBU 30 1,000 lb JDAM munitions internally, with four or more external weapon positions, which would dramatically reduce stealth characteristics.

JSF will carry long range precision radar, electronic counter measures and advanced processing capacity. Its costs will be contained, however, by reducing integral avionics and weapon systems. It will depend on external sources for target and threat information[25]. In contrast to the F-22 or the B-2, it is very much the product of concepts of operations calling for interconnected systems, or "system of systems". Some of those systems will be examined below but connectivity dependence does raise complex questions about exports, foreign access to sensitive US information sources, international military co-operation and dependence by purchasers on systems remaining under US control and driven by US political and military priorities.

Indeed, even within a totally homogeneous US operational environment, the responsiveness in crisis of JSF will be heavily influenced by the readiness and flexibility of the associated systems. When total systems costs are factored into crisis response, the comparative cost effectiveness of B-2, and especially of F-22, is to say the least, thought provoking. Moreover, in 1997, a Congressional Budget Office analysis noted that the total cost of 438 F-22s, 1,000 F/A 18 E-F, and

---

24. USAF Presentation, Shepherd Air Power Conference London, 27 Feb 97.
25. Ibid.

3,000 JSF would amount to $350 billion, stimulating concurrent budgetary pressure at least until 2010[26]. The potential US multirole force mix is likely to stimulate debate for some time before the first JSF is due to enter Service in 2007.

UCAV POTENTIAL

If a large amount of the information necessary for JSF to operate effectively is to be provided from outside the aircraft and the pilot's responses are increasingly complemented by automation, how far can JSF itself be replaced by a UCAV? All the advantages noted above for a fighter UCAV apply equally to a multirole UCAV. Satellite and datalink relay will allow ground control far away from a theatre of operations, reducing manpower deployment for outposts, protection and logistic support. Removal of aircrew reduces casualty risk and political sensitivity. Combat "crews" would remain in sanctuary and most combat training could be carried out in a simulator. Current US development of miniaturised munitions will further benefit a smaller UCAV structure.

It is highly probable that "black" UCAV programmes already exist in the US. McDonnel Douglas built a 28% sized JSF prototype, while Lockheed Martin has been examining UCAV feasibility since 1993. The Royal Air Force has included a UCAV option in its preliminary studies of a "Future Offensive Air System" to replace Tornado GR4 in RAF Service

Offensive use of UCAVs, however, may require automated self protection systems to compensate for lack of on board situational awareness. If a UCAV is to be updated in flight to enhance mission flexibility, omni directional receiving antennae are required, which will take up further precious space and increase vulnerability to jamming. Moreover, if the UCAV is to operate within a "system of systems", with JSF, the cost and political implications of the whole enter the equation.

UCAVs are, nevertheless, strong and possibly early candidates for the defence suppression role. They can be pre-programmed against known installations and cued to respond to unprogrammed threats within their radius. Low observable UCAVs could loiter for many hours outside detection range carrying GPS-guided munitions and make a formidable contribution to the initial establishment of air supremacy for exploitation by manned aircraft.

---

26. Martin Marietta representatives to the author in 1977.

For the foreseeable future, however, providing a UCAV with situational aware-ness either autonomously or from a secure control location outside a theatre is likely to be a major task. The comprehensive replacement of manned combat aircraft by UCAV remains many design, development and experimental years away.

THE MISSILE OPTION

Competition for several offensive tasks may also arise from surface or subsurface launched cruise (CM) or ballistic missiles (BM).

The US and friends only possess ballistic missiles with nuclear warheads, although US commercial studies of ballistic conventional submunition delivery have existed for at least 20 years. As long as concerns about collateral damage and indiscriminate casualties remain, deep attack by BM, even with conventional warheads are likely to be politically unattractive. Long range targets may emerge, at several levels of intensity, which are entirely military and remote from the civil-ian population. Where such targets are clearly identified and static, attack by BM without risk of friendly casualties may be preferable. At present, however, payload limitations and costs of single shot weapons do not encourage heavy investment in BM precision guidance or sub-munitions.

In practice, therefore, the General Dynamics BGM 109 Tomahawk Land Attack Missile (TLAM) is the sole western competitor to air delivered PGMs. Its maximum range with a 700lb payload is in the region of 1100 miles[27]. Two hundred and eighty eight were fired in the Gulf War and they have been employed against targets in Iraq on several occasions since. TLAM, like all autonomous guided missiles, is a direct product of the introduction of the micro-processor.

The weapon depends for its guidance on the conversion of photographic images to digital form for comparison with its pre-programmed route features. No mid course alterations are yet possible. The weapon requires a distinguishing feature some 4-5 miles away from the target itself to provide final attack position update. TLAM is usually costed at approximately $1 million a unit.

TLAM is widely deployed on USN ships and submarines and is to be supplied to the Royal Navy. It is difficult to detect and intercept and, with GPS/INS updates to increase terminal accuracy, is a flexible and formidable weapon.

---

27. JDW, 6 Mar 96, p 46.

At present, however, it lacks penetration against hardened or horizontal surfaces, while special facilities to receive alternative imagery are required before the missile can be reprogrammed. It is best suited to attack static targets with a highly visible profile. At approximately $1 million a weapon, TLAM is not a cheap option. If the delivery platform is a naval vessel, the total costs of the system may be partly subsumed in other roles, but should be included in cost comparisons and investment appraisals.

NON LETHAL WEAPONS

Both air and sea launched CM may have a stronger long term future in a complementary offensive role. For example, Tomahawk missiles scattered wire filaments over Iraqi electrical power installations in the Gulf War to induce short circuits and cut power to military command posts at the very start of the air campaign.

It is possible that the USAF's AGM 86C air-launched cruise missile (ALCM) will carry a non-nuclear electro-magnetic pulse (EMP) generator, powerful enough to produce a burst of microwave energy strong enough to disable unprotected electronic components on radars, guidance systems, communications, computers and vehicles. Such a weapon would either disarm an opponent, or make him very vulnerable to follow up attack with less sophisticated weapons.

Anti-traction super lubricants could be dispersed over air bases or road surfaces; polymer adhesives could immobilise individuals and equipment and liquid metal embrittlements could weaken bridges, ships, vehicles or aircraft. CS gases and other incapacitating aerosols could also be delivered by air.

Delivery of such non-lethal substances by cruise missile would relieve a manned aircraft from the risk of a lethal response from the target, thereby reducing the reluctance of many air forces to indulge in such an asymmetric exchange. Temporary disablement or neutralisation of equipment has considerable attraction in any confrontation where coercion is sought with minimum collateral or permanent damage. Alternatively, temporary neutralisation can be exploited by conventional forces.

Overall, Western air forces are approaching the use of offensive alternatives to the manned aircraft with justifiable caution. In the foreseeable future, it is difficult to avoid the conclusion that the greatest and most versatile cost-effectiveness lies with the manned aircraft, stand-off PGM combination. Trends towards operational dependence on multiple external systems should be accompanied by copper-bottomed guarantees of their availability, responsiveness, invulnerability and accessibility to allies and coalition partners.

THE ATTACK HELICOPTER

At the end of the century, there can be no doubt about the contribution of the attack helicopter to offensive air operations. In some countries, its employment has been constrained by the tendency of armies to see it simply as an extension of battlefield fire power and by inter-service turf wars over command and control. With reduction in the occurrence of large scale traditional ground force confrontations and the advent of helicopters such as the McDonnell Douglas Apache, its potential as a complement to fixed wing aircraft is considerable.

The AH 64D Apache is equipped with Longbow fire control radar, integrated GPS, a target acquisition and designation sight, pilot low level night vision sensor, TV and FLIR sensors, terrain following/avoidance and Doppler navigation radar and can carry any combination of AIM 92 Stinger AAM, Sidewinders and Maverick PGM, in addition to Hellfire anti-tank missiles. Within 30 seconds, the masthead Longbow radar can detect, classify, prioritise and display up to 256 tracked, wheeled, air defence, helicopter or aircraft targets. Apache has a combat radius of 253 miles with internal fuel, endurance of slightly more than three hours and a maximum speed of 227 mph (261 km/h).

This is far more than extended artillery, as its use to destroy Iraqi radars in the opening hours of Desert Storm illustrated. It is capable of defence suppression, deep strike and armed reconnaissance as well as close air support.

Apache cannot be refuelled in flight and therefore must be transported to participate in expeditionary force operations. One variant has foldable rotor blades but, even then, and with the mast dismantled, only one helicopter can be airlifted at a time. Nonetheless, transported in numbers by sea or deployed aboard a carrier, it will be a formidable, if slower responding, contributor to joint or combined operations.

For its full potential to be exploited, it needs enlightened ownership and imaginative concepts of operation.

The example of its employment in The Netherlands is well worth emulation. Its Apaches are operated by the RNLAF but normally deploy under army command and control. They also train for operations not involving ground forces. Priorities in crisis or conflict would be determined in a Joint-Service context, thereby guaranteeing the helicopter's availability to the army except when a higher national offensive priority elsewhere was defined. Hopefully, such a deployment pattern will enhance the fixed-rotary wing interface in joint offensive air operations.

RECONNAISSANCE

Since the end of the Cold War, demands for reconnaissance have increased for two reasons.

First, a need to focus primarily on one country, one theatre of operations and one dominant conflict scenario, has been replaced by a requirement to monitor several regions and activities ranging from clandestine weapon development to the non-compliance of peace-keeping agreements by small units. In addition, all the traditional reconnaissance roles may be required at any level of future conflict.

Second, when force is being used with precision in small quantities, accurate information is essential. Without it, precision is impossible. Up to date knowledge about an opponent's location, direction, strengths and weaknesses is required to exploit aerospace power's attributes of speed, reach, responsiveness and concentration of force, with or without precision.

Fortunately, the technology revolution has considerably enhanced all aspects of reconnaissance, from acquisition of information, through fusion and discrimination to dissemination. They are the essential components of the "system of systems". Its components are manned aircraft, UAV and satellites, with many future investment priorities and relationships still to be decided.

THE AIRCRAFT

SR-71 Blackbird and the U2 variants are veterans of the Cold War. Blackbird has been progressively updated since it entered USAF service in 1966. It carries SAR, infra red and optical sensors, radio and radar signal receivers, signal direction locators and ground and satellite data links. In 1997, it was completing trials of a new SAR real time data link and transmission of telescopic film imagery. The aircraft's sensors can give a snapshot of forces deployed in the Gulf in one mission at less than a day's notice, from heights in excess of 85,000 feet at speeds over Mach 3.

SR-71 was retired from USAF service in 1990 because of funding pressures and anticipation of replacement by satellites and UAVs. As explained in Chapter 7, satellite capacity is rapidly expanding, but the US UAV programme proceeded more slowly than expected. Consequently, two SR-71s were reactivated in 1995 and limited funding allocated in 1997.

U2 is scheduled to remain in service until 2020. From heights over 70,000 feet, it uses long range SAR incorporating both moving and fixed target indicators to collect imagery at night and in all weathers. It is, however, more vulnerable to high altitude air defences, it has limited digital processing and limited band width datalink requiring a forward-deployed ground station and, despite its apparent greater favour than the SR-71 with the USAF, it could become an earlier candidate for replacement by UAV.

The new technologies are fully exploited in a further handful of extremely complex and expensive specialist reconnaissance aircraft: typified by EC-135 Rivet Joint, RC-135S Cobra Ball, and EC-8 JSTARS.

Rivet Joint collects and relays data from electro-magnetic emissions from surveillance radars, missile guidance systems and many communication frequencies. They are identified, located to within less than a mile, analysed partly by computer and partly by operator and despatched via satellite and several other systems to many agencies and, when relevant, directly to Patriot batteries or to individual aircraft to warn of impending attack. While Rivet Joint cannot locate targets accurately enough for PGM attack, it can indicate a narrow area, in which other systems can search.

EC-135's wide range of sensors make it a difficult aircraft to take by surprise and its considerable value, at all levels of intensity since 1989, has induced detachments of up to 200 days a year for the 16 aircraft fleet.

The three USAF RC-135S Cobra Ball aircraft have a specific task of detecting missile launches, primarily by electro optical systems and electronic emission sensors. US funding in 1997 was directed towards "fusing" Cobra Ball information with that derived from Defense Support Programme satellites and from Rivet Joint to provide pre launch, launch location and trajectory data in real time to ground and airborne defences. Details are likely to remain classified but such "cueing" will be indispensable for systems such as the YAL airborne laser.

The Joint Surveillance Target Attack Radar System (JSTARS) was conceived in the 1970s to see and track Warsaw Pact ground forces and follow on echelons at night and in all weather. Two development aircraft provided unprecedented battlefield information to the Coalition commanders in the Gulf War. JSTARS can detect, locate, track and automatically classify moving surface targets up to 250 kms distant at speeds from 5 to 150 mph depending on the radar mode. It can either survey up to a million square millimeters in one pass or revisit a designated area for closer inspection at the same time, showing different information to different operators. The combination of SAR and moving target indicator (MTI) plus memory store allows sequential imagery to discriminate, for example, between temporarily stationary and disabled vehicles.

JSTARS data is almost entirely processed by computer. An early systems specification envisaged 220,000 lines of software code. By 1996, they had grown to 750,000. Four data processors can each perform over 600 million operations per second[28]. Fourteen data bases enhance raw radar information, covering cartography, topography/visibility, order of battle and weapons. Secure, encrypted line of sight, real time surveillance and control data link connects JSTARS to a Ground Support Module (GSM) and from there to units world wide. Other communications link it to AWACS and other aircraft.

Over Bosnia, although it did not perform in that more difficult environment as well as in the Gulf, it monitored the movement and location of aid convoys and potentially threatening movements by the warring factions. In future, its arrival in theatre could contribute to crisis control by monitoring the scale and direction of different activities over a wide area.

JSTARS can reveal a battlespace to an unprecedented degree, conferring considerable information dominance and facilitating accurate and timely disposition of friendly air and surface forces. And yet, in 1997, the US Quadrennial Review cut procurement by six aircraft, offering the residue to NATO[29]. JSTARS costs approximately $180 million dollars and requires a crew of 21 for normal missions and up to 34 for endurance beyond 20 hours. Unlike AWACS or Rivet Joint, it cannot detect threats to itself and, therefore, needs sanitised air space or protection. Its detection slant range is approximately the same as the combat radius of the S-300 SAM and its radiating presence cannot be concealed. Its dependence on a line of sight GSM creates a vulnerable ground position in theatre which must itself be secured against hostile action. Finally, even though it can draw upon its area visibility data base to forecast target reappearance, its single sensor effectiveness was inevitably degraded by Balkan topography.

Despite its comprehensive exploitation of many of the products of the technology revolution, JSTARS may prove to be operationally constrained more than any of its contemporary sophisticates, because of its Cold War lineage by primary dedication to large scale land encounter manoeuvre and consequent reduction in cost effectiveness and flexibility across a wide spectrum of conflict over less suitable terrain.

Despite the Strategic Defence Review, Britain is likely to proceed with its Airborne Stand-Off Radar (ASTOR) requirement which is similar to JSTARs in concept, but mounted in a civilian airframe such as Gulfstream IV. Although conceived at the end of the Cold War, ASTOR is likely to have widespread utility.

---

28. Northrop Grumman Briefing Notes, Los Angeles April 1996, p 3
29. JDW "Contracts", July 1997, p 2.

THE UAVS

The potential of the UAV to replace manned reconnaissance aircraft and complement satellite activity is illustrated by two US vehicles: the General Atomics Predator and the Teledyne Ryan Global Hawk, costing $3.2 million and $10 million respectively. Reconnaissance UAVs, such as the Israeli Pioneer family and the US Pointer, have been operational for many years, but Predator and Global Hawk have considerably greater endurance: 24 hours and 42 hours respectively, and particularly benefit from increased sensor and communication capacity with reduced volume and costs.

Global Hawk.

Predator carries SAR, IR sensors and optical lens with SATCOM links and communication channels to other aircraft. It does not require a line of sight command post on the ground in theatre. With a ceiling of 24,000 feet, it is not immune to air defences but it has a lower political profile than a manned aircraft. Its particular value is to supplement the more distant sensors of Rivet Joint or JSTARS by monitoring electro-magnetic emissions at very low level and searching areas of radar shadow.

Predator did disclose one problem of UAV operations: volume constraints on payload. An anti-icing system competed for space with a SIGINT fit on the wing leading edge, thereby reducing payloads, while other reports suggested that system compression was inducing mutual magnetic interference[30]. Nonetheless, by 1997 a programme of 44 Predators had been funded.

Global Hawk, which began flight tests in 1998, is in a very different category. It is almost the same size as the RAF Harrier. It will cruise at 65,000 feet carrying a 2,000 lb pay load which includes SAR, MTI, electro optical and IR sensors which can be employed simultaneously. It can survey 40,000 square miles and focus on 1,900 spot targets in 24 hours by day or night and in all weathers, with a resolution from 100 km of 30 cm. Multiple SATCOM and line of sight wideband data links can transmit 50 megabytes per second, allowing real time relay of video imagery. Its ground mission control unit can be located anywhere in the world, and is costed at $20-25 million. Costs of the overall system have been contained by extensive use of commercially available components.

Unlike Dark Star, a third UAV under development, Global Hawk is not stealthy, relying instead on automatic pre-programmed evasion of known threats and on a variety of on board defensive systems. The inclusion of stealth features would have increased the unit cost anywhere between $40 million and $150 million. It will also be evaluated as a communications platform certainly for radio relay and possibly replacing airborne command and control aircraft. At 60,000 feet, it would have a surface communication radius of 150-200 miles, providing links with mobile forces or any other group using hand held receivers and transmitters. The logistic and manpower savings from such an innovation would be dramatic. In Bosnia, line of sight surface communications required several outposts on hill or mountain tops, each with up to 100 troops, and each relying on regular logistic support.

Meanwhile, several air forces, including the USAF, have opted to include reconnaissance in multirole configurations by carrying pods with electro-optical sensors. The RAF Tornado GR1A will be equipped with a Lockheed Martin system which will provide a dual waveband, electro optic day/night stand off simultaneous visual and thermal sensor up to a range of 45 km with real time downlinks and on board recording. Retention of the venerable RAF Canberra PR9 reconnaissance aircraft is likely to be a short term anomaly for the RAF.

At present, all reconnaissance aircraft and UAV systems have to deploy into or near a theatre of operations. Global Hawk will extend range, but in exchange for

---

30. AWST, 7 Apr 97, p 39.

reduced endurance on station. When accurate information is a prerequisite for precise application of combat air power and reconnaissance platforms require secure airspace, there could well be a 'chicken and egg' problem in expeditionary force priorities. The increasing need for global awareness plus the forward basing, manpower and logistic requirements of the specialist aircraft suggest that a steady progress towards their replacement by UAV and satellite is inevitable.

Exactly when the aircraft and even UAVs will actually be replaced by satellites remains conjectural, for reasons explained in Chapter 7. It is possible that a reduced long range UAV force will be retained indefinitely. The increasing inter-dependence of complex and expensive sensors, communications and weapons is, however, likely to widen the technological and operational divide between the US and all other air forces, with widespread implications for coalition warfare (see Chapter 3) and for national procurement programmes. Considerable co-opera-tive effort in Europe will be required to prevent the gap widening even further.

In a period of dwindling defence funding, the balance of investment between manned, uninhabited and space vehicles will require resolution. Difficult prob-lems of coalition interoperability lie ahead, with multi-billion dollar international aerospace industrial competition lurking below them.

AIR MOBILITY

Technological innovation has intruded less dramatically on air transport opera-tions. Automated systems have reduced aircrew numbers, as in C-17, C-130J and the proposed European Future Large Aircraft (FLA).

The greatest combined impact can be seen in the avionics, flight control system, engine performance and low speed wing aerodynamics of the C-17, but at a reported unit cost of $262 million[31]. The aircraft can carry 157,000 lbs over 2,700 miles and land on airstrips of 1,000 yards.

The accuracy of air drops has been enhanced by GPS in the cockpit and guid-ance systems on the air-dropped loads themselves, facilitating resupply at night and in all weather at various levels of intensity.

One traditional constraint on air transport operations has been increased by the proliferation of mobile and hand-held SAM. Transport aircraft have always needed a benign air environment to avoid disastrous losses. One Italian G-222 was shot down over Bosnia while on a humanitarian mission and many other UN

---

31. AWST, 17 Feb 97, p 37.

transports were threatened or fired upon. Fortunately, technology has also provided some protection, with automated warning and counter measures activation against both IR and radar homing weapons. There is, however, no antidote, other than armour, to heavy calibre anti aircraft guns.

The vulnerability of transport aircraft, however, reinforces the need for air control and defence suppression, even in the lowest intensity conflicts.

MARITIME OPERATIONS

With the demise of the Soviet blue water navy and the end of the potential requirement to mount convoys across the Atlantic, maritime air operations have increasingly focused on coastal waters and overland power projection from the littoral. There is however a residual anti-submarine task arising from the continued operational deployments of SSBNs and from the expansion of diesel boat fleets in several regions.

The major contemporary maritime patrol aircraft (MPA) update, of the RAF Nimrod, to MR4 standard largely comprises automatic sensor fusing and processing within overall computerised and integrated communications, defensive aids, engine control, electronic support, navigation, weapons and flight management. The sensors and weapons themselves are largely unchanged, but their individual potential effectiveness has been considerably enhanced. Several of the new components for Nimrod 2000 have also been adapted from commercial use.

The US Navy vies with the USAF at the forefront of aerospace technology evaluation and application, but in similar areas which overlap. For example, electronic counter measures (ECM) roles have been combined, with the USN EA 6B taking over the functions of the USAF EF111 Raven. JSF, JSOW, independent development of the SLAM ER stand off air-to-surface weapon and separate naval programmes of air and area ballistic missile defences demonstrate that growing role convergence and the projection of maritime air power over land, rather than technology innovation, are driving US naval aviation procurement.

Naval air power, projected by the aircraft carrier, has been uniquely enhanced by the PGM. Even the largest USN ship will only carry about 60 attack or multi-role aircraft. Those numbers can only be reinforced by deploying another carrier. Consequently the firepower enhancement afforded by PGM has been gratefully, if tardily, welcomed by the US Navy.

Provided it can be positioned swiftly, the US carrier group is a formidable military instrument. As a carrier moves through international waters, it is not dependent for diplomatic clearance for overflights, nor on land bases in theatre for operations. It may deploy with nuclear weapons which could be politically unacceptable on forward air bases. Mobile and comparatively small, it is a very difficult target for conventionally armed surface-to-surface ballistic missiles, even assuming an opponent has access to real time intelligence and targeting integration. Inside its short range air defence escort screen and protected at distance by F-14s armed with BVR AMRAAM, it is also a difficult target for opposing aircraft, even armed with modern stand off anti-shipping missiles. Delivering PGMs, its comparatively small numbers of attack aircraft can threaten a wide variety of targets on land. In small scale scenarios, when an opponent only has a small air force or embryonic air defences, its political and military value is considerable.

If a carrier is on station in or near a crisis area – and hopefully, intelligence has identified it in time and political decisions have been taken to allow deployment, it can be a formidable deterrent. If the crisis area and critical target arrays are within reach of the relatively short legged carrier borne aircraft and if the carrier is not inhibited by shore based missile carrying aircraft, mines, narrow seas, or by weather, it can be a force for the first hours, preparing an environment for exploitation by land based air and ground forces.

A nuclear powered carrier can, in theory, sustain a 30 knot speed for thirteen years without refuelling but, unless her escorts have a similar endurance, the operational advantages of nuclear power are constrained. The need to replenish with aviation fuel and weapons stocks, however, can act as a brake on high tempo operations. A conventional carrier will usually replenish with fuel every four days and with fresh food every eight. A realistic wartime cruise endurance would be approximately 100 days.

The large carrier battle group has therefore become a very versatile political instrument among the uncertainties of the post-Cold War world. Its arrival in crisis or regional conflict is a palpable sign of US interest. In March 1996, Chinese missile tests and military exercises in the seas near Taiwan prompted the despatch to the region of the USS Independence and USS Nimitz. The reassurance of such carriers put Chinese threats against Taiwan into perspective, illustrating the realities of military power in the region and demonstrating continued US support for the government in Taipeh.

In the context of such a confrontation, the cost effectiveness of the large carrier may be strongly argued, especially if China should develop ballistic missiles with the accuracy to neutralise air bases and other military installations in Taiwan. There are, however, several other factors to be included in the balance sheet of carrier cost effectiveness.

Combat radius of carrier-borne aircraft is constrained by weight and size. In the Gulf War, aircraft attacking Iraqi targets from carriers in the Red Sea were dependent on shore-based tankers for inflight refuelling. Many countries have important military and industrial installation within 200 miles of coastline but several of the more problematical, in the Middle East and Asia, are located well beyond the unrefuelled reach of current and proposed carrier borne strike/attack aircraft. If tankers, or other support aircraft, have to be deployed into theatre to enable carrier operations to take place, the attribute of unimpeded political and operational independence is obviously devalued. This factor, relevant to JSF procurement for carrier deployment, awaits debate.

Even the largest carriers are susceptible to wind and sea states for both launching and aircraft recovery. Co-ordination of attacks between carriers and with land based aircraft can be dislocated far more than operations from air bases on land, with consequent impact on tanking provision, concentration of force and route deconfliction.

While operating in blue water, escorted carriers are difficult to locate and attack by air but they must approach within range of land based aircraft to attack targets on shore. As in the Gulf, they risk entering coastal minefields. If F-14s have to enter potentially hostile airspace to establish a defensive perimeter for the carrier, the advantages of beyond visual range engagement may be eroded by SAM below them. Moreover, as implied above, the ability of a carrier group to remain in station "over the horizon" is limited by its need to refuel and restock. For example, British carrier operations over Bosnia in 1995 were dependent on logistic support, as well as on reconnaissance, inflight refuelling and co-ordination, from bases in Italy.

In March 1997, the US Congressional Budget Office estimated that the savings from cancellation of carrier CVN 77 would be $6.4 billion[32]. Total costs of a US carrier and its air wing were estimated to be approximately $9 billion, with annual operating costs for the battle group of about $800 million per year. Battle groups usually comprise one or two cruisers with Aegis air defence systems, three or four air defence destroyers or frigates and one or two logistic support vessels. It may also be assumed that a carrier group will have unspecified submarine escort.

The same Budget Office report related a USN assertion that only one quarter, or less, of a carrier fleet could be deployed overseas in peacetime because of time required for repair and refit, stateside duty time and transit time outbound and

---

32. Congressional Budget office, "Reducing the Deficit –Spending and Revenue Options", Washington DC, March 1997.

inbound. A fleet of twelve carriers was considered insufficient to discharge the US policy requirement for carrier presence in the western Pacific, the Indian Ocean/Gulf and the Mediterranean, without planned gaps. If that argument is translated into operational, available cost effectiveness, the real cost of each USN carrier and its aircraft rises from $9 billion to $36 billion.

Such outlays are beyond the reach of all but the USA. There are also obvious examples of wasteful role competition and equipment duplication which can be avoided by smaller powers. The examples in 1997 and 1998 of Royal Air Force Harriers deployed on Royal Navy through-deck cruisers on the other hand, should encourage much greater utility of the combined Harrier force. The embarked aircraft will continue to depend on land based in-flight refuelling and longer range AEW, but the off-shore advantages of the smaller ship can be exploited.

Sooner or later, the viability of a separate small fixed wing naval air arm with its expensive support tail, will be questioned. Only by total integration of the Harrier force can its full potential be realised. With the advent of JSF, such considerations will become paramount.

CONCLUSION

The attitude of the United States Navy, in refocusing towards operations over land, demonstrates the symbiotic relationship between the technology revolution and the post-Cold War environment.

Had the Cold War not ended and the focus on massive land confrontation in Central Europe not changed, there would have been less intense international competition to find markets for sophisticated aerospace equipment. Had US forces not been reduced, and many overseas bases abandoned, there would have been less requirement for systems which could react globally from North America. Increasing international economic interdependence prompts interest among several states in containing destabilising crises and conflicts far from their own frontiers. Economic growth and national consciousness, quite apart from regional tension, have encouraged other states to invest, albeit in small numbers, in sophisticated weapons and systems.

The technology revolution has therefore come to have an ambivalent impact on western aerospace power. In the wrong hands, even a small number of opposing aircraft equipped with modern weapons can threaten unwelcome casualties on an expeditionary force. New generations of mobile SAM threaten all air operations with a materially insignificant, but politically unacceptable, loss rate.

Unease or straightforward hostility to US hegemony has stimulated interest in competitive Russian built aircraft, air-launched missiles and SAM. International market competition will ensure that expeditionary forces will encounter the most sophisticated weapons and systems at any level of conflict. But the winning and sustaining of control of the air and suppressing enemy air defences will remain prerequisites, at any level of intensity, for all military operations, whenever a potential opponent has some air assets.

Consequently, technological superiority is not a desirable luxury for the Atlantic Community and friends. In virtually any foreseeable circumstances it will be needed to offset numerical inferiority, distance, accessibility or vulnerability to indiscriminate weapons – or any combination of these.

The cumulative impact of the revolution is to enable aerospace power, at the threshold of the 20th Century, to determine the dimensions of a battlespace and to become a politically attractive, highly cost effective instrument in many different environments.

CHAPTER 6

AIR POWER IN THE INFORMATION AGE
Squadron Leader P C Emmett

"All the business of war, and indeed all the business of life, is to endeavour to find out what you don't know from what you do; that's what I called guessing what was at the other side of the hill".

the Duke of Wellington[1] 1769-1852

INTRODUCTION

A N ERA OF CHANGE is one of both opportunity and danger. In planning for future conflict it is essential to look beyond the superficialities of change and understand its mainsprings, not only to guide design adaptation in the existing means of air power, but also to be ready, if necessary, to engage in new forms of warfare in which air power may require a new economy of means or take on new roles. Air power has often had to undergo major and rapid adaptation to the changes wrought by technological innovation. It owes its very existence as a field of human endeavour to the early pioneers of flight and to the industrial innovations by which powered flight was first made possible. The application of air power through the 20th Century has seen several major phases of evolution (Figure 6.1), in which the underpinning technologies have, at times, given a decisive advantage to those air forces that were able to exploit them in moments of danger. A classic example of this is radar, which was introduced by the RAF just in time for operational exploitation during the Battle of Britain. Employed within a highly efficient raid-reporting system, radar enabled Britain's scarce air defence assets to be fielded with maximum economy of force against a numerically superior enemy. The RAF's success in 1940 sparked an immediate 'radio war'[2] – largely unforeseen in 1939 – involving a protracted series of electronically-based innovations, leading to a new form of conflict that is known today as Electronic Warfare (EW). Radar and EW had a most profound effect on both aircraft design and air power doctrine, changing, indeed, the way we conduct air warfare.

What has been called the Information Age has seen an explosive growth in software-intensive electronic networks of all descriptions. In recent years, the defence of electronic networks has become as pressing a concern as the defence of territory. For the proponents and practitioners of air power, this is not an issue

---

1. Wellington, A W (Ist Duke of), Cited in *Croker papers*, vol 3, 1885, 276.
2. Cockburn, Sir Robert, 'The Radio War', *IEE Proceedings-A* on Historical Radar, 423.

TECHNOLOGY PHASE	FLIGHT CAPABILITIES	OPERATIONAL CAPABILITIES
EARLY MECHANICAL	Manual flight control Synchronised machine gun High-performance engines	Aerial reconnaissance Sporadic ground attack Aerial dog-fights
DEVELOPED MECHANICAL (hydraulics, electromechanics, jet propulsion)	Power-assisted control surfaces (leading to large aircraft) Navigation aids Supersonic speeds	Manoeuvre and agility Longer range, better targeting Aerial saturation bombardment
ELECTRONIC	Avionics Sensory capabilities Air/Ground Communications	Radar early warning Electronic Warfare Improved Command & Control
EARLY SOFTWARE	Autonomous functions Fly-by-wire (single, piloted aircraft) IT in combat planning	Precision strike Battlespace awareness Highly co-ordinated air plans
DEVELOPED SOFTWARE (prospective capabilities)	Autonomous flight Fly-by-swarm (massed, small unpiloted aircraft)	Co-operative engagement Adaptive Weapon Intelligence Software Warfare

Figure 6.1

which can be safely set aside for others to resolve. Its threads are diverse and inter-twine more closely with military affairs than may at first be imagined. The command of modern air power depends on networked information systems every bit as much as do the spheres of banking and finance. Many civilian and military communications bearers are held in common and utilise the same commercial IT products. Moreover, combat systems are software-intensive and have their own vulnerabilities. Since attacks upon electronic networks have already become fair game in warfare, any vulnerabilities in the civil information infrastructure could place significant constraints upon the application of air power unless the threats are forestalled in advance of conflict. This new means of strategic coercion recog-nises no frontiers and cannot be repulsed by physical force alone. It can be developed by any rogue state or even sub-state actions at a low cost-of-entry and its offensive use is currently far better understood than are the possible defences against it. Like the terrorist the information warrior tends to strike randomly and there are no ready means for identifying the culprit.

DAWN OF THE INFORMATION AGE

The present era is most frequently described as the Information Age.[3] In a period suffused with technological novelty this concept sits oddly, because information in itself is not a technology and has long been valued in all fields of human endeavour. The above quotation demonstrates that its military worth was well appreciated by the Duke of Wellington, for example, and information was equally prized by Sun Tzu, who described it as 'foreknowledge'.[4] Recognition throughout history of the importance of information indicates that the term Information Age is a misnomer. The pervasive use of computer technology, the most visible product of which is an unprecedented volume of information, accounts for the present popularity of Information Age concepts. This interpretation matters because unless the roots of change are formally recognised, they cannot be nurtured to advantage. What has underpinned the transformation of both society and military affairs in the late 20th Century has not been information *per se*, but the computer in all its manifestations. This involves embedded computing in industrial plant and in the combat domain as much as it does the now familiar desk top technologies. It is not only information that emerges from computers but diverse control functions and what is hidden can be as important as what is seen.

It may or may not be an age of information, but it is most certainly an age of bandwagons. In a technology domain which is complex and ever changing, the fear of ignorance and of being left behind drives the spread of shallow messages that are both seductive and anxiety-generating: *information is power; information is control; information is progress.* Since it is easier to understand what flows out of computers than to rise to the more daunting challenge of actually looking inside them, uncritical embrace of these ideas, across all levels of the social strata, has allowed them to become the most popular but least qualified icons of Western belief. Faced with the perils of real investigation, the information vogue provides a ready-made substitute.

The spread of Information Age ideas throughout the 1980s finally caught up with the hitherto immune military in the post-Gulf euphoria of 1991. The Gulf War, military commentators pronounced, was the first 'Information War'.[5] With the barriers suddenly down the information bandwagon once again rolled. The mood of the time was aptly captured in the words of one senior commentator

3. Lyon, D, *The Silicon Society*, Lion Publishing plc, Tring, UK 1986, 97.
4. Sun Tzu, *The Art of War*, Hodder and Stoughton, London, 1981, 90.
5. Camden, A D, *The First Information War*, AFCEA International Press, Fairfax, USA.

who called for: 'A battlefield filled with information'.[6] Following so soon after the 'peace-dividend' and military downturn, this was good fortune indeed for the commercial providers of information systems,[7] who invested heavily in persuading the military to buy information systems which could deliver information faster and send it farther.[8] The rushed procurement of military information systems, which they were understandably eager to promote during the 1990s, was unprecedented in peacetime and has transformed the previously bespoke military command, control and communications infrastructure to uncertain effect. While military change was both inevitable and essential, the manner and speed of introduction of information-based concepts has outpaced the capacity of the operational and research communities to learn how to defend, operate and exploit a computer-intensive and information-rich battlespace.

Western policy makers remain fully engaged in establishing a common understanding of Information Warfare (IW), a concept which has at least three principal connotations loosely involving operational knowledge, information systems and the human mind.[9] In its most recent definition of IW the USAF has adopted a pragmatic approach and this is employed as the baseline interpretation of IW for the purposes of this discussion:

> *Any action to deny, exploit, corrupt or destroy the enemy's information and its functions while protecting Air Force assets against those actions and exploiting its own military information operations.*[10]

The various definitions of IW have undergone successive modifications in order to accommodate its many competing interpretations. Some authorities have stressed the importance of enemy command and control systems and the

---

6. AFCEA 45th Conference Report, 'Electronic Systems Gain Spotlight at Convention, *Signal*, August 1991, 123.

7. In the strictest sense, an Information System is any means for communicating knowledge from one person to another, from simple verbal means using analogue devices to fully computerised methods. For the purposes of this chapter the term represents any computer-based system which provides information or information linkages to a user. It therefore excludes embedded computers which provide functional control over physical processes (eg, fly-by-wire).

8. Mowerly, B P, Report on Commercial Providers: 'Delivering More, Faster, and Farther Drives Information Signal Opportunities', *Signal*, August 1995, 50

9. Successive DoD draft definitions of: IW during the 1990s attempted to be all-embracing through references to *information* (reflecting the battlefield dimension), *information-based processes* (covering the human and social aspects) and *information systems* (to include computer hardware and networks).

10. USAF Information Warfare Fact Sheets, www.af.mil:80/news/factsheets/Information_Warfare.html dated 20 October 1997.

competition for information as a goal in its own right,[11] while others have argued for a wider concept of IW which fully embraces the human mind and the complexities of the social dimension.[12] [13] Significant confusion concerning the relationship between IW and the longer established concept of Command and Control Warfare (C2W)[14] has triggered extensive debate as to the military responsibilities for IW and what it should entail.[15] As discussed in another chapter these developments have unfolded at a time when there are few legal guidelines as to what information-based activities are legitimate, either in peace or in war.[16] Many nations and non-state agents are currently investing in offensive IW capabilities, but methods of IW defence are at an immature stage of development. For these reasons and because the threshold for entry into IW activity is low, the destabilising potential of IW should not be underestimated. A global military experiment is in progress whose outcome is highly uncertain. Advanced, software-intensive, information-rich societies are increasingly exposed to diverse threats from rogue states and from non-state agents, empowered and emboldened by the new economics of computer-based force. A root and branch analysis of this new economics of force – which involves combat systems as much as it does the desktop computer technologies – is a prerequisite to effective preparation for future conflict.

THE NEW ECONOMICS OF FORCE

In warfare, the software weapon is a two-edged sword. Like any sword it not only cuts both ways but can be made so heavy and unwieldy that it loses all utility. This statement fully applies to both the command and combat domains. The undoubted potential of information systems in the command process must be weighed against new vulnerabilities, new dependencies upon civilian communication bearers, new complexities in command and control and new difficulties in

11. Hutcherson, N B, *Command and Control Warfare: Putting Another Tool in the War-fighter's Database*, Air University Press, Maxwell AFB, 1994.

12. Stein, Prof G J, 'Information Warfare', *Airpower Journal*, Spring 1995, 31.

13. Emmett, P C, Corcoran, M J, Ferbrache, D and Macintosh, J, An Analysis of the Military and Policy Context of Information Warfare, DERA Report No DERA/CIS3/58/8/5 dated June 1997.

14. The origins of C2W can be traced to Counter C3I in the early 1980s. C2W comprises 5 'pillars' or means for undermining the command and control effectiveness of an opponent. These are: physical destruction, EW, military deception, psychological operations and operational security.

15. Emmett, ibid.

16. See Chapter 4 by Dr K A Kyriakides on Air Power and International Air Law.

extracting what counts in the moments of danger from the amount of information available. The power of embedded computing in weapons and weapon platforms has transformed the combat environment in ways which require new approaches to the engagement, as well as new thinking about the design of weaponry and the numerical availability of their platforms.

A new economics of force has emerged whose consequences are not yet widely recognised or understood. This involves information but, at a more fundamental level, it is being driven by software. Software is the repository of computer power in all its varied military applications, the key to its exploitation and the source of its most intractable constraints and vulnerabilities. Operational software delivers function as well as information and must perform in a highly networked, interdependent and hazardous battlespace. Networked information systems need a collective performance under stress which satisfies the physical challenges and time constraints of conflict – challenges which are not nearly so acute for commercial information systems. Where operational software is concerned *more does not equal better*. As fast as the information infrastructure has grown, new software-based means have been developed which are able to break it. The larger it grows, the harder it becomes to control. As operational software makes more information available, the greater the inferences that can be read into it by further processing.

When there is ample time and system availability is high, a computer-intensive and information-rich environment works with deceptive ease. This has been the case in the Gulf War and the Bosnian conflict. In the absence of effective Iraqi counter-attacks on the coalition communication infrastructure during the Gulf War, the disparate computer systems fielded at short notice provided an immense communications network which achieved a remarkable ninety-eight per cent availability rate.[17] Despite this information-rich environment, there remained significant information and communication weaknesses on which the opponent was, fortunately, unable to capitalise. As one commander observed:

"One of the failures of the whole damn war was intelligence...absolutely terrible...when battalion commanders and regimental commanders crossed the line of departure, they didn't know what was in front of them.[18]"

During the Gulf War the total volume of satellite communications traffic alone peaked at an unprecedented 68 megabits per second[19], and comprised at least half

---

17. Toma, J S, 'Desert Storm Communications', Chapter in Campen, ibid, 1.

18. *US Naval Institute Proceedings*, US Naval Institute Press, Maryland, November 1991, 58.

19. Anson P and Cummings D, in Campen, ibid, 123.

the total, but the task of getting the right information to the right units in a timely fashion was actually impeded by the sheer complexity and quantity of information transactions. On the ground, trucks and helicopters often took on the role of getting photographic reconnaissance to troops about to go into combat.[20] The Computer Assisted Force Management System[21] used by the USAF for generating Air Tasking Orders (ATOs) was incompatible with US Navy systems, resulting in ATO transmission times of up to seventeen hours and the requirement to deliver ATOs to units afloat by helicopter.[22] Over Bosnian airspace on 2 June 1995, a USAF F-16 was shot down by a mobile Serbian missile battery whose location had been identified and stored in an intelligence database, but the information was not made available to those preparing the ATO for the mission.[23] This same pattern is also showing up regularly in field exercises, but it is a lesson which has yet to be amply demonstrated in conflict. A report on a US Army desert war game held in March 1997, involving more than 6,000 troops, the most modern computerised combat equipment and 1,000 vehicles, concluded that the sheer quantity of information available to those taking part overwhelmed operational efficiency and resulted in a tripling of friendly fire incidents compared to levels involving conventionally equipped troops in previous desert exercises.[24] Intelligence failures have always existed, but in information-saturated environments they may rapidly multiply. In periods of acute operational stress and under directed attack, truly robust and adaptive systems are necessary in which scaling strategy-to-task becomes a vital requirement. Software-based processing can be made almost limitless and unless it is constrained within an orderly doctrinal concept of battlefield exploitation, information saturation is the inevitable consequence.

The problem of design scaling involving the computer affects equally the combat domain. In the procurement of advanced weapons and weapon platforms, software is frequently cited as a cause of project lateness or failure.[25] As costs have escalated, fewer combat systems than ever can be afforded at the very time that the global proliferation of cheap precision weaponry threatens unprecedented rates of attrition in all physical terrain. This long and well recognised

---

20. Campen, ibid, 58.
21. CAFMS was forerunner of CTAPS (see footnote 11), which provided computer assistance in the generation of air tasking orders during the Gulf War.
22. Campen, ibid, 42.
23. News report on role of National Security Agency in F-16 downing, *Washington Post*, 16 June 95.
24. US Army, Report on Exercise Ivy Focus – March 1997, US Government Printing Office, Washington DC, May 1997.
25. Canan, J W, 'The Software Crisis', Chapter in *Military Air and Space Communications*, AFCEA International Press, Fairfax, 1990, 66.

procurement trend is widely accepted as the inevitable price of combat effectiveness in an era of high-technology, but it is primarily a cultural and not a technological phenomenon. This ability to trade and to scale in software-intensive projects was not fostered in the operational culture which developed during the Cold War. In that game of competitive procurement with the Soviet Union what counted most was combat sophistication during the short conflict in conventional arms that was expected to precede a nuclear exchange, as well as the ability to sustain a credible nuclear threat. Credibility was everything and economy of force counted for little. Indeed, the super-power contest of outspending, unnerving and debilitating the weaker Soviet economy, was central to the Western flanking strategy in which technology was a key component.[26] That generally meant packing every conceivable sophistication into weapon platforms in order to produce maximum psychological effect. The apogee of this strategy was arguably the Strategic Defence Initiative or 'Star Wars' project, a set of largely impossible schemes which were deliberately over-hyped[27] in order to intimidate the Soviets during the era of the Strategic Arms Reduction Talks. It was a fertile period for the multiplication of technological means. The needless continuation of a cultural habit that was first established to debilitate the Soviet Union, now threatens to do the same to the West.

AN OPERATIONAL STRATEGY FOR SOFTWARE

The explosive growth of operational software is not an inevitable product of technological sophistication, but a cultural phenomenon which has affected the military and civilian sectors in equal measure. Any artefact, hard or soft, can be scaled-to-task or made more efficient by design or policy choice. The overburdening of embedded computers arises because of blind and unselective reliance on software to execute an excessive number of functions – the unfiltered trivial along with the essential – in the absence of any systematic linkage between software production and the desired operational effects.

A technological turning point for combat engineering was the availability from the early 1970s of cheap semiconductors which freed programmers from the constraints of ferrite core memory space. The quantity of software in combat systems multiplied throughout the 1970s and 1980s and the trend continues

---

26. Reagan, R, Whitehouse Background Statement, in *Military Air and Space Communications*, ibid, 8.
27. Snyder A, *Warriors of Disinformation: American Propaganda, Soviet Lies and the Winning of the Cold War*, Arcade Publications, 1997.

unabated today. An F-4 Phantom of the Vietnam era contained very little computer code. The F-16C developed in the 1970s contained 236,000 lines of code.[28] By the 1980s the amount of software in advanced aircraft projects such as the B-1B,[29] typically exceeded one million lines of code, while several advanced tactical fighters under current development will contain in excess of ten millions of lines of on-board software. Multiples of the amounts of on-board software are employed in ground-support systems. The procurement difficulties which followed the escalation in software costs led to the coining of the term Software Crisis.[30] By 1990 DoD expenditure on software was running at $30 billion a year or around 10 per cent of the defence budget and software remains a frequent cause of project failure and over-expenditure. No amount of engineering can solve the underlying problem – the operational need to achieve economy of software-based force. The Software Crisis is one which cannot be solved by anything other than a coherent operational strategy for software and reform of the post-Cold War defence procurement culture.

Modification of software is now a primary means by which to upgrade systems and keep them ahead of the threats. Adaptation of software can also give new capabilities to existing combat systems without the need for physical modifications. Modifications to the US Army's Firefinder radar were implemented prior to the outbreak of the air war, just in time for the Firefinder to play an important role in the detection of Scud missiles after launch and in the provision of rapid predictions of their probable target points.[31] The Thermal Imaging and Laser Designators[32] fitted at short notice to a number of RAF aircraft during the Gulf War, were similarly enabled by some rapidly implemented software modifications.[33] Software adaptability has become fundamental to operational performance but, even if the need has been recognised, software changes can be greatly hindered when programmes are large, monolithic and complex. They also become risky. The probability of introducing one or more errors during a 'bug-fix' has been estimated to lie between 15 and 50 per cent,[34] depending on programme size and complexity. The first attempts to launch the US Space

---

28. Kitfield, 'Is Software DoD's Achilles' Heel?', *Military Forum*, July 1989, 28.

29. According to Canan, J W, in *Military and Space Communications*, 1990, 66, the B-1B contains 1.2 million lines of computer code.

30. Canan, ibid.

31. Report in *Signal*: 'Trashing Iraqi Scud Sites Shows Firefinder's Metal', August 1991, 27.

32. Thermal Imaging and Laser Designator

33. Jackson, P, 'TIALD Designated a Success', *RAF Yearbook Special*, 1991, 33.

34. Boehm, B W, *Software Engineering Economics*, Prentice-Hall, New Jersey, 1983, 383.

Shuttle resulted in failure because of a software error which had been introduced two years earlier, when another error had been fixed. On average, the new error would have manifested itself once in every 67 times.[35]

It would be unwise to anticipate or rely upon future technological fixes to the Software Crisis because there are physical and logical ceilings beyond which computing cannot go. Every ounce of operational advantage must be extracted from software, but that means living with the art of the possible and being aware of the hazards of exceeding basic design limits. Professor Mike Underhill, Chairman of the Electronics Division of the Institution of Electrical Engineers, has warned for many years of the dangers of a condition known as 'metastability' in flip-flops – the basic building block of computers – in which ever higher interrupt rates and computer clock speeds can lead to ambiguous logic states.[36] This may seem a trivial consideration, but it is an especially important factor in fly-by-wire systems and one that remains poorly recognised by software design engineers. Extensive reliance on software to execute flight and mission critical functions means that safety-critical software increasingly controls modern combat aircraft. The undoubted flight performance advantages this brings can and must be exploited. Fly-by-wire control functions must also be as rigorously tested as possible, but no system of testing yet exists which can check more than a small fraction of possible execution paths. Mathematical tools based on formal methods[37] are of considerable value, but there are intractable limits to the amount of code which can be checked using these formal methods. The spectacular loss of the Ariane-5 rocket on 4 June 1996 demonstrates that even the most rigorous and expert software testing can and does fail. Even when the hardware and software components of a fly-by-wire system have been subject to rigorous testing, there remains the problem of training pilots to cope with unfamiliar cockpit environments and to keep pace with software updates. The European Airbus project has suffered acutely from this particular problem.[38] The tragic consequences of a failure to keep aircrew aware of program changes in an avionics computer occurred

35. Lin, H, 'The Development of Software for the Strategic Defence Initiative', *Scientific American*, December, 1985.
36. Underhill, Professor, M J, 'The Magic of Marginal Electronics', *Electronics and Communications Engineering Journal*, December 1993, 359.
37. Examples of which include the Malvern Program Analysis Suite (MALPAS), extensively used in the nuclear industry, and the Southampton Program Analysis and Development Environment (SPADE),which has been employed on the Eurofighter project.
38. Sedbon, G and Learmount, D, Report on findings of French Commission of Enquiry into A320 Airbus Crash, *Flight International*, 4 January 1994, 11.

in 1979, when an Air New Zealand airliner crashed into a mountain in the Antarctic. They had not been kept abreast of changes to basic navigation data used for calculating flight paths.[39]

Software is the now the primary repository of command and combat power in the Information Age, but the West is in significant danger of drowning in it. Scaling-to-task is the only realistic strategy, which means living within sensible limits of software-based means. It is a strategy which can commence from the moment an operational decision has been made to pursue, but software continues to be perceived as a black art in which operational intervention has no place and the potentially rich dividends of the strategy remain unclaimed.[40]

AIR POWER IN TRANSITION

The technologies of the Information Age present both opportunities and threats to air power. Computer-based command aids such as the Contingency Theatre Automated Planning System[41], for example, are transforming the process of air mission planning and tasking. Exploitation of information technologies can undoubtedly assist in the deployment and co-ordination of diverse air assets at an unprecedented level of detail. In circumstances where tactical surprise can be executed over an opponent whose dispositions are well known in advance, as in the Gulf War, this method has proven its effectiveness. Dangers could arise, however, if excessive dependency on cyclically-generated ATOs, led to such a culture of digital dependency that neither operational squadrons nor air commanders are effectively prepared for the more daunting challenges of fluid tactical engagements against capable opposition. Computer-assisted mission planning could be reduced to an irrelevancy in a bloody and rapidly unfolding conflict, or be made to cease altogether by means of its in-built vulnerabilities. The culture of digital dependency can be countered by training for the unexpected and lessened through the provision of tactical communications which have in-built resilience under operational stress (see discussion on tactical air operations

---

39. Lin, ibid.
40. Emmett, P C, 'Software Warfare: The Militarization of Logic', *Joint Force Quarterly*, Summer, 1994, 84.
41. The Contingency Theatre Automated Planning System is an air planning and tasking tool which is an amalgam of several computer systems, including CAFMS, and has been developed by the US as a standard and their common platform for air mission planning. It is scheduled to be replaced by the Theatre Battle Management System in 1998.

below). In the Information Age, continued reliance on the centralised command, control and communications of past practice might be decidedly unwise.

A major threat is now posed by software-based attack upon the networked infrastructure of the ground-based air command and control environment and this will endure as long as software offence remains stronger than software defence. It is important to recognise that it is the temporal nature of the software threat – the number of simultaneous events and the complexity of their interactions – which makes the software threat so insidious and difficult to counter. One-to-one counter-measures against known software threats are relatively straightforward, but they are of limited value in the moments of danger against novel modes of attack. The software threat can take a variety of forms, but essentially involves malicious software (including software viruses and hidden software switches) and unauthorised access into computer networks or 'hacking'. Incidents of hacking into military networks continue to increase yearly. In 1995, the US Defence Information Systems Agency used openly available hacker tools to test the security of 26,170 unclassified DoD computers. They found that 86% of computers could be penetrated by exploiting the trusted relationship between the machines and their host networks and that 98% of penetrations were not detected by system administrators or users[42]. In March 1994, a British hacker named 'Datastream Cowboy' attacked the air command and control computer systems at Rome Laboratories and obtained sensitive information from ATOs.[43] At the height of the conflict in Bosnia, the Serbs were particularly adept at using information technology to monitor the movements of UN forces.[44] Computer security measures designed in peacetime may be found difficult to enforce during conflict. Many of the computers used in the Gulf were privately owned,[45] and this hindered the introduction of effective security measures.

Software-based attacks are normally indistinguishable from the day-to-day software infections that increasingly pervade the commercial digital environment. It is no accident that, at the height of the Cold War, Bulgaria was the major producer of malicious software.[46] A co-ordinated and well-timed attack could

---

42. Report of the Defense Science Board Task Force on Information Warfare – Defense, 21 November 1996, 2-15.

43. Ibid.

44. Moss, N, Report into computer hacking in which Air Commodore R Holt comments upon the Information Warfare capabilities of Serb forces, *European*, 10-16 October 1996.

45. Macedonia, Major M R, 'Information Technology in Desert Storm', *Military Review*, October 1992, 34.

46. Moss, ibid.

slow the much prized flow of battlefield information – at a decisive moment – to a manually processed trickle. This could be achieved by diverse methods but, in very general terms, will involve a successful penetration of a network followed by malicious action against databases or network control systems. Detection is most unlikely and the commercially available 'firewall' can, in most cases, be circumvented with intelligent effort.[47] Network access can normally be gained remotely or, failing this, by means of direct physical access and the use of insiders. Attacks need not be confined to operational and tactical networks, but could be directed at a nation's information infrastructure with the aim of causing maximum disruption at a strategic level. In an all-out software offensive attacks could be staged simultaneously using diverse and largely untraceable means. In the networked form, the problem lies less with anticipated damage than the damage that arises from unexpected interactions which cannot be known in advance. These are termed multi-order effects and involve a complex interplay of human, social and technical factors. An attack on the wealth-creating potential of a Western state would be especially dangerous because social disruption and chaos might develop before restoration of the information infrastructure could be put into effect. It is not beyond the bounds of possibility that this could induce irreversible political and social changes in Western states, who will remain exposed to such dangers until the growing imbalance between software offence and software defence is countered.

The ability to operate in degraded modes during moments of danger is the crucial operational requirement, but this is lacking in commercially-produced information systems; post-attack recovery of data is presently just sufficient to satisfy the commercial requirement. Software Warfare of this kind – like Electronic Warfare – is just another agency for the attainment of timed denial, and the timing of software denial can be made exquisitely precise. Denial may not always be the aim, but deception. This could achieved by hacking into an operational network and changing basic mission or logistics data, such as the flight path of a tanker mission, or inserting false statistics on weapon availability. The volume of data in mission planning tools is such that detection by command units is unlikely prior to the execution phase. Error-checking by human operators is generally not feasible and could only be achieved at the cost of planning delays. This suggests that autonomous verification tools, based on independent checking protocols, should be developed in tandem with mission planning tools.

---

47. News Article, 'A Hacker Writes – How to Break into a Corporate Network', *Network News*, 19 March 1997.

Unauthorised access and abuse of commercial computer networks will always be possible – at all levels of classification – because no computer security measure in a complex, changing and highly innovative environment can be made absolute. Bespoke security systems can greatly improve security – at a price – but they are slow to procure and are often obsolete by the time they have been delivered. A middle way between commercial and bespoke IT products is that of 'blended procurement'[48] in which commercial products having bespoke security features would be developed in close co-operation with commercial vendors, while legacy bespoke systems could be upgraded at low cost using advanced, commercially available technologies. The central role of human operators remains crucial, as does the internal threat which continues to account for the majority of hacking incidents. There is no simple panacea to these threats, except that of being at all times prepared to cope by team effort and leadership with the challenges of uncertainty.

The desk top technologies of the Information Age by no means establish the whole pattern of computer-based change as it affects air power. The transformation of the air command and control environment has been complimented by a transformation in air combat power. Many technologies have played an important part in the air power revolution, but the vital capabilities of precision and smartness available in modern weaponry, as well as diverse avionics and flight control functions, stem from the same technological root which has transformed the command environment – the power of the computer. The scaling-to-task of the software basis of computer-power is a primary consideration, but the diffusion and global exploitation of this vital medium also demands close attention. The benefits of this deeper analysis in the context of air power, can be illustrated by considering the significant challenge to the future effectiveness of air power posed by precision weapons and their global proliferation. An important difference between the software of desk top and combat systems is that the former is overwhelmingly commercial in origin, and exposed to interference over electronic networks, while the latter is overwhelmingly bespoke and generally embedded. Combat software is, therefore, not easily accessed through direct electronic means, except using the bespoke communications capabilities likely to be available only to the owning state, or by advanced manipulation at the production stage. This means that the vulnerabilities which were described the desk top technologies do not apply to anything like the same extent to combat systems. Software vulnerabilities in combat systems undoubtedly exist – and have been

---

48. Emmett, Corcoran, ibid.

exploited in the past – but they can be countered by rigorous verification regimes and do not pose anything like the same threat. This understanding matters, because it means that future growth in software-intensive combat capabilities is likely to be largely unimpeded by software-based attacks.

SOFTWARE WARFARE

Intelligence estimates leave little doubt that the preferred weapon-of-influence of rogue states may be cruise missiles and their derivatives.[49] Ultra high-cost and highly sophisticated manned aircraft of the F-22/Sukoi 32 genre are less afford-able. Ballistic missiles will continue to pose a significant threat for the foreseeable future but lack the intelligence and flexibility of cruise missiles. Small weapon systems are easier to hide and if vital centres can be hit precisely, then small payloads are sufficient. The air-breathing power units of cruise missiles gives them extremely long range and the technologies needed for accurate navigation can be purchased in the international marketplace. The surface-launched Tomahawk, for example, has a range in excess of 2,400km and greater ranges than this are likely to be commonplace in future cruise weaponry. Terrain contour matching during low-level flight enables the Tomahawk missile to avoid air defences and optical sensors take over for the attack phase, homing the missile on targets with remarkable precision.

Smartness and range are the key attributes of today's cruise missiles, but their major threat to the future air defence of Western states lies primarily in their intrinsic economy of force. Smartness derives from the on-board computer programs, which can be copied infinitely. This is something new in warfare – a military asset which defies physical destruction and transcends the cost-benefit conventions of military economics. Software – the 'logical' – is an asset which doesn't need the large industrial base that is required to produce sophisticated manned aircraft – the 'physical'. Its qualitative attributes count for everything while its numerical strength is an irrelevancy. Nor do the physical components of cruise missile technology require much industrial sophistication. Cruise platforms could be manufactured by a determined opponent in larger numbers than manned aircraft. This makes cruise missiles especially attractive to states which cannot afford to manufacture or purchase sophisticated manned aircraft and unit costs are likely to continue to decline as the necessary knowledge and software are

49. Institute for Strategic Studies, *Strategic Survey 1996-7*, Oxford University Press, 1997.

disseminated over electronic networks. The technological sophistication of manned aircraft has grown steadily over several decades driven, fundamentally, from the need to evade air defences and survive air engagements. But cruise missiles, surface-based point-defence systems notwithstanding, have as yet no effective airborne predator and can perform under many levels of electronic threat until their self-destruction at the target point.

The numerical threat which cruise missiles may one day pose is worth relating to the physical and psychological damage inflicted by the V1 'flying bombs' during the closing years of WWII. At a stage when the RAF was at an historic peak of strength, more than 3,500 of these first and primitive cruise missiles, about a third of those launched, penetrated a layered air defence comprising fighter aircraft, guns and balloon cables. Add in the factors of smartness and stealth likely in future cruise weaponry and a most potent threat emerges. It may not require many successful penetrations to have a decisive psychological effect, for example, on the continued participation of a key member of a coalition or the provocation of a non-involved state. The Scud attacks against Israel during Gulf War came close to drawing her into the conflict, thereby endangering an already fragile US-Arab coalition; more accurate attacks using cruise missiles could cause graver psychological damage with fewer assets. In today's media-dominated and global society, perception is everything.

A particularly dangerous development could be the emergence of offensive co-operative capabilities based on the continuous exchange of mission data (logical co-operation) between cruise platforms. The Co-operative Engagement Capability under development by the US Navy is a forerunner of this kind of warfare. Fully developed logical co-operation would see cruise missiles flying and reacting co-operatively as a swarm, turning upon anything which moved against it, and engaging ground targets through combined action. Such capabilities could emerge with further but achievable physical adaptation of cruise platforms and become a significant threat to manned aircraft. The power of logical co-operation in the air engagement would derive from the ability to compute the available escape routes for a manned aircraft and to achieve multiple weapon positioning in anticipation of the pilot's available manoeuvres. Software-based air warfare of this kind is a prospect for which there is yet scant recognition or preparatory strategy. Its emergence is unlikely to be impeded by the undoubted difficulties in the design and procurement of software-intensive systems, but defensive preparations could certainly be advanced by a procurement strategy which established software as an operational entity or weapon in its own right.

The proliferation of cruise missiles faces the West with a major prospective threat. It is one that the existing operational culture senses but it has not yet been able to address the root issues. Consideration of physical performance continues to dominate the design and procurement of military systems, while the many distractions of the information vogue have obscured the latent power of the logical or software dimension. The root of the cruise missile threat lies neither in information nor information technologies. The computer is the vital enabling technology and information is an important by-product of it, but the root source of the cruise missile threat lies in the stored machine instructions – the software – which control the responses of cruise missiles at every level of detail.

Recognition of the underpinning role of software in future air combat will be the beginning of the end of the conventional air engagement as it has been understood in the era of pure physical-on-physical contention. Although software in weaponry normally controls a particular physical entity, it can also be unified using communications and real-time co-operation within a much wider physical and logical context. The speed, complexity and spatial dimension of the modern battlespace means that only software can close on software and it must be made to work through the paradigm of the logical-on-logical and the co-operative many, not the precocious few. The human element remains vital (see discussion on pilot skills below), but this unified logical dimension is as new and important to warfare at the close of the 20th Century as the electromagnetic spectrum was in its middle decades. Just as rapid advances in electronics under the aegis of EW were fundamental to dominance of the electromagnetic spectrum, so too will systematic exploitation of software become central to achieving dominance in the logical battlespace. The strategic answer to the threat of software-based air warfare is to develop inexpensive airframes and enable them to co-operate using all the unexploited, latent power of software. Specifically, this means designing military systems which exploit in a co-ordinated and systematic fashion the key characteristics of software, particularly its co-operative ability, intelligence and adaptability, in order to achieve maximum economy of software-based force. This has been termed Software Warfare (SW)[50] because it involves logical-on-logical actions as much as do virus attacks within computer networks.

THE RISE AND RISE OF THE STORED MIND

Unless forestalled, the gradual shift from the physical to the logical in the warfare of the Information Age may be accompanied by a significant shift in the global balance of military power. Much more than cruise missile technology is involved.

---

50. Emmett, ibid.

Software-based empowerment affects the whole panoply of military capabilities from intelligent undersea mines to satellite technologies. The dust-cloud of concepts thrown up by Information Age fads has obscured this wider prospect of danger. The forward trend is not one of continued Western empowerment through information technology, but of a growth in diverse offensive capabilities of previously weak non-western states which threaten to expose the West on a number of vital technological flanks. Many other important characteristics of software remain to be exploited, including diverse means for creating 'artificial intelligence' in combat systems and the development of synthetic environments in the modelling of complex battle environments. Such capabilities can be exploited regardless of economic prowess.

The increasing prevalence of computer-based systems of all kinds does not presage autonomous warfare, but rather the resolution of the decision-making component of conflict into two domains – one geared to the speed and analytical capacity of the human mind, the other to the software-based processing capabilities of the computer. Clausewitz represented warfare as two men wrestling.[51] In a direct bodily contest, fighting unfolds as a complex series of interactions, as each seeks the advantage, involving the physical and mental domains. What is new in today's warfare is an artificial mental activity representing, effectively, a third player in human conflict – the domain of stored mind (Figure 6.2). This is further illustrated in Figure 6.3 as a domain of such networked scale and complexity that events can no longer be dissected as sequences but are increasingly dominated by simultaneous chains of events. What was initially introduced to enhance the command element, has cast the human mind in a self-created 'processing space' of such scale and complexity that events within it increasingly defy human comprehension or management. This renders it both difficult and unwise to execute the command function by means of the sequential mission planning methods that have been traditionally employed. Command-by-influence remains the only realistic option. This would cast the commander more in the role of the conductor of an orchestra. From the morass of independent players he selects to play only those which count most in the moments of danger. Where detailed intervention and direction is needed it is given, but otherwise he or she concentrates on the co-ordination of the whole around higher goals and accepts the uncertainties of this command mode.

The disparity between the human and software-driven players in conflict must also lead to a physical polarity in the battlespace, with the human players avoiding

---

51. Clausewitz, C, *On War*, Princeton University Press, New Jersey, USA, 1976, 75.

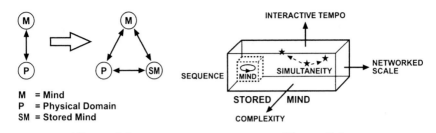

Figure 6.2
The third player in human conflict

Figure 6.3
The increasing extent of the Stored Mind

danger by operating from remote or otherwise safe locations. Human governance of the whole process of conflict remains essential if the irreplaceable qualities of judgement, intuition and creativity are to be continuously brought to bear upon an opponent, thereby introducing uncertainty and driving innovation in the technologies. The human players in warfare do not change, what changes are their roles and their responses to the fast changing element of danger. The proliferation of precision weaponry represents a growth in the element of danger which also affects the prosecution of land warfare. While manned aircraft will also experience a growth in the element of danger, their speed, flexibility and mobility – as well as their unique sensory and communications vantage points – will continue to allow them to operate remotely or to escape danger zones when necessary. The peculiarities of the Gulf War mean that it must be interpreted cautiously, but it demonstrated a major shift in the balance of critical destructive mass conveyed by air as against land-based power. This important interpretation was poorly heard in the noise of instant, information-based assessments of the Gulf War which have distorted military theory ever since. The sensory and communications dominance established by airborne platforms, such as the Joint Surveillance Targeting and Reconnaissance System, also demonstrated the growing importance of the airspace high-ground to the theatre command elements. After almost a century of gestation – its relative advantages against surface power greatly magnified by the computer – air power is finally coming of age as the most widely effective means for conducting high-intensity warfare.

The ability to exploit, dominate and protect air and space-based communications is a vital factor affecting all tactical activity. Information is indeed important in all facets of warfare, but it must also be able to pass through regions of air and space vulnerable to electronic attack and still be routed to those who most need it in a timely fashion. Information routeing is a far from trivial problem and involves the command and control philosophy as much as it does bandwidth and the available communication technologies. Information systems are increasingly networked and physically distributed at sites which must co-ordinate diverse air planning and tasking activity over extremely large geographical regions. This is not just a future capability but one that is the subject of current operational trials. The first intercontinental air command and control experiment took place in August 1996 during the Joint Warrior Interoperability Demonstration (JWID)[52] held at Ft Bragg, USA,[53] [54] involving co-operative air planning and tasking across the Atlantic between five participating nations. A highly distributed, networked and information-rich environment is a significant challenge for air power which may, over time, lead to major revisions in the concept of centralised command and control traditionally held to be sacrosanct.

THE INFORMATION CHALLENGES OF TACTICAL AIR OPERATIONS

In the past decade there has been a substantial growth in communications technologies of all descriptions, which has been led by advances in the commercial sector. The major effect of these advances has been to extend the physical range by which high bandwidth data communications can be achieved, allowing an unprecedented degree of horizontal interaction between computer nodes and their operators. Where once an air commander sat in a sector or major HQ and had a reasonable expectation of knowing the recognised air situation, he or she can now be confronted with increasing volumes of information of all kinds – the essential along with the trivial – which are able to flow and to multiply freely between many centres over electronic networks. But more does not mean better and it most decidedly means worse if it swamps essential information during periods of operational danger. Fundamentally this is a problem of information selection and routeing – the establishment of a process for deciding what information is required by whom and how urgently it is needed.

---

52. The Joint Warrior Interoperability Demonstration is a US-led international effort, held annually, which allows a large measure of operational experimentation in the exploitation of emerging technologies.
53. Emmett, P C, 'Concept of Operations for a Global Air Command and Control Demonstration', DERA Report No. JWID133/UK5/1, July 1996.
54. Emmett, P C, 'Interoperation of CTAPS and ICC Supported by Coalition Air Planning over Distributed APS', DERA Report No. JWID133/UK5/2, September 1996.

The other major challenge air commanders will increasingly face is how to maintain central authority over electronic networks. This is a human and doctrinal problem as much as a technological one, but it is the technologies which are presently setting the pace with doctrine lagging far behind. Central command authority (whether in an orchestrating role or otherwise) and distributed air planning and tasking are not inherently contradictory. For command authority to be effective over dispersed sites a solution to the information routeing problem is the crucial requirement. With information routeing protocols established, synthetic environments could be constructed to unite physically distributed sites and provide tomorrow's air commander with a fused and coherent picture of the essential air situation over all regions. More than this, synthetic environments could allow computer-based 'what-ifing' and the diverse information synergies which are the key ingredients for the emergence of tactical surprise within air campaigns. This would be a step to removing the plethora of information systems which have so rapidly filled command centres in recent years, each addressing only one segment of the command process. The problem and the solution outlined do not differ fundamentally from past practice. What has changed, is the granularity of information that can now be made available, the speed with which it can flow and the complexity of its interactions.

Considerable resources have been vested in the use of computers at command units and the installation of broad band communication links between them, but remarkably little consideration has been given to the information routeing problem. This has two key facets: the technological problem of routeing from an information source to an already identified group of receivers and, secondly, the much more intractable problem of how to identify what information counts from the morass that may be available and who most urgently needs it. Since there are limits to the amount of information the human brain can handle at any one time, an information-rich environment can fast become a decision-poor one and an air commander's nightmare. However much the technologies change, the ultimate decision maker – the human brain – has remained much the same.

The challenges of air tactical communications need first to be set in the context of the peculiarities of military communications in general, as shown in Figure 6.4. The backbone of military organisation is the command chain. It is necessarily hierarchical in nature because there must be, at all times, a focal point for decision making at the command head to support all tempos of operation and to allow fast reactions and responses by the military body. Command, subordinate commands and the individual command units have traditionally been linked by point-to-point communications as shown on the left hand side of the figure. Communication is then said to be sender-oriented (or 'push') since is it is up to the sender of information to decide when information is transmitted and who should receive it. The flow of information tends to be vertical up and down the command chain. This is a significant disadvantage when the volume of information which flows is large, because each sender acts as a potential choke point. With the growing precision and long reach of guided weaponry, the command nodes in this form of communication architecture are also increasingly vulnerable to C2W.

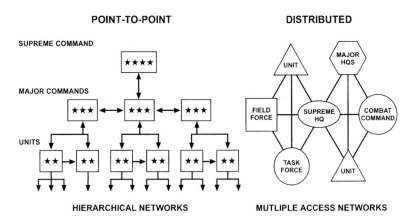

Figure 6.4
Communications Architectures

The right hand side of the figure represents an alternative communication architecture based on multi-access electronic networks in which information exchange is essentially horizontal in nature and can flow around electronic networks using autonomous communications routeing. This can be described as receiver-oriented communications (or 'pull') because it is the receiver who decides which information he or she wishes to access. Receiver-oriented communications are a significant advance on sender-oriented communications, because they avoid the difficulties which can occur in an hierarchical communication system when the overwhelming of a few individuals may impede the timely flow of information. Its inherently distributed form is also a clear advantage in C2W, because command information is replicated at many nodes and central authority can be maintained during an attack. There remains, however, the major difficulty that the individual receiver of information may still be confronted with information-overload and there must be some mechanism by which he or she can be first alerted to the need to pull necessary information off the network. Users of the Internet will well recognise how easily the multiples of information that are so freely available can lead to side-tracking and needless distractions. Information volume and the potentially excessive choices offered by information processing software remain a core problem in both architectures.

There is also the deeper issue of how to decide what information counts in each operational exigency. The networked scale, complexity and degree of simultaneous activity in the modern battlespace – itself a product of computerisation – means that tactically significant information is increasingly transient in nature. Information held in computer databases tends to reflect yesterday's conditions. Add in the factor of military deception and the magnitude of today's emerging communication crisis becomes apparent; somehow the command and combat elements must respond to these monumental challenges in a time-scale that is far more compressed than it was in the pre-digital era.

Challenges of this order should be set into an historical context. The actors and their artefacts change, but armies throughout history encountered these problems many times. They differ extensively by degree but not in nature, and the lessons of the past are there for the taking. Information has always had an intrinsic tendency to multiply, whether by rumour, by paperwork or by computer. Effective communications systems have been those which avoided information saturation by establishing well-defined human communication protocols and deciding *in advance of conflict* the *minima* of information which units need to receive. The Romans based in Britain in the late 4th century AD faced the threat of multiple invasions by Saxon and Pictish tribes. Under the exceptionally able command of Theodosius, they responded with a highly sophisticated signalling system based on hilltop outposts, the scale of which was not seen again in Britain until the advent of Watson Watt's brilliantly conceived RDF Chain Home reporting system some 1,600 years later.[55] By operating primarily with information minima, by rigorous training and by rehearsal, the Roman legions (until the collapse of Rome) and the RAF in WWII were both successful in fending-off the attackers. Information minima allowed the human command and combat elements to respond to attacks in the moments of intrusion and concentrate their forces. The exploitation of information in today's battlefield can be approached using similar principles.

---

55. Interestingly, the RAF occupied many of the earlier Roman signalling sites. RAF Staxton Wold, one of the earliest Chain Home sites, for example, had been a Roman signalling station and HQ No 73 Signals Wing, responsible for Sector RDF operations, was based at Malton (Derventio), also an important Roman headquarters.

WELCHMAN – FATHER OF JTIDS

What are arguably the deepest and most lucid investigations ever conducted into the problems of air tactical communications were made by Gordon Welchman, a largely forgotten figure who worked during WWII at Bletchley Park and was closely involved with the breaking of the Enigma codes.[56] At Bletchley, Welchman made an extensive study of the tactical communications employed in the German *Blitzkreig* and by Rommel in the North African desert campaigns. This was to stand Welchman in good stead when, in later years, he emigrated to the United States and undertook studies for the MITRE Corporation into air command and control and the disastrous use of computers during the Vietnam War. The flexible radio interconnectivity which the Germans developed for their Blitzkreig offensives served as a model for Welchman's conception of the Joint Tactical Information Distribution System (JTIDS), a system of interlocking communication nets that provide robustness and autonomous distribution of essential tactical information. The procurement of JTIDS has been late, considerably over-budget[57] and the digital technology employed has consequently failed to keep pace with advances in computing and communications. Welchman saw JTIDS as only the tactical forerunner of a much wider communications concept which would provide tactical unity to all land, sea and air arms. In a sea of poorly conceived, vulnerable and non-interoperable communication systems, JTIDS remains a solid island of tactical communications excellence whose operational advantages are slowly beginning to be recognised. Indeed, as Group Captain Peach agrees in Chapter 3, JTIDS may soon become the minimum entry standard for coalition. Welchman may be fairly described as the father of JTIDS.[58] The following words describing his experiences in the late 1960s deserve quotation because they are especially poignant for today's computer-intensive, information-saturated military culture:

"Everyone seemed to be thinking about what happened at command posts. There was too much talk of using computers. I was asked to concentrate on what was involved in the actual attack...the pilot would get his briefing well ahead of time, and would be able to study the problems he was likely to encounter. (quoting the typical experiences of one pilot)....*out of some sixty-five F-4 missions flown, only five had gone as originally briefed. Not one of his positive missions had gone as originally briefed. They had occurred only because he was redirected or had acted on his own initiative to take advantage of some unexpected opportunity"[59].*

---

56. Welchman G, *The Hut Six Story: Breaking the Enigma Codes*, McGraw-Hill, New York, 1982.
57. Allard, Col C K, *Command, Control and the Common Defence*, Yale University Press, 1990, 204.
58. Recognition of Welchman's accomplishments in his country of birth is surely long overdue.

In Vietnam the USAF was up against a clever and capable opponent. Over-reliance on the information held in computers at command units led them to waste capable men and machines attacking the targets of yesterday's battlespace. The above quotation demonstrates that communications for the air battle must support a balance between aircrew initiative and the air commander's stated mission. At times, detailed direction will be both possible and advantageous (as in the Gulf War); at other times the ebb and flow of battle will dictate an *Auftragtaktik* approach in which all the initiative, skills and leadership that can be mustered at squadron level will be crucial. Since there is no easy disconnect between the two *modus operandi*, the supporting communications have to be made flexible enough to allow command intervention at decisive moments or in critical engagements while supporting the continuous horizontal flow (and fusion) of essential tactical information in pre-arranged formats. This means ensuring that new information and directives reach the right squadrons at the right time and that they know in advance how they should react. It was one of Rommel's great tactical advantages that he was able to command his forces centrally from any point in the battlefield at the moment of his choosing.

PILOT SKILLS, TACTICS AND UNCERTAINTY

The ability to exploit essential flight characteristics – height, range, speed and manoeuvrability has generally been decisive in air engagements. Exploitation of these characteristics will always have its limitations because not every situation can be foreseen, or is necessarily computational. The physical presence of a pilot, who can make on-the-spot assessments and react to events immediately using human judgement is, therefore, likely to remain an irreplaceable advantage in the decades to come however much air power roles may change, or whatever degree of autonomy is introduced into weapons and unmanned platforms.

It was Clausewitz who said that war is fundamentally about fighting.[60] Military theory either spawns outwards from the hard edges of fighting or becomes so beset by the abstraction and dogma that it can hardly be understood by those who fight, as has happened in recent years with IW. Fighting in the air is fundamentally about flying, a basic tenet which should be kept uppermost in the development of every air communications innovation or theory of air power. The

---

59. Welchman, ibid, 202, 271.
60. Clausewitz, ibid.

advent of autonomous, co-operative weaponry does not remove the need for a manned and *unpredictable* element in air combat. The great strength of air power is that of mobility in three dimensions and the uncertainty this can create in the mind of an enemy. The ability to communicate provides the basis not only for the co-ordination of mission execution with the air commander, but is essential for effective co-operation between cockpits. Uncertainty is enhanced if air communications allow fluid co-operative manoeuvres. The history of air combat demonstrates that whenever the innate strengths of air power have been enslaved to over-rigid and predictable application, it has resulted in operational failure and avoidable losses. It was a lesson the RAF first learned the hard way in 1940. 'Johnnie' Johnson likened the RAF's textbook 'vic of three' tactics in 1940 to parade drills for the air, as the following account of early fighter tactics by Johnson testifies:

"The climb that sunny morning was uneventful except for the odd command from a section leader to 'get in closer'....All my attention was concentrated on keeping this immaculate station; I could not even look behind or to my starboard side even for a second...They were sitting ducks for the lively, roaming Messerschmitts." [61]

The co-operative engagement was originated during WWI by such pioneers as Oswald Boelcke, who first developed the paired attack formation that became the classic fighter tactic which is still in use today. Boelcke's tactics necessarily had to be based on visual communication, but a multiplicity of co-operative functions can now be established using modern communications and are opening up a wide range of novel tactical possibilities. This requires something of a cultural shift for aircrew who have lived through the long tactical stasis of the Cold War era, but that era is now decidedly over. The technologies of the Information Age and the increasing degree of autonomy in weaponry will not displace pilot functions, as many predict, but begin, once again, to offer ample challenges for flying and air tactical skills. It should also be remembered that, at times, technologies will be denied, or fail, and that even the most modern sensors are not immune from the effects of weather. Even during Desert Storm it was not all 'gin-clear' flying days that many had expected and the worst weather in that region for a decade resulted in the cancellation of 15% of coalition air sorties in the first ten days.[62] Targeting was also often frustrated in the missions that flew because dense cloud cover often prevented the positive identification of targets, as required in the rules of engagement. Even such basics as the interruption of power supplies may at

---

61. Johnson J E and Lucas P B, *Courage in the Skies*, Stanley Paul & Co, London, 1992: 41.

62. Winnefield, J A, Niblack, P and Johnson, J, A League of Airmen – US Air Power in the Gulf, RAND Publications, 1994, 124.

times deny a swathe of IT systems. Fighting in the air then becomes more than ever a contest of individual skills and co-operative team effort.

The ground environment in the Information Age offers equal challenges. Co-operative air planning and tasking over wide area communications networks today allow unprecedented co-ordination of air activity on an inter-continental scale – tomorrow it will be global. This could be exploited, for example, in the attainment of simultaneous pressures against a coalition of powers for maximum impact, or as a highly effective counter-measure to C2W, but will require new thinking about air command and control. Centralised air command remains essential, but concepts of operations must be developed which will enable it to be executed over widely separated sites using electronic communication networks.[63] Global communications could lead to global air warfare in which the air and space high ground will be decisive in achieving a communications advantage. Global air campaigns of this sort must allow for the rapid passing of essential tactical data between disparate geographical regions which previously did not need linking. This is not least essential in countering the threat of long range cruise missiles, for which effective long-haul data links will be needed. JTIDS presently has a UHF radio horizon of 300 nautical miles at 30,000 feet and much less for low level activity, limiting its utility at high altitude and greatly diminishing it at low altitudes. Extension of JTIDS relay capabilities using satellite communications would be highly desirable in future equipment programmes, as would an increase in the available bandwidth using data compression.[64]

THE WEST IN DANGER

The Western response to the Information Age has been chiefly characterised by rush and by excess. In the military sphere, excess throughout the Cold War has led to the near abandonment of any concept of economy of force. A mirage of false opportunities represented by Information Age concepts have led to the rapid transformation of economic and military environments to uncertain effect, and significant risks have been introduced which could and should have been avoided. The rush to computerise at any cost has led to widespread failures of software-intensive programmes across the full spectrum of civilian and military affairs. It has led to an imbalance between software offence and software defence which,

---

63. Emmett, ibid.
64. Emmett, ibid.

unless swiftly countered, will sooner rather than later be exploited by an opponent.

It is a cause for grave concern that Western society is now fully afloat upon an uncommanded digital sea in which storm conditions are increasingly predicted. The West should first demonstrate that it can successfully overcome the Year 2000 Problem (or 'Millennium Bug') before it embarks on any further large-scale information experiments. The British government's Central Computer and Telecommunications Agency has published a six volume assessment of the Year 2000 Problem.[65] Estimates suggest that up to 80% of all computers and software in use today may not cope with the date change, resulting in the temporary failure of many systems and businesses. Lacking IT personnel in the required numbers to make the changes, many companies are outsourcing the work overseas. Few verification protocols are either available or in operation to guard against malicious software.

The growing threat to the financial and economic well-being of Western society has important security and defence implications. Quite apart from its well-publicised vulnerabilities the networked infrastructure on which economic prosperity depends is increasingly capable of chaotic behaviour, such is its global presence and the uncontrolled diversity of the computer patchwork of which it is comprised.[66] A new form of civil defence is urgently required to defend the software-intensive and highly networked infrastructure on which economic and financial security now rests, but this cannot be organised as a uniquely national operation. Western armies, navies and air forces are geared to the defence of territory, but the establishment of means for defending the electronic networks on which Western prosperity increasingly depends has hardly commenced. When it comes, the defence of the information infrastructure is likely to be a three-layered operation involving the social preparedness of populations, the global management of networks and the development of software-based network defences under the aegis of SW.

If present vulnerabilities deepen, the defence (or recovery) of the civilian infrastructure may require organisation along the lines of a full-scale international military operation. Many military and civilian communication bearers are shared and expertise from one domain could be employed in supporting the defence of the other. Whatever the organisation approach it should be explicitly defensive in character. The spread of IW concepts around the globe has stoked a threat which

---

65. Tackling the Year 2000 Problem, CCTA Guide (in six volumes), HMSO, 1997.
66. Bugliarello, G, 'Telecommunications, Politics, Economics and National Sovereignty – A New Game', *Airpower Journal*, Spring 1996.

was previously minimal, while the rapid growth in Western communication networks has provided many high-value targets for rogue states and terrorists. In the clutter of 'cyberwar', 'netwar', and IW ideas, the very concept of warfare as a 'peacetime' activity has introduced a new and potentially destabilising factor into international relations. This has come at a time when the very concept of the nation-state is increasingly being called into question. These developments led Vladimir Maronenko, a senior figure in the Russian establishment, to condemn the irresponsibility of the rush to IW in the following stark warning of the dangers of a new arms race:

"The danger of unsanctioned intervention in the operations of information systems has increased abruptly...the danger of an information war breaking out is coming to the fore, and information warfare will soon rank second only to thermo-nuclear war in its consequences." [67]

Experience has shown that every 'revolution' in human affairs has brought its prophets, those of doom and destruction somewhat more frequent than those who offer future promise. At the risk of falling into the former category, the West is talking itself into an information catastrophe. Somewhere, it is assumed, there are 'experts' who have the IW experiment in hand, but baseless theorising is more in evidence than hard experience and the voices of informed caution are few. IW is not the expression of something new but the last gasp of the culture of technological excess. In this uncertain era, the practitioners of air power have a duty to defend the essential advantages of their chosen profession of arms and to adapt it swiftly to the new economy of force. With sister Services and with international allies, a programme of co-operation is urgently needed to establish joint and coalition defences for electronic networks on which they so depend. Every soundly conceived innovation must be exploited, but the Information Age will remain a time of danger for the West until the imbalance between software offence and defence is resolved.

---

67. Maronenko is Deputy Director General of the Federal Government Communications and Information Agency and is quoted here from an Itar-Tass report dated 25 July 1996.

CHAPTER 7

AIR POWER IN THE SPACE AGE
Major General W E Jones

INTRODUCTION

A GROWING AWARENESS within and outside Western defence establish-ments is that Space represents a fundamental international security commitment which will continue to grow in importance into the 21st Century. The thrust behind this commitment is pervasive. Increasingly, multi-billion dollar national and international government and commercial interests assume virtually uninhabited access and exploitation opportunities while operating in accordance with international agreements, government licensing, and accepted operating standards.

Two indicators bring this assessment into focus. Currently, over 150 countries routinely access primarily communications-based satellite data and services. Basically, there are no real sanctions to impede any nation from obtaining or using information derived from space. Therefore, trends projected by various agencies which publish global and regional historical information and forecasts, reflect a global market opportunity for the 21st Century and hedge the rate of growth as dependent on the health of the major industrial economies. The associated rate of growth in communications, the relative pricing balance between the terrestrial and space alternative markets, and the amount of government sponsored financing for the civil, commercial and military space sectors. For the immediate future the United States, Western Europe through ESA, Japan, Russia, China and India appear to be the major actors involved in capitalising space. Figure 7.1 summarises basic interests to date. Information at Figure 7.2 provides an estimate that global space is an approximate $77B industrial base employing approximately 856K people with revenues expended to capitalise space growing to $121B by the turn of the century. More importantly, information at Figure 7.3 indicates that the revenues generated from selling services in just one sector, telecommunications, represents approximately $550B in 1996 from the US alone and that the global market could be 3-4 times this figure. Although initial commercial interest lies primarily in the area of communications, there is a growing interest in remote sensing and navigation. Representative growth rates are summarised at Figure 7.4. Likewise, civil and associated scientific endeavours continue to explore opportunities for advances in exploration, environmental monitoring, medicine, basic research, and domain knowledge. Additionally, Western international security is inextricably linked to space-based indications and warning assessments of situations and trends on global and regional scales. Finally, from a near term military combat perspective, national and alliance defence operations increasingly capitalise on the high ground of space to gain and maintain terrestrial situation awareness and understanding, determine appropriate courses of action, employ military forces, and assess the impact of operations throughout the period of any crisis world-wide. At the same time, extensive access to space-derived information by potential adversaries is forcing military planners to ponder the consequences of losing the element of surprise as transparency increases.

In the aggregate, military space is evolving much like the aeroplane. In the early years of aviation, reconnaissance represented the dominant air power role. As the operational and tactical advantage of surveying from the high ground across a theatre of operations was demonstrated, self protection and air superiority became fundamental necessities. When long range aerial bombardment entered the operational inventory, a separate air component resulted. Over time, continued air power maturity fostered increasing operational roles including rapid mobility and the ability to survey and control air operations across broad **frontal** combat areas.

	Communications	Remote Sensing	Navigation	Science	Launch
US	•	•	•	•	•
ESA	•	•		•	•
JAPAN	•	•		•	•
RUSSIA/CIS	•	•	•	•	•
CHINA	•	•		•	•
INDIA	•	•		•	

*With annual spending for space in excess of $500M.

ADAPTED FROM EUROCONSULT, GOVERNMENT SPACE PROGRAMS, WORLDWIDE PROSPECTS, 1996-2006.

Figure 7.1
International Space Interests

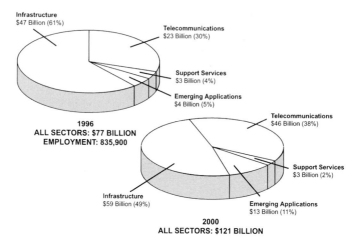

Infrastructure
$47 Billion (61%)

Telecommunications
$23 Billion (30%)

Support Services
$3 Billion (4%)

Emerging Applications
$4 Billion (5%)

1996
ALL SECTORS: $77 BILLION
EMPLOYMENT: 835,900

Telecommunications
$46 Billion (38%)

Support Services
$3 Billion (2%)

Infrastructure
$59 Billion (49%)

Emerging Applications
$13 Billion (11%)

2000
ALL SECTORS: $121 BILLION

* Adapted from: State of the Space Industry, 1997 Outlook, developed by SpaceVest,
KPMG Peat Marwick, Space Publications & Center for Wireless Communications

Figure 7.2

All Sectors: $121 billion

	1995	1996	1997	1998	1999	2000	Compound Growth
DIRECT – Fixed Transponder Services							
Transponder Leading	4300	5000	5770	6584	7505	9000	90%
Mobile Satellite Services	780	850	1450	2400	4500	8000	841%
Direct-to Homes Services	1800	2856	4600	6800	9400	12000	320%
INDIRECT – Fixed Satellite Services							
Cable Distribution [1]	8586	9273	9737	10223	10735	11271	22%
Long Distance Service-US [2]	2174	2239	2306	2375	2446	2520	13%
International Telephone [3]	2440	2538	2614	2692	2773	2856	13%

1. Represents revenue based on US carriers only. World-wide market is anticipated to be about 40% of US market figure.
2. Approximately 3% of service is due to interconnectivity between ground cable and satellites and support backup and heavy traffic periods.
3. Only includes service via US providers. Revenue for non-US connections have not been included. Based on total worldwide communications revenues of $550 Billion and using a similar percentage as US international to national revenue, the world-wide figure could represent 3-4 times this amount or higher if one considers the increased satellite utilisation rate of developing nations.

SOURCE: STATE OF THE SPACE INDUSTRY, 1997 OUTLOOK; DEVELOPED BY SPACE VEST, KPMG PEAT MARWICK,
SPACE PUBLICATIONS, & CENTRE FOR WIRELESS TELECOMMUNICATIONS.

Figure 7.3

Telecommunications Revenues ($ Millions)

Selected Industry Growth Rates 1996-2000

Mobile Telecommunications Services	800%+
Satellite Ground Stations & Hand Held Receivers	50%+
Position Location through the Global Positioning System	320%+
Remote Sensing & Geographic Information System Application	100%+

SOURCE: STATE OF THE SPACE INDUSTRY, 1997 OUTLOOK, DEVELOPED BY SPACE VEST, KPMG PEAT MARWICK, SPACE PUBLICATIONS & CENTRE FOR WIRELESS TELECOMMUNICATIONS.

Figure 7.4

Industry Growth

Space is evolving along a similar path. In the early years, Cold War intelligence-driven reconnaissance represented the dominant space role. Later, capabilities to communicate, navigate and provide remote sensing entered the inventory to enhance terrestrial operations. Space is currently at the threshold of evolving into the operational domains of self protection and superiority, including the evolution of intelligence-based reconnaissance into intrusive surveillance. The current military space discourse can be summarised as a growing awareness that western satellites can indeed be degraded or information denied. This awareness is promoting interest in providing a level of self protection which will likely become a near term priority for space systems provisioned by western alliances. Such a commitment is consistent with a long-standing priority placed on protecting terrestrial forces. At the same time, a growing discourse is associated with the necessity to provide theatre-wide and even global reconnaissance and surveillance as air power returns to its core operational competencies centred around long range and precise application of force. For space superiority and other combatant roles, political consensus and a generally accepted military vision of the future remain primary impediments to the pace of expanded military space evolution.

In the political domain, the overarching premise of non-militarised space for combat continues to dominate the international security debate. The NATO and US experience with the Strategic Defence Initiative offers a graphic example. Since space has yet to be weaponised, air power theorists have chosen not to deal seriously with the implications of conducting military operations in space or to terrestrial centres of power from space. Moreover, the evolution of air power theory to embody space warfare has largely been ignored. The resulting incremental approach to dealing with the evolving fourth dimension of warfare is placing air power on the same course as the land army's addressal of air forces through the 1940s. At the point when political consensus is realised to weaponise

199

space, based either on the emergence of a compelling military threat or to deny the impact of adversary space forces to allied international security interests, the same debate that resulted in establishing a separate air power component may be inevitable.

Finally, it is important to recognise that this paper attempts to offer a basis upon which to expand the traditional institutional level dialogue surrounding air power – a dialogue which tends to focus on posturing for execution in supporting and supported terrestrial operational roles in an uncertain future and is currently dealing with the definition and implementation of Information Warfare and even Dominance. The overarching premise of this paper is that air power is being drawn into an expanding international security situation which includes space. From all current indications, this expansion will occur incrementally. In the near term, integration and control of information from space into weapon and weapon systems will represent the institutional priorities. Later, political impera-tives to protect the major international investments and financial interests in space and deal with a yet to materialise compelling military threat may result in the weaponisation of space. Therefore, air power in the Space Age projects into an approximate 20 year horizon in which space has yet to be weaponised, but the dependency on space forces in combat support roles has increased exponentially.

TRENDS IN SPACE

As air power theorists begin to consider the appropriate role of space within or outside the institutional framework, forecast capabilities are summarised below that will likely be resident in a Combat Support role early in the 21st Century and available to support Combat roles in Space as political and military imperatives evolve over time.

SPACE SUPPORT OPERATIONS

COMMUNICATIONS

Aerospace America forecasts a 961 commercial/civil communication satellite inventory by 2005, see Figure 7.5. The market opportunity of wireless informa-tion exchange, nationally and internationally, has become widely recognised with substantial inventory and capacity forecast within the next decade. With this inventory, virtually every facet of modern society, including military activities and

	Broadband	Data Relay	Direct Broadcast	Mobile	Telecommunications
US	63	3	17	448	12
ESA		3			
EUROPE			3	6	4
JAPAN		2	2		2
RUSSIA			5	140	6
RUSSIA/CANADA				5	
CHINA			3		4
CHINA/RUSSIA				2	
SINGAPORE					1
SINGAPORE/CHINA			2		
FRANCE	60				1
GERMANY				5	1
MEXICO				12	
BRAZIL			1		2
BRAZIL/US				54	
BRAZIL/FRANCE					3
NORWAY				4	
BELGIUM				4	
ITALY		7	1		2
LUXEMBOURG			4		
SWEDEN			2		
HUNGARY			1		
AUSTRALIA				6	1
ARGENTINEAN			1		
SOUTH KOREA					3
GREECE					1
UAE				1	
EGYPT			1		
INDIA			4	2	2
PAKISTAN					1
ISRAEL			1		
IRAN					2
INDONESIA			4		2
IND/PHILIP/THAI				2	
THAILAND/LAOS			2		
THAILAND					1
PHILIPPINES					3
TAIWAN			2		
MALAYSIA			1		
VIETNAM					1
INTERNATIONAL			1	14	3
MIDDLE EAST			1		

ADAPTED FROM AIAA PROPOSED COMMUNICATIONS SATELLITES WORLDWIDE: 1977-2005.

Figure 7.5
Civil/Commercial Communications Satellites

operations, will be seen, heard, manipulated and distributed. Services provided include Broadband capacity for high-speed voice, data, and video; Data Relay for data, voice and navigation; Direct Broadcast for TV, radio, data and networking; Mobile communications for voice, data, messaging, position determination and video; and Telecommunications for voice, TV, radio, data and networks.

In a national or international security role, satellite communications are fundamental to military operations. Intelligence gathering and dissemination; conferencing; information query and exchange; force and resource status and replenishment needs; deployment; mission planning, tasking and rehearsal; employment; and mission assessment are all enabled through satellite connectivity and will be increasingly so in the years ahead. The essential nature of military operations requires flexibility and on demand response (given the uncertainty in time and location of military commitments), encryption, anti-jam, low probability of intercept and detection, and survivability features for satellites and supporting terrestrial infrastructure.

In the early 21st Century, two levels of satellite telecommunications appear to be emerging. A limited number of systems, owned and operated by the military, will continue to service the need for highly protected and assured connectivity. The continued evolution of legacy systems should fill this need. However, the majority of operational throughput and secure telecommunications needs will likely be provided by commercial or commercial-based systems. As the commercial market place is increasingly driven to provide secure, tamper-resistant and interoperable capacity to meet the demands of the national and international market place, the military can capitalise on the opportunity to conduct information exchange with significantly fewer and less complex organic resources.

REMOTE SENSING

The conventional view on this subject is that remote sensing from space is the exploitation of the electromagnetic spectrum to reflect, radiate, refract or scatter to determine the state of the terrestrial domain. Basically it is a means to sense the earth's surface and air below without regard to boundary, sunlight, weather and, in some cases, foliage or soil characterises this portion of space operations. National security, science, agriculture, forestry, real estate, geology, environmental, and law enforcement are among the interests involved. A broader view of this area embodies the ability to survey and determine the status and operational profile of satellites or other objects in or transiting space.

On an international scale, a number of countries are forecast to possess the ability to sense and assess the terrestrial and space domains in the early part of 21st Century. From a terrestrial perspective, Figure 7.6 summarises the countries and anticipated ability to image in the early 21st Century. Representative types of information available and operation utility are summarised in Figure 7.7. This

COUNTRY	HIGHEST RESOLUTION (M)*			FUTURE
	Panchromatic	Multispectral	SAR	
USA	1-30	4-30		1M Pan, 1 Multspec
RUSSIA	2-4	2.5-4		5-40M SAR
FRANCE	5-10	10-20		
INDIA	6	23-36.25		
EUROPEAN COMMUNITY			30	
ISRAEL	1-2			
JAPAN		18.3	18	
CANADA			10	
CHINA & BRAZIL		20		

*Does not include any classified capabilities possessed by any country.
ADAPTED FROM KPMG REPORT, THE REMOTE SENSING INDUSTRY, JUNE 1996.

Figure 7.6
Commercial International Remote Imaging

information is but one indication of the information which will be increasingly available in the international community in the near future. On a broader scale, the ability to obtain and fuse information from a variety of sources has provided the impetus for highly specialized disciplines such as Measurements and Signature Intelligence or MASINT. In the current US MASINT Information Sheet, this activity is described as collecting information from a variety of sources, i.e. '... radar, laser, optical, infrared, acoustic, nuclear radiation, radio frequency, spectroradiometric, and seismic sensing systems as well as gas, liquid, and solid materials sampling and analysis.' In military applications, MASINT target signatures are then converted into threat recognition and identification profiles that support mission planning, I&W, TW/AA, TMD, SAR, strike operations, non-co-operative target identification, and space control. Additionally, the potential to obtain rapid reconnaissance, provide virtual real time surveillance of any terrestrial area, fusion information for battlespace understanding, and command and control air power globally and discretely across an entire theatre of operations is

APPLICATIONS	OBSERVABLES
Mapping, Charting and Geodesy	
Image Mapping	Vegetation, Geolocation control points
Terrain Characterisation	Soil, moisture, Vegetation, Topography, Steams, Land covering
Feature Extraction	Ground LOCs, Wetlands, Airfields, Water, Land cover
Elevation	Land surface altitude
Area Search	Terrain and cultural features changes
Strategic Industry and Resource Monitoring	
Exploration/mining	Liquid and material quantification, Cratology, storage tanks, LOCs buildings
Facilities	Tanks, Bladders, Berms, LOCs, Drill rigs
Material Processing	Ground scarring, Land clearing, LOCs
Seaport Usage	Vessels, Storage, Containers, Dredging
Power Supply	Hot objects, Effluent, Cooling towers, Boilers
Underground facilities	Tailings and waste, Thermal, exhaust vents
CW/BW production	Raw materials, Waste, Cratology, Energy use, Storage
Contingency Planning	
Trafficability	LOCs, Obstacles, Terrain, Drainage, Soil Moisture, Water depth
Landing/Drop zones	Cleared areas, Soil, Vegetation, Trees, Rocks
Amphibious	Beach Composition, Tide Marks, Vegetation, Berms, Wetlands, Soil/Sand
Airfield Analysis	Runways, Taxiways, Ramps, Revetments, POL, Berms, Hangers
NEO	Airfields, Ports, Harbours, LOCs, Heliports
Mission Planning and Operations	
Area orientation/Mission rehearsal	Terrain, LOCs, Waterways
Operations planning	Target analysis
Mission Assessment	BDS (Fire, Smoke, Craters, Scarring, Debris)
Theatre Surveillance	CC&D, Military units, Track activity, Bases, Logistics facilities, Terrain, LOCs
Naval OB	CC&D, LOC usage, Buoys, Platforms, Construction, Water depth
Land OB	CC&D, Field of Fire, Topography, Vegetation, Mine fields, Cratology, Trenches, Berms, Water, Trackage patterns CW/BW
Air OB	CC&D, Thermal, Bases/Runways, Construction, Radar units, Aircraft
Missile OB	CC&D, TELs, Track/Vehicle activity, Terrain, Rail
CW/BW OB	Component ID, Soil Foliage, Decontamination
Treaty Monitoring	
START	CC&D, Land Scarring, Underground facilities, Silo construction, Trafficability, Boat type, Thermometry, Assembly plants
CW/BW	LOCs, Chemical/Waste Storage, Test Grids
CFE	Tanks, Artillery, Planes, Missiles, Area Delimitation
Environmental	Chemical spills, Erosion, Vegetation, Oil Slicks
Nuclear Weapons Proliferation	
Monitoring	Storage Sites, Thermal reactors, testing signatures

Figure 7.7

now on the planning horizon. Likewise, the ability to survey and control activities transiting space or in space is in this same planning window. However, the West has accrued no exclusive licence to this horizon. Unless measures are implemented to deny or constrain future adversaries from exploiting this same type of information and control capabilities in time of crisis, allied deployments, order of battle and combat operations could be compromised.

NAVIGATION

Precision navigation and timing is now a fact of life in the international security and domestic communities. The US Global Positioning System and Russian GLONASS Applications of precision are pervasive and make precise air operations a current and growing reality. In the future, the West may simply not be able to control access to precision prior to entering into situations involving the use of force. Western commercial ventures are already authorised to provide high precision and global access at market driven pricing. Extensive satellite based access is forecast by the early 21st Century.

Given the international security implications of precision to enhance as well as degrade allied military operations, government sponsored activities will continue to focus on ensuring higher precision access, even in disturbed/jamming environments, through capabilities such as GPS while denying or degrading access to adversaries during times of crisis.

SPACE COMBAT OPERATIONS

The means to attain and sustain space superiority or to employ military forces against terrestrial centres of power is now a question of political will, military cultural acceptance, and priority. Kinetic, laser, high power micro-wave and numerous other weapon system options are feasible, near term alternatives to be deployed either in space or as terrestrial systems to ensure space superiority and neutralize weapons transiting space, such as ballistic missiles. Before any system alternative is actually pursued, debris will most certainly become a consideration. In a significantly reduced gravity environment, surgical weapons with limited or no debris effects appear to offer distinct advantages, but at the same time place stringent demands on weapons systems. Additionally, hyper-velocity munitions, REVs, lasers and a host of other options can also be developed to engage high priority terrestrial centres of power.

There also appears to be renewed interest in pursuing a military Space Plane currently termed as a Space Maneouvre Vehicle. A capacity to access space or transit space to a terrestrial centre of power offers definite unique advantages. From a space or terrestrial perspective, combat options to posture and execute a weapon in space or against terrestrial centres of power can be held in a terrestrial sanctuary until required to achieve a security objective. Such an option allows western alliances to possess a capacity to employ military force quickly, avoid tactical surprise of coercion by future adversaries, engage politically during pending crisis, and maintain a weapons free space during a period of relative peace.

At this juncture, it is difficult to forecast the events that will lead to the weaponisation of space. However, the need to counter high precision, ballistic and cruise missiles, with ever increasing range, remains a necessity which could reasonably become compelling at some point in the 21st Century if western alliances become significantly threatened-politically and militarily.

Since the end of WWII, the Western containment policy and deterrent strategy manifest primarily in a Eurocentric forward defence security framework, coupled with the political imperative to retain a weapons-free space domain, foreclosed expanded space alternatives, other than 'enhancing' terrestrial operations. The failed attempt to deploy a primarily space-based system to counter Soviet Union ballistic missiles targeted at NATO (including the US) brought into the public domain the choice between accepting the risk of western survival if MAD/deterrence failed versus pursuing active defences, including the weaponisation of space. The collapse of the Soviet Union and resulting phased demobilisation of both the East and West, including nuclear weapons, temporarily lessened the intensity of the political debate and associated military imperative to continue. However, the Gulf War experience and the continued global proliferation of weapons of mass destruction and ballistic missiles with increasing precision and range result in recent renewed focus to seek some level of terrestrial-based defences. In such an environment, air power alternatives have been constrained to terrestrial pre-, early boost- or post-phase interdiction. The classic Air Interdiction role represents the current air power commitment with the planned Airborne Laser providing an expanded capacity for early boost phase operations within a decade against ballistic missiles. Cruise missiles, especially those with low signatures, remain a significant challenge.

Given the near term western focus on ballistic missiles, as these weapons of potential mass destruction continue to proliferate, the resulting threat could possibly provide the leverage to bridge the political debate to interdict, with high probability, weapons entering or transiting space with space based alternatives. If the proliferated threat becomes compelling, alternatives other than terminal defences with associated fallout of employment/destruction occurring over defended territory, will likely receive serious consideration and space could become weaponised as a perceived to be necessary defensive-based measure. However, there is no current indication that this political threshold is actually approaching.

Additionally, if such a capacity is pursued, the means to attain rapidly space superiority will also be available as an extension of the capacity to ensure the integrity of the western military posture and maintain geo-political advantage. From purely a military perspective, interdicting a satellite or other object in space at low or medium altitudes represents a much simpler military task than sorting and neutralising actual ballistic missile re-entry, within a relatively short operational time profile.

Once space is weaponised for defence, other roles may logically follow. The ability to interdict terrestrial centres of power from space will likely be developed when military planners can ensure some reasonable level of space superiority to virtually foreclose the interdiction opportunity to potential adversaries. As mentioned earlier, the asymmetrical advantage of employing precision firepower at the discretion of western alliances as a show of force, or to achieve a political objective at the moment of maximum leverage cannot be overstated. However, there is no indication that the political threshold to weaponise space is approaching. A political and military imperative has yet to materialise.

MILITARY IMPLICATIONS

Against this background, in recent years the military establishments are beginning to consider appropriate space roles and responsibilities relative to exploitation and, to some limited degree, the protection of security interests. At this juncture surface combatants generally view space as a means to provide additional information for potential or evolving crisis areas. There is also growing interest in integrating space-derived information into weapons and weapon systems to expand the operational envelope of air, sea and land forces and execute precision operations. Additional interest has recently been spawned by ballistic missile defence, since no component to date assumes sole responsibility for any current or future warfighting role, except sub-surface naval operations. Air forces, currently tasked – in the US – with the primary responsibility of capitalising military space, have somewhat de facto assumed the role of establishing doctrine, influencing command relationships, and planning. To date, all of the military services assume space forces will operate in a supporting role as additional force structure to assist in achieving terrestrial-based political objectives. However, at the point when the West approaches the threshold of protecting expanding international security interest in space and even weaponsing the ultimate high ground, the realisation that space will become a supported theatre of operations in which lethal measures can, in fact, be taken as a politically acceptable option cannot be avoided.

From an air power perspective, the emergence of combatant operations in space can logically evolve along one of two paths. In the first model, space is treated as a separate warfighting domain. The unique nature of space, the global influence, span of control and multi-dimensional utility of space forces, and the direct linkage of interests in space to national and international command authority decision-making dictate establishing a separate service. In the second model, space becomes integrated as a basic extension of air power theory, doctrine, planning and operations. Basically, space to an airmen becomes a logical extension of air power.

An overarching premise that airmen should consider when evaluating the pros and cons of either path, is that the degree to which air power is relevant in the 21st Century will likely be based on the protection of the full spectrum of interests that determine the economic and social well-being of a nation or alliance. Space now, and increasingly so in the future, represents a fundamental interest that must be protected. It is therefore, the second path of integration that air power theorists should promote.

If approached from the integrated model, air and space become a continuum which will dictate a somewhat different question and answer to space-related issues.

- From an airman's *operational* perspective, there is no fundamental demarcation between air and space.
- The basic tenets of air power theory, doctrine and strategy apply.
- The basic goals of warfare systems provisioned by airmen remain: reach anywhere, quick reaction, rapid and decisive impact, and survival.
- Operationally, space forces can be executed in a separate, dedicated organisation to prosecute command and control. Space forces will operate simultaneously in supported/combatant and supporting/force enhancement operational roles. Much like mobility forces, space operations simultaneously influence terrestrial operations in multiple theatres around the globe and in space which requires a separate activity to plan and employ.
- Decisive operations in air and space are now required to achieve a political objective through the use of military force. Victory in air and space are inextricably linked.

It is also essential to note that basically the same considerations that apply to provisioning terrestrial air forces, apply to space. The implications of stealth/low observables, concealment and deception, Information Warfare, attrition, fratricide, etc, all apply. The implications of the unknown if stealth/low observables and concealment are deployed for space forces involve virtual instantaneous impact at the time of employment. However, in the broadest context, regardless of where these measures are applied, i.e. space, aircraft, UAVs, cruise missiles or surface forces, the type of impact is basically the same. If the opponent is not aware of intent or presence until the time of execution or impact, significant leverage is a definite potential. The higher leverage of space involves omni-presence and the ability to respond rapidly. Therefore, planning for space needs to include physical protection, measures to-determine mission profiles of on-orbit objects, detection and protection against unauthorised intrusion as counter IW measures, and means to replenish rapidly if space forces are destroyed.

An additional consideration that is certain to confound military planners as space dependence continues to grow, is the impact of civil, commercial, and military interests operating in the continuum of space. Orbits and geography are as one with all three interests in proximity. During periods of crisis, airspace control means will, by necessity, need to accommodate situations in which international consortia place intense pressure on national command authorities to ensure uninterrupted operations. From a business perspective, billions of investment dollars and revenue will not be viewed otherwise. In such an environment, considerations of space denial as a viable operational objective become foreclosed. Therefore, capabilities that limit, preclude fratricide or impose controlled deniability of disruption, will assume increased priority to deal with this growing reality.

FORCE STRUCTURE PLANNING

As space continues to evolve in both combat and combat support capabilities, the character of air power will inevitably change.

SPACE SUPPORT OPERATIONS

With an institutional vision to conduct decisive military operations across an entire theatre of operations and in space, the need for a pervasive surveillance and control capacity will be recognised and pursued (a general assessment of alternatives is at Figure 7.8). Assuming current trends continue, within a relatively

Characteristics	Satellites	Aircraft	UAVs	Ground Ops
Area of Influence	Global	Limited	Limited	Limited
Employment Opportunity	Unrestricted	Threat & Overflight Right Dependent	Limited Threat Overflight Right Dependent	Threat & Basing Right Independent
Forward Mobility	Limited – C3[2]	Substantial[2]	Moderate[2]	Moderate[2]
C3 Capacity Required	Substantial	Moderate	Limited	Limited to Substantial
Personnel	Moderate	Substantial	Moderate	Limited to Substantial
Cost	Low to High[3]	High	Low	Low to Moderate

1. Line of sight to the Horizon, either Intermittent or Continuous based on Force Structure.
2. Basing, Maintenance, and Logistics
3. Based on mission – Limited area (High) versus Global (Low)

Figure 7.9
Enduring Realities

short period, space will become the defining domain to provision reconnaissance, surveillance and control of broad areas in space and across terrestrial areas while providing discrimination and targeting for precision operations. For terrestrial operations, augmentation with ever decreasing levels of legacy aircraft, UAVs, and ground elements will fill the gap in capacity not provided from space. With such a capacity, coalition air, land and sea components may conduct decisive operations while deploying and sustaining far less mobility and sustainment forces and infrastructure than currently planned. Also, the opportunity to divest major segments of marginal utility, narrowly focused frontal capabilities such as ground based radars, UAVs, and aircraft may become apparent. Theatre wide, global, and space international security interests, Joint/Coalition imperatives, operational cohesion, resource realities, mobility constraints, forward sustainment, and investment efficiencies/priorities/opportunities will all weigh heavily and promote a sustained evolution into a more heavily weighted space commitment. The perspective offered for consideration, is that the resources simply are not currently available and will likely be less so in the future to provision for comprehensive layers of ISR forces. A basic planning pre-requisite to maximise the highest pay-off medium and supplement where necessary provides a basis to achieve the desired outcome with substantially less investment, but more importantly, with far fewer personnel at risk during combat.

As basic space technologies continue to mature and compete favourably to replace terrestrial alternatives, the operational features that must receive increasing focus include connectivity to in-theatre forces, information fusion, and information cycle times to ensure that space support forces operate inside the operational tempo of allied combat elements and well inside the operational tempo of any opponent. Currently, GPS is considered the only space system that enhances the operational tempo. With the planned enhancements to counter hostile actions, restrict access, and provide improved accuracy, this Space weapons system that arguably introduced precision into military operations will increasingly grow in utility and ubiquity. In so doing, it will continue to pioneer the interdependency between Space and terrestrial forces.

Additionally, as western terrestrial forces continue to be down-sized (in an international security environment without a compelling military threat), and increasingly dependent on rapid and decisive operations, the air component must attempt to dominate the information domain. By concentrating on focused and fused information flow, proper influence can be exerted on the development of space and other capabilities that can be directly integrated into theatre level operations. At the same time, the geographic location of information processing elements (from satellites or any other source) will become less important than efficient, assured, and mission responsive integration. The very nature of the space support functions – reconnaissance, surveillance, navigation, remote sensing, telecommunications (each involved with the direct real time control and execution of combat forces) – become the discriminators needed by senior commanders. Combat support information processing elements are postured and sustained within or in proximity to the forward combat theatre, with fused information distributed to appropriate operational and tactical echelons.

As the interdependency between Space and terrestrial operations continues to grow, equal focus will be given to the protection and capacity to sustain space operations. In the post-Cold War era, space became viewed as somewhat 'sacrosanct' regarding counter military operations in the minds of many senior decision-markers. In reality, space forces are no different in this regard from terrestrial forces. Lethal and non-lethal measures, including Information Warfare, can be taken to destroy or degrade space forces to a degree similar to those of terrestrial forces. Although an increased level of difficulty is incurred to execute such operations against space forces, denying asymmetrical advantages will logically dictate that such measures be planned and fielded by future adversaries. Given the lead time to replace/enhance space forces in peace time as reliability continues to increase, measures will need to be implemented early in the planning and provisioning process to ensure operational availability when needed.

SPACE COMBAT OPERATIONS

The traditional debate surrounding Space Combat Operations represents a more contentious subject and includes the two dimensions: attaining and sustaining space superiority; and employing weapons from space against terrestrial targets. Addressing first the question of space defence/superiority, it is unlikely that a single component will ever possess the directed role, responsibility, resources, and political consensus to carry out provisioning and combat operations to defend space. The entire history of western military experience argues that this is true. The defence role can be viewed much like Theatre Air Defence. If the defence/space superiority portion of Space Combat Operations is considered from a premise of international importance and approached from a joint/coalition perspective, legitimate roles become more clear. Specifically, as air power theorists approach the defence of space, they must take into consideration that lethal combat forces executed from land or sea for ballistic missile defence can also serve in a Space Combat Operations role (commonly termed ASAT) and become a responsibility of the Army and the Navy. The navy component can also contribute the ability to deny access to space by positioning capabilities such as AEGIS Cruisers at strategic locations in international waters. When inserting payloads into space, regardless of the inclination chosen from any specific location, transiting objects are subject to interdiction. For the Air Force, air and in space forces employed as an extension of the traditional air superiority role become – defacto – an extension of air power. Finally, each component involved in operations to neutralise adversary capabilities, such as command centres, ground processing stations, and space launch complexes will contribute to ensuring space is exploited primarily by allied forces.

When considering weapons from space – the second part of Space Combat Operations, the basic determination can be reached that this role is an extension of Air Interdiction. As such, the Air Force can be viewed as the logical component to supply and employ space forces in support of joint operations. Figure 7.9 provides a summary of the evolving component roles.

There is also one additional aspect of combat operations that warrants discussion as space dependency evolves. This aspect involves the degree to which dependency on off-board sources impacts upon the provisioning of weapon systems that penetrate to execute a combat role. Implied, but rarely debated, is that off-board dependency equates to significant reductions in internal capacity for combat aircraft. The premise offered is that off-board sources provide the capacity to **expand** the operational envelope and that tactical aviation sent into

Army	Navy	Air Force
BMD	**BMD**	**BMD**
Mid-Course, Terminal	Mid-Course, Terminal	Mid-Course, Terminal
Space Combat OPS	**Space Combat Ops**	**Space Combat Ops**
DEF – Ground-Based	DEF – Sea-Based	DEF – Air- and Sea-Based
OFF – Ground-Based	OFF – Sea-Based	OFF – Air- and Sea-Based
Non-Lethal I/O Ops	**Non-Lethal I/O Ops**	**Non-Lethal I/O Ops**
Land Component	Sea Component	Air and Space
Influence	Influence	Component Influence
		Force Application from Space

Figure 7.9
Recommended Roles

'harm's way' simply must continue to possess the internal organic capacity to survive and execute significant operational missions.

Without question, off-board derived and real time information offers the opportunity to conduct higher probability ingress and egress operations; re-target and route plan; and contribute to theatre-wide situational awareness. Doctrine needs to evolve and tactics need to be revised accordingly to expand the operational envelope as the quality of off-board information continues to improve. However, off-board information denial simply must not equate to mission failure for air power. In the final analysis, history, command authorities and the public forum will continue to judge airmen based on the role air power actually plays in achieving a political objective.

Before offering some final thoughts about the institutional considerations facing Western air forces, the chapter considers force structure planning for space-based investment. In the final analysis, the pace at which space matures within Western military air forces will be directly related to the pace of investment. The argument that space represents a fundamental security interest might play well in academic circles, but unless decisions are made to capitalise the end objective, status quo will continue. The premise offered to guide such deliberations is that real investment must be tied to real opportunity. In this vein opportunity is bounded by political reality.

Pragmatically, an argument that space should be capitalised across the board as a fundamental military imperative is interesting, but unlikely to achieve institutional, much less international level attention and consensus. However, leading edge technology promoted as a hedge against evolving threats and even the weaponisation of space to protect fundamental security interests, represents legitimate options and ones against which limited resources have traditionally been allocated. The combatant side of space represents the real near and mid-term reality for Western air forces.

In planning the force posture for the next $10 - 15$ years, space has matured to the point of representing an alternative, not simply an enhancement option, when force structure opportunities are debated. At this juncture, there are several opportunities for expanded space operations. As mentioned earlier, the most fundamental shift involves the transition of reconnaissance and narrowly focused frontal surveillance activities to theatre-wide and even global surveillance. Within western military forces, dependence on large airframes to transport remote sensing and communications devices are reaching a point of becoming financial and operational liabilities as Air Vice-Marshal Professor Mason hints at in Chapter Five. As contingency operations and resource allocation deliberations have demonstrated, these systems are inordinately expensive to develop and field; difficult to mobilise, deploy and sustain; require special care and investment during employment; and provide utility in only limited operational areas.

If the problem of force posturing and resource allocation is addressed in the planning process, windows for change can be defined. For example, airframes at definable points in the aircraft flying hour programme one must receive major sustainment investment, commonly termed Service Lift Extension Programme (SLEP), to remain airworthy. Engine replacements, reskinning, structural integrity upgrades are among the type of investments involved. A planning process injected into the resource allocation deliberations, offers the opportunity to transition from large airframe dependency to legitimate space alternatives, as space demonstrates potential to achieve greater operational utility with fewer expended resources. Such a process also provides the basis for near term investment in space, including survivability measures to offset forecast threats that also impact terrestrial forces-lasers, jamming, IW, etc – and ensure availability within the periods of traditional major investments such as SLEP. Perhaps such considerations can only occur within an institution in which air and space are considered a continuum.

Another opportunity involves inter-agency co-operation which has the unfortunate legacy of a somewhat tainted history. Within the civil sector there is a continuing interest in developing the next version of reusable access to Space and is manifest in programs such as the US NASA – sponsored X-33. Such a development affords the opportunity for the military to capitalise on a civilian based initiative to develop the leading edge technology for a space vehicle with the production potentially phased as part of an integrated derivative. A much broader national and international consensus should result to satisfy the military need with much less expenditure.

In the aggregate, a *'going it alone'* approach for the US with an internal institutional focus is the least likely path to achieve the required level of national and international influence and resulting force posture required for the 21st Century. Western air forces are at the point of addressing the need for a much broader perspective when dealing with the reality of capitalising space while retaining legacy force postures during periods of transition. At the same time, increased inter-agency co-operation is now an imperative. At least now common interests are definable.

FINAL THOUGHTS

The growing importance of space notwithstanding, as the western international military establishments begins to debate and assess the proper role of space, the relative balance between space and terrestrial operations, may be determined in the short term by the degree of self-sufficiency retained in traditional service terrestrial components versus dependence – space activities within components, various intelligence organisations, the commercial/civil sector, host nations/alliances, etc. Throughout the 20th Century, each of the military components air, land and sea – postured forces based on institutional self-sufficiency and, to some degree, alliance interoperability. Until the 90s, the institutional underpinning of self-sufficiency represented the core of all service component force structure planning and provisioning. By any measure, this orientation served western alliances well based on the results of 2 world wars, the Cold War, and numerous regional contingencies and peacekeeping operations. However, the end of the Cold War, associated western alliance demobilisation, recent operational experience in the Gulf War and Bosnia, and funding reductions for the military have prompted an increased level of service/component interdependency. The current force planning discourse can now be characterised as 'Joint/Coalition' with interdependency a fundamental prerequisite in force posturing decision making. See Chapter 3 by Group Captain Peach for a discussion on coalition operations. Such a dynamic presents an opportunity for accommodating a broader view about the evolving role of space in planning future military force postures.

For the air component, extending self-sufficiency versus interdependence considerations to space can logically be based on the extent to which air power is postured to fight both in-contact and near operations set against the theatre-wide campaign. If air power continues to be postured as primarily an extension of the land campaign and employed to enable surface manoeuvre and sequential attrition warfare, limited justification exists for it to evolve except in the fields of precision and lethality. However, within western alliances there is every indication that air power theory (to the extent that relevant theory exists for the 21st Century) and planning – especially in the USA – appear to be returning to a basic orientation of long range, theatre and even global influence. Since an Air and Space Power, Aerospace, or Space Power theory has yet to emerge, the evolution of space in the context of air power continues along a piecemeal path. In the 21st Century, the extent to which the air component provisions combat support operations to executive an organic theatre ability to provide intelligence, telecommunications, surveillance, weather, precision navigation and the associated information packages for battlespace understanding, terrain analysis, targeting, ingress/egress operations, and post strike assessment is now a fundamental challenge.

The reality faced by air power theorists and military planners is that the basic laws of physics, military threat and sheer magnitude of force structure required for the theatre and global tasks essentially foreclose continued reliance on terrestrial alternatives for ranging, surveying and controlling operations requiring extensive depth and breadth – the very essence of air power. Additionally, available technology is no longer a limiting factor. Self-sufficiency, although a laudable objective may no longer be achievable. Over time, the considerations may broaden and may become the appropriate combat role for space to ensure domain superiority and interdict terrestrial centres of power. Legitimate choices are now on the planning horizon.

The basic dilemma faced by air power theorists, but largely unstated, is the degree to which increasing combat support roles and combat capabilities transition to space under the current rubric of '... space as an extension of air power'. The reality is that as space continues to evolve the migration of certain traditional surface and air capabilities to space is a distinct possibility with the resulting space component organised in a separate joint/coalition arrangement in a supported/supporting role.

There is also a practical consideration facing Western air forces that intend to engage in the space domain. To the extent that space forces become institutionalised within the air component, airmen must become conversant with the credibility and limitations of these supporting forces. Space, in a Combat Support role, will soon become the dominant component to provide the information that will, without question, significantly impact and even determine the course of events in combat or related roles. Training, doctrine, and unit integration are as fundamental in this regard as any current or planned air combat or combat support element. At the same time, the same basic principles that apply to training, organising and equipping terrestrial air elements must also apply to space. Coherent employment of air power will simply not occur otherwise.

CONCLUSION

Arguably, no single chapter can adequately address the compendium of cultural and operational issues associated with the evolving role of Space and its impact on the western international security posture. However, a stark reality faced by airmen is that Space has matured to the point of representing a legitimate alternative, not simply an additive force. Given this reality, the time to develop seriously the proper role of Space in the context of air power has arrived. If this chapter serves only to expand the discussion, then it has served a useful purpose.

As we look to the immediate future, Space represents a fundamental and increasingly important national security commitment for the 21st Century and beyond. Economic, civil, military and international interests are involved. Given the international security implications of continued space exploitation, it is only logical to assume that military operations will continue to expand and that space warfare will become reality in the 21st Century.

The perspective of this chapter is that the degree to which air forces remain relevant in the 21st Century may be determined based largely on the protection of the full spectrum of interests that determine the economic and social well-being of a nation. It is, therefore, imperative that air power theory be revised to integrate Space as a continuum of air operations. Setting such a course will require a fundamental revision of the long-standing tenets which have underwritten the provisioning and execution of air forces since the 1940s.

To this point, Western air forces have yet to seriously deal with the implications of dependency on non-assigned forces (i.e. Space) and divesting the premise of self-contained operations which has served air power well since the end of WWII. As air power returns to its basic role of theatre-wide and even global/space domain influence, capabilities with limited range and scope of influence will become of increasingly limited value. When surveillance and control capabilities transition to Space – air mobility, flexibility and sustainability will increase as less infrastructure is required in forward theatres. Also, with significantly less people engaged in forward combat areas, the utility of air power will continue to increase and become the instrument of choice to resolve conflicts and protect Western security interests. In the final analysis:

> *'Victory smiles upon those who anticipate the changes in the character of war,*
> *not upon those who wait to adapt themselves after the changes occur'*
>
> Guilo Douhet

CHAPTER 8

AIR OPERATIONS AND AIR LOGISTICS
'FIGHTING AND STUFF'
Wing Commander D J Foster

"I git thar fustest with the mostest men" [1]   *Lieutenant General Nathan Bedford Forrest*

INTRODUCTION

TO WIN IN BATTLE we must concentrate combat power in time and space. Strategy and tactics define the questions of what time and what place; but these are the ends, not the means. The means of victory is **concentration**, and that process is the focus of this. There are only four key factors to think about if we seek success in concentration. Thinking about these factors is not a simple task. For although few in number, their impact, dynamics and interdependencies are hard to grasp. This is a problem as much of perspective as of substance. It concerns the way we think, as much as what we are looking at. The factors are not functions, or objects, or even processes. They are best thought of as conditions representing the nature of what we are dealing with in seeking concentration; they are:

Variability – Uncertainty – Synchronicity – Complexity

In this analysis we take a systems view of the world to look at basic concepts, to arrive at a way of looking at things, rather than to present a set of answers. The ideas are fuzzy, so we use simple words and pictures. Simple words like "***stuff***". This means fuel, and spares... bullets, bombs and missiles... tools, machines, power and water... food, maps and toilet paper... and anything else we need to keep us in the fight. The use of simple language is not a trivialisation; it forces us to focus on essentials. One of the problems we face is the way we think. Here we attempt to look at things from a new angle, to break out of the old frame of reference, to think out of the box, to reflect on the basics.

In the widest sense of the term, which is how we will use it, logistics is the crucial enabler for all operations including air power. However, logistics on its

---

1. Widely used misquote of : "I always make it a rule to get there first with the most men".

own is not worth talking about. It is not independent. It exists only as one half of a partnership that governs the success or failure of concentration. The aim of this Chapter is to develop a simple, holistic description of the partnership of operations and logistics, of the dynamics of what General Forrest might have called "*fightin n'stuff*", to provide a perspective for effective thought and action.

First the Chapter explores the fundamental nature of the partnership. We start at the point where operations and logistics meet, then step down into the world of stuff to take a look at what happens there. Once we have a picture of the basic mechanics of logistics we move on to look at what links activity in the world of operations to work in the world of stuff. This perspective is used to examine how the particular nature of a military force governs the way things happen in practice. Here we look at the differences and similarities in the structure and dynamics of the partnership in the separate cases of land, maritime and air power, to determine how the partnership works. In conclusion we offer a view of what really matters in managing the partnership to achieve our goal of effective concentration of air power.

Why is understanding this so important? Logistics governs the tempo and power of operations. For us, and for our enemy. We have to think about the partnership of operations and logistics because it is a target. A target for us, and for our enemy. Like any target, we need to understand its importance, vulnerabilities and critical elements to make sure we know what to defend, and what to attack. All military commanders, at all levels of command, rely on the success of this partnership. How well they understand it will make a big difference to how well it works for them, and how well they work for it.

> **"A *real knowledge* of supply and movement factors must be the basis of every leader's plan; only then can he know how and when to take risks with those factors, and battles are won only by taking risks."**
>
> *Field Marshal A C P Wavell*

Real knowledge in this context is *deep* knowledge, not simply how long it takes a force to move from A to B, or the numbers of weapons needed to take on a particular enemy strength; but an understanding of the likely behaviour and response of the logistics system, in the face of the real demands, of real operations, as they develop and as they are executed. So this is a tale of two systems, and how they work together as one : operations and logistics – "fightin n'stuff".

PART ONE

THE NATURE OF FIGHTIN N' STUFF

Operations and logistics sit alongside each other; they overlap (Figure 8.1). Imagine the overlap as the area where aircraft or air and space systems are loaded before launch, and recovered after an engagement. Between the two systems there is an interface where information and objects are exchanged, in both directions. This 'communication' takes time and energy. Logistics gives operations the stuff needed to bring a weapon to readiness. Stuff includes fuel and things that go bang, but also serviceable parts for the weapon, and personal kit for its operators. Lack of stuff usually gets the most attention; it is what makes the most noise, where the pain seems to come from, where failure first becomes apparent. But often it is not where we find the real cause of failure; lack of stuff is the symptom, not the disease.

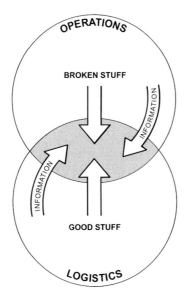

Figure 8.1
Operations/Logistics

Logistics gives operations information. We sometimes overlook the importance of getting this right, and then we fail. To be effective, operational planning must have a good indication of how the logistics system is likely to perform under load. But operators are not mind readers, they have to be told what can and cannot be done.

Even less well understood is how much our success depends on operations getting stuff and information back to logistics. First, a lot of stuff is scarce and critical. Broken stuff of this kind is a potential resource. The quicker we mend it and get it back into circulation, the higher our readiness states will be for high tempo air operations. Consider the priority given to the operational turnaround to get an aircraft fuelled and armed and back on line for the next mission. The same urgency is needed in regenerating critical aircraft components, for exactly the same reasons. Second, logistics needs information. Some of our stuff runs out of life, and some we break. Some stuff we consume, like fuel. Timely and accurate information on actual and potential usage, in terms of breakage, failure and consumption, is important. Without this rapid feedback on changing circumstances the logistics system cannot respond and adapt, and support performance will deteriorate.

Now we have a simple view of the key transactions between operations and logistics. But what happens inside the two systems? What drives the transactions? We start our next phase of exploration in the world of stuff.

To get answers, we need to look at logistics as a complete system, and we need to stand well back to get the whole picture. We need to think about: what the system is for, what it includes, what it produces, what happens inside it and what is needed to feed it. How it is put together, what it handles, and how it works. The fundamental purpose of logistics in our context is to **enable** the focusing of air combat power, in time and space. That is what it is for, but what is it? This analysis proposes that we can see it as just a few very simple processes (Figure 8.2).[2]

Clearly, before we can do anything we have to bring new stuff into the system from outside: we **buy**. This is a fundamental process, but we are concerned in this discussion with the problems of fighting with the stuff we have already got our hands on. We will not consider here the planning, budgeting and programming issues, the 'shopping' and procurement problems, important though they are.

What do we do with stuff once we have it? We **move** it around the system. When it is not moving we **store** it. This all takes people, information, facilities, transport, management and time. We **mend** stuff we have broken, and stuff that

---

2. 'A New Look at Wholesale Logistics', D J Foster, *USAF Journal of Logistics*, Fall 1995.

fails. This takes skills, tools and spare parts, and time. For complex stuff each different piece usually needs its own very specific skills, tools and test equipment. We put stuff together to **build** more complicated stuff. Again this takes skills, tools, and equipment that are specific to the task, and more time. Each process is very simple. It is true that within the **mend** box we find very skilled and intricate engineering activity, but in essence all that does is generate more demands for more stuff. It is tempting to identify a separate process showing us **replacing** stuff we have consumed, but this is merely a special case of the general cycle. When we consume stuff the flow is only one way. There is one caveat. Figure 8.2 shows operations as the only source of broken stuff. This is just a schematic simplification. Stuff breaks and is consumed in the logistics system itself, during building, mending and moving processes.

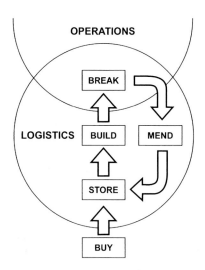

Figure 8.2
Processes

These are simple processes. What makes logistics such a puzzle is that we put hundreds of these simple processes into a complex network of relationships, and then populate the network with thousands of families of components, subsystems and parts, all moving around the network from one simple process to another, sharing pathways, hitting bottlenecks, and waiting. Waiting for parts to arrive to complete a set and fill the last hole in a component. Waiting for repair facilities to be free.

Consider what this means, at each stage. First we have to find all the parts we need, and get them together in one place. Then we have to put them together as a set. This takes time, tools and skill.

Only when the last part arrives and is fitted, when the last hole is filled, can we move on to the next stage. And we do not know what will arrive last, and how long it will take. Building creates delays, and they add up. For an individual part, no journey through the network will be like any other. This fact is simply a result of the complexity and interdependence of the network itself. Delay in the time taken by one process will add to the delays in processes further down stream. The resulting **variability**[3] in how long things take is a fundamental condition of any logistics system. Once we start dealing with the assembly of complex mechanical and electronic stuff, and the test and repair of components, we enter a world of probability distributions and queuing. We cannot rely on a precise schedule. How long it takes all depends on who else wants to do the same thing at the same time.

This is important and bears emphasis. Logistics is made up of very simple processes, but these are arranged in a network of interdependencies that, when acting on the many different units of stuff that are needed to support each weapon, create a complex, busy, dynamic system full of **variability** (the first of four key factors). To be successful this system must respond to the demands caused by activity in the operations system; not just what is wanted now, but what may be wanted later; not just what is wanted by operations, but what is wanted by parts of the whole logistic system to complete work needed to continue productive throughput. This leads us to the second key factor.

How and when demands will emerge is a source of **uncertainty** for the logistics system. We do not know what will fail next, nor exactly when. *This is the core problem* for the partnership. We want continuous forward motion; to get this we seek certainty and speed. But, because of the very nature of logistics, we face uncertainty and delay. The crucial question is: how can we organise a logistic system to meet these demands effectively, when we know that the time taken to do things in any logistic system will always be variable?

A good way to understand a process is to start with the end product and work backwards. In this context we need to stand at the front line of air operations and look to the rear (Figure 8.3). In simple terms, the final output from air operations

---

3. *'The Machine that Changed the World',* J P Womack, D T Jones, D Roos, New York. 1990. *'Theory of Constraints',* E M Goldratt, New York, 1990.

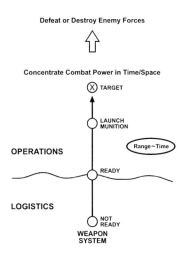

Figure 8.3
Mission

is an engagement, where a target is hit. To do this we have to concentrate combat power in time and space and this requires weapon systems loaded and fit to fight. This point of readiness is where operations and logistics touch. In the world of operations, we are first concerned with range between the loaded weapon system and the target. This range translates into seconds, minutes or hours, depending on the weapon system. Whatever measure is used, the cycle of action – ready, aim, fire – is relatively quick. But an even more important factor is opportunity. The target is often moving or fleeting and only visible or vulnerable for short periods of time. The cycle of action is not only quick; the opportunity to act is often fleeting. So readiness is crucial (see Air Vice-Marshal Professor Mason's views on technology in Chapter 5, balanced by Arthur Williamson's Challenges in Chapter 12).

The activities that happen after – ready, aim, fire – we call recovery and regeneration. The weapon system is off-line while we check serviceability, remove and replace failed parts, and reload with fuel and munitions. Time taken for recovery and regeneration is influenced by the complexity of the tasks and the availability of good stuff to replace the bad (or to fill holes in weapon racks), and skilled people and the necessary tools and equipment to do the job. There are three types of output from this process. Firstly, a loaded weapon system: this goes back into the operations world. Secondly, information: this will include failure rates, time taken to replace components and perhaps new ways of doing work faster. We will also get information on how fast we are using our stocks, how many holes need to be filled. The third output is bad stuff that has been removed and replaced; this bad stuff will be input to the logistics system. The detail of what happens to the good stuff when it returns to the world of operations is outside the scope of this paper. For our purposes, of understanding what influences the task of concentration, we now need to follow the bad stuff back into the logistics black hole.

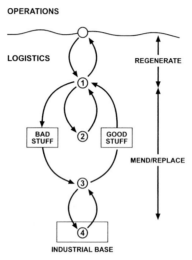

Figure 8.4
Support Echelons

In the air logistics world we talk about echelons of support (Figure 8.4). As we move back from the interface with operations the complexity of work that can be done at an echelon increases. Typically, a first echelon task would be simply to remove and replace a black box in a system, or to re-arm. At second echelon we might test functions and replace modules that can be simply plugged in or pulled out of the system. To address more complex maintenance and repair tasks, for example to do internal work on an aircraft power plant, we would expect to go back to a third echelon, where we have concentrated the skills, spares, tools and test facilities to gain economies of scale, and a focus of expertise. Finally, for work such as complete rebuilds, or for small populations of very complex equipment, or processes involving exotic materials, we may move back to a fourth echelon, often to the commercial manufacturer. Where we put our echelons, and what capabilities we give them, largely determines the shortest possible time it could take to mend or replace things. How long work really takes is determined by the way we operate within this structure; in short, how effective we are as a team.

In operations we focus on opportunity and range, and we think in seconds, minutes or hours. In logistics we are first concerned with the time it takes to 'mend' something, which will be at least hours and sometimes days. But, more crucially, when we think about moving stuff, we step into a world of distance and much slower speeds. Our units of time quickly move from hours to days to weeks as we move back through echelons 1 to 4. We stop looking at the clock and start reading the calendar. Remember, it is not just the physical transportation that takes time; it is the preparation for movement, shipping delays, and simple queuing for resources and facilities that really dominate the system. And we are not moving just one package through the system; we are moving thousands, all competing for space and attention at every stage. To understand the nature of this movement, we need to take a look at pipelines and how they interact with the stuff that moves through them.

What do we mean by a pipeline? Often the first image that comes to mind is of very long tubes of metal crossing the tundra – pipelines getting fuel from A to B. But *any means* of transporting stuff can be understood as a pipeline. We can think of a convoy of trucks on a road, men on bicycles struggling along jungle tracks in Vietnam, or a production line in a factory. Whatever their shape, size and components, when we describe them in systems terms all pipelines have three basic characteristics: capacity, length and flow rate. This means: how big and how heavy can each lump of stuff be? How many lumps of stuff can we have in the pipe at any one time? How far apart are the ends of the pipe? How fast can we push the lumps of stuff down the pipe? And most important of all, how long does it take between putting a specific lump of stuff in the pipe, and getting it out at the other end? Also, for many pipelines, more capability often means less flexibility. Setting up a pipeline, or changing where we put the ends, are the classic problems of the fireman. The faster the flow of water and the wider the bore of the fire-hose, the more effort it takes to move. It takes more manpower, and it takes more time. Heaven help the fireman if he has put the fire engine in the wrong street; he cannot stretch the hose, and he will have to empty it and roll it up before he can move the engine to where it is really needed.

It gets harder; in logistics we have to deal with many pipelines of different capabilities, in a complicated and busy network. The most obvious problem in a network is how to have control over the many flows that merge and diverge. If we are not careful, we can overload smaller pipes by putting them downstream of bigger pipes. To keep the flow going we may have to speed up flow in a smaller pipe, or restrict flow in a bigger pipe that happens to be upstream. It is like plumbing. Coupling copper and plastic pipes of different sizes is not easy. In the transportation world one of the biggest challenges is getting this transfer right.

Because of the uncertainty of demand, and the variability of the many processes connected by the logistics system network, the natural tendency even in a well designed system, is for backlogs to build up and for flows to interfere with each other. Forward motion slows down, and sometimes stops. In extreme cases, the system can be paralysed. How can we deal with this natural tendency? To some extent the solution lies in good plumbing. We anticipate surges in flow and droughts in supply, and design our system to be flexible. The most important technique is to position spares, and spare capacity, at well chosen points in the system so that when there is any interruption in supply we can use the local **buffer** to produce what we need to fill the hole and keep forward motion going. We may think of buffers as header tanks, or reservoirs, producing steady pressure and uninterrupted flow. The goal is always to maximise throughput of the whole system. Buffers are essential but they take up space and cost money. The aim is to keep them to a minimum. Too much stuff in buffers is just as bad as too little. There is a golden rule: 'just in time, not just in case'. He who breaks this rule loses his gold.

There is one more pipeline characteristic we need to consider: invisibility. Despite attempts to track progress, most pipelines are opaque. We know what went in, but we often cannot see exactly where things are now. If a package is late we will know, but not how late it may be. We take a bad thing and make it worse. We hide things when we put them together on pallets in batches to get economies of scale. This is the result of an inevitable trade-off. The aggregation of stuff for transportation gives us a cost benefit, and moves more stuff faster. But it also makes the task of finding and redirecting individual items much harder. It reduces flexibility.

As a result of our analysis we can now propose the fundamentals of any logistic system as:

Variability of Process
Uncertainty of Demand
Capacity and Flexibility of the Network
Design and management of Buffers

The first two are conditions, two of our four key factors that relate to the general nature of the partnership we are examining. The second two are the basic characteristics of any particular air logistic system we may construct. As we step up out of the world of stuff and cross the interface with the world of air operations we meet the third of our key factors. It is not a condition of either world. It is the fundamental quality of the partnership between operations and logistics – *synchronicity*. What does this strange term mean?

The goal of the air operations system is to concentrate air combat power in time and space. To make that possible, the logistics system has to concentrate stuff in time and space, and it has to be useful stuff. What is *useful* is defined directly by the needs of air operations. Simply because they share the same stuff, and feed each other with stuff and information, the processes in both systems need to be synchronised. But this is not easy to do, for two main reasons. First, people working in operations and in logistics will tend to have very different time horizons. Air operations are focused on range, and fleeting opportunity; logistics is seeking continuous flows often over long distances. This leads to different mind sets, a different sense of how fast things need to get done, and how reactive to be. Second, each world has a different view of what constitutes a unit of work. The focus on stuff is different. This creates another tension between the systems that makes keeping in step hard. What is this different focus?

Logistics processes tend to batch repair work and to palletise stuff into shipments to get production and transportation economies, but this inevitably holds some things up. On the other hand, processes in direct support of operations focus on holes to be filled, and therefore on the individual things that are needed to fill those holes. The urgency in the operations world to bring unserviceable weapon systems back on line creates an imperative to get everything done immediately; from this point of view any delay is bad.

Our problem is to get and maintain synchronicity between two systems: each with a natural tendency to look at the world differently and march to different drummers. The solution lies in good system design and good planning processes, and people who are comfortable with ambiguity and constant change. We have got to remember the environment will always be unsteady. To succeed we need to be flexible enough to accommodate uncertainty of demand and variability of process. The truth is that logistic systems will never be easy to deal with: they are simply too complex, too dynamic, and too big. We cannot ever fully control them; we can only prepare them and sustain them. Additionally, the partnership with air operations is complex, dynamic and dependent on many actors. The resulting condition of *complexity* is the last of our four key factors. It is clear that, whatever else we do, to deal with the challenge of complexity we will always have to do a lot of thinking and organising before the shooting starts, if we are to hope to win.

PART TWO

THE DYNAMICS OF FIGHTIN N' STUFF

We have looked at the fundamental nature of the partnership. Now we need to examine how it works in practice by looking at the similarities and differences in the application of land, maritime and air power. In the case of air power we will look a little deeper. But first, we need to think about power projection in general terms (Figure 8.5).

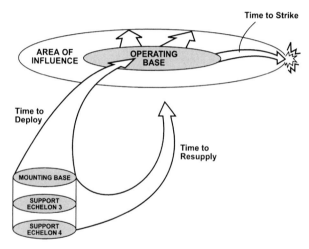

Figure 8.5
Power Projection

For any operation, the crucial determinants of effective power are the time to strike, and rate of striking. From a logistics point of view, the crucial determinants of effective support are: time to deploy, but in terms of useful packages of capability; and time to resupply, but in terms of useful amounts of useful stuff. Getting the bombers into theatre quickly is of little value if you have not got anything there for them to drop. So how does the nature of military power determine how operations and logistics work together?

For land forces, most of the support capability is relatively close to the operating base, and everyone is close to the battlefield. The echelon structure, with stocks, is massive, slow to deploy, and relatively slow to move. We can imagine a force tethered by a large, unwieldy pipeline. It is true that in manoeuvre warfare forces may detach from the pipeline, but not far and not for long. In the Gulf we saw an operation lasting less than 100 hours resulting in an advance of perhaps 300 km. But this was at full stretch, after massive preparations, and with no enemy strikes against our own logistics. The army structure moves as one; it flows in waves across the ground. Movement is punctuated by pauses to resupply and regenerate. When the forces are engaged, rate of consumption can be much faster than rate of resupply. Launch of the next offensive operation can be whenever the commander judges that enough forces are reloaded and in position to meet opportunity. Risk assessment is all. Opportunity may most often be due to enemy weakness, and may be unpredictable in time and weight of effort needed. Small forces can have big effects if used suddenly, in the right place. Surprise and shock action pays off. This possibility puts a premium on mobility of logistics on the battlefield.

For naval forces, the operating base can always be moving. Because of this it has to be at the end of a long and flexible pipeline, that will of necessity be narrow and will be broken from time to time. Pipeline capacity is low and flow can be interrupted. For this reason a naval force needs more stocks and more 'mending' capability on board the operating base. Like land forces, a navy has to take its buffers into the fight. Because of this, it is more critical to get things right before deployment; catching up is hard. Maximum power is fixed at the start of the operation when the fleet leaves its home port, and diminishes rapidly once engagements occur.

What does the partnership look like in the case of air power? The list of characteristics is well known, but what do the words mean? We can propose the following interpretation. Air power measures by the clock rather than the calendar. Air power can go anywhere, can attack scattered targets, attack deep targets, and attack simultaneously over a wide area. Air power can be very precise; and can be responsive: in the range of capabilities, in deployment, in the tempo of operations. But we must stress the conditional nature of all these capabilities, because to do all these things we have to get our bases in place, our capability to regenerate stuff on line, and our rounds, men and equipment in place to reload at the rate we need. And then keep it going. This, of course, is logistics.

So, for land based air, there are similar challenges as in the cases of land and maritime forces, but also some unique opportunities to get sustained, flexible, combat power by carefully synchronising operations and logistics. The operating base is static, once deployed. But new bases can be activated relatively quickly and the forces can be redeployed between bases quickly, and over long distances. As a result, air forces can build up power at the base to a schedule, and adjust the schedule while build up is in progress. More power can be brought to bear faster, and in different places, far apart – what we may call 'switchability'.

The capacity and flow speed of supply pipelines for air power can be increased given time, and use of an air bridge can redirect the flow of force multiplier stuff very quickly, stuff like the critical spare parts that keep weapons on line. With an air bridge direct to the operating base the pipeline can be brought right up to the weapon systems. This capability is crucial for air power because it relies completely on technically very complex and somewhat fragile systems operating far from support echelons. Despite steady improvement in reliability and main-tainability of aircraft systems, for the foreseeable future operations will continue to generate significant failure rates, resulting in a great deal of difficult and time consuming test and repair work. With fast, reliable pipelines vulnerable regenera-tion capability can be kept further back from the threat. This means the number of support forces near the battle can be reduced, and this, in turn, reduces the requirement for force protection. If fewer personnel and less equipment are sent it does not take as long to deploy a force and it does not cost as much to keep them in place. We talk about reducing the mobility footprint. Fast reliable pipelines mean the flow around the repair loop can be speeded up, and buffers of spares can be smaller. This reduces cost and releases funds for other purposes. For complex aircraft spares, moving them faster is usually much cheaper than buying more.

The reach of air power means that commanders can often choose to put an operating base near or on a good transportation hub, readily maximising flow and so maximising air combat power. Air forces are not constrained to line up with the enemy forces on a shared patch of ground and make the best of the infrastructure that happens to be there. Deployed air forces 'en masse' are not limited by a finite magazine of weapons and the need to disengage and return to port for rearming. A word of caution: an important element of air power flexibil-ity comes from having a choice of weapons, but this choice can generate more uncertainty. For example it introduces the question of what weapons to ship out in what order before the shooting starts. As platforms become more multirole the logistic support 'command' function mounts. The commander will need to assess which of the roles to deploy (typically air superiority or recce) with PGMs or ARMs to follow. Of course, this process is entirely scenario and context driven. But there probably will not be time to deploy all the stuff for every conceivable role and specialisation. Here co-ordination between air operations and air logis-tics planning is critical. In general, air transport cannot move large quantities of heavy stuff, so we have to look far enough ahead to have time to send the bulk of weapons by sea. Nevertheless, well planned and adaptive resupply can match the consumption of stuff by air forces even under conditions of a sustained tempo of operations generated by a fast sortie cycle. If resupply is effective air forces can reload and retask quickly and continuously. To achieve this there must be good information and effective, integrated movement and repair processes.

When we look at sharing stuff in air coalition operations, we normally mean basic stuff like fuel and other consumables. Even though we often fly a similar type of aircraft, the marks and detailed logistic support requirements vary so much that sharing aircraft engines and parts is hard to do. For a detailed examination of logistic interoperability problems in coalition operations, see Group Captain Peach's Chapter 3 on Coalition Operations.

We have seen that differences in the nature of the forces and their application naturally leads to differences in approach for the fundamental logistic processes of stocking, sustainment and regeneration. These differences in process determine how forces set up their structure, how they distribute stuff around the structure, in what quantities, and the rules that must be followed to best manage their activities to achieve success. So now we understand the nature and dynamics of the partnership: what is critical to success, what really matters most in doing *'fightin n'stuff'*.

CONCLUSIONS

The goal for the partnership is to achieve **_concentration_.** To get the right stuff to the right place at the right time, and to keep on doing it. This has to be achieved in the context of four conditions: **_variability, uncertainty, synchronicity,_** and **_complexity._** To deal with these key factors we have to have two things, the right attitude and the right fitness: doctrine and capability. The right attitude helps us identify what must be done; fitness provides the energy and flexibility to do it. The right attitude is to think first and most about just five things.

1. The operations/logistics partnership is a target for our enemy – protect it.

We must try always to think of an enemy looking for the decisive points in the partnership. What we want to make strong, he will try to weaken. Where we want agility, he will want to paralyse us. What we can do to our enemy, we can do to ourselves by lack of attention. So all concerned with operations and logistics must protect and care for the partnership and the things it needs for success. This includes stuff and information and people. Also, we must not forget, the corollary is just as important: the operations/logistics partnership of the enemy is a target for us, we must attack it.

"The layman tends to associate air superiority with destruction of enemy aircraft ... it is not the only approach. A potentially vulnerable sequence of events (the aircraft chain) must take place before an aircraft fires a missile or drops a bomb ... it is possible to eliminate an air force by successful attacks on any point in this chain."[1]

Colonel John Warden III USAF

2. Think about the physics.

Stuff is heavy and it fills space. Anything we want to do needs to take account of the weight that will have to be moved, over what distance, with what effort. Usually this all comes down to time, a delay between the idea and the act. If we think about the physics we can know the earliest time we can finish any task, and we can separate the possible from the impossible. It is crucial to determine the scope of the physical logistics task early in any planning process. Planners must know how long things take, and why they take that long.

3. Think about what needs to be done when – and tell everybody.

Once we have given instructions and the stuff is in the pipeline it will fill that space until it emerges at the other end. The goal is to make sure that the stuff coming out of the pipe is exactly what is needed at that point in the operation. If it is not then we have lost an opportunity. Useless stuff is doubly useless. Useless in itself, and wasting space and effort and time. Moving useless stuff delays operations. Even in a shooting war extra missiles are a luxury if there are already enough for the next three days, but aircraft are grounded for lack of engines. In setting priorities it is important to think about what might have to be done, even if it is not part of the current plan. It might be tempting to insist on maximum numbers of all alternative weapons choices being shipped to a base, but if there is no thought given to the sequence of arrival of the right mix, the enthusiastic but undisciplined outloading of weapons might put back the earliest time action can be taken. For example, changes to Rules of Engagement or other operational factors, such as prevailing weather conditions, may introduce limits on which weapons we can use legally or effectively. Also, priority of order of arrival will change with conditions, and with the nature of the force deploying. For example, the political need to respond quickly and show an air presence may lead a commander to take the risk of using the first air transport sorties to get aircraft turn-round crews and weapons into theatre before deploying all the force protec-

---

4. 'The Air Campaign'.

tion elements. The logistics planner must have a seat at the command table when the decisions are taken.

4. Think about defining useful packages of stuff

Stuff is only useful when all the pieces to complete the jigsaw are assembled. Until the last piece arrives, there is nothing but something complicated with a hole in it. It is vital to know exactly what is needed to make a useful contribution to the operational goals, and to manage effort to complete unfinished jigsaws, not simply to start more. Useful stuff often has a sell-by date. If it arrives too late it has no value and the effort expended has been wasted. The sell-by date must be clear to everyone who is helping to build the jigsaw. And it is important to work on the right jigsaw first. In any operation there is a need to relate stuff in the pipelines to joint operational goals, not to single service or single unit priorities. It is no good having all the tanks serviceable if the force cannot get enough aircraft armed and ready to provide air cover; or ensuring that the bomber wing gets priority at the expense of its supporting aircraft.

5. Think about what has already been started.

The length of a pipeline is measured in time not distance. There will always be a lag in the system and it is important to remember what has already been set up to happen later. Constantly changing instructions can waste a lot of energy just moving stuff around to no real purpose. Poorly conceived interventions driven by narrow understanding of local and transitory pain can generate instability and failure in the system.

So, there are five things to think about. But thinking is not enough. We have got to be clever and fit to win. It is important to conclude with some thoughts on the fitness we must seek to guarantee a robust partnership of operations and logistics.

We need systems that can cope with damage, disruption and confusion. Remember, we expect variability in performance, just by the nature of the logistic processes. We need simple rules, simple procedures and a clear view of the mission. People must be in no doubt what they should be trying to achieve. This might be compared with the notion of 'mission command'. We must not build systems that are rigid and too dependent on fixed infrastructure; this mistake is usually the result of seeking local efficiencies without considering the impact on overall system effectiveness. The partnership has to be *resilient.* We need systems that can respond quickly and effectively to change. Remember, we expect uncertainty in demand just by the nature of the activity we are supporting. We need to be ready and able to redirect and accelerate, and we must be open to learning as we go and to exploiting new knowledge immediately. We must not become so focused on what we have planned for that we fail to recognise and respond to what is really happening. Both partner systems have to be ***adaptive.***

We need a partnership that concentrates effort on meeting operational objectives so that every action adds the maximum value to combat power. As much as we can, we must link what we do in the logistics system directly to the contribution in combat readiness. We must not work to measures of output at intermediate sections of the pipeline; we must measure all performance in terms of the outcome at the business end of the pipe. Logistics has to be ***focused on operational outcomes.***

What we always face are trade-offs, in time, investment and operational opportunity. One of the purposes of deliberate planning, and the exercising of systems for real, is to highlight these trade-offs, to understand their interdependencies, and to learn how to get the best result even when we do not have all the facts. A robust partnership will beat a tidy plan, every time. The focus of trade-offs at the operational level is the commander. His planning and execution must be centred all the time on the need to synchronise operations and logistics. Making trade-offs is unavoidable; variability and uncertainty see to that. But making better trade-offs, faster than the enemy, is how we win. Knowing what we are doing helps. And doing as few stupid things as possible and as many clever things as we can is important. We need knowledge on what is happening, why, and how it will change things. Information on the performance of critical success measures in the process is crucial to gaining these insights. Knowing what the critical success measures are comes from good analysis and design – from asking the right questions, from thinking clearly about the system we are working in.

Experience teaches that most often things go wrong because of poor understanding and poorer communication, because of lack of clear focus on essentials, on what really matters. Too often we work at doing things right, not on doing the right things. We measure efficiency rather than effectiveness. Thinking about the nature of things is hard. But it is what we must do if we are to truly understand and be effective.[5]

"Gentlemen, the officer who doesn't know his communications and supply, as well as his tactics, is totally useless."

Lieutenant General George S Patton USA

---

5. Understanding Organisations', C Handy, Oxford, 1993.

PART III

MILITARY CONTEXT

CHAPTER 9

AIR POWER IN JOINT WARFARE
Dr. Philip A G Sabin

INTRODUCTION

IN RECENT YEARS, Western nations have placed ever-increasing emphasis on 'jointery' in their approach to military planning and operations. In Britain, for example, the power of the Ministry of Defence and of the Central Staff has been growing steadily compared to that of the single services, and the 1990s have witnessed further major steps towards integration, through the establishment of a Permanent Joint Headquarters, a Joint Rapid Deployment Force, a Joint Services Command and Staff College, and a series of joint doctrine publications.[1] This shift towards 'jointery' raises important questions regarding the role of air power theory and doctrine in the new joint environment.

The present chapter will explore this issue by addressing several key questions which arise. How useful is it today to focus on 'air power' as a distinct sub-category of military power as a whole? What distinctive characteristics do aerospace vehicles possess? What missions can such vehicles perform as part of a joint military effort? What variables determine the most appropriate balance between air and surface assets in any specific scenario? In what circumstances are synergistic benefits from the combination of air and surface assets most attainable? What does all this imply for the most appropriate command and control arrangements for air power in a joint environment?

There is no space here to do more than scratch the surface of these complex issues, but the chapter will aim to highlight the most important characteristics and dilemmas, thereby helping to establish a clearer theoretical framework for further more detailed study of the issues concerned. The central argument of the chapter is that a new balance needs to be struck in military theory and doctrine, with more of a focus on various different joint campaigns rather than on the old categories of air, land and sea power, but with a continuing need to address the distinctive role of aerospace vehicles within this new joint perspective.

---

1. See *British Defence Doctrine,* JWP 0-01, (London: Ministry of Defence, 1996).

THE DISTINCTIVENESS OF AIR POWER

When 'classic' air theorists such as Douhet, Mitchell and Trenchard produced their ideas in the 1920s, it was fairly clear what constituted 'air power', given the distinctive nature of the instruments involved in land, sea and air warfare respectively.[2] Not surprisingly, nations developed three separate armed services to run warfare in the three different realms. Since then, however, technological advances have gradually but inexorably blurred the boundary between air and surface power, as more and more diverse military instruments have emerged which straddle the boundary concerned.

Although the traditional manifestation of air power, namely the manned, fixed-wing, land-based combat aircraft, retains its primacy, it has now been joined by helicopters, carrier aviation, airborne and airmobile forces, cruise and ballistic missiles, surface-to-air missiles (SAMs), and a rapidly increasing range of unmanned aerial vehicles (UAVs) and space satellites. Ownership of these new capabilities is spread much more evenly among the armed services, with the precise pattern differing between different nations, and there is no longer any kind of straightforward equation between 'air power' and the capabilities held by any particular air force. For these reasons, settling on a precise definition of air power is becoming an increasingly problematic task.[3]

Given the growing trend towards 'jointery' in military affairs, devising a clear definition of 'air power' may actually no longer matter all that much. It could be argued that the whole process of dividing military power up into air, land and sea components is in fact outdated and anachronistic, and that the practice survives only because the single services have a vested bureaucratic interest in championing their own core components as part of their continuing struggle for status and resources. If this were true, then joint doctrine publications should perhaps supersede rather than supplement existing handbooks like the British AP 3000 and BR 1806, produced on an essentially single-Service basis.[4]

It is certainly the case that all forms of military power are subject to the same basic strategic logic associated with a violent interactive contest between competing political entities; hence the continuing influence of insightful theorists like

---

2. See Phil Meilinger (ed.), *The Paths of Heaven: The Evolution of Airpower Theory* (Maxwell AL: Air University Press, 1997).

3. See Philip Sabin, 'Modern Air Power Theory – Some Neglected Issues', *The Hawk Journal*, 1994, pp.5-7.

4. See AP 3000, *Air Power Doctrine* (UK: Royal Air Force, 2nd ed., 1993), and BR 1806, *The Fundamentals of British Maritime Doctrine* (London: HMSO, 1995).

Clausewitz and Sun Tzu, even though they based their ideas purely on land conflict in eras now long ago. This pervasive strategic logic must certainly form the basis of all modern military theory.[5] The problem is that military affairs are now so complicated and diverse that **some** form of analytical sub-division is vital within this overall framework, if one is to move beyond vague generalisations which try to cover every aspect of the subject at once.

The traditional argument for producing distinct theories of air, land and sea power has been that these sub-sets of capabilities are sufficiently similar internally, and sufficiently different from other forms of military power, that useful specific theories may be produced which do indeed move beyond the vague generalisations necessary when trying to cover modern military power as a whole. However, the proliferation of different types of systems complicates this capability-based approach, and produces an intractable dilemma which is illustrated in **figure 9.1.**

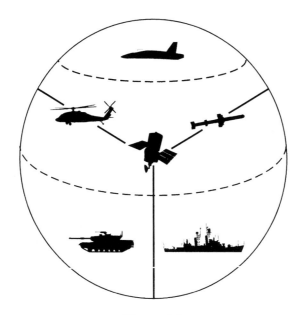

Figure 9.1
Broad and Narrow Interpretations of Air Power

---

5. See *British Defence Doctrine* (op cit), chs.2-4, and Edward Luttwak, *Strategy: The Logic of War and Peace* (Cambridge MA: Harvard University Press, 1987), esp. ch.11.

If we adopt a highly restrictive definition of air power, limiting ourselves say to manned fixed wing aircraft, this makes the internal similarities within the set far greater, but it artificially excludes other systems such as missiles and satellites which would play a key part in an integrated air operation. Any resulting theories would have only tactical rather than strategic validity, rather like separate theories devised for tanks or for submarines. If, on the other hand, we adopt a broad definition which brings in everything from missiles and satellites to helicopters and UAVs, as well as the surface bases or platforms from which these systems operate and which are integral to air operations, the scope of air power becomes so wide that we risk a 'lowest common denominator' effect which forces doctrinal generalisations almost as great as those for military power as a whole.

A further problem lies in the overlap between doctrines produced for the three environments of air, land and sea. For example, maritime warfare is now so dependent on various forms of missiles and aircraft that, by including the warships on which these systems are based, virtually the whole of modern navies would fall within a broad definition of 'air power'! One could try to avoid this overlap by devising purely single service doctrine, but this flies in the face of the current shift towards joint campaigns, and it is very hard to defend intellectually when different services field similar capabilities as at present. In an age when British aircraft carriers operate Harrier jets from both the Royal Navy and the RAF, having separate doctrines for the two air arms seems distinctly anachronistic.

The only way to avoid this dilemma is to move to an altogether different way of subdividing military doctrine. There are strong arguments for moving beyond the traditional 'input based' subdivision in terms of air, land and sea power, and shifting instead towards an alternative 'output based' framework organised around different types of joint campaigns. This would involve replacing single service or environmental doctrine with truly integrated bi- or tri-service doctrine for various joint campaigns, as illustrated in **figure 9.2.**

Peace support operations (PSOs) and counter-insurgency operations obviously deserve consideration in their own right, due to their highly distinctive political characteristics. At the other extreme, there is a strong case for analysing 'strategic' warfare as an integrated whole, since the same political dynamics of coercion and deterrence apply whether pressure is exerted through a nuclear threat, an air or cruise missile attack, a maritime blockade or a raid by special forces. In each case, the object is to coerce the opponent into coming to terms, or to cripple his ability to resist, as with the highly successful air and submarine offensive against the Japanese war effort in WWII.

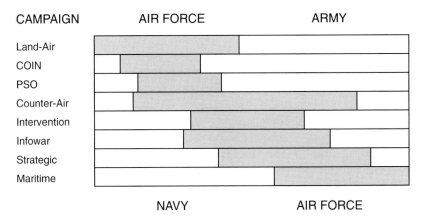

Figure 9.2
A Campaign Based Framework for Joint Doctrine

As regards operations against the enemy armed forces in conventional campaigns, there are strong grounds for dividing these up not on the basis of one's own capabilities but on the basis of joint operations against various **enemy** capabilities. Hence, counter-air operations against opposing air and air defence forces may involve not just one's own aerospace systems but also ground-based air defence, or surface force attacks on enemy bases or aircraft carriers. Similarly, land-air warfare involves the integrated use of one's air and surface forces to defeat the enemy army, while maritime warfare entails an equally joint campaign against opposing submarines and surface warships.

Given the current Western focus on 'expeditionary warfare', it is probably worth having a separate doctrinal category for intervention operations, to consider the special challenges of amphibious and airborne attacks which have always been the archetype of joint warfare. Finally, given the growing prominence of information technology and 'cyberspace' in modern military affairs, there is a case for an integrated focus on 'information warfare', bringing in not only electronic warfare as traditionally defined but also new preoccupations such as computer hacking and the winning of the media war.

Hitherto, such campaign-specific doctrines have tended to be produced by the lead service in each area, and have often taken insufficient account of the contribution of other forms of military power, with the result that thinking became fragmented and ill co-ordinated. This happened to some extent with recent

British thinking about peace support operations, as the campaign in Bosnia unfolded.[6] A key benefit of the continuing shift towards 'jointery' is that it should foster more integrated consideration of the various campaigns, across traditional service boundaries.

However, this campaign-based approach does have serious limitations of its own. For one thing, there is obviously considerable interaction and overlap between different campaigns, just as there is between air, land and sea power. Moreover, armed forces are inevitably organised more around inputs than outputs, given the very different specialist skills required to operate armoured vehicles, ships and aircraft, so campaign-based doctrine will always involve working 'against the grain' of service force structures. Since the same forces may find themselves engaged in a wide variety of campaigns, from PSOs to strategic coercion, a purely campaign-based doctrinal framework would require even junior officers to familiarise themselves with the operation of all types of air and surface assets across the whole range of possible scenarios!

Given these practical problems, what is really needed is a shift of the **balance** between input based and output based analytical frameworks, rather than a wholesale move from one to the other. Although it is now increasingly difficult and anachronistic to distinguish a separate category of 'air power' within military power as a whole, it is still worth paying specific doctrinal attention to the distinctive contribution of aerospace **vehicles** to the various different joint campaigns. Not only does this offer a useful analytical sub-category within each type of joint campaign, but it also permits certain generalisations across the campaigns, hence making it easier both for airmen and for surface commanders to appreciate the dynamics involved.

The way forward thus lies in a twin-track approach to doctrinal development. On the one hand, there is a need for truly integrated doctrine concerning various different joint campaigns - a project far wider than can be addressed in this volume. On the other hand, there is also a need for continued thinking about the distinctive contribution of land forces, naval vessels, and aerospace vehicles to these joint campaigns. This thinking will not simply correlate with existing service boundaries, since armies and navies now deploy significant air as well as surface capabilities; hence, there needs to be true tri-service consideration of the aerospace dimension. The rest of this chapter addresses some of the issues that arise from this one specific aspect of the overall doctrinal agenda.

---

6. See the British Army manual *Wider Peacekeeping*, and Andrew Lambert & Arthur Williamson (eds.), *The Dynamics of Air Power* (Bracknell: RAF Staff College, 1996), Part II – 'Air Power in Peace Support Operations'.

CHARACTERISTICS OF AEROSPACE VEHICLES

Missiles, satellites, UAVs, helicopters and fixed-wing aircraft all share one central distinguishing feature compared to surface forces - namely **flight.** Some of the vehicles use aerofoils to support themselves within the ocean of air, while others 'fly' on a ballistic trajectory inside or outside the atmosphere, but this internal distinction is much less important than the fundamental contrast with other vehicles which move across the surface of the earth. It is this fundamental contrast which makes some degree of separate doctrinal consideration of aerospace systems worthwhile, even within an increasingly joint framework.

Since all weapons except mines and torpedoes involve projectiles which 'fly' through the air to their targets, there must obviously be a cut-off, if only to eliminate bullets and shells from consideration! Probably the best approach is to consider only those air vehicles with a maximum range of at least 100 miles. This discounts the vast majority of tactical systems such as SAMs, anti-ship missiles, battlefield rockets and so on, since their operational effectiveness depends so heavily on the location of the surface launching platform. By contrast, vehicles which meet this criterion will have sufficient range and/or endurance for 'flight' to be the primary distinguishing characteristic of the system in operational terms. As was argued in our previous book on **The Dynamics of Air Power,** this central attribute of 'flight' leads to certain fundamental and distinctive strengths and limitations of aerospace vehicles compared to surface forces, as shown in **Figure 9.3.**[7]

The first strength, 'freedom of movement', refers to the ability of aerospace vehicles to traverse land and sea, independently of the surface terrain and of surface obstructions. The second innate strength, 'pace', reflects the order of magnitude speed advantage which aerospace vehicles enjoy, travelling as they do at hundreds or even thousands rather than tens of miles per hour. The third strength, 'perspective', arises from the unique elevated viewpoint which height above the surface confers.

To set against these three innate comparative advantages, flight also brings three concomitant limitations compared to surface forces. One is 'detachment', which makes it difficult to interact sensitively with the surface environment in the same way as an infantry unit or a patrolling warship. The second is 'impermanence', since flight usually requires considerable expenditure of energy, so that endurance away from an established base is measured in hours rather than the

---

7. See Philip Towle, 'The Distinctive Characteristics of Air Power', in Lambert & Williamson (op cit).

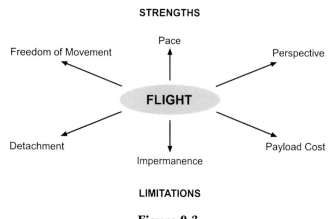

Figure 9.3
Distinctive Characteristics of Aerospace Vehicles

weeks for which surface forces can remain on station away from a local or home base. The third innate limitation flowing from the nature of flight is 'payload cost', since it is much more expensive to transport a given load or to deliver a given weight of ordnance by air than by land or sea. Satellites obviously suffer less from impermanence, due to the unique nature of the orbital environment, but the penalties they pay in terms of detachment and payload cost are even greater than for other aerospace vehicles.

As discussed in our previous volume, these innate strengths and limitations give rise to certain consequential characteristics of aerospace vehicles, such as the ability to **penetrate** deep into enemy territory (and to withdraw just as readily), through enjoying freedom of rapid movement. This chapter will build upon our earlier discussion of such generic characteristics, by assessing how the various attributes of aerospace vehicles affect their ability to contribute militarily in different types of joint campaigns.

AEROSPACE MISSIONS

The RAF's **Air Power Doctrine** lists 19 separate contributions which air power can make during peacetime, crisis or war.[8] However, it is possible for analytical

---

8.   AP 3000 (op cit), pp.17-26.

Systems like cruise missiles, perhaps launched from naval vessels
and flying long distances to strike targets deep inland, make it much
more difficult to define 'air power'

purposes to reduce this wide range of applications to just five core mission
capabilities, from which almost everything else flows. The five basic missions
which aerospace vehicles can perform as part of a joint campaign are as follows:

- they can **observe** opposing forces, both visually and electronically;
- they can **intercept** opposing aerospace systems in flight;
- they can **attack,** or threaten to attack, opposing surface targets;
- they can **transport** friendly forces or supplies.
- they can **support** friendly forces by facilitating communication,
  command and control, navigation, meteorology, and so on.

In every one of these five areas, the potential contribution of aerospace vehicles has grown substantially over time as technology has advanced. Developments
in sensors such as radar have revolutionised the observation capabilities of aero-

space platforms, and have enhanced the ability to track and intercept enemy systems in flight. Weapons advances such as precision guidance have greatly increased the potential for aerial interception and for the successful attack of surface targets.[9] Surface attack and the transport mission have also benefited from larger, more efficient aircraft and from the advent of helicopters. Finally, the support function has been transformed by developments in electronics and satellites. Hence, whereas in WWI air assets played only a marginal role in the overall course of the conflict, in recent campaigns such as the Gulf War, aerospace capabilities have been decisive in determining the outcome.[10]

However, one must never forget that the ability of aerospace vehicles to perform the missions outlined above depends not just on unilateral progress in aerospace technology, but also on a dynamic measure-countermeasure contest. What seems to have happened is partly that aerospace technology has advanced faster than the technology of surface forces, and partly that the growing dependence on electronic systems has brought greater differentiation, so that superior air powers such as the United States or Israel can take full advantage of the new technology while inferior air powers like Syria or Iraq can find themselves utterly outclassed. Today, air battles tend to be decided sooner and in a more one-sided fashion than in the drawn-out attritional air campaigns of the World Wars, leaving the losers with little or no aerospace capability, while allowing the victors to use their dominant aerospace assets much more effectively to influence the surface conflict.[11]

This polarisation of effectiveness between superior and inferior air powers will not necessarily continue as starkly in the future. As technologies such as passive SAMs, laser weapons, stealthy airframes, and cruise and ballistic missiles spread to more nations, it may become harder for superior air powers to use aerospace vehicles with impunity while denying their use to the opponent. Also, as satellites and UAVs proliferate, it may become more difficult to impose the same degree of information asymmetry as the Iraqis suffered from during the Gulf War. However, the net effect of such trends seems more likely to be to salvage the utility of certain aerospace systems for inferior air powers, rather than to reduce the utility of advanced aerospace vehicles for superior air powers.

---

9. See Richard Hallion, 'Precision Air Attack in the Modern Era', in Richard Hallion (ed.), *Air Power Confronts an Unstable World* (London: Brassey's, 1997).
10. For more details of this shift, see Tony Mason, *Air Power: A Centennial Appraisal* (London: Brassey's 1994).
11. See Philip Sabin, 'The Counter-Air Contest', in Lambert & Williamson (op cit).

As far as Western nations are concerned, the real limits on the contribution of aerospace capabilities to joint warfare will stem from the enduring limitations of aerospace vehicles, as discussed in the previous section. In some ways, higher payload cost will become a progressively less significant disadvantage of aerospace systems, as the emphasis in military affairs as a whole continues to move away from massed forces relying on 'dumb' weapons to smaller strike forces relying on precision guided munitions (PGMs) and on the essentially weightless weapon of electronic information. However, this will be offset to some extent by escalating system costs, as concerns over survivability prompt even greater investment in expensive 'high tech' solutions such as stealth, stand-off weapons, cruise missiles and satellites. Given this continuing cost escalation, aerospace vehicles are likely to remain a scarce resource as overall inventories shrink to fit within restrictive defence budgets.

The contribution of Western aerospace systems in joint warfare will also be constrained by the limited range of missions they can perform, stemming ultimately from the inherent detachment and impermanence of the systems concerned. Sometimes the overall objective of the joint campaign will be limited and specific enough that aerospace vehicles alone will be able to achieve it, as with Israel's destruction of the Osirak nuclear reactor in 1981, or the US punitive strike against Libya in 1986. More usually, there will be a need for surface forces to undertake missions which aerospace assets are ill-equipped to perform directly, such as occupying territory, providing protection and succour, consolidating control, and conducting detailed intelligence investigations. The best balance between aerospace and surface assets to achieve the joint objective in particular scenarios will depend on a wide variety of factors, as the following section will discuss.

KEY VARIABLES

It has become commonplace in modern joint doctrine to point out that the relative contribution of air and surface forces to any particular campaign will vary, depending on the specific circumstances. Sometimes aerospace assets will play the leading role, while at other times they will make only a subordinate contribution to the joint effort. In order to move beyond this bland generalisation and to obtain rules of thumb which will help decide the best balance in any particular case, it is necessary to discuss the many variables which bear upon this highly complex problem.

RAF Harrier GR7s operating off HMS Invincible in the Persian Gulf in a clear embodiment of joint warfare

One set of variables concerns the nature of the antagonists' overall objectives. As a general rule, aerospace assets are likely to play more of a role the less **complex** and **ambitious** that side's overall objectives, and the less political **commitment** both sides have to the struggle. As was noted in the previous section, aerospace vehicles are best at achieving straightforward, limited tasks such as destroying particular fixed and known facilities, or imposing pain through punitive strikes. They also offer a means of exerting military power while putting fewer personnel at risk for a shorter time than in surface force actions, hence appealing to politicians who want a 'limited liability' option because the conflict does not affect their own state's vital interests.

The trouble is that these three variables of complexity, ambition and commitment often point in different directions. In all-out contests like the World Wars, the objective is usually pretty straightforward, involving smashing the enemy forces by any means possible. However, this is also a very ambitious objective involving high political commitment on both sides, so the greater weight of massed surface forces tends to be required to reach a decision.

In more limited campaigns fought for less ambitious objectives and with a lower degree of political commitment, there is often a temptation to rely much more heavily on aerospace assets. However, surface forces tend to be needed as well because the overall mission is usually more complex and politically constrained, requiring subtle engagement **with** (as distinct from simply engagement **of**) the surface environment. Hence, it is not possible to make sweeping generalisations such as that aerospace capabilities contribute more in limited than in all-out wars (or vice versa). The balance may vary significantly in both cases, depending on the precise political context and on the other variables discussed below.

As was pointed out in the previous section, a second set of variables concerns the nature and sophistication of the aerospace capabilities available to the powers involved. The more advanced one's aerospace panoply, the larger the contribution it is likely to make, both because of its greater absolute capabilities and because it will be less vulnerable to disruption by the opponent. As indicated by various past experiences, ranging from 'air policing' in the inter-war period, up through Allied air operations in the last year of WWII, and culminating with recent aerospace operations in the Gulf War and over Bosnia, aerospace assets may have most to offer precisely when they enjoy an asymmetric advantage over enemy air and air defence capabilities.

This leads on to the third set of variables affecting the contribution of aerospace assets, namely the nature of the contending surface forces. In general, air power will be more important the lighter the friendly surface forces, and the heavier the enemy surface forces. The less heavily equipped one's own surface forces are, the more that air transport will be able to contribute despite payload cost limitations, and the more need there will be for air power to provide fire support to offset the weakness of the surface forces' organic firepower (as during the UN deployment in Bosnia). Conversely, the heavier the enemy surface forces, the more concentrated a target they will offer for aerial observation and attack, and the more dependent they will be on supplies and industrial infrastructure which can be disrupted from the air.[12]

The Vietnam war offers a telling illustration of this dynamic, since a key reason why US air power was more effective in 1972 than during the earlier 'Rolling Thunder' campaign seems to have been that the enemy had by then

---

12. This may, of course, be offset to some extent by the fact that heavier enemy forces will have better air defence capabilities, thereby reducing the asymmetric aerospace advantage discussed earlier in this section.

moved from a guerrilla strategy to a conventional offensive using heavier main force units.[13] Other past campaigns indicate that a very important additional factor is the **morale** of enemy surface forces. Whereas highly motivated forces like the North Vietnamese or like the Germans in Normandy may be able to withstand prolonged and heavy air attack, similar attacks on troops whose morale is shaky may produce demoralisation and panic which greatly magnifies the physical impact of the air bombardment. Several Middle Eastern armies have suffered such a psychological collapse under air attack, from the Turks facing Allenby in 1918 to the Arab forces in 1967 and the Iraqis during the Gulf War.[14]

In Vietnam, the physical environment and the nature of the enemy
limited the effectiveness of the aerospace contribution, except in the
vital mission of air mobility

13. See Mark Clodfelter, *The Limits of Air Power: The American Bombing of North Vietnam* (New York: Free Press, 1989).
14. See Andrew Lambert, 'Shattering Impact: The Psychology of Air Attack', in Hallion (op cit).

A further key factor during these Middle Eastern campaigns was clearly the nature of the battle area itself, and this is the final category which must be considered when judging the likely contribution of aerospace assets. Several component factors stand out here, namely the geographical **extent** of the area, the amount of terrain **cover** to conceal surface forces, the prevailing **weather** conditions, the **tractability** of the area in terms of surface movement, and the **accessibility** of the area in terms of the availability of air bases and the ease of deploying surface forces there. Clearly, aerospace vehicles will be at a comparative advantage in an extensive battle area, with clear skies and little terrain cover, with lots of surface obstacles such as watercourses which impede friendly and canalise enemy surface movement, and with suitable local airfields to offset its distance from friendly home bases. Given this 'ideal' prescription, it is not hard to see why air power played such a dominant role during the Gulf War!

Usually, these environmental factors will not be so happily correlated, so their implications for the air contribution in joint campaigns will be more equivocal. For example, the jungles of Vietnam decreased the tractability of the environment and so made the ubiquity offered by air movement more valuable, but they also provided excellent cover from aerial observation and attack. Conversely, during the Battle of the Atlantic, the extensive and open nature of the arena was offset to some extent by poor weather, the lack of air bases, and the complete tractability of the medium, allowing vessels to proceed in any direction and to hide in the vastness of the ocean.

Since these many variables so often point in different directions, the problem is to decide their relative importance, and to determine which of them deserve higher priority when trying to judge how large a contribution aerospace assets should be expected to make. There is no simple answer to this problem, and perhaps the best way forward is to consider separately each of the five different air missions identified in the previous section.

For aerospace observation, the important thing is to be able to use the advantage of perspective, while avoiding problems of obscuration or lack of discrimination caused by the detached nature of the observing platform. Clearly, perspective is of most help in an extensive battle arena, where it would take multiple surface observers to cover the area required. Aerospace observation platforms will be least inhibited in arenas where there is little terrain or climatic cover, and where enemy forces or other targets of interest are heavier and so more visible from a distance and less able to blend into the environment. This said, terrain cover or irregularities obviously block surface observation as well, and there may still be significant **relative** advantage in having an aerial perspective, especially where built-up areas are concerned.

The second mission, intercepting opposing aerospace vehicles in flight, clearly depends primarily on what aerospace capabilities the opponent possesses. Experience suggests that this will be a key mission in all circumstances except those where the enemy is simply incapable of mounting a challenge, or (at the other extreme) where his aerospace forces are too potent to be tackled successfully by one's own air vehicles. In the latter event, surface-based air defences may be a better bet, either to impose attrition on superior enemy aircraft, as the Arabs did during the Yom Kippur war, or to intercept incoming missiles, as the **Patriot** system did during the Gulf War. Another important variable is the extent of the battle area, with fighter aircraft being more cost-effective than SAMs in defending large territories, due to their greater flexibility of deployment.

When one considers the third aerospace mission, namely attacking surface targets, virtually all the variables discussed earlier come into play, and it is very hard to identify generic priorities among them. The two principal requirements for a large role for air vehicles in this mission area are clearly that such vehicles can actually destroy or disrupt certain specified targets, and that this does actually contribute significantly to the achievement of the overall strategic aim. Hence, air attacks will have most to offer if one has good intelligence about concentrated and vulnerable targets which are crucial to the enemy's will or ability to resist, and if the attacks do not jeopardise one's own protective objectives regarding friendly forces or civilian populations.

The fourth mission, air transport, is much simpler, in that the most important variable is clearly whether friendly surface forces are light enough to be moved and supplied by air. Other key requirements to make air transport worthwhile despite the comparative cheapness and flexibility of surface alternatives are intractable terrain and an extensive battle area, so that the freedom and pace of air move-ment come into their own. Hence, air transport contributes hardly anything in contests between heavy naval vessels on the open seas, but it is much more impor-tant for the lighter marine forces involved in amphibious operations, where it helps to overcome the intractability of the coastal divide. The accessibility of the battle area by air and surface means is obviously another important variable, as is the level of enemy air defence capabilities, given the vulnerability of transport aircraft.

The final mission, embracing various forms of support ranging from naviga-tion to communications, is clearly a function primarily of the sophistication of one's own aerospace assets, given the way in which capabilities in this area have been revolutionised by space based electronic devices such as GPS. Such support will be even more important in extensive, distant, and featureless theatres like the high seas or the deserts of the Persian Gulf, but it will play an increasingly vital role in all situations as the technology develops and proliferates.

Aerospace capabilities like this NAVSTAR GPS satellite make a
growing contribution to joint warfare in which electronic information
matters at least as much as heavy physical presence

Future scenarios are obviously infinitely variable, and the only way to get a
proper sense of how large a contribution aerospace assets should be expected to
make as part of a joint campaign is to prepare a detailed military estimate for that
specific case. However, the generic variables outlined in this section may help to
organise one's initial thinking in the face of the many complexities involved. The
following table summarises which factors are likely to have **most** impact on the
prominence of each of the five basic aerospace missions, and it offers a rough-
and-ready framework for estimating the importance and nature of the
contribution which aerospace assets may be expected to make in different possible
contingencies.

255

Variable	Aerospace Mission				
	Observe	Intercept	Attack	Transport	Support
Political Objectives					
COMPLEXITY	●	●	●		
AMBITION			●	●	
COMMITMENT			●		
Aerospace Forces					
FRIENDLY CAPABILITY	●	●	●		●
ENEMY CAPABILITY		●	●	●	
Surface Forces					
FRIENDLY WEIGHT			●	●	
ENEMY WEIGHT	●		●		
ENEMY MORALE			●		
Battle Area					
EXTENT	●	●	●	●	●
COVER	●		●		
WEATHER	●	●	●	●	
TRACTABILITY			●	●	
ACCESSIBILITY	●		●	●	●

Figure 9.4
Key Variables Affecting Aerospace Contributions

AIR-SURFACE SYNERGY

Whatever balance of aerospace and surface assets is appropriate in a particular joint campaign, one should strive to ensure that the combination is a synergistic one. 'Synergy' is an over-used concept, especially in joint operations, and it is all too easy to assume that any combination of forces is necessarily beneficial and synergistic. In fact, synergy means that the whole is greater than the sum of the parts, and this only happens if specific mechanisms come into play. Without such mechanisms, one has mere complementarity, with the effect of the two forces simply being additive. It is even possible that the two forces may interfere with one another and have an overall effect which is less than the sum of their individual parts. An obvious example would be the initial operations in Bosnia, when the coercive potential of NATO air power was offset by the reciprocal vulnerability of UN ground forces to hostage-taking. Thus, not all combinations of forces are necessarily beneficial.[15]

15. For a fuller discussion of the theory and practice of synergy, see Andrew Lambert, 'Synergy in Operations', in Lambert & Williamson (op cit).

The basic mechanism by which synergy is achieved is that one force offsets the limitations of the other (and perhaps vice versa), thereby allowing one or both forces to have a greater individual impact than if the same force had been employed in isolation. The effect is similar to 'force multiplication', with the difference perhaps being that force multipliers tend to be support systems such as communications or GPS which have no effect on the enemy in themselves, whereas synergy is generally achieved through the combination of two fighting forces, each of which could have some impact in its own right, but which work even better if used in combination. The distinction is a subtle one, and both types of effects will be discussed here, under the general heading of 'synergy'.

As noted earlier, a key limitation of air vehicles is impermanence, which results in routine dependence on surface bases or launching platforms. One way in which surface forces can combine synergistically with air vehicles is by providing or protecting these surface installations, from which the air vehicles can then operate. Without such nearby bases or launching platforms, the air systems would be forced to operate at long range from more distant points, with all the attendant problems of higher fuel requirements (at the expense of military payload), longer transit times, and slower responsiveness to crises at the front. In many cases, limitations on the maximum range of air vehicles would make them altogether incapable of conducting operations in the area required, without surface forces to facilitate nearby basing.[16]

Today, these constraints are not quite as great as in the past, thanks to the advent of longer range aircraft and missiles and of air-to-air refuelling, which allow operations even at intercontinental ranges (as in some B52 raids during the Gulf War). However, long range air operations still involve severe penalties in responsiveness and sortie rates, so unless the mission merely requires a one-off attack like the US raid on Libya, it remains more efficient to operate from bases nearby. Only satellites escape the range problem altogether, because of their more permanent and globally pervasive presence.

Operating from nearby bases does have the twin drawbacks that the bases may be limited in capacity and may be vulnerable to enemy action due to their proximity to the opponent. These drawbacks are particularly acute in maritime warfare, since warships generally offer more cramped and fragile operating platforms for air vehicles than bases on land. However, this is offset to some extent by

---

16. A classic instance of synergistic air-surface co-operation was the US 'island-hopping' campaign in the Pacific War, when Marines seized successive atolls and constructed airbases on them during the drive on Japan. On the importance of base location for air operations, see Price Bingham, 'Operational Art and Aircraft Runway Requirements', *Airpower Journal*, Fall 1988.

the mobility of the warships – a particularly important factor in the case of missile-firing submarines, since it allows them to hide very effectively in the vastness of the oceans. Given this continuing and highly complex trade-off involving range, responsiveness, capability, vulnerability and cost, the debate over the respective advantages of sea-based and land-based air systems is unlikely to abate in the foreseeable future.

In maritime warfare, the scope for other forms of air-surface synergy is limited because of the lack of terrain cover and the focus on physical destruction of enemy forces as the primary outcome of air or naval action. Some synergistic mechanisms do exist in operations involving submarines, but in surface maritime warfare there is less need for air and naval units to attack together in order to gain synergistic benefits. Several surface naval battles from Midway to the Gulf War have been won entirely by air action, without any direct clash between the surface forces concerned. By contrast, in land-air warfare the historical pattern has been very different, and synergistic co-operation has usually been central to the success of the joint effort.

Because enemy land forces are often able to hide from air attack by dispersing into entrenchments or terrain cover, the effect of air superiority over land has not usually been to destroy enemy land forces outright, as in carrier engagements at sea. Instead, the effect has been more to gain a temporary advantage over the opposing land forces, which fades away over time unless exploited by a simultaneous offensive by one's own land forces. Hence, air action alone has historically produced mostly short term or contingent effects in air-land warfare, making synergistic co-ordination with land forces vital to capitalise on the significant but temporary advantages gained.

This mechanism is visible in many ways, spanning the spectrum of air missions. The disproportionate ability of the superior air power to conduct air observation has often resulted in an asymmetric intelligence environment, indecisive in itself, but greatly facilitating manoeuvre warfare by friendly land forces.[17] Air attacks directly against enemy land forces have historically had 'suppressive' effects very similar to those of artillery, pinning the forces down, denying them mobility, and causing psychological shock, but not creating much lasting destruction unless the enemy was forced to move in order to counter or escape a friendly land offensive (as at Falaise in 1944).

---

17. A classified study by Alfred Price suggests that this may in fact have been the most significant contribution of air power in past air-land campaigns.

The shattering of the retreating German forces at Falaise in 1944 illustrated
the enormous synergistic benefit of co-ordinated air and land forces

Air interdiction of enemy supply lines has also tended to do little more than
cause temporary shortages at the front, which can be made good over time unless
exploited by simultaneous land action.[18] Similarly, strategic air bombardment has
tended to be most effective not when conducted independently, but when friendly
surface forces have been poised to exploit and accelerate the weakening of the
enemy's war effort and determination, as in the final defeat of Germany in 1945,
and as in Iran's eventual acceptance of a cease-fire in 1988 under the twin pressures of Iraq's missile bombardments and its renewed successes at the battlefront.
The same synergistic logic applies to air transport and air assault, which are very
good at facilitating the surprise seizure of key points by light airborne or airmobile forces, as long as there is rapid relief by heavier land units to save the 'coup de
main' force from being overrun (as at Arnhem).

18. See, for example, Eduard Mark, 'A New Look at Operation STRANGLE', *Military Affairs*, October
1988.

What is interesting about the Gulf War is that this pattern of air power merely 'setting the stage' for decisive action on land was modified, due to the enhanced ability of PGM-equipped aircraft to inflict permanent attrition on the Iraqi forces. Whereas previously night had offered a sanctuary for enemy land forces and allowed them to rest, move and replenish supplies so as to negate the impact of daytime air attack, now the night was even more dangerous for the Iraqis than the day, due to the opportunities it provided for 'tank plinking'. Hence, unlike the long preliminary artillery bombardments of WWI, it was worth continuing the air campaign against the Iraqi army without an immediate land attack.

There were still plenty of synergistic benefits once the ground war started, since the chronically demoralised Iraqis could now at last surrender, and since those who tried to flee or counterattack thereby exposed themselves to even faster attrition from the air. However, the relationship between air and land assets was much more balanced than in the past, with air systems bearing a major part of the burden of destruction rather than mere suppression. Although one should not generalise too much from this uniquely favourable situation, it does illustrate that air and land assets are now equal partners, and that in some cases land forces may be used to set up the conditions for a decisive air attack, rather than vice versa. Given the advantages which Western states enjoy in air capabilities, and their unwillingness to risk the level of casualties which major ground fighting involves, there is likely to be considerable pressure (as in Bosnia) to capitalise on this aero-space-led approach to land-air warfare in the future.

As regards synergy in general, the key is to co-ordinate air and surface planning, and to think through synergistic mechanisms in each particular case, while also being alive to the contrary possibilities of interference. Sometimes it may be better to let one type of force handle the mission on its own, for example by relying on long range air and missile strikes guided by satellite intelligence rather than placing surface forces in harm's way. In the more common cases where joint engagement is appropriate, the benefits must be maximised by proper co-ordination, for instance by having both air and surface forces concentrate first on winning the air battle so that they can then both turn to winning the surface battle (as in Lebanon in 1982). This need to maximise the co-ordination of assets in order to achieve the greatest synergy raises the final, vexed question of how the aerospace components of joint forces are best handled in terms of command and control.

COMMAND AND CONTROL

The issue of aerospace command and control is simply one aspect of the general problem of controlling powerful assets in war. This problem involves two funda-mental and related choices – between centralisation and decentralisation, and between specialisation and integration. Centralisation has the advantage that scarce assets may be focused at the decisive point rather than frittered away in penny packets, while decentralisation has the advantage that it is easier for the assets to respond quickly to threats and opportunities at the local level. Specialisation encourages commanders to develop the 'vision' to employ the assets to best strategic effect, while integration makes it easier to co-ordinate the employment of the assets with the use of other arms within the same command and control structure.

Neither of these are straight 'either-or' choices, and there have been many instances of intermediate options being adopted to try to get the best of both worlds. Although trade-offs are inevitable whatever solutions are adopted, some solutions are clearly 'less bad' than others in particular cases. For example, in 1940, the French approach of assigning armour support to infantry armies in a decentralised and integrated fashion proved markedly inferior to the German approach of massing their armour in specialist 'Panzergruppen', focusing these at a decisive point for the breakthrough, but having enough decentralised command to allow panzer leaders like Guderian and Rommel to use their initiative and exploit local opportunities as they raced ahead of the infantry armies slogging along behind.

The long-standing preference of air theorists faced with this command and control dilemma has been for specialisation and centralisation. They have argued fervently that air assets should be controlled by a separate air force, not limited to supporting the army or navy, but capable of focusing air attacks against strategic targets as the most cost-effective way of employing this form of power. Air theo-rists have also been strong supporters of centralisation, because of the cost and scarcity of the assets involved, and because these assets return to established bases after each raid, making them much more amenable to central direction by a higher commander than are surface forces which remain continuously engaged and so rely more on the initiative of the commander on the spot.[19]

Airmen have largely had their way on these issues, thanks to the gradual emer-gence of separate air forces earlier this century. However, armies and navies now

---

19. See Meilinger (op cit).

field increasingly significant air fleets of their own, especially if one includes missiles and UAVs as well as fixed and rotary wing aircraft. These two services tend to take a more equivocal approach to the command problems outlined above, preferring a rather greater degree of decentralisation and integration in their air arms. The different philosophies have produced certain tensions over the ownership and employment of particular air assets, as in the debates in Britain regarding the support helicopter force and the doctrinal consequences of acquiring Apache attack helicopters.[20]

The problems of each service running its own air war became evident in Vietnam, when control of the US air effort was disastrously fragmented.[21] To avoid such problems, the accepted procedure today is to have a Joint Force Air Component Commander (JFACC), drawn from the service providing most air assets, who is responsible to the Joint Force Commander for co-ordinating the whole air operation via a joint air planning staff. However, the growing pervasiveness of aerospace vehicles within military power as a whole means that not all such vehicles fall within this highly centralised framework. Satellites are handled separately at the national level, while some helicopters, missile systems and UAVs remain much more under the immediate control of surface commanders. There also remain some fundamental underlying tensions between different services over whether the balance in command and control arrangements has been struck correctly.[22]

New information technology is improving procedures in several ways. In the USA, for example, the new Contingency Theater Automated Planning System (CTAPS) addresses several of the shortcomings evident from the Gulf War, such as the difficulty of modifying the Air Tasking Order (ATO), and the problem of integrating naval forces into the process without proper electronic links. Once its teething problems have been overcome, CTAPS should also make planning less cumbersome, while allowing a wider range of air vehicles to be incorporated into the ATO so that the risk of fratricide is minimised.[23] The continuing revolution in command and control technology will no doubt widen options further, to the point where every tank, aircraft and ship may have access to a real time electronic picture of the entire battlespace, but this does not in itself resolve the

---

20. See, for example, Grahame Keating, 'Back to the Future- Britain's New Royal Flying Corps', *RUSI Journal*, April 1996.
21. See William Momyer, *Air Power in Three Wars* (Washington DC: USGPO, 1978), ch.III.
22. See, for example, J L Whitlow, 'JFACC: Who's in Charge?', *Joint Force Quarterly*, Summer 1994.
23. See Marcus Hurley, 'JFACC: Taking the Next Step', *Joint Force Quarterly*, Spring 1995.

problem of where the locus of command and control of the various aerospace assets should lie.

Would one solution be to re-absorb air forces back within armies and navies, thereby removing some of the inefficiencies associated with the current tripartite structure of air command? Those who see a long term technological trend away from manned aircraft towards missiles, UAVs and satellites do sometimes argue that this trend will progressively remove the rationale for separate air forces altogether.[24] It is certainly true that air forces which focus unduly on manned systems may create problems for themselves as technology and threats develop. It is also true that there are profound cultural obstacles to the assumption of command by airmen without personal flying experience 'at the sharp end'.[25] However, the idea that command and control tensions and inefficiencies could be resolved by reintegrating all aerospace assets back into surface forces is fundamentally flawed, because it flies in the face of the unique characteristics and growing importance of aerospace vehicles.

For one thing, manned aircraft seem likely to remain far more efficient than one-shot missile systems for superior air powers like Britain and the United States, especially now that the focus is on conventional rather than nuclear warfare. Even if improvements in sensors, communications and artificial intelligence mean that it becomes sensible in due course to remove personnel from the vehicles themselves, the systems will have the same essential characteristics as at present. Since the justification for specialised air forces lies in the need for a coherent overall vision of how to win control of the air and exploit this in strategic terms, and has little or nothing to do with the technical skills of piloting the vehicles involved, any shift towards unmanned systems should be irrelevant to the broader command and control dilemma.

Furthermore, splitting all aerospace vehicles between armies and navies runs directly counter to the freedom of movement of the systems concerned, and their ability to transcend and ignore what in surface terms is a fundamental divide between two entirely different media. Imposing an artificial division running through the heart of the aerospace continuum would be profoundly damaging, and is exactly the kind of thing the institution of the JFACC is designed to prevent. It is hard to believe that any modern state which has hopes of winning rather than losing the all-important contest for air superiority would want to wind

---

24. See, for example, the correspondence in *The Times* on June 20th, 26th and 30th and July 4th and 8th, 1997, and 'Missiles threaten to down the RAF', *Sunday Times*, August 24th, 1997.
25. On the role of these factors in the US Air Force, see Carl Builder, *The Icarus Syndrome* (New Brunswick NJ: Transaction, 1994).

the clock back to the command and control arrangements of the start of this century. The real issue is how to handle in terms of command and control the very real physical difference within the aerospace realm between the atmospheric and orbital environments, and this issue is discussed by General Jones elsewhere in this volume.

There will never be a wholly satisfactory solution to the problems of aerospace command and control, given the fundamental trade-offs outlined at the start of this section. The important thing is to learn from experience which compromise approaches work better than others. The current dispersion of aerospace assets among all three services might seem gravely inefficient, but in fact, it does at least approximate to such a 'least bad' compromise approach. There are strong grounds for believing that command and control arrangements should depend primarily on the varying characteristics of the vehicles themselves, with the more scarce and potent assets which depend the most on fixed land bases being subject to centralised tasking by specialists, while less capable but more numerous and less base-dependent assets can be decentralised and integrated more with the operations of surface forces. Above all, there must be continuing progress towards jointery, so that commanders at all levels and of all types of forces understand the overall shape of the aerospace battle and can see what mix of air and surface assets is appropriate and how they should be co-ordinated to achieve maximum synergy.

CONCLUSION

The welcome and long overdue shift towards 'jointery' in Western military forces needs to be reinforced by a new tri-service doctrinal framework organised more around different types of joint campaigns, and less around the increasingly problematic traditional categories of air, land and sea power. However, there will remain a need to consider the specific role of aerospace vehicles within and across these various joint campaigns. Although air **power** is increasingly difficult to define, due to the proliferation of related systems among all three services, these systems themselves all share the distinctive attribute of **flight,** and so have characteristic strengths and limitations which need to be considered on an organised analytical basis.

The missions which aerospace vehicles can perform in joint warfare may be reduced at the most basic level to the five generic categories of 'observe, 'intercept', 'attack', 'transport', and 'support'. How large a contribution aerospace systems can make to the overall campaign within each of these mission categories is highly situation specific, but one may identify a range of key variables under the broad headings of 'political objectives', 'aerospace forces', 'surface forces', and the 'battle area', which may help in deciding the most appropriate balance of effort between air and surface capabilities.

Whatever balance is appropriate, it is important to ensure that the combination produces synergy rather than interference. Attaining synergy through proper co-ordination of effort is of particular significance in the context of air-**land** operations, although air assets are no longer the junior partner which they once were. The command and control of aerospace forces will remain a matter of striking the right balance among conflicting imperatives, with centralisation and specialisation of command being more appropriate for the scarcer and more potent assets, while decentralisation and integration may be possible for less capable and base-dependent systems. However, even if unmanned aerospace systems do gradually attain greater prominence as technology advances, there will remain a very strong case, especially in countries enjoying aerospace superiority, for all three Services to retain their identity within an increasingly joint framework.

CHAPTER 10

AIR POWER AND COERCION
Group Captain A P N Lambert

INTRODUCTION

THE WARFIGHTING PARADIGMS of the Cold-War era require consider-able revision if they are to have utility in the turbulent inter and intra-state relations of the new Millennium. The geographical imperative to defend West Germany as far forward as possible that the Cold War placed on commanders required massed armies and a defensive style of warfare more redolent of WWI than the manoeuvre attacks of WWII. Now, thankfully, all that is past – for the time being at least. Abrasive Foreign Policy, however, did not die with the end of the Cold War; inter-state rivalries, ethnic friction and belligerent criminal activi-ties have, arguably, increased in number if not in intensity since the ending of bipolar equilibrium. Moreover, the pre-democratic anarchic nature of much of the world suggests that there are still great opportunities for despotic adventurers to exploit their weaker brethren using military muscle. While we may see rela-tively few eruptions such as the Falklands or Gulf Wars in the immediate future, we should ponder that each event did, like many others probably will in the future, largely catch us on the hop.

Air Power's utility in this boiling cauldron of world affairs is now acknowl-edged by all but its most extreme detractors. Its speed of reaction is highly responsive to political needs; it commits and risks the minimum number of personnel; it can deliver enormous punch from which it is almost impossible to hide; and can do so now with a precision that both opens up new coercive possi-bilities and minimises casualties[1]. As the USAF School of Advanced Air Power Studies paper has argued[2], the Balkans Air Campaign, executed under the code-word Operation DELIBERATE FORCE, showed that Air Power is likely to be a key, and possibly decisive, ingredient in any future operation.

---

1. For a treatise on the fundamentals of coercion see Michael Clarke, *Air Power, Force and Coercion*, in *The Dynamics of Air Power* by Lambert and Williamson (eds), MOD London, 1996.
2. Air University Paper, The Balkans Air Campaign, in *Air Power Journal*, Summer 1997, pp 67-85.

If force is to be used, current Western sensitivities demand that its aim should fall far short of total military defeat and outright military occupation, with their concomitant requirement to garrison the delinquent state. If force is to have a utility in military operations short of total war, its use will probably be in the context of a more subtle, and hence coercive application.

Coercion, in its strict interpretation, focuses on the use of force, and it is true that in every international relationship where one side seeks to influence another's behaviour the threat of the use of force is always present, either overtly or implicitly. In reality, however, states almost always prefer other instruments either as precursors to the use of force, or, at the very least, in parallel with it. A Western response to a crisis is thus likely to be both ad hoc and multi-faceted, involving humanitarian aid, quiet diplomacy, persuasion through the megaphone of the media, opprobrium through the UN, economic sanctions and, if all those fail, the threat or the use of force. The interaction between the panoply of instruments suggests that they should never be examined in isolation; it is their combined effect that provides the leverage and, if we are to comprehend their impact as perceived by the decision makers in the target state, we must consider them as part of a whole.

Many theories attempt to explain coercion; but deriving a theory that enjoys universal support is fraught. To the left of arc is the Schelling approach of graduated response, where costs are increased slowly, allowing the victim time for sober reflection, and logical compliance. At the right of arc stands Douhet, with his massive punishment strategy, designed to destroy civilian resolve. Whether these two strategies lie on the same spectrum or are, in reality, on different axes is still an open question. My fundamental assumption is that war is, however, an event between human beings, with individual and collective aspirations, and with individual and collective risks.

For the purposes of this chapter the word coercion includes both compellence and deterrence, but the focus will be primarily on the compellent aspects. The chapter does not attempt to argue the pros and cons of any particular taxonomy; but it suggests a more objective view of the processes involved. It reviews the historiography and concepts that underpin coercion, and finishes by suggesting some coercive lessons from recent campaigns. In parallel, it reviews some of the deficiencies in extant work and applies psychological and decision making principles to the mechanics involved.

USE OF FORCE

In its most stark form, force destroys something, thereby depriving an opponent of its use, hence limiting his future courses of action. At one extreme, the destruction of the Grande Armée in 1815 finally thwarted Napoleon's ambitions and it laid France open to occupation. Conversely, at the other end of the spectrum, the application of even a relatively small amount of force may be enough to persuade the victims that any further resistance is futile, and they then elect to comply in order to avoid further attrition. Examples of such coercion include the "gunboat diplomacy" of the colonial era, or even the Air Control of the Middle East in the 1920s. Such a differentiation echoes the thoughts of earlier nuclear theorists.

> Thomas Schelling, in his 1960s analysis of nuclear power, distinguished between "brute force" and "coercive force". "Brute force" referred to those cases where military power was used to destroy something, purely to deny it to an adversary, or to exert force in such a way as physically to prevent a certain behaviour.
> "Coercive force", on the other hand, referred to the use of violence as a way of hurting or punishing an adversary, and there was, therefore, an implicit bargain between user and victim to deter or compel a certain type of behaviour.[3]

If we are to understand the use of force it is necessary to distinguish the primary purpose of an operation – whether it is principally to *Deny* a victim his military options or to *Coerce* him.

DENIAL

There are times when one is not interested in whether an enemy is coerced or not; for example, if he is disarmed, although he may still be vindictive, he is still disarmed. Denial, in the form of constraint or destruction, aims to reduce an opponent's war-making capability or potential, either by preventing movement or deployment, or by altering the balance of power. This can be achieved through the destruction of his forces, or by more subtle means, such as the containment of forces through destruction of bridges, the sowing of minefields[4] or by confinement through blockade. Denial prevents the victim from waging war as he intended, and it normally also alters the victim's expectation of success. Perhaps from enduring physical damage on his lines of communication, from watching his

---

3. Michael Clarke, op cit, p67.
4. NB British policy now eschews mine operations.

command functions paralysed, or from seeing his means of waging war destroyed, the victim is forced to recognise that, unless he accedes to the assailant's wishes, the balance of power will be irretrievably altered, that he will lose to his opponents, and may lose quickly. A good example of a denial campaign is the attritional warfare of WWI where the intention on both sides became the destruction of the enemy's army. Once the army had been destroyed, the vanquished state would feel compelled to surrender. This linkage is important and will be returned to below.

Often unavoidably, past denial campaigns have degenerated into a slogging match, an attritional process that continues as the pendulum of advantage swings from one side to the other, until the balance of power finally becomes irrevocably altered. Indeed, many denial campaigns degenerate still further, into a match where the contest is less over who achieves a military advantage, more over which side can tolerate the most pain. It becomes rather more a contest of stamina – who can endure losses for longer. In effect, not which side can win, but which can come second-last.

Denial campaigns thus frequently achieve a momentum all of their own and can become difficult to terminate, even well beyond the culminating point of defeat. The reasons are many. First, is the element of self-delusion. For good psychological reasons commentators frequently become fixated by losses, rather than the more important factor, what remains. For example, commentators waxed lyrical over losses on (e.g.) the first day of the Battle of the Somme, but neither they nor the public seemed interested in the more important criterion – the balance of forces remaining. With this fixation, propaganda machines go into overdrive as they talk up enemy losses while minimising one's own. Nations thus become deluded into thinking that the enemy is close to exhaustion, he cannot sustain further losses and victory must, therefore, be just around the corner. Second, habituation to own losses can take place. Provided the loss rate is not perceived to be too severe, and the cause deemed important enough, then populations, leaders and even military personnel adjust to a slow rise in casualty rates.[5] Third, as the war progresses, leaders become progressively identified with the outcome of the war, and surrender without success is seen not only as a waste of the investment in the war, but more importantly, as a betrayal of those who have

---

5. In WWII, loss rates amongst bomber crews grew progressively throughout 1943 and early 1944. Bomber crews of the USAAF coped with their personal vulnerability provided they had a reasonable chance of survival. "BGen Eaker felt strongly that for a man to stay and fight he needed at least an even chance of survival". Tour lengths were adjusted to balance crew survival against operational needs. Mark K Wells, *Courage and Air Warfare*, Frank Cass, London, 1995, p. 103.

given their lives in the cause. A willingness even to consider negotiations is seen as debasing their sacrifice. – "How can we give up now, after so many gave so much?" – Finally, at a personal level, failure in the war may also be regarded as a failure of the government, perhaps with dire personal consequences for its leadership. For example, how could the senior leadership of the Nazi party have entertained any thought of surrender? – To have done so would have been tantamount to signing their own death warrant.

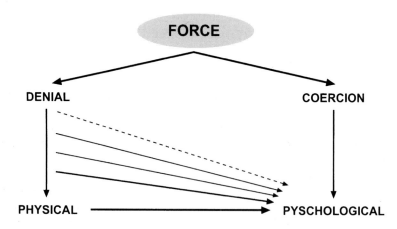

Figure 10.1
Physical and Psychological Aspects of Force.

Denial is fundamentally a physical act, but inexorable attrition seems to portend inevitable defeat. Progressively and surreptitiously, this produces a psychological reaction, and hence a measure of coercion. Even in WWI, capitulation occurred far short of annihilation of the German army. Indeed, the German army felt it had been stabbed in the back by its political leadership. The psychological result of denial is critical to understanding the processes. At one end of the spectrum a denial tactic that physically constrains produces frustration at the very least. At the other extreme, an attritional campaign becomes progressively coercive as casualties mount, and the progressive destruction of the military power-base, and the prospect of impending defeat, are highly compelling, even far short of total destruction. That said, evidence suggests that where an enemy feels that there is **no** way out he may, like a cornered animal, fight fiercely to the death. This was the choice that the allies gave Hitler, which inevitably meant that the allies would have to march on to Berlin.

Denial also has the unfortunate side-effect that the sheer size of the operation, and the scale of destruction may produce considerable collateral damage, and, at the very least, destroy items of great sentimental or cultural value. This may produce a sense of outrage, encouraging even the war's detractors to rally to the cause, and making the rest determined to fight all the harder.

However, if the study of warfare is confined only to denial, the most physical of wartime phenomena, it rather misses the point. At all levels, war is fought by human beings, each with his own hope of success and fear of failure, each with his own prospects of reward and fear of retribution. And it is based on these, and even more subtle and diffuse beliefs, that the individual will fight and die, or give up in surrender or flight. Erroneously, the quality of a force is often measured in numbers and weapons when, in reality, morale, resolve and commitment are often more decisive. Indeed, no two apparently evenly matched armies ever fight to mutual destruction; at some point one side gives up and the other is victorious.

In his analysis of coercive methods, Alexander George distinguished between "coercive diplomacy" as an alternative to "military strategy"[6]. This somewhat arcane distinction is difficult to draw, and is more in the mind than in reality. Indeed, Clausewitz accentuated the fact that force is always used as an instrument of policy, and that the aim of war itself is to "compel the enemy to do one's will". Force, or the threat of the use of force, is used right across the spectrum of conflict, and to seek to draw a line between the use of force for "coercive diplomacy" and war-fighting is simplistic. Force is always used to compel; in reality, the purpose of "war fighting" is less to annihilate, but far more to coerce – be it to persuade the enemy to comply with demands, to compel an army to surrender, or just to run away.

COERCION

Fundamentally, Coercion is about persuasion, and it is hence a psychological activity[7]. It seeks to: dissuade an adversary, to persuade him to do what he would

---

6. A L George, *The Limits of Coercive Diplomacy*, Westview Press, Boulder Colo, 1994, p 10.
7. British Defence Doctrine, British Military Doctrine, and many classical theorists all allude to the importance of psychological factors in war. Indeed, the basis of the British Army's Manoeuvrist Approach is not so much to destroy an army but rather to undermine the enemy''s resolve to continue the fight. The secret lies in how to invest in that of wartime success lies in investing in the precise destruction that will produce the maximum profit in terms of the return in its subversion of enemy resolve. In other words, what damage will produce the earliest submission?

prefer not, or to desist from what he is currently doing. But, like beauty, coercion is in the eye of the beholder. From an analytical point of view, it is the perceptions of the victim that matter, and not the intentions of the coercer. At one extreme, the atomic attacks on Japan at the end of WW II were highly coercive. Hiroshima was the HQ of the Japanese 2nd Army; it was a road/rail/port complex, but its destruction could equally have been accomplished by 210 B-29 sorties[8] in just one raid. The destruction of Hiroshima and Nagasaki, therefore, by single weapons produced profound psychological intimidation. As Japan saw it, the aim was not to deny an important facility to the Japanese – the purpose was simply to demonstrate not only Japan's profound impotence to do anything in response, but also her abject vulnerability. The implication was clear: the next would surely fall on Tokyo[9], and hazard the life of the Emperor. These supreme events, together with other misfortunes, combined to put inescapable pressure on the leadership both to surrender, and equally, giving them a pretext for so doing. At the other end of the spectrum, coercion is the only realistic option open to terrorists who could not engage in classic warfare.

In terms of presentation, coercion enjoys an advantage over Denial. Denial removes or destroys an object; the choice of target rests with the assailant, and responsibility for any casualties or collateral damage is his alone. Coercion, on the other hand, threatens to destroy something only while the victim remains in his delinquent state. Thus the burden of choice passes to the victim – cease your criminal activity or suffer the consequences.

In a coercive process, there are many different audiences each with his own agenda and perspective. What might appear a simple process of a coercer attempting to coerce a victim, is in fact far more complex. The coercion may have to gain acceptability from a whole range of third parties, ranging from the public opinion of the coercing party, to allied leaderships and their publics' opinion, through supra-national organisations, and the patron(s) of the victim state. Finally, but by no means least, the coercer will hope to establish his credibility more widely if he wishes to be taken seriously in the future by any other putative malefactor, who will be watching the current contest with interest.

---

8. Pape, *Bombing to Win*, Cornell Univ Press, 1996, , p.105.

9. Recent research suggests that a third weapon was available, that it would have been dropped on or near Tokyo on the night of 17/18th Aug, just before dawn, in imitation of the power to create a false dawn, a new Rising Sun. Night would be turned into day, lest anyone had missed the god-like power the US possessed.

DETERRENCE

The most effective form of coercion is a stated (or even implied) threat that does not have to be carried out because it is believed and feared, thereby deterring an adversary from a particular course of action. Unfortunately, the success of a deterrent threat frequently goes unrecognised since the object of the threat may be deterred even from contemplating a particular course, or he may reject it at an early stage. In consequence he appears to do nothing. British naval policy of the Victorian era, to maintain a standing navy twice the size of the next nearest competitor, was a manifestation of such a policy. Indeed, the success of a deterrent can best be measured by the paucity of challenges against it.

Unfortunately, unless the asymmetry of power is vast, deterrence based on conventional weapons is inherently contestable, and an adversary may have few reservations in reacting aggressively to test and explore the credibility of a threatened use of force. Indeed, just like a naughty schoolboy, a belligerent may try to assess what constraints are operating and where the point of punishment really lies; there will always exist, therefore, a tension between a threat and calling its bluff. In Bosnia, for example, the Serbs frequently tested the UN's resolve, to find what level of atrocities or military activity was likely to precipitate UN punishment. At Srebrenica, in particular, the West had implied that it would react strongly if this "safe area" was attacked; this, the Serbs did not believe. In the event, NATO Air Power attacked just 2 tanks and then largely stood by while the town was overrun, the men massacred, women raped and the town ethnically cleansed. This reinforced the Serbs' perceptions and gave a "green light" for an attack on the other safe areas, Zepa and Gorazde.

In simple theoretical deterrent contests, such as exemplified by the "Chicken" game, one contestant can gain psychological dominance over the other by various subterfuges which demonstrate an absence of constraints, – one such subterfuge might be to say that "I have an incurable disease and will die anyway". The essence is to demonstrate that "there are no constraints upon me, whereas you have everything to lose".

An adversary's reaction to a deterrent posture may be far less in contemplating a trial of strength, but rather in identifying and exploiting the weaknesses of those doing the deterring. One example of an unsuccessful deterrent strategy but a successful coercive strategy, was the 1982 terrorist truck-bombing of the US Marine barracks in Beirut, with the unexpected and sudden loss of 300 men. The US presence in Beirut was designed to demonstrate her power, to overawe and deter the factions then operating in the Lebanon. In response, Hizbollah's aim was simple: to puncture the myth of overwhelming US power by exploiting her extreme vulnerability to human losses, thereby compelling her to withdraw. At no time did Hizbollah seek to alter the balance of power vis-à-vis the USA, since to have done so would have been somewhat futile.

Both Bosnia and the Gulf War demonstrated a further phenomenon, that of self-deterrence. Given the West's sensitivities, not only to receiving casualties, but in inflicting them as well, the use of force may backfire, and become counter-productive. Western public opinion would have little sympathy for a posture based on chemical warfare, but even in conventional warfare, where enemy casualties became too large then the West may back down. In Bosnia, a sensitivity to casualties, and a desire to remain on the touchline, deterred the UN from applying its air power effectively. In the Gulf War the perceived scale of casualties amongst the fleeing Iraqis on the Al Basrah road produced popular revulsion, and the perception of "massacre" was a key ingredient in the early termination of the conflict.

COMPELLENCE

Coercion, poorly targeted, or applied too slowly, can exhibit many of the disadvantages of Denial, and can often embroil one more deeply in a war. Unfortunately, a slow pace means that the target may have time not only to habituate to the pain, but also to take effective countermeasures. The graduated response strategy of **ROLLING THUNDER** against the North Vietnamese fitted this model, and there is considerable evidence not only that it failed either to coerce or deny, but also that it gave the population time to become hardened to the bombing, time to upgrade their air defences, time to put their industry on a war footing, time to garner allies, and time to mobilise.

Unfortunately, in the highly complex world of UN operations and multinational forces, constraints frequently swamp capabilities, and what was conceived as an overwhelming demonstrative application of coercive force often serves to say more about a coercer's constraints, weaknesses and lack of resolve, than it implies about his determination. NATO's raid on Udbina airfield in 1994 gave such a message. The damage inflicted was minimal, and easily repaired. In contrast, what was supposed to demonstrate NATO's overwhelming power probably said more to all sides about the constraints under which NATO laboured, giving a perception of political weakness and lack of commitment. The effect was thus the opposite to that desired; and like Srebrenica, it encouraged the belligerents to redouble their efforts.

Compellence is harder to achieve than deterrence since threats that failed to deter are unlikely to compel, and victims are normally willing to pay higher costs to retain possessions than the assailants are to take them. Moreover, because it is psychological, coercion is also heavily time-dependent. The instantaneous loss of the 300 men from the truck-bombing in Beirut was far more stressful than the same loss spread out over several months, as British experience in Northern Ireland amply demonstrates.

Some military activities which pass for coercion have, in reality, no intention of compelling; their aim is to establish a future credibility, or just to bolster the morale of own or allied personnel:

> The most obscure form of hurt is pure punishment, perhaps where a threat has failed and force is used to punish the adversary to re-establish the credibility of threats for the future. Punishment not designed to re-establish credibility is mere revenge and has no utility of itself, except perhaps for the satisfaction or morale of those inflicting it.[10]

In a similar vein, domestic politics often become a more important outcome than the coercion of an opponent. In the period before an election governments have been known to execute raids on delinquent states to demonstrate their standing on the world stage, rather more than in the hope of achieving a desired coercive outcome. Such operations should not really be judged as genuine coercive attempts – nevertheless, an examination of the use of coercion as an electoral tool might, on the other hand, prove interesting to a researcher interested in conspiracy theory!

MECHANICS OF COERCION

At its simplest level, that of the individual, coercion is typified by a "carrot and stick" approach, of inducements against stressors: rewarding compliance, while threatening to punish intransigence. Individuals are highly impressed by asymmetries of power and vulnerability, and the consequent implications for their own life expectancy. The use, or the threat of the use, of force is thus always accorded a high priority in personal decision-making and it inevitably produces a significant psychological reaction. The reaction varies with personality type, perspective, and the perceived vulnerability of the victim. Where force is targeted directly, the reaction might vary from submission and compliance, to outrage and a desire to fight back at all costs.

---

10. Clarke, op cit, p. 70.

Psychologically, victims are more impressed by a forthcoming stressful event than they are by an equivalent inducement. In other words, an inducement has to be significant to match a smaller but credible physical threat. Moreover, fear of failure is often more important than hope of success. Success, once achieved, becomes the new norm, whilst failure carries huge penalties. Unlike denial, which concentrates on damage done thus far, coercion accentuates prospective damage. Moreover, rates of destruction are more highly regarded than levels of destruction, and the victims' perception of future events is derived from extrapolation.

At the individual level the coercive processes can be inferred from classic psychology. At the collective level, the processes are not so straightforward. Four principal decision-making theories enjoy currency: realism, with decisions taken by a unitary rational actor; organisation theory, where decisions are more the result of "turf battles" between bureaucratic self-interest groups; social psychology, where decisions are the product of small elites, who brainstorm ideas; and cognitive psychology, where decisions are taken by individuals each of whom is subject to stressors.[11] This chapter cannot give space to weigh the theories, rather, it will blend the salient points of each, and examine how coercion has impacted on decision makers.

If stress is the prime agent of coercion, then violence is its prime instrument. A campaign that seeks to persuade without violence will have to offer very strong inducements indeed, or it will most likely fail. Similarly, a threat of violence without the substance is not likely to enjoy much credibility and, as Robert Pape has argued,[12] the most effective option may be a denial campaign which, he argues, should focus on the military.

ASYMMETRY

Effective coercion is also not about a fair fight. To be successful, a coercer needs to demonstrate his asymmetry, both of power and invulnerability, to force the perceptions that he has the initiative, and that the opponent is utterly defenceless. The effect of this stark asymmetry is not new. Rommel made the famous remarks that:

---

11. Holsti, O R, *Crisis Management*, in *Psychological Dimensions of War*, by Glad, E, Sage Pubs, 1990, p. 121.
12. Pape, R A, op cit, p 15. – "When coercion does work, it is by Denial."

...anyone who has to fight, even with the most modern weapons, against an enemy in complete control of the air fights like a savage against modern European troops, under the same handicap, and with the same chance of success.[13]

The enemy's air superiority has a very grave effect on our movements. There's simply no answer to it.[14]

In the 1991 Gulf War, the Iraqi soldiery faced a similar imbalance. As the Coalitions growing air superiority demonstrated, Iraqi forces could do little to prevent allied air power from having free rein across the whole country; they were incapable of preventing aircraft operations, and unable to prevent aircraft from attacking targets at will. Even their best efforts seemed impotent. In contrast to the Vietnam War, where aircraft losses had been significant, coalition losses in the Gulf were measured in fractions of one per cent.[15]

In both these circumstances the Allies enjoyed overwhelming power, and the few vulnerabilities were largely mitigated by a commitment that would tolerate substantial casualties. However, in operations where commitment is low, or the constraints imposed are high, then the tables may be turned. The coercer's overwhelming combat power become progressively attenuated as the capability is passed through a mesh of constraints. Meanwhile, his force deployment may itself offer a vulnerability ripe for the picking. In Bosnia in 1995, for example, UN forces were taken hostage as a counter to the very limited NATO bombing.

Asymmetry of power alone is thus not a very effective predictor of coercive outcome, and any putative coercer needs equally to examine the balance of vulnerabilities and the relative constraints for himself and his victim. Similarly, conventional balances of power can be misleading since alternative means of fighting may also render simple calculations of power obsolete.

---

13. Lewin, Rommel as Military Commander, (Batsford 1968), p.162 in ibid., p. 383.

14. Field Marshal E Rommel. Letter to his wife, in R P Hallion, 'Strike from the Sky,' p. 205.

15. Therefore, an important deduction is that there is not only the obvious physical reason for destroying the opponent's Air Defences and Command and Control system, – it is a fundamental first step in convincing the opponent of his vulnerability, – that the screw can and will be tightened at the whim of the coercer.

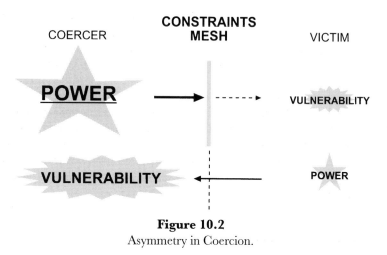

Figure 10.2
Asymmetry in Coercion.

SELECTING A VICTIM

A vulnerability is only exploitable if coercion targets people that can have an effect on the outcome. Historically, coercion has been regarded as focusing on one or more of 3 groups of the population.

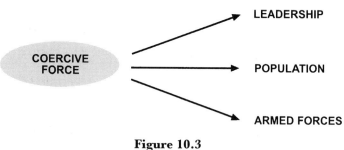

Figure 10.3
Targets of Coercion.

Hiroshima targeted the leadership, the Strategic Bomber Campaign of WWII was originally conceived to target the morale of the enemy's population, and the Gulf Air Campaign proved most effective in destroying the resolve of the Iraqi Army .

The effectiveness of coercion rests in its exploitation – on an understanding of the decision making and psychological processes involved: on deciding whom to hurt and what potential destruction the victim will find unbearably painful. The "whom" requires an objective assessment of who are the true power brokers. Who in the target group has the power to respond in the desired way, and has the power to carry the oligarchy with him? To take an obvious example, in the final stages of the Pacific War in 1945 should the US seek to coerce the emperor, the political leadership or the Japanese army? Similar choices would have had to be made against communist states, where factions in the communist party may have been more influential than a political figurehead. Similarly, in Iran Ayatollah Khomeini would probably have been a more lucrative coercive target than the nominal government.

COUNTER-COERCION

It is important to remember also that while an assailant is focusing on his target audience, whichever that might be, the nominal "victim" is almost certain to attempt counter-coercion. Probably, because of the likely asymmetry in conventional power the victim may use methods other than military force, or even other forms of military power, such as WMD or guerrilla tactics, the use of ballistic missiles, laser weapons or even Information Warfare.

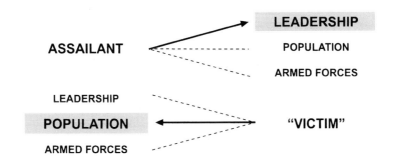

Figure 10.4
Potential Targets of Coercive Force.

And, since Western democracies are susceptible to persuasion, the most profitable target may be judged to be the population. So, while the US was busy coercing the North Vietnamese leadership through bombardment, Ho Chi Minh was busy coercing the US population via the Media. An attack on the population or the armed forces would normally lead to pressure on the existing leadership to surrender or comply, but this is not inevitably true. In 1917, the Germans helped the Bolsheviks undermine the existing leadership, thereby substituting a non-compliant leadership with a compliant one.

Selection of the most lucrative group is difficult. Pape argues that attacks on civilians are unlikely to be effective:

> Social scientists have long studied the effectiveness of both threats to civilians ("punishment") and threats of military failure ("denial") for deterrence. Punishment threatens to inflict costs heavier than the value of anything the challenger could gain, and denial threatens to defeat the adventure[16]....
>
> The evidence shows that it is the threat of military failure .... and not threats to civilians, ... which produces the critical leverage in conventional coercion.[17]

Indeed, while leaderships and forces have proved susceptible to coercive force, populations frequently have not. The reasons perhaps lie not only the size of the target audience, but, more importantly, on the fact that the population's demotivation is often difficult to translate into a desirable outcome, especially if the target state is a dictatorship and, in surrender, the dictator is possibly facing his own demise. In Hitler's case it is likely that he would have accepted almost unlimited destruction of his population before he agreed to surrender. In any case, deliberate attacks on non-combatants are now clearly considered unlawful. For the West, therefore, on non-combatants are unlikely to be acceptable, but, conversely, our vulnerability to civilian casualties makes civilians an attractive option for others not fettered by the rule of international law. Indeed, the SCUDS fired against Israel in the Gulf War almost unhinged the Coalition, and the War of the Cities in the Iran/Iraq War was certainly a factor in bringing that conflict to a conclusion.

But anti-leadership strategies can also be unpredictable. Against Qaddafi, the 1986 bombing raid of Libya seems to have had mixed results. Anecdotal evidence suggests that the accidental death of a young girl – "one of my daughters" – in the Azziziyah barracks did more to persuade him of his personal vulnerability – with the result that he quickly retired into the desert. That said, in the aftermath

---

16. Pape, op cit, p. 7.
17. Pape, op cit, p. 10.

of the attack, terrorism did not decline but actually increased, culminating in the bombing of Pan Am 103 over Lockerbie 2 years later. Whether this was because by then he felt far less vulnerable – since it had become clear that no further attacks would be countenanced by the US Administration, is not certain.

In the Gulf War the *de facto* power brokers were the thousands of individuals in the Iraqi army who decided to desert, surrender or just run away. It mattered not a jot what the Ba'ath party wanted, or what Saddam intended, the power to continue the war had largely passed to the mass of the soldiery. And it is doubtful that they were concerned whether Kuwait could or could not be retained: what mattered to them was primarily their own survival in the face of the huge asymmetry of power demonstrated against them, amplified by coercive psychological operations that moulded Iraqi perceptions of their personal vulnerability.

VICTIM'S PERCEIVED VULNERABILITIES

Having selected the target group, there is a need for an assessment of the victim's vulnerabilities – what does he value, but more importantly, for what is he prepared to make any sacrifice? Maslow, in his study of the "Hierarchy of Needs" drew attention to the most fundamental requirement for every individual, that of the actuality (or illusion) of security. Weapons have always challenged individual and group securities which is why coercion applied to threaten the individual is always highly influential, with the degree of coercion proportional to the perceived risk posed.

The exact vulnerability will clearly differ from one individual or culture to another. Determining it is one of the more difficult assessments to be made, and is without any guarantee of success. For example altruistic unitary rational actor might be persuaded by devastation of his infrastructure since this would make life intolerable for his people, and costs would outweigh any anticipated benefits. Conversely, a despot might find that attacks on his population were perversely beneficial – they might focus the population's anger elsewhere, even reduce the number of mouths to feed/support, and provide a cause célèbre in the media battle. Certainly, Mohammed Fara Aideed seemed keen to exploit such a concern in Somalia.

Pape has argued that exploiting vulnerabilities is not the prime determinant of success. In his analysis the successful coercer should target the enemy's benefits, not his costs:

> The key to success is.... the ability to thwart the target state's military strategy for controlling the objectives in dispute.
>
> To succeed, the coercer must undermine the target state's confidence in its own military strategy.
>
> *Once a state is persuaded that objectives cannot be achieved, levels of costs that were bearable as long as there was a chance of success become intolerable. The target then concedes in order to avoid suffering further losses to no purpose.*[18]

However, if frustration of benefits is the only measure, it is difficult to see why the Japanese did not surrender far earlier than they did, when it became clear that their aims had been thwarted. In fact, they only gave up only when the failure could no longer be hidden and costs became unacceptable. Moreover, Pape's model combines tens, if not thousands or even millions of individuals into a single anthropomorphic entity, a "unitary rational actor" that, in reality, does not exist. The "state" does not have "a" view or "an" opinion. Some individuals will be persuaded others will not. The key is in compelling the power brokers – who may, or may not, be the leadership, and who may, or may not, have a single view.

Groups, of course, have their own dynamics. Under relatively benign conditions a group often presents a united front and speaks with a single voice. However, as the pressures mount, small groups tend to become more cohesive against a common enemy, while larger units fragment, and may ultimately even compete against each other. But even cohesive groups are rarely entirely objective. Dominance competitions, or factional self-interest pressures mean that the decisions may not be rational, weighing costs versus benefits. Even the view of a small elitist group is not entirely logical, since the leader can assume an overwhelming control of decisions. But even these small groups are impressionable. Successes are briefly hailed but rapidly become the new norm, while the risk of an obvious and decisive failure is very dangerous. Experiments have shown that people are disproportionately averse to suffering a loss from the status quo, and may prefer to yield a gain, rather than be responsible for a failure.

Against leaders, or small groups such as the Tikriti Clan that supports Saddam Hussein, tailoring the coercion is difficult:

> Predicting the response of any individual to coercive pressure is a highly subjective exercise at best because it turns on estimating the balance of incentive between the coercer and the target.[19]

---

18. Pape, op cit, p10.

19. Tim Zimmerman in *Coercive Diplomacy and Libya*, in *The Limits of Coercive Diplomacy*, op cit, p. 203.

This unpredictability means that leadership strategies can be fraught with danger. One option would include targeting the leader's self worth: his perception of immortality, of how history will regard him, and whether he has brought honour, or disgrace upon himself and his peers. Removal of the leader by 'decapitation' is another coercive option. One could argue that no one could have been worse than Hitler, and his removal would have placed a more compliant leader in power, who could then be compelled through a sense of his own vulnerability. However, even a successful decapitation strategy is fraught. Killing the leader might not produce compliance, but might equally likely precipitate a sense of outrage, and the replacement of a rogue by one that was even more extreme, and who may have less control of the reins of power. For example, had Saddam Hussein been killed during the Gulf air war, there would have been at least a chance that he would have been replaced by his heir apparent, the arrogant Uday, with almost totally unpredictable results.

Recent revolutionary changes in the *modus belli* suggest that certain non-violent coercive mechanisms may also be highly persuasive. While non-violent weapons cannot produce such immediate and decisive effects to challenge security, they can have more long term surreptitious threats that affect the individual's perception of his longer term prospects. For example, an information warfare weapon that targeted a dictator's bank accounts and demonstrated that his retirement security blanket could be removed might be highly influential.

APPLICATION

Since coercion is inherently a psychological mechanism, the application of stressors needs to be considered.

Incremental Force. Schelling's concept of an incremental application of force is highly theoretical, and assumes complete rationality on the part of the victim – somewhat difficult in the stresses of war! It is difficult to find a campaign where it has succeeded; but worse – its employment has frequently led up a *cul-de-sac*[20] or an escalation ladder. Indeed, the evidence from the ROLLING THUNDER campaign against Vietnam suggests that the initial graduated response strategy produced results the opposite of those intended. In early 1964 McNamara directed the JCS to develop a programme of "graduated overt

---

20. On 3 Sep 96, a number of CCM were fired against Baghdad, after a flagrant incursion by Iraqis into the Kurdistan area in N. Iraq. It did not modify Saddam Hussein's behaviour; indeed 14 mths later, in Nov 97, it looked as though a further attack would be needed.

military pressure"[21] which it was believed, Hanoi could not withstand. It began on 2 Mar 65, and built up progressively with ever increasing intensity. Why did it fail – since it demonstrated capability and resolve, and allowed the victim a chance for rational calculation of losses v gains? Perhaps the answer lies in the psychological process. Selye's General Adaptive Syndrome, see Figure 10.5 below, explained that as stressors mount, so too does performance, with the individual achieving a peak at "a". However, more stress, beyond the critical level cannot be dealt with by the individual, and faced with competing demands, he loses rationality, and his performance falls, ultimately to a point of confusion – "b"[22].

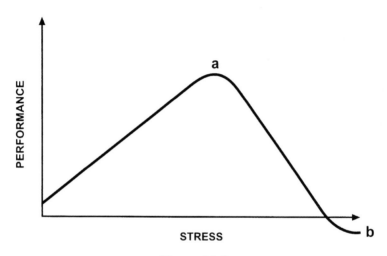

Figure 10.5
Selye's General Adaptive Syndrome.

In logic, coercion, which is fundamentally the application of stress, should produce a similar effect. Thus, if this is true, as the total coercion increases so too would the performance of the target audience. There is considerable evidence to support this hypothesis. In London in 1940, the relatively slow build up to the Blitz allowed Churchill time to prepare his population, time to pass emergency legislation, time to encourage longer hours of work, time to deploy his air defences and scope to demonise the Nazi threat.

---

21. Clodfelter, *The Limits of Airpower*, Free Press, NY 1989, p.45.
22. After Selye, General Adaptive Syndrome, *Understanding Stress*, by Sutherland &Cooper, Chapman & Hall, London 1990, p13.

During the employment of the Schelling strategy in Vietnam, a similar phenomenon seemed to be operating. Attacks grew in intensity, and the target area chosen was gradually moved further north[23]. However, the graduated response had little effect on North Vietnamese resolve, its war effort, or support for the Vietcong. Indeed, realising the air war would be limited, "Northern leaders used the air offensive to create popular support for the war"[24] The Leadership dispersed its oil reserves and evacuated urban centres. "Rolling Thunder's gradually increasing severity acclimated the North Vietnamese to the campaign..."[25] "In terms of its morale effects .... the US campaign may have presented the [North Vietnamese] regime with a near ideal mix of intended restraint and accidental gore."[26] These analysts agree with this hypothesis, therefore, that Incremental Stress did actually improve the performance of the target audience by :

- Giving the victim opportunity to take countermeasures, and to habituate to the stress.
- Giving a Sense of Purpose.
- Externalising the threat.
- Encouraging the population to rally round.

In sum, it can prove counter productive, and may be just what the victim leadership wanted.

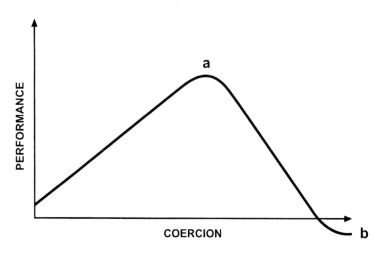

Figure 10.6
Performance Linked to Coercive Impact.

Taking the argument one stage further, and continuing to apply sound psychological stress principles, if it is true that the victim reaches a point of maximum performance at point "a"; it is also the point at which the victim is most focused on the task in hand, and his rationality is maximised. If the coercer wants to bargain with his victim, this would be the optimum point of bargaining. Provided it is clear to the victim that the coercer can, and most probably will, apply further stress, the victim should be at his most compliant. That said, for all the reasons given above, he may be unable to act rationally and compliance will only be achieved through levels of coercion that place the victim(s) into psychological confusion. Evidence from Iraqi POWs suggests that the bombing had certainly taken them to this point, depicted by "b" on the graph, see Figure 10.6.

According to one specialised clinic:[27]

> The Iraqis had been exposed to conditions specifically designed to lead to the development of Combat Stress Reaction (CSR). The incredibly intense and successful allied air campaign subjected many Iraqis to extraordinary stressors, including the constant fear of imminent death, frequent witnessing of the deaths and injuries of comrades, sleep deprivation, lack of food and water and disruption of command and control channels. Any of these circumstances separately would be expected to predispose a soldier to the development of CSR while their combination would multiply the risk.[28]
>
> All the EPWs [POWs] reported ... anxiety, depressed mood, sleep disturbance and fear. Other CSR symptoms reported by most of the EPWs included intense memories and dreams, exhaustion, irritability, guilt ... noise sensitivity, disciplinary problems, psychotic disturbances, dissociate slates, poor concentration and constricted affect. Homicidal ideas were expressed by half of the EPWs ... to kill their own officers.[29]

Unfortunately, it was not possible to quantify the level of trauma, nor to correlate it against particular attacks. Nevertheless, it was clear that all had been exposed to frequent bombings; several POWs indicated that bombings had occurred almost continuously. The least frequent was every two to three days. Living conditions were miserable with little food or water, and starvation was common. Soldiers lived in small groups, they often witnessed death or injury and

23. Pape, op cit, p. 185.
24. Clodfelter, op cit, p.138.
25. ibid.
26. Hoeffding, RAND Corp., in ibid.
27. J M Marcum and D W Cline, 'Combat Stress Reaction in Iraqi Prisoners of War', Bulletin of the Menninger Clinic Vol. 57, No 4 , Fall '93, p. 479.
28. ibid. p.480.
29. ibid.

medical care was largely non-existent; there was a marked schism between officers and enlisted soldiers. Soldiers were asked to rate their combat effectiveness at
the start of the ground war; all replied they were at 0%.

Many methods of coping were employed: "by far the most common response
involved prayer. Another common sustaining thought was of family members.
POWs often expressed fear for their family members, indicating that they would
have deserted except for anticipated reprisals against loved ones".[30] The strength
drawn from their small "buddy" groups was important to sustain them but they
openly discussed surrender and a third actively considered suicide.[31]

Fear of the allies grew progressively and eventually outweighed the fear of
death squads; at least 160,000 soldiers deserted. Until G-Day few prisoners were
taken, largely because of the Iraqi obstacles and minefields, but once these had
been breached the trickle became a flood; 87,000 gave up, most without a fight.

ANALYSIS

In stressful situations individuals make a model of the anticipated events, and
from this attempt to predict the outcome. Where an individual anticipates success
he commits himself more fully to the enterprise, and vice versa.

> The reasons for this may lie in the concept of self-efficacy. Self-efficacy theory was
> developed within the framework of social learning theory. The theory is founded upon
> the simple postulate that people's perceptions of their own capabilities influence how
> they act, their motivation levels, their thought patterns and their emotional reactions in
> demanding situations. Perceived self-efficacy is high when the individual believes that
> he can perform an act or a completed task. It is low when failure or inability is antici-
> pated. Self-efficacy has nothing to do with the outcome of the behaviour; it is purely to
> do with whether or not people believe that they could be successful.
> Even where self-efficacy is raised by bogus feedback about performance success, it will
> still engender greater effort in subsequent similar tasks.[32]

---

30. ibid. p. 484.

31. The confusion can be further amplified by counter-intuitive strategies, where compliance is
punished and intransigence seems ignored. This seems to be irrational and the victim thus
becomes at a loss to predict the future or map a course for his survival. Under such stresses, the
victims search for certainty, for some hope of salvation and for effective leadership. In essence they
search for someone to act in loco parentis. And this is what the Coalition Psywar did.

32. G M Breakwell, *Coping with Threatened Identities*, Wiley 1986.

The effect of such a perception is that where a leadership or a group believes in their prospects of success they are likely to invest heavily in terms of effort, treasure and commitment. Conversely, where the perceived self-efficacy level is weak, the group is likely to be far more diffident over the chances of success. In each case, the predictions often become self-fulfilling prophesies. For the coercer, the task must be both to recognise the level of self-efficacy, and expect that his effectiveness in undermining resolve will need to be all the more severe. He will need additionally to demonstrate clearly to the victim that his perceived level of confidence was entirely misguided.

Studies by Professor Quester parallel this concept and suggest that victims are very impressed when their expectations are exceeded.[33] Anticipation is the key to the victim's psychological defences. If the level of destruction fails to meet his expectations, the victim is likely to be pleasantly surprised, more resolved to resist, and thus less likely to be coerced. It reinforces his self-efficacy prediction. Conversely, if the level of destruction is patently far greater than he expected, his ability to cope is inadequate, his credibility as a leader suffers and his extrapolation of the future is likely to be very painful. His belief in himself is thus in question, and so is the rationale upon which he based the investment of time, effort and money. He has thus become far more susceptible to coercion. The V1 and V2 attacks against London in 1944 were militarily insignificant, yet they brought an outcry amongst the population which felt secure in its expectation of a rapid victory. The SCUD attacks in the Gulf produced a similar effect.

For this, and the stress-curve reasons, the initial application of force needs, therefore, to be well beyond the victim's expectations. Equally importantly, the victim must believe that the worst is yet to come, and what will happen next will be utterly intolerable. This is fundamental; if the victim believes the worst is past then he needs only ride out the storm, and wait for it to pass. However, if the worst is yet to come then the future is bleak and unpredictable. – "Surely he won't go as far as ... (destroying A or B etc)?" It is vital, therefore, not to let the victim know when the coercer is approaching the end of his target list!

UNCERTAINTY OF SUCCESS

Unfortunately, coercion is, like any psychological event, not susceptible to measurement nor can one always have a high degree of confidence in its predic-

---

33. G Quester, *Psychological Dimensions of War*, by B Glad (ed).

tions. It is fraught with uncertainties, both for the coercer and his victim. Indeed many, if not most, air campaigns begin in the belief that they can quickly coerce the target group, but the absence of any response seems to suggest that another remedy is required. The first week of DELIBERATE FORCE probably fitted this mould. If a coercive aim fails, the putative coercer may have to fall back to a Denial strategy, where the outcome is physical, and the effect of the destruction can be more easily and more accurately measured and judged.

However, the victim's increasing commitment through costs already incurred, or "sunk" costs, together with the identification of the government with the war, means that termination may prove almost impossible for the existing leadership if the war just continues as it is. Termination may still need to be achieved by other means. One example is a psychological blow – a devastating overwhelming shock leaving no room for alternatives – or perhaps a cataclysmic event that provides at its very least a pretext for surrender, as, for example were Hiroshima/Nagasaki.

ACHIEVING COMPLIANCE THROUGH A CONCATENATION OF PRESSURES

Analysis of Operations ELDORADO CANON and DELIBERATE FORCE suggest that successful coercion often hinges on the synergy obtained from the confluence of a variety of pressures.[34] For example, for President Qaddafi in 1986, the combined effect of Soviet displeasure, Libyan military unrest in the aftermath of the bombing, improved European counter-terrorist activity, a dramatic defeat in Chad and the real prospect of another raid, combined synergistically to persuade him to reduce his support for the terrorists,[35] – certainly for a time.

In Bosnia, the cumulative effects of economic sanctions, the bombing, the (consequent) inability to deploy troops, the increasing military successes of the Moslems and Croats and strong diplomatic pressure all peaked at the same time; they combined to convince the Serbs that the high-water mark had passed and the tide had now turned.

---

34. A L George, *The Limits of Coercive Diplomacy*, Westview Press, Boulder Colo, 1994.
35. Tim Zimmerman, op cit, p 216 et seq.

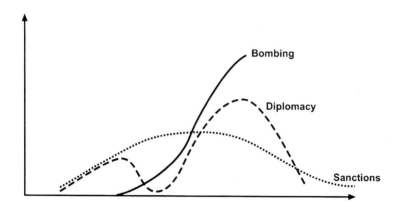

Figure 10.7
The Concatenation of Coercive Pressures.

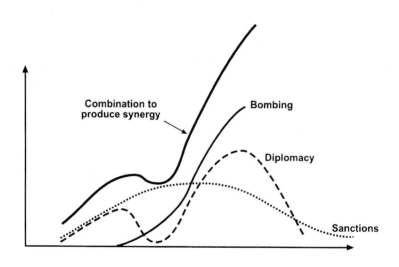

Figure 10.8
The Combination of Coercive Pressures to Create Synergy.

Perhaps the secret is to phase the pressures so that they peak at the same time, with synergistic results. For example, perhaps the sanctions have reduced the stockpiles, and what transport can get through, has to carry food not weapons. Meanwhile a lack of weapons, combined with the widespread destruction of the bombing means that what forces there are left cannot move to the battle areas.

Failure has a psychological effect, and both patrons and the mediators apply progressively increased pressure. Fear of imminent failure is highly stressful, and the leadership, given the right inducements and pretext, elects for a settlement.

In the mind of the victim, therefore, I argue that a coercer seeks to induce a number of perceptions:

- That the victim is impotent to withstand the onslaught.
- That all options are moving against him. And the pressures are mounting synergistically:

    First, the victim should feel isolated from his Patrons.

    Second, not only is there now no prospect of victory or success, but the tide of war is moving inevitably in favour of the enemy.

    Third, that the victim's losses will grow and any temporary gains are likely to be lost.

    Finally, a Diplomatic Offensive piles on the odium.

- If his predicament is now hopeless, and his aims are thus impossible, why should he or his people endure any further pain?

    Given the awful alternatives, and perhaps, with suitable inducements by the assailant, compliance becomes the least bad option.

- Nevertheless, the assailant will need to avoid the prospect of humiliating the victim, since this is likely to produce a hardening of attitudes culminating perhaps in a fight to the death. A way out must be available.

Even a cataclysmic coercive finale may be required either to persuade or as a pretext to achieve an end state. Indeed, a demonstrable failure may be seen as the only justification for compliance, and thus satisfy the contract (that we will only surrender under the most extreme duress) between leadership and population in the target state.

CONCLUSIONS

Air Power has a positive and powerful role in direct coercion throughout the spectrum of conflict. Bombing, by itself does not create a political **solution** to the dispute but it can contribute powerfully to coercion and even break a deadlock. The key points are as follows:

- In addition to evaluating a victim's value sets, the coercer needs also to assess the target's expectations.
- Demonstrative use of force has rarely proved successful. It often says far more about a coercer's resolve and constraints, and allows the victim to identify a coercer's weaknesses.
- Incremental use of force also allows the victim to habituate, to prepare his populace, and to deploy countermeasures.
- Threats by the coercer to use force will be tested; a bluff will be called.
- A victim may tolerate considerable pain if he believes victory is within his grasp.
- To coerce successfully, an assailant needs to apply decisive (high intensity, short period) force which exceeds the victim's expectations.
- The victim needs to be convinced that worse is to follow, and that tomorrow's pain will be intolerable.
- If coercion fails then the campaign should switch to denial. The balance of power should be altered so that the victim's prospect of victory evaporates. This has 2 outcomes:
  Remotivates the victim's adversary and provides him with the political acceptability for negotiations.
  Imminence of defeat convinces the target that further pain is not worth enduring.
- The effectiveness of the campaign is likely to be magnified by synergy with other pressures:
  Diplomatic pressure, especially through patrons.
  Sense of isolation
  Inducements.
  Victories by the target's enemy.
  Prospect of further coercion.
- However, a significant, highly coercive, cataclysmic event may still be required to persuade the victim to cease operations.

Finally, coercion is like the relationship of schoolmaster and schoolboy; it is not a one-shot event. The schoolboy might comply for now but he is sure to try again, and the coercer should therefore always be prepared to see his activity as part of a continuing process. That is the dilemma for short, sharp military interventions.

CHAPTER 11

STRATEGIC BOMBING:
WHAT IS IT, AND IS IT STILL RELEVANT?
Lieutenant Colonel Mark A. Bucknam USAF[1]

History shows that strategic bombing strategies are the least effective ways to use air power…. [S]trate-gic air power cannot be decisive. The most it can do is to reduce the costs that friendly land and theater air forces have to pay to defeat enemy forces on the battlefield.

Robert A. Pape, *Bombing to Win*

Air power is an inherently strategic force….Air power changed things by compressing the line between the strategic and tactical levels. Aircraft can routinely conduct operations that achieve strategic effects. To a great extent airplanes obviate the need to confront terrain or the environment because of their ability to fly over armies, fleets and geographic obstacles and strike directly at a country's key centers.

Colonel Phillip S. Meilinger USAF, *10 Propositions Regarding Air Power*

EVER SINCE OPERATION DESERT STORM, military officers and defence professionals have taken a renewed interest in strategic bombing. Varying interpretations of the Gulf War bombing campaign generated questions over the military and political efficacy of strategic bombing, and its future relevance. As the last decade of the 20th Century draws to a close, debates about strategic bombing are alive, if not well. Perhaps the biggest obstacle to clear thinking about strategic bombing is the lack of consensus over the meaning of 'strategic', and the concomitant disagreements over what separates strategic bombing from other bombing operations. This chapter begins by presenting an historical context for understanding strategic bombing; it addresses the continu-

---

1. The views expressed in this article are those of the author and do not reflect the official policy or position of the United States Air Force, Department of Defense, or the US Government.

ities and changes in the practice and thinking about strategic bombing, giving particular attention to the implications of the changes. Next, the chapter focuses on the defining characteristics of strategic bombing, and it ends with some thoughts on the future relevance of strategic bombing.[2]

SOME BACKGROUND ON STRATEGIC BOMBING

The idea of strategic bombing predates any actual experience with using airplanes in war. As Air Vice-Marshal Tony Mason has pointed out, a decade before man achieved powered flight at least one British officer forecast what we, today, would call a revolution in military affairs based on aeronautical developments. That officer, Major J.D. Fullerton, suggested that: "future wars may well start with a great air battle,....[and that] the arrival over the enemy capital will probably conclude the campaign."[3] Four years before the Wright brothers' inaugural flight at Kitty Hawk, the Hague Conference of 1899 imposed a five year ban on aerial bombing.[4] In 1908, H.G. Wells's *The War in the Air* offered an ominous vision of air power's military potential, and three years after that, two Italian officers conducted the first recorded bombing operations in history. On 1 November 1911, Captains Moizo and Piazza dropped a total of four bombs on their Arab and Turkish adversaries near Tripoli.[5] Obviously ideas about strategic bombing ran far ahead of experience.

---

2. Readers familiar with the historical evolution of strategic bombing might want to skip to section two, and pick up with the discussion on the continuities and changes in strategic bombing. Before jumping ahead, however, they should note that ideas about strategic bombing were forged during the first half of this century in the context of total wars between great powers. Nuclear weapons, the Cold War confrontation, and technological limitations no doubt helped to impede fresh thinking about strategic bombing despite experience in limited wars, such as Korea and Vietnam. Now that total war and nuclear Armageddon seem remote, it is appropriate to question which connotations of strategic bombing one should retain, and which ones one should discard.

3. Cited in Air Vice Marshal Tony Mason, *Air Power: A Centennial Appraisal*, Brassey's, London, 1994, p. 3, citing A.F. Hurley, *Billy Mitchell, Crusader for Air Power*, Indiana University Press, Bloomington, 1975, p. 142.

4. Tami Davis Biddle, 'Air Power,' in *The Laws of War: Constraints on Warfare in the Western World*, ed. Michael Howard, George J. Andreopoulos, and Mark R. Shulman, Yale University Press, London, 1994, p. 141-2.

5. Mason, *Air Power*, op. cit., p.10-11; and Lee Kennett, *The First Air War: 1914-1918*, The Free Press, New York, 1991, p. 18.

FIRST WORLD WAR

In the First World War, strategic bombing passed from the realm of ideas into practice. German Zeppelins gave way to Gotha bombers as the Central Powers attempted to sow panic in London and Paris. The Allies responded with their own raids against military and industrial targets in German, Austrian, and Turkish cities, but losses rendered deep daylight operations costly for both sides. By 1916, much of the long range bombing was being conducted at night.[6] In Italy, Guilio Douhet was court-martialed and jailed for openly criticising his uniformed superiors, after they refused to support his plans to mount massive bombing operations against Austrian cities.[7] And the war ended before the Allies could carry out their most ambitious plans for bombing Germany.[8] The impact of air power in the war was aptly described by historian Lee Kennett, who concluded that: "While the role of the air weapon in the Great War was a modest one, the role of the Great War in the rise of air power was anything but modest."[9]

The bifurcation between strategic and tactical bombing began in WWI, and the defining characteristic of strategic bombing was its independence from battlefield operations. As historian George Williams noted, this meant that strategic aviation was anything that took place beyond the range of friendly artillery, or about fifteen miles from friendly lines (twenty-five kilometres).[10] The British formation created late in the war for strategic bombing was called the Independent Force, and its commander was indeed independent from the ground force chain of command.[11] In conducting these independent, or strategic, bombing operations, the British, French, and American planners expected to produce

---

6. Kennett, *The First Air War*, op. cit., pp. 50-56.
7. Giulio Douhet, *The Command of the Air*, translated by Dino Ferrari, Coward-McCann, New York, 1942, reprinted Office of Air Force History, Washington, 1983, pp.vii-viii.
8. Kennett, op. cit., p. 216.
9. Kennett, op. cit., p. 226.
10. Williams is worth citing: "A word on how American aviation officers defined 'strategical' aviation is in order here. From the arrival of the first US Air Service staff officers overseas, the term connoted independent operations—independent, that is, of direct support of ground units on the battlefield, as the British conceived air's primary mission. To the Board of Officers convened at Pershing's GHQ, 'strategical aviation' could be defined as 'attacking enemy elements, whatever their nature, at a distance usually more than 25,000 yards from friendly troops'; tactical aviation fell inside that distance, or 'roughly within the extreme zone of long-range artillery.' " George K. Williams, ' "The Shank of the Drill": Americans and Strategical Aviation in the Great War,' *The Journal of Strategic Studies*, vol. 19, no. 3 (September 1996), p. 409, citing Major Frank Parker, 'The Role and Tactical and Strategical Employment of Aeronautics in an Army', (2 July 1917).
11. Mason, op. cit., pp. 30-36.

two effects: demoralisation, and disruption of enemy war industry – allied bombing failed to produce either.[12] Thus, Kennett's conclusion is especially appropriate to strategic bombing, for while it had little, if any, effect on the course of the war, the war had an enormous impact on strategic bombing theory.

INTER-WAR YEARS

The unprecedented carnage and costs of WWI spurred political leaders to seek international conventions against various means of war, while at the same time focusing military minds on ways of avoiding the slaughter and stalemate of trench warfare. If liberal minded politicians hoped it had been the 'war to end all wars', then professional soldiers, seamen, and airmen took *total war* as the basic planning assumption for wars of the future. For those who came to champion strategic bombing, air power seemed to offer a means of winning wars quicker, cheaper, and, in the end, with lower casualties than other forms of military power. Moreover, before the days of radar, when the most advanced bombers often flew as fast and as high as pursuit aircraft, the idea that the bomber would always get through must have seemed like the stark reality of today's ballistic missile threat, rather than some overly alarmist prediction.

After WWI, there was no consensus among military officers about the proper role for air power in war. Some officers – including a number of airmen – believed that air power's greatest contribution would come from attacks against an opponent's ground fighting potential, that is, via interdiction and air support operations near the battlefield.[13] However, strategic bombing theorists in Britain and America shared the basic assumption that any future war between great powers would be total war, and that air power could best contribute to victory by directly attacking an enemy's 'vital centres'.

Despite these shared assumptions about total war and vital centres, those who placed their faith in strategic bombing lacked a common conception of what

---

12. Thus the links between strategic bombing and the objectives of coercion and denial (discussed later in the paper) stretch all the way back to the Great War. Strategic bombing was also conducted in retaliation for German bombing of Allied cities, though to some degree these retaliatory attacks probably had a coercive dimension, as opposed to being purely for punishment. Williams, op. cit., 392; and Kennett, op. cit., p. 55.

13. See for instance, Wing Commander J.C. Slessor, *Air Power and Armies*, Oxford University Press, London, 1936, reprinted AMS Press, New York, 1982, pp. 200-215; and George K. Williams, 'The Shank of the Drill,' op. cit., pp. 380-425.

might constitute an enemy's 'vital centres'. Two broad schools of thought emerged: one suggested targeting enemy morale by bombing cities, the other focused on enemy war industry. These two concepts of strategic bombing grew from experience and, more importantly, from faith born in WWI.[11] Given the state of bombing accuracy in the 1920s and 30s, and the fact that factories existed in and around major cities, attempts to distinguish between the two schools of thought now seem more theoretical than practical. In general, it is safe to say that British strategic bombing doctrine was geared toward affecting enemy morale or will to fight, while American doctrine was based on paralysing an enemy's industry and, hence, his ability to fight. In reality the two concepts of strategic bombing overlapped, and the generalisation above should not obscure the fact that officers in both countries understood this overlap, and often held opinions which differed from their service's official doctrine.[15]

SECOND WORLD WAR

At the beginning of WWII, RAF Bomber Command losses forced a shift from daylight attacks to night-time bombing, with detrimental, if unacknowledged, implications for bombing accuracy. It was late in the summer of 1941 when the Butt commission reported that only a third of the crews claiming to have hit their targets had actually managed to navigate to within five miles of them. For heavily defended regions, only ten percent got within five miles, and, of course, these fractions only applied to those crews claiming to have hit their targets; fully one third of all crews to take off, returned to admit that they had not managed to bomb their primary targets.[16] On 14 February 1942 the Air Staff issued a directive to Bomber Command formalising a policy of area bombardment. The objective of these area attacks was to undermine "the morale of the enemy's civil population and in particular, of the industrial workers."[17] Later that month Air

14. Lacking any real means of obtaining information for accurate bomb damage assessment, British and US air campaign planners in WWI reasoned as best they could about what effects the bombing was having on German war fighting potential and morale. See, for instance, George K. Williams, ' "The Shank of the Drill",' op. cit., pp. 386-395; and Mason, op. cit., pp. 35-36.

15. Tami Davis Biddle, 'British and American Approaches to Strategic Bombing: Their Origins and Implementations in the World War II Combined Bomber Offensive,' *The Journal of Strategic Studies*, vol. 18, no. 1 (March 1995): pp. 91-145.

16. Alan J. Levine, *The Strategic Bombing of Germany, 1940-1945*, Praeger, London, 1992, pp. 30-31.

17. Citation apparently taken from original directive, though not footnoted. Ibid., p. 36.

Marshal Sir Arthur Harris took over at Bomber Command, and he soon insti-
tuted a program of massive raids against Germany's industrial cities.[18] Harris was
sceptical of strategies based on bombing bottlenecks in the German war economy
and those based on attacks against civilian morale. He derisively referred to both
as 'panacea targets'. In Harris's view, area bombing would slowly grind down the
entire German economy while simultaneously forcing the Nazis to divert their
war-making efforts toward defensive measures.[19] It was unashamedly inelegant –
a brute force approach to winning the war. Though a variety of uniformed and
civilian agencies continued to press for attacks against weak links in the Nazi war
machine, Harris strenuously resisted all efforts to alter his campaign of grinding
attrition.[20]

The US Army Air Force (USAAF) was slow to make any substantial contribution of its own to the bombing of Germany.[21] Plans to build up Eighth Air Force
in England were repeatedly delayed, as US bombers were diverted to the
Mediterranean theatre.[22] When the Americans finally began deep bombing operations in earnest in 1943, they kept to their doctrine of high-altitude daylight
attacks against selected targets.[23] Early unescorted missions against Schweinfurt
and Regensburg suffered such appalling losses that the USAAF refrained from

---

18. Harris launched the first raid of over 1,000 bombers against Cologne on the night of 30-31 May
    1942. Sir Arthur Harris, Marshal of the RAF, *Bomber Offensive*, Billing & Sons, Worchester, 1947,
    reprinted by Stoddard Publishing Co., Toronto, 1990, pp. 109-119.

19. Ibid., pp. 74-89, 165; and Levine, op. cit., p. 38.

20. Harris, op. cit., 219-224; and Alfred C. Mierzejewski, *The Collapse of the German War Economy, 1944-
    1945*, The University of North Carolina Press, Chapel Hill, 1988, pp. 71-85.

21. Eighth Air Force's first combat mission with heavy bombers flew on 17 August 1942; the force was
    made up of twelve B-17s escorted by spitfires, and it struck a marshalling yard in France. The first
    attack on Germany did not come until 27 January 1943, when just over fifty B-17s attacked U-boat
    facilities at Wilhelmshaven. Eighth Air Force did not hit a target in Germany's Ruhr industrial
    region until 4 March 1943, when a mere sixteen B-17s attacked a marshaling yard in Hamm.
    Though Eighth Air Force gradually built up in size during the spring of 1943, nearly all of its
    combat operations were directed against marshaling yards in France or coastal targets (especially
    U-boat facilities) in Holland, France, or northern Germany. The first significant USAAF attack
    against German industry came on 22 June when 182 heavy bombers struck targets in the Ruhr
    region. Kit C. Carter and Robert Mueller, *Combat Chronology: 1941-1945*, Center for Air Force
    History, Washington, 1991, pp. 33, 88, 102, 148.

22. DeWitt S. Copp, *Forged in Fire: Strategy and Decisions in the Airwar over Europe*, Doubleday, Garden City,
    New York, 1982, pp. 357-424.

23. In practice, American precision bombing of selected industrial targets often destroyed built up
    urban areas, inadvertently producing the same effect as area attacks. See, W. Hays Parks, '
    "Precision" and "Area" Bombing: Who Did Which, and When?,' *The Journal of Strategic Studies*, vol.
    18, no. 1 (March 1995): 145-175.

venturing deep into Germany again until long-range fighter escort aircraft arrived in the winter of 1943-44.[24] In early 1944, Allied bombers were committed to an intense campaign against German aircraft production and the Luftwaffe, before being diverted in the spring to operations in support of the upcoming Normandy landings.[25] By the summer of 1944 the Combined Bomber Offensive was directed, in part, against German oil production, though significant resources remained tied up in support of the ground campaign.[26] In the autumn of 1944, after General Eisenhower had relinquished control over bomber operations, the Allied bomber forces attacked the German transportation and oil systems again.[27] By this time, the Allies had an abundance of bombers and crews, and they had achieved air superiority over Germany; the effects of unfettered strategic bombing were devastating to German cities and the German economy.

In any analysis of strategic bombing in WWII, it must be remembered that more bombs were dropped in the first four months of 1945 than in the first four years of the war.[28] Moreover, bombing accuracy improved as the war progressed, and much of the bombing before September of 1944 had been diverted to other than strategic targets.[29] One consequence of this escalation in strategic bombing at the end of the war, when ground forces were advancing against Germany on every front, has been a complete lack of consensus, then or now, over the effects of the bombing.[30]

In the Pacific, the Japanese surrendered without an invasion of their home islands, after being subjected to months of naval blockade, urban firebombing by air power, and two atomic bombs. Many observers, particularly airmen, were quick to see this as proof of the effectiveness of strategic bombing; others remained less certain or entirely unconvinced. Analyses of the Japanese decision to surrender are numerous, yet to this day the role of strategic bombing in prodding that surrender remains a contentious issue.[31] Factors other than strategic bombing, which might have compelled the surrender include, the impending invasion of the home islands, the naval blockade, Soviet entry into the war against

---

24. Levine, op. cit., pp. 106 and 110.

25. Ibid., pp. 118-122, 126-132.

26. Ibid., pp. 143-155.

27. Ibid., pp. 161-171.

28. Over 690,000 tons of bombs were dropped by the RAF and USAAF in the first four months of 1945; fewer than 500,000 tons of bombs were dropped prior to January 1944. Major General Haywood S. Hansell, Jr., USAF, *The Air Plan that Defeated Hitler*, Higgins-McArthur/Longino & Porter, Atlanta, 1972, p. 200, citing Office of Statistical Control, Headquarters, A.A.F., and British Air Ministry, London.

29. Ibid., 201; and Harris, *Bomber Offensive*, op. cit., 235-6.

Japan, and the Japanese perception that the Allies had relaxed their demand for unconditional surrender and would permit Japan to retain its emperor.[32] No doubt, a combination of factors led to the surrender and, as Group Captain Lambert argues in Chapter 10, establishing the importance of any one of them is problematical.

Whatever the effects of strategic bombing in WWII, bombing critics and proponents alike have found ample evidence upon which to base their arguments. Clearly, strategic bombing did not affect the German or Japanese will to fight in the way that pre-war theorists had postulated. Had bombing ever motivated the citizens of the Axis nations to rise up in protest, the coercive mechanisms of these states stood ready to ensure that the fascist regimes remained firmly in control.

---

30. Historian Max Hastings gives significant credit to the USAAF for winning air superiority and for its work in the oil campaign. Alfred Mierzejewski claims that Allied destruction of the German transportation system at the end of 1944 and early 1945 caused the German economy to collapse, while Richard Overy sees the indirect and diversionary effects of the bombing playing an important role in winning the war. Meanwhile others, such as economist John Kenneth Galbraith, who served on the US Strategic Bombing Survey team, and, more recently, Robert Pape, a US political scientist, claim that strategic bombing was an utterly ineffective adjunct to the Allied war effort, and an outright waste of resources. Max Hastings, *Bomber Command*, Michael Joseph Ltd., London, 1979, pp. 346-352; Alfred C. Mierzejewski, *The Collapse of the German War Economy, 1944-1945*, The University of North Carolina Press, Chapel Hill, 1988, pp. 177-187; Richard Overy, *Why the Allies Won*, W.W. Norton & Co., London, 1995, pp. 129-133 (For a fuller treatment by Overy, see *The Air War, 1939-1945*, Stein and Day, New York, 1981; and *War and Economy in the Third Reich*, Clarendon Press, Oxford, 1994.); John Kenneth Galbraith, *A Life in Our Times: Memoirs*, Houghton Mifflin, Boston, 1981, p. 206; and Robert Pape, *Bombing to Win: Air Power and Coercion in War*, Cornell University Press, Ithaca, 1996, pp. 309-313, and 316-318. As a guide to understanding measures of effectiveness in military operations, see James G. Roche and Barry D. Watts, 'Choosing Analytic Measures,' *The Journal of Strategic Studies*, vol. 14, no. 2 (June 1991): pp. 165-209.

31. Major General Haywood S. Hansell reckoned that strategic bombing was the primary cause for the Japanese surrender, and he cites an excerpt from the US Strategic Bombing Survey (USSBS) to that effect. The summary report of the USSBS contains a more restrained conclusion that stops short of giving strategic bombing the degree of credit that Hansell gives. Haywood S. Hansell, Jr., *The Strategic Air War Against Germany and Japan: A Memoir*, Office of Air Force History, Washington, 1986, pp, 263-267; and *The United States Strategic Bombing Survey, Summary Report (Pacific War)*, GPO, Washington, 1946, reprinted Air University Press, Maxwell AFB, Alabama, 1987, p. 106. Robert Pape gives strategic bombing no credit for the Japanese decision to surrender; he argues that: "Contrary to the assertion of the Strategic Bombing Survey….in actuality the naval blockade, invasion threat, and Soviet attack ensured that surrender would have occurred at *precisely* the same time even if there had been no strategic bombing campaign." [emphasis in original] Pape, *Bombing to Win*, op. cit., p. 135.

32. USSBS Summary Report (Pacific War), op. cit., p. 106; and Pape, op. cit., p. 135.

On the other hand, studies on the morale of bombing victims have not supported the contention (often made during the war by governments attempting to bolster morale) that bombing only served to stiffen morale.[33] Sustained strategic bombing probably hurt enemy morale, but not in ways that would win the war.[34]

Similarly, the effects of strategic bombing on the Axis's war-making industries, seemed to show that modern industrial economies were less fragile than strategic bombing theorists had assumed. Yet the economic devastation of Germany and Japan were plain for all to see. Like a team of successful stock market investors counting their gains, no amount of explaining or economic theorising could convince them that their strategy had not worked. Many airmen were similarly convinced of the decisive contributions of strategic bombing toward winning the war; no matter what the critics said, the results seemed to speak for themselves. The enduring debate over the efficacy of strategic bombing in WWII bears testimony to Winston Churchill's post-war assertion that: 'Air power is the most difficult of all forms of military force to measure, or even to express in precise terms.'[35]

KOREAN WAR

When North Korean forces invaded South Korea in June of 1950, the American Joint Chiefs of Staff saw the move as a possible diversion, preparatory to some military action in Europe.[36] The concept of total war still dominated American military thinking, and the advent of atomic weapons seemed only to have solidified USAF ideas on strategic bombing. Air planners identified key industrial targets in North Korea as the proper object of strategic bombing, and as soon as General MacArthur agreed to release B-29s from battlefield support operations around the Pusan perimeter, the heavy bombers went to work against the North.[37]

---

33. See, for instance, Irving L. Janis, *Air War and Emotional Stress: Psychological Studies of Bombing and Civilian Defenses*, Greenwood Press, Westport, Connecticut, 1951; and Stephen T. Hosmer, *Psychological Effects of US Air Operations in Four Wars, 1941-1991: Lessons for US Commanders*, RAND, Santa Monica, 1996.

34. Obviously this generalization seems less true for the Pacific theater. Still, it is difficult to argue convincingly that bombing, by itself, could have won the war in the Pacific, especially if one discounts the effects of atomic bombing.

35. Winston Churchill, *The Gathering Storm*, 1948, cited in Robert Debs Heinl, Jr., *Dictionary of Military and Naval Quotations*, United States Naval Institute Press, Annapolis, 1984, p. 6.

36. Matthew B. Ridgway, *The Korean War*, Da Capo Press, New York, 1967, p. 34.

By mid-September 1950, when the Inchon landing took place, North Korea's industry had already been smashed.[38] Destruction of the North's industry had no perceptible effect on the war, and when the Chinese intervened in late 1950, rumblings of possible atomic attacks by the US brought British Prime Minister Clement Atlee to Washington seeking guarantees from President Truman against their use.[39]

The Chinese intervention ended Truman's reluctance to allow incendiary attacks against North Korean cities, and the USAF firebombed the North's capital, Pyongyang, in early January 1951.[40] During most of 1951 and the first half of the following year, bombing operations were diverted from strategic attacks, to interdiction of supplies bound for communist forces at the front.[41] By mid-1952, with the war stalemated on the ground, coalition air forces took a new tack; they now began a campaign of 'air pressure' designed to compel the communists to negotiate a settlement to the war. In June 1952, UN aircraft destroyed most of North Korea's hydroelectric generation facilities and Pyongyang was bombed again in July and August.[42] In early 1953, after Eisenhower became President, he signalled to the Chinese that he was willing to widen the war, and to use atomic weapons, in order to end the fighting in Korea.[43] In May 1953, US aircraft bombed irrigation dams in North Korea, thus threatening the North's rice crop.[44] Toward the end of July, after three years of war, an armistice was signed and the fighting stopped.[45]

The lesson most American military professionals learned from the Korean War experience was to never again get involved in a limited war, especially a ground war in Asia.[46] For USAF leaders, this meant staying focused on the real mission of the Cold War, preparing for war against the Soviet Union. As a recent USAF monograph on the war explained, the Air Force began the war with a faith

---

37. Wayne Thompson and Bernard C. Nalty, *Within Limits: The US Air Force and the Korean War*, GPO, Washington, 1996, p. 12.
38. Ibid., p. 20.
39. Max Hastings, *The Korean War*, Simon & Schuster, New York, 1988, pp. 179-180.
40. Robert Frank Futrell, *The United States Air Force in Korea, 1950-1953*, GPO, Washington, 1983, p. 278; and Thompson and Nalty, op. cit., pp. 26 and 52.
41. Thompson and Nalty, op. cit., pp. 44-50.
42. Ibid., 51-52.
43. Ibid., 54-55; and Futrell, *Korea*, op. cit., p. 667.
44. Futrell, op. cit., pp. 666-669.
45. Thompson and Nalty, op. cit., p. 56.
46. Richard K. Betts, *Soldiers, Statesmen, and Cold War Crises*, Harvard University Press, Cambridge, Massachusetts, 1977, p. 167.

in strategic bombing and: "Far from undermining these principles, three years of limited warfare had reinforced them, persuading the leadership of the Air Force that the United States should stand ready to attack the Soviet Union and not divert its strength against aggression by proxy."[47] In order to trump the Soviet superiority in conventional arms and manpower, the US relied on a strategy based on its growing nuclear arsenal. Although the US would again conduct conventional strategic bombing in a limited war, the term 'strategic' became increasingly associated with nuclear weapons and the total war connotation of strategic bombing endured.

VIETNAM WAR

Like Korea, Vietnam was another limited war fought in the shadow of the Cold War. Like North Korea, North Vietnam lacked a modern industrialised economy; thus, it too relied on external sponsorship from China and the Soviet Union for nearly all of its arms. Unlike the Korean War, however, the war in Vietnam had a dual nature. It was part guerrilla war, fought by the Vietcong who were mostly indigenous to South Vietnam, though dependent upon support from the North. And it was part conventional war, with regular North Vietnamese units fighting in company, battalion, and even multi-battalion strength, as early as 1965.[48] In fact, the guerrilla nature of the war predominated until the Tet offensive in January of 1968, and the conventional nature of the struggle did not become apparent to many observers until it took the unmistakable form of the Easter offensive in the spring of 1972. Despite the predominantly unconventional nature of the war in 1964, the USAF proposed, and the Joint Chiefs of Staffs supported, a list of ninety-four 'strategic' targets in North Vietnam. Striking these targets, it was believed, would cripple the North's ability to support the Vietcong, and might compel the North to abandon its aims to unite the country under communist control.[49]

---

47. Ibid., p. 60.
48. The first large scale contact between US and North Vietnamese regulars took place in November of 1965 in the Ia Drang Valley of South Vietnam. See, for instance, Lt Gen Harold G. Moore, USA (Ret) and Joseph L. Galloway, *We Were Soldiers Once and Young*, Random House, New York, 1992.
49. Fundamental to this strategy was the USAF's and the JCS's expectation that they would be permitted to blockade North Vietnam, or attack targets such as Haiphong Harbor, in order to cutoff the North's external arms supplies. See, for instance, Admiral USG. Sharp, *Strategy for Defeat: Vietnam in Retrospect*, Presidio, Novato, California, 1978, pp. 46-49.

When the US decided, in early 1965, to bomb North Vietnam, the USAF proposed striking all ninety-four targets in less than a month.[50] For a variety of reasons this did not happen, and the bombing operations, called Rolling Thunder, became a graduated campaign that quickly lost any strategic aim it might have had. As historian Earl Tilford noted: "In the summer of 1965 the focus of Rolling Thunder switched from strategic persuasion to interdiction."[51] And after President Johnson agreed to send an additional forty-four American combat battalions to Vietnam, "the bombing of the North was subordinated to the ground war in the South."[52] In the spring of 1967, after two years of bombing, and with Rolling Thunder increasingly looking like an abject failure, air power was turned against 'strategic' targets in the North with some degree of consistency. By this time, the list of strategic targets had grown to 359, and the US had nearly half a million soldiers in South Vietnam.[53] Rolling Thunder had, from the start, been shaped by the ground war and by American domestic politics; in March 1968, shortly after the embarrassment of the Tet offensive and Robert Kennedy's declaration of his intent to seek the White House, President Johnson went on television to announce a halt to all bombing above the 20th parallel in Vietnam, and his withdrawal from the upcoming presidential race. Johnson would later further restrict bombing to targets south of the 19th parallel, though strikes north of that continued sporadically until April 1972, under the overall rubric of Rolling Thunder.[54]

In late March 1972, the North Vietnamese launched a conventional ground attack, spearheaded by tanks, into South Vietnam; this 'Easter offensive' quickly threatened to defeat the South Vietnamese army. President Nixon responded by ordering the Linebacker air campaign and the mining of Haiphong Harbour, the North's only major port and the point where most arms entered the country.[55] Linebacker saw the first large-scale use of laser guided bombs, and US air power severely damaged the North's military supplies, military support facilities, and transportation network.[56] By June, the focus of the bombings was shifted to targets

---

50. Earl H. Tilford, Jr., *Setup: What the Air Force Did in Vietnam and Why*, Air University Press, Maxwell AFB, Alabama, 1991, p. 104.

51. Ibid., p. 111.

52. Ibid.

53. Ibid., pp. 135 and 142.

54. Ibid., pp. 151-153. Note: the 19th parallel is about equidistant (120 nautical miles) from the border of North and South Vietnam (17th parallel) and the North Vietnamese cities of Hanoi and Haiphong (21st parallel).

55. Ibid., pp. 224-228.

56. Ibid., pp. 235-236.

essential to the North's long-term war-fighting potential, and in early October the objective of Linebacker changed again. The aim now was to force the North Vietnamese to accept a negotiated settlement to the war.[57] With a peace agreement apparently at hand, President Nixon ordered a halt to the bombing on 18 October 1972.[58]

Political developments in the US soon gave the North Vietnamese hope that they could gain more by stalling at the peace table.[59] When the talks broke down in December 1972, Nixon ordered Linebacker II. During Linebacker II, the US military were permitted to extend the target list and night raids by B-52s on targets around Hanoi took place for the first time in the war.[60] Though fifteen of the eight-engine bombers were lost during the eleven-day campaign, before it was over the North Vietnamese ran out of surface-to-air missiles and were left defenceless against future air attacks.[61] Whereas President Johnson had let Chinese leaders know that he had no intention of harming the regime in Hanoi, President Nixon remained ominously silent on the matter.[62] Also, under Nixon relations between the US and Vietnam's principal sponsors, China and the Soviet Union, had warmed considerably.[63] Time was no longer on the North's side and Hanoi beckoned the US back to the negotiating table, and rapidly agreed to points it had previously refused to accept. Though some observers felt that Nixon's negotiator, Henry Kissinger, gave away too much in the subsequent talks, a peace treaty was signed near the end of January 1973, ending America's longest war.[64]

As with WWII, many airmen were convinced that air power had delivered success (such as it was) in Vietnam. The lessons of Vietnam seemed to confirm the faith that senior Air Force leaders had in strategic bombing. The lessons were so deeply impressed upon the Air Force as an institution, that at the end of the 1980s, just a few years before the Gulf War, historian Mark Clodfelter could confidently assert that: "The conviction that the manufacturing and distribution

---

57. Ibid., pp. 236-237.

58. Ibid., p. 238.

59. Ibid., pp. 248-250, and 253.

60. Mark Clodfelter, *The Limits of Air Power: The American Bombing of North Vietnam*, Free Press, New York, 1989, pp. 184-186.

61. Ibid., pp. 193 and 198.

62. Ibid., pp. 138, 155-157, and 205-206.

63. Ibid., pp. 172 and 204.

64. Betts, *Soldiers, Statesmen*, op. cit., p. 30; and Tilford, *Setup*, op. cit., p. 291; Clodfelter, op. cit., pp. 200-201.

of goods are the keys to war-fighting capability and will remains firmly planted as a cornerstone of Air Force thinking."[65] Clodfelter also believed that:

> Because most air chiefs think political limitations prevented air power from gaining a victory in Vietnam, they have not revamped the fundamentals of strategic bombing. Their unspoken belief is that since Linebacker II demonstrated bombing effectiveness, political leaders *must* realise that bombing can win limited wars if unhampered by political controls. [emphasis in original][66]

THE GULF WAR

After Linebacker II, it would be nearly twenty years before either Britain or the US would take part in a strategic air campaign. In January 1991, Operation Desert Storm marked a new era in strategic bombing. During the forty three-day campaign, coalition air forces devoted just under fifteen percent of their air-to-ground sorties, and about thirty percent of the their precision guided munitions (PGMs) to attacks against strategic targets.[67] Though coalition planners had developed twelve categories of targets, they identified eight of those categories as the 'strategic core', these were: 1) leadership facilities; 2) command, control, and communications targets; 3) nuclear, biological and chemical warfare capabilities; 4) military support facilities; 5) SCUD missiles and their support facilities; 6) electric power; 7) oil refineries; and 8) key bridges and railway facilities.[68] Colonel John Warden, the architect of the strategic campaign's precursor – a plan he called Instant Thunder – believed that strategic bombing, by itself, could achieve the War's objectives. His Instant Thunder plan was soon incorporated into an overall theatre campaign plan, which had four phases. Instant Thunder served as the basis for Phase I. While senior military leaders were willing to use Colonel Warden's plans and ideas about strategic bombing, they did not share his confidence that air power alone could win the war.[69] Significantly, planners tasked with

---

65. Clodfelter, op. cit., p. 209.

66. Ibid., p. 208 .

67. Thomas A. Keaney and Eliot A. Cohen, *Gulf War Air Power Survey Summary Report*, GPO, Washington, 1993, pp. 64.

68. Ibid.

69. Richard G. Davis, *Decisive Force: Strategic Bombing in the Gulf War*, GPO, Washington, p. 20; and Colonel Edward C. Mann, III, USAF, *Thunder and Lightning: Desert Storm and the Air Power Debates*, Air University Press, Maxwell AFB, Alabama, 1995, p. 170.

linking political objectives to Iraqi centres of gravity (COG) identified certain Republican Guard units, and their avenues of escape from the Kuwaiti theatre, as 'strategic' targets; this was fundamentally at odds with Warden's thinking, for he had planned to ignore Iraqi ground forces.[70]

The number of strategic attack sorties peaked during the first two days of Desert Storm and steadily declined for the next ten days, before levelling off, so that as Richard Davis, a USAF historian, noted: "For the last two-thirds of the Gulf War the Coalition conducted the strategic air campaign at a minimum level."[71] As with earlier wars, the Air Force judged strategic bombing in the Gulf War most favourably, while others remained less convinced of its effectiveness. The authors of the *Gulf War Air Power Survey Summary Report* refrained from rendering any over-all assessment of strategic bombing, confining their judgements instead to evaluations of individual target sets within the 'strategic core'. Predictably, critics of strategic bombing, such as Robert Pape, dismissed it as ineffective.[72]

CONTINUITY AND CHANGE IN STRATEGIC BOMBING

The foregoing highlights of the history of strategic bombing set the context for the following discussion, and they should help to remind the reader of what has changed and what has endured for strategic bombing over the past eight decades. Two major changes in the concept of strategic bombing stem from a change in the geopolitical environment and advances in aerospace technology. However,

---

70. As Davis points out, the reason the Republican Guard units do not show up on the list of 'strategic core' target sets is that the responsibility for targeting of the Republican Guard was passed from the 'black hole' planners to planners responsible for air operations in the Kuwaiti theatre of Operations (KTO). This was done for administrative convenience to ease command and control arrangements, not because the importance of the Republican Guard was being downgraded. After giving a good synopsis of coalition air and ground efforts against the Republican Guard, Davis says that the theater commander "overemphasized its military threat to Coalition ground operations and underestimated its political function to maintain Hussein's regime". Based on this assertion, which would seem to strengthen the case for including the Republican Guard as a 'strategic' target set, Davis goes on to suggest that: "The *Republican Guard* ground forces in practice and actuality were not, and could not be, a 'strategic target' system." It is unclear whether Davis is writing about all Republican Guard forces, including those outside the vicinity of the KTO (in which case his argument would be logical), or whether he is writing strictly about the Republican Guard units in the KTO (in which case his final assertion would seem to be a *non sequitur*). Davis, op. cit., pp. 20-21, citations in footnote from p. 72; and Mann, op. cit., footnote, p. 170.

71. Richard G. Davis, *Decisive Force: Strategic Bombing in the Gulf War*, GPO, Washington, p. 43.

72. Keaney and Cohen, *GWAPS Summary Report*, op. cit., p. 90; and Pape, *Bombing to Win*, op. cit., 251.

Figure 11
Aspects of the Gulf War – Strategic bombing is intended to directly fulfil
political or strategic military objectives

two overarching continuities – the distinctions between coercion and denial, and
between 'strategic' and 'tactical' – tend to obscure some other important shifts in
the concept and practice of strategic bombing. The taxonomy surrounding such
concepts is discussed in detail by Group Captain Lambert in Chapter 10 of this
book.

The changed nature of the geopolitical environment that came with the end of
the Cold War hardly needs elaborating here. The implications for strategic bombing, however, are significant and should be borne in mind throughout the
following discussion. The Cold War, like the two world wars before it, can be
viewed as a total war between mutually incompatible political systems. This total
war assumption is evident in NATO's late 1980s definition of strategic bombing:
"strategic air warfare are air operations designed to effect the progressive destruc-

tion of the enemy's war-making capacity."[73] The US Air Force doctrine from the same period reflects similar thinking: "The objective of the strategic attack mission is to destroy or neutralize an enemy's war-sustaining capabilities or will to fight."[74] In both definitions, the assumed strategic objective is military victory. Though military victory is a valid strategic objective in total war, it might not be the ultimate objective in all limited war scenarios, or in other situations calling for the use of force. See Group Captain Peach's 'Spectrum of Conflict' model in Chapter 3 for a non-linear view. Today, prospects for total war seem remote, and even large scale limited wars appear unlikely. If one takes older definitions of strategic air attack as a starting point, given the current geopolitical environment, strategic bombing will be irrelevant **by definition**. Undoubtedly 'destroying an enemy's war-making capacity' will seem out of place when a conflict's objectives are likely to be much more limited than the military subjugation of one's adversary. The problem rests with the old definitions of strategic air attack, and the assumptions that underpin those definitions. As the following discussion will show, the concept of strategic bombing has evolved since the end of the Cold War, but the evolution is incomplete, or at least it is not universally recognised. Any analysis of the relevance of strategic bombing must begin with a clear understanding of what it is, and what it is not. But first, it is worth examining other changes and continuities in strategic bombing.

Conflict	CEP (feet)*	Quantity (bombs)
World War II (B-17)	3,300	9,070
Korea/South East Asia (F-84/F-105)	400	176
Desert Storm (F-16)**	200	30
Desert Storm (F-117)	<10	1

Effect of accuracy (CEP) on quantity of 2,000-pound bombs needed to achieve a 90% probability of hit on a hypothetical target measuring 60 x 100 feet.

* CEP stands for circular error probable, which is a measure of bombing accuracy.
** The figures for F-16s in Desert Storm reflect accuracy for unguided bombs, not PGMs.

Figure 11.1
Comparison of Bombing Accuracy and Bomb Quantities[75]

---

73. US Department of Defense, *Dictionary of Military Terms*, Greenhill Books, London, 1990, p. 373.
74. *Air Force Manual 1-1, Vol I: Basic Aerospace Doctrine of the United States Air Force*, GPO, Washington, 1992, p. 6.
75. Mann, op. cit., p. 107.

The second obvious change in strategic bombing relates to aerospace technology and the increased capabilities that advanced technology affords air planners today. The table shows a comparison of bombing accuracy and the quantity of bombs needed to achieve a ninety percent chance of hitting a hypothetical building-size target (Figure 11.1). What the table does not show is the tremendous reduction in the number of aircrew members put at risk to destroy a given target. As Colonel Warden likes to point out when using this example: "In the Gulf War, one bomb dropped by an F-117 flown by one man had a 90% probability of hitting the same target which in WWII took a thousand planes and ten thousand men."[76] Perhaps even more dramatic than the improved accuracy and decreased risk to fliers, is the huge reduction in logistical, training, and administrative effort needed to support the more precise bombers. According to Warden, munitions requirements for the entire air campaign during Desert Storm could have been supported with just six C-5 cargo planes a day, if all aircraft had been using PGMs.[77]

The precision and the survivability of modern aerospace systems have changed dramatically, and in a way that makes strategic bombing not only more useful for certain situations, but politically more attractive in almost all situations – regardless of its usefulness.[78] Recent trends toward high-tech munitions compliment the traditional focus on developing more capable aircraft. Increasingly, developments in both munitions and aircraft are denying potential adversaries the sanctuaries of darkness, underground shelters, and (eventually) bad weather.

---

76. Colonel John A. Warden, III, USAF (Ret), 'Air Power in the Gulf,' *Daedalus Flyer*, 36, no. 1 (Spring 1996): p. 15.

77. Colonel John A. Warden, III, USAF, 'New War', briefing to the USAF Air Command and Staff College, 30 August 1994.

78. As Eliot Cohen pointed out: "Air Power is an unusually seductive form of military strength, in part because, like modern courtship, it appears to offer gratification without commitment." Eliot A. Cohen, 'The Mystique of US Air Power', *Foreign Affairs* 73, no. 1 (January/February 1994): pp. 108-123. A counter to this technological change argument is that such precision and survivability applies mainly to the United States, and only to others when they join with the US in operations such as Desert Storm and Deliberate Force. I would suggest, though, that while precision and survivability are enhanced by some high technology intelligence and communications systems unique to the US, these qualities are valuable in their own right and have the potential to change the nature of strategic bombing for all technologically advanced nations. I would also argue that political constraints, rules of engagement, and military doctrine and military politics are at least as important as high technology intelligence and communications in terms of the factors enhancing or inhibiting strategic bombing. Manned and unmanned reconnaissance aircraft are not the exclusive purview of the American military. Moreover, high-speed, wide band width communications are available to any modern nation wishing to have them, and willing to pay for them.

Though the technology sword cuts both ways (as Squadron Leader Peter Emmett argues in Chapter 7), technological advances offer a change in kind not just degree, over earlier concepts of strategic bombing. These changes are the cornerstone of a new war-fighting concept, called parallel warfare, and seem to have breathed new life into older theories of strategic paralysis.[79]

Though the geopolitical environment and technology have changed, an enduring feature of strategic bombing has been the distinction between its use as a tool for either denial or coercion.[80] Just as air planners in WWI expected strategic bombing to have both a physical (denial) effect and a psychological (coercion) effect, strategic bombing strategies today can be geared to the same options; that is, they can either target an enemy's ability to resist (denial), or they can target an enemy's will to resist (coercion). These two options are not mutually exclusive, but before considering them in combination, it will be useful to think of them in their idealised, forms. In its purest form, the concept of denial relates to one's efforts to physically impose a solution on an adversary. When one pursues a pure denial strategy, one does not much care if the enemy's will is broken or bent to one's own; one uses force for its physical effects, to achieve one's ends.[81] Coercion, on the other hand, is used to change an adversary's will. In its pure form, coercion could act through punishment of the enemy – actual, or merely threatened. There is no requirement for coercion to be linked to the military situation. The act or threat of punishment is directed against whatever the enemy values, or whatever is most likely to give one leverage in influencing the enemy's will; the targets could be

---

79. See for instance, Colonel David A. Deptula, 'Firing for Effect: Change in the Nature of Warfare', *Defense and Air Power Series*, Aerospace Education Foundation, Arlington, Virginia, 1995; Colonel John A. Warden III, USAF, 'Employing Air Power in the Twenty-first Century', in *The Future of Air Power, in the Aftermath of the Gulf War*, Richard H. Schultz, Jr. and Robert L. Pfaltzgraff, Jr. (eds.), Air University Press, Maxwell AFB, Alabama, 1992, pp. 57-82; and Colonel John A. Warden III, USAF, 'Air Theory for the Twenty-first Century', in *Battlefield of the Future*, Barry R. Schneider and Lawrence E. Grinter (eds.), Air University Press, Maxwell AFB, Alabama, 1995, 103-124.

80. This is not meant to suggest that the concepts of denial and coercion are unique to strategic bombing, or air power; they certainly apply to the other forms of military power. For a fuller treatment of these concepts see Michael Clarke, 'Air Power, Force and Coercion', in *The Dynamics of Air Power*, Group Captain Andrew Lambert and Arthur C. Williamson, eds., MOD, RAF Staff College, Bracknell, Berkshire, 1996, pp. 67-85.

81. Strategies of annihilation represent denial in this extreme form. Another extreme form of denial would be the utter destruction of an adversary's war-making capacity. Whether targeting an enemy's people or his things, whenever force is employed without regard to changing an adversary's intentions, denial is the concept at work. As an example consider the Israeli air strike on Iraq's Osirak nuclear facility in June 1981. The objective was to deny Iraq its nuclear program for the short term, regardless of what Iraq's leaders wanted.

economic, symbolic, psychological, or even the enemy's civilian population.[82] In summary, denial strategies are designed to achieve one's objectives by causing a physical effect, coercion strategies aim to change the will of an adversary.

The neat conceptual distinctions drawn above rarely apply in practice. However, it is a mistake to conflate the two concepts of denial and coercion into one, or to see all warfare as coercion.[83] Experience has shown that attempts to overcome an enemy's will to fight, without seriously attacking his capability to fight will most likely, end in frustration. In fact, it seems that the best way to overcome an enemy's will to resist is to deny him the capability to do so. Denial might be the most effective means of coercion, but that does not mean that all uses of force are intended for coercion.[84] In fact force has long been used, and will continue to be used, to destroy things one would like to deprive an opponent from having. Inevitably, warfare is a struggle that involves both denial and coercion, and each side attempts to defeat its opponent's ability and will to fight. But specific military activities in war, or operations other than war, can be conducted strictly for denial or coercion.

---

82. Coercion can be used to maintain the status quo (deterrence), or to alter it (compellence). Counter-value nuclear deterrence strategy, which targets enemy cities exemplifies an extreme form of coercion. Demonstrations of force, especially those without any effect on the military situation are examples of compellence. The NATO airstrikes in Bosnia prior to Deliberate Force came close to pure coercion, because they were not intended to affect the military situation so much as the will of the Bosnian Serb leaders.

83. This is a mistake Robert Pape makes in *Bombing to Win*. Because he sees all warfare as coercion, he fails to consider the possibility that the Republican Guard and other 'strategic' targets were struck during the Gulf War for the simple physical effects the strikes achieved. Pape viewed strategic bombing in the Gulf War through the lens of coercion, thus drawing his conclusions about the bombing's effectiveness on the basis of whether or not it coerced Saddam Hussein. I would suggest that the coalition, especially the US, was less interested in coercing Saddam Hussein out of Kuwait, than in effecting a certain level of destruction against Saddam's war-making abilities. The US apparently wanted to reduce Saddam's ability to threaten his neighbors, and to weaken his internal power base. General Colin Powell made this clear when he was first briefed on Colonel Warden's 'Instant Thunder' plan. The JCS Chairman said: "I don't want them to go home – I want to leave smoking tanks as kilometer fence posts all the way to Baghdad." Powell is also reported to have said: "We need to destroy – not attack, not damage, not surround – I want you to destroy the Republican Guard." Strategic bombing of Republican Guard units, Weapons of Mass Destruction (WMD) facilities, C3 targets, etc., had nothing to do with coercion. The two Colin Powell citations are, ironically, from Pape, op. cit., p. 224, who is citing, respectively, Diane T. Putney, *Air Power Advantage: Planning the Gulf Air Campaign*, Office of Air Force History, Washington, 1993, p. 7; and, General H. Norman Schwarzkopf, *It Doesn't Take a Hero*, Bantam, New York, 1992, pp. 381-382.

84. This is, in essence, what Pape concludes. Pape, op. cit., pp. 329-331.

Despite the broad continuity of strategic bombing as a tool for either coercion or denial (or both), the target sets and the presumed mechanisms for coercion and denial have changed. Whereas early air power theorists once believed that attacks on enemy civilians might lead to a breakdown in social order, and a collapse of the enemy's will to fight, direct attacks on an enemy's population are no longer seen as a viable or effective strategy – at least not in the UK or America.[85] The last time the US conducted incendiary attacks against enemy cities occurred in the first half of mankind's experience with strategic bombing, during the Korean War.[86] Nothing during the Vietnam War compared to the attacks on civilians in WWII. In fact, the Johnson administration seemed to be more concerned, ironically, with avoiding civilian casualties when bombing targets in North Vietnam, than in bombing operations over its ally South Vietnam. In the Gulf War, strategic bombing came under extremely tight controls after several hundred civilians sheltering in the *Al Firdos* command bunker were killed in an F-117 attack on the facility.[87] The trend in strategic bombing for coercion is toward targeting things, not people. In Chapter 10, Group Captain Andrew Lambert addresses the utility of bombing operations for the purpose of coercing enemy troops.

Just as targeting for coercion has changed, so too has targeting for denial. In WWI, WWII, and much of the Cold War, enemy industry featured prominently as a 'vital centre', which captured the attention of those who were concerned with strategic bombing. Working under the assumptions that war between great

---

85. This generalization does not necessarily apply to nuclear strategy. The qualifier about the UK and America is meant to apply to western democracies. Other belligerents continue to conduct indiscriminate attacks against enemy civilians. The Bosnian Serbs shelled civilians to intimidate them into leaving their homes and villages, as part of the Bosnian Serb strategy of ethnic cleansing. The Croats did the same thing to Serbs living in the Krajina region of Croatia in August 1995. Also, Iraq launched ballistic missile attacks on Tehran during the Iran-Iraq War. Indiscriminate attacks against civilians is probably unacceptable in the UK and America for at least four reasons. First, western liberal democracies are based on values and moral principles which could be seriously undermined by such attacks. Second, experience from WWII has shown that such attacks probably will not work. Third, the idea and practice of attacking enemy civilians was a product of total war; such extreme means would almost certainly be inconsistent with strategic objectives in a limited war or operation other than war. Finally, the UK and US are probably more vulnerable to these sorts of attacks than the societies they are most likely to fight, thus there would be a practical incentive to refrain from civilian attacks in the hope for mutual restraint.

86. The Korean War ended in 1953, and 1956 is the mid-point between the first strategic bombing in 1915 and the current year, 1997.

87. Rick Atkinson, *Crusade: The Untold Story of the Persian Gulf War*, Houghton Mifflin, New York, 1993, pp. 285-290.

powers would be total war, and that great powers were modern industrialised states, air power theorists and air planners naturally fixed their sites on their enemies' industries. The focus on industry carried over into the Korean War and the Vietnam War. Though the role of airmen in advocating and planning strikes against industry in those two wars has long been caricatured and criticised, exploring that issue is well beyond the scope of this chapter.[88] It seems safe to say, however, that airmen in both of those wars might fairly be criticised for being too slow to accept the political realities of limited war, and the implications of those realities for their total war concepts of strategic bombing. This linkage between an enemy's industry and his ability to fight continued in both USAF and RAF doctrine until the end of the Cold War – and beyond.[89] Compared to planners in earlier wars, coalition air planners during the Gulf War conducted more analysis and made fewer assumptions about the objectives of the war and about what constituted their adversary's 'vital centres'. Fresh thinking about 'centres of gravity' and the means of linking targets to political objectives have been the most valuable legacies of the Gulf War for air strategists today.[90]

The second enduring feature of strategic bombing is inherent in the term itself, that is, there is some bombing that is 'strategic', which is somehow different from other bombing operations – especially bombing for tactical purposes. Though the distinction between 'strategic' and 'tactical' remains, the definition of

---

88. For a more sophisticated, if somewhat turgid discussion of what air force leaders and planners advocated in these wars see Robert Frank Futrell, *The United States Air Force in Korea, 1950-1953*, GPO, Washington, 1983; and Futrell's two volume work *Ideas, Concepts, Doctrine: Basic Thinking in the United States Air Force, Vol. I, 1907-1960 and Vol II, 1961-1984*, Air University Press, Maxwell AFB, Alabama, 1989.

89. According to *AFM 1-1*, "Strategic attacks are carried out against an enemy's centers of gravity including command elements, war production assets, and supporting infrastructure (for example, energy, transportation, and communication assets)." *AFM 1-1*, op. cit., p. 11. Though starting to break out of the mold linking strategic bombing to enemy industry, the 1993 version of RAF air power doctrine still contained passages such as the following: "Strategic air offensive action is directed at undermining the enemy's ability and will to continue his aggression by attacking industrial, political and economic target sets, rather than direct action against the enemy's forces." *AP 3000, 2nd Edition: Air Power Doctrine*, Royal Air Force, London, 1993, p. 72. As of this writing, both the 1991 USAF doctrine and the 1993 RAF doctrine have not been superseded, though both are under revision.

90. See, for instance any of the articles listed above by Colonel Warden, or see his seminal work, Colonel John Warden III, USAF, 'The Enemy as a System', *Air Power Journal* 9, no. 2 (Spring 1995): pp. 40-55. See also, Lieutenant Colonel Maris McCrabb, USAF, 'Air Campaign Planning', *Air Power Journal* 7, no. 2 (Summer 1993): pp. 11-22; and Major Jason B. Barlow, USAF, 'Strategic Paralysis: An Air Power Strategy for the Present', *Air Power Journal* 7, no. 4 (Winter 1993): pp. 4-15.

strategic bombing has changed in a way that is often unrecognised, or under-appreciated. The simple notion of independence from battlefield operations, which in WWI meant anything outside the range of friendly artillery, is obviously outdated. But what distinguishes 'strategic' from 'tactical' today? Agreeing to a definition of strategic bombing is a fundamental prerequisite to any meaningful discussion of its future relevance.

WHAT IS STRATEGIC BOMBING?

In order to define strategic bombing, it is helpful to note what it is not, as well as what it is. According to USAF doctrine, strategic bombing is a particular type of aerospace mission that falls under the heading of 'force application'. Force application, in turn, is a subdivision of air-to-surface combat operations, exclusive of 'aerospace control' missions.[91] The other 'force application' missions besides 'strategic attack' are interdiction and close air support. So strategic bombing is a mission, and it is not an aerospace control mission, nor is it close air support or interdiction. This taxonomy provides a useful beginning for defining strategic bombing, but it lacks sufficient descriptive detail. The defining characteristic of strategic bombing is the objective or purpose for which it is conducted; strategic bombing is bombing intended to contribute **directly** to the achievement of polit-ical or military strategic objectives.[92] It is meant to affect the conflict as a whole. Aerospace control missions, interdiction, and close air support usually have a direct or indirect impact at the operational or tactical levels of war.

The levels of war are conceptual tools that are useful in so far as they facilitate thinking about, and planning for military activities. Ideally, actions at one level should be consistent with, and in support of, actions at the other levels. Moreover, in planning military operations and setting objectives, the levels should be considered as hierarchical. One should start with strategic objectives and design

---

91. Under existing USAF doctrine, 'force application' is a subdivision of air-to-surface bombing operations. Bombing operations other than 'force application' come under the separate broad heading (or role) of 'aerospace control', which includes offensive counter air (OCA) and defensive counter air (DCA) missions. *AFM 1-1: Basic Aerospace Doctrine*, 1992, p. 6-7.

92. The inaugural British Defence Doctrine, JWP 0-01, identifies four levels of war, the top two being the 'grand strategic' and the 'military strategic'. For ease of conceptualization and presentation, I will follow US practice of using only three levels of war: strategic, operational, and tactical. Throughout the remainder of this paper, 'strategic objective' can be taken to mean either 'grand strategic' or 'military strategic'.

campaigns or military operations which will achieve the strategic objectives, before planning the operational level objectives of the campaigns. In planning one starts at the top and works down. In execution things work the other way around. One conducts engagements designed to achieve tactical objectives, these tactical objectives should build upon one another so as to achieve operational ends, which in turn should fulfil the strategic objectives.

The labels strategic, operational, and tactical can be, and have been, used to describe military activities in conflicts as diverse as WWII, the Gulf War, and peace support operations in the former Yugoslavia. The flexibility and utility of these labels has some drawbacks though, for in what way can one compare the strategic level in WWII to the strategic level in Bosnia? Furthermore, how distinct were the strategic and operational levels in the Gulf War, which was prosecuted as a single campaign in a relatively small theatre of operations? As one moves down the conflict spectrum from total war to limited war, to operations other than war, the various levels of war seem to merge. Tactical engagements are more likely to have strategic implications, and in order to achieve the desired nuances of policy, senior civilian and military leaders will want to control details at the tactical level. In trying to differentiate between the levels of war at the lower end of the conflict spectrum (i.e. limited wars and operations other than war), one soon gets the sense one has when looking at an Escher staircase; what initially appears to be a straightforward ascent or descent to a different level, inevitably leads one back to where one started, so that strategic, operational, and tactical become indistinguishable.

A way out of this dilemma is to recognise that the defining characteristic of things strategic is that they are linked **directly** to the ultimate or political objectives involved, and that things tactical are relevant to what goes on at the level of an engagement and, most importantly, they are not mutually exclusive. Moreover, some strategic objectives can be pursued **directly** with each engagement, thus obviating the need for the intermediate operational level objectives. The hierarchical relationship between the levels of war, which is an essential concept for planning military operations, is not the defining characteristic of 'strategic' or 'tactical'.[93] Finally, it must be recognised that even when all three levels seem relevant in a given situation, an activity, such as bombing, could serve objectives at all

---

93. The whole concept of 'levels of war' depends on a hierarchy; in fact, the hierarchy is inherent in the word 'level'. While 'strategic' and 'tactical' are labels given to the levels of war, they have meanings rooted in concepts of strategy and tactics which predate models of the 'levels of war'. Once one adds the concept of operations linking strategy and tactics, the way is prepared for some hierarchical model, and it is difficult to conceive of operations outside the context of a hierarchy.

three levels.[94] The key is to plan and conduct air operations so that they compliment each other, or at least so that bombing at the tactical or operational level does not undermine accomplishment of strategic level objectives.[95]

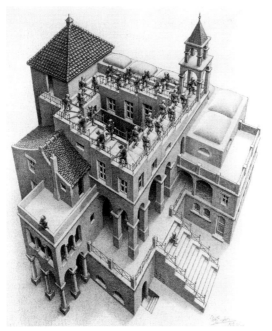

Escher Staircase[96]

---

94. The bombing of German oil targets in the summer of 1945 illustrates the ability of one activity to serve objectives at all three levels. At the tactical level, the bombers served as bait to draw Luftwaffe fighters into combat with allied fighters. At the operational level, the loss of oil affected the German Army's ability to conduct armored operations, thus facilitating Anglo-American advances. At the strategic level, shortages of oil undermined the overall Wehrmacht war effort; it forced changes in training and operational policies, and it eliminated the major source of nitrates needed for Nazi munitions production.

95. For instance, it could be argued that during the Vietnam War, American carpet bombing of Vietcong controlled parts of South Vietnam was operationally or tactically useful, but it probably undermined the higher-level American objective of shoring up the legitimacy of the government in Saigon.

96. M.C. Escher, Copyright: Cordon Art B.V. Exclusive representatives of the worldwide Escher copyrights.

Strategic bombing, then, is bombing which is intended to directly fulfil strategic or political objectives in war or in operations other than war. Such bombing is not usually conducted in order to achieve control of the air, nor is it intended for interdiction, or close air support missions. What distinguishes strategic bombing from these other air-to-surface bombing operations, is its defining characteristic – its direct connection with strategic or political objectives. In total war, the primary strategic objective is to win the war. In limited wars and operations other than war, the strategic objectives can be quite varied and changing; indeed the main strategic objective might have little to do with traditional notions of military victory. Of course this begs the question: is strategic bombing relevant when the objective is something short of destroying an enemy's ability and will to fight?

FUTURE RELEVANCE OF STRATEGIC BOMBING

Perhaps one of the greatest impediments to a modern appreciation of strategic bombing is the historical baggage that adheres to the term. This sentiment is reflected in the epigram of a recent report from a distinguished multinational panel which studied strategic air warfare: "The great obstacle to progress is not ignorance, but the illusion of knowledge."[97] Given the early record of strategic bombing, one can hardly fault political and military leaders (especially if they are well versed in history) if they conceive of strategic bombing as the bluntest of all military instruments. But the reality is that strategic bombing today could, under the right circumstances, be a very precise instrument. As DELIBERATE FORCE – the two and a half week bombing campaign against the Bosnian Serb Army in the summer of 1995 – showed, precision bombing can effect strategic level objectives.[98] That said, it must be conceded that whenever the military dimension of a conflict is overshadowed by considerations of 'proportionality' and retaining the 'consent' of the belligerents (as in Bosnia before the summer of 1995), any proac-

---

97. 'Aerospace Power for the 21st Century: A Theory to Fly By', White Paper from the Strategic Aerospace Warfare Study Panel, Air University, Maxwell AFB, Alabama, 4 October 1996, p. iv.

98. At Dayton, the Serbs revealed that the entire bombing campaign caused fewer than 25 deaths, including Bosnian Serb soldiers. Ambassador Christopher Hill, US State Department, interview with Lt Col Robert Owen, USAF, 27 February 1996, USAF Historical Research Agency, Balkans Air Campaign Study, File H-1, p. 16. The statement that Deliberate Force achieved strategic level objectives is based on the assessment of the Contact Group's chief negotiator, US Assistant Secretary of State Richard Holbrooke. Holbrooke and senior NATO officials concluded that Deliberate Force coerced the Bosnian Serb leaders to negotiate at Dayton. Colonel Robert Owen, USAF, 'The Balkans Air Campaign Study: Part II', *Air Power Journal* 11, no. 4 (Winter 1997).

tive use of force, including strategic bombing, might be inappropriate, regardless of its precision.

Even when a proactive use of force is deemed appropriate for accomplishing a given military or policy objective, opinions still vary on how useful strategic bombing might be for achieving those objectives. Colonel John Warden is a staunch advocate of air power's strategic potential, while at the other end of the spectrum, Robert Pape argues that strategic bombing has not worked in the past and will not work in the future. Debates over the usefulness of strategic bombing are often characterised by the debaters talking past one another. The apparent differences in opinion stem largely from differences in definitions and assumptions about strategic bombing and the nature of warfare.[99] Rather than trying to generalise about strategic bombing, or take sides with either Warden or Pape, the remaining discussion addresses the likely utility of strategic bombing, as defined above, across the spectrum of conflict, from operations other than war, to total war.

OPERATIONS OTHER THAN WAR

At the low end of the conflict spectrum, military operations other than war, there are several types of operations which seem to fit the parameters of the above definition of strategic bombing – though it might surprise some people to think of them as strategic bombing. First are punitive attacks such as the US strike against Libya in 1986. Though some observers claim the political objective of the strike was to kill Muammar Qaddafi, or to compel him to desist from any future support of terrorism, Caspar Weinberger makes the argument that the US objective was simply to make Qaddafi pay a price for his past support of terrorism.[100] Whatever effect the attack had on Qaddafi, it bolstered domestic political support for the Reagan administration, and it destroyed some things that Qaddafi valued, including some military aircraft. The French allegedly made a punitive strike against a residence in Pale on 23 July 1995, the day after two French peacekeepers were

---

99. See footnote 82 for an example of how Robert Pape's assumptions affect his conclusions. For a discussion of, and challenge to, Colonel Warden's assumptions see, Colonel Richard Szafranski, USAF, 'Parallel War and Hyperwar: Is Every Want a Weakness?', in *Battlefield of the Future: 21st Century Warfare Issues*, Barry R. Schneider and Lawrence E. Grinter, eds., Air University Press, Maxwell AFB, Alabama, 1995, pp. 125-148.
100. Caspar Weinberger, *Fighting for Peace: Seven Critical Years in the Pentagon*, Warner Books, New York, 1990, p. 197.

shot and killed by snipers in Sarajevo.[101] Israel has had a tradition of using air strikes to punish those it believes are behind terrorist attacks against its citizens.[102] The precision and survivability of modern air power could make punitive airstrikes more attractive in the future.[103]

Closely related to punitive strikes are symbolic bombing operations for political signalling. Such bombing operations could be used to either reinforce a deterrent threat, or to demonstrate a willingness to make good on a threat to compel. These coercive bombing operations meet the definition for strategic bombing whenever they are conducted to deter or compel at the political level. For a discussion of coercion at the operational level, see Chapter 10 by Group Captain Andrew Lambert. Some of the early NATO air strikes in Bosnia fit this category of strategic bombing, as did early bombing operations in the Rolling Thunder campaign.[104] Many of the characteristics of air power help to make it a tempting tool for political signalling, especially in peace support operations where one might want to use minimum force, while communicating the ability to employ much more. Experience, however, suggests that symbolic strikes are unlikely to be effective, especially if the party being coerced places a high value on whatever is at stake.

Preventive air strikes represent another military operation below the level of war that fit the definition of strategic bombing.[105] In a preventive attack, the

---

101. 'Zepa Safe Area Falls to Bosnian Serbs; Western Allies Threaten Air Strikes', *Facts On File Yearbook 1995*, Facts On File Inc., Np, 1996, 530.

102. Barry M. Blechman, 'The Impact of Israel's Reprisals on Behavior of the Bordering Arab Nations Directed at Israel', *Journal of Conflict Resolution* 16, no. 2 (June 1972): 155-181; and Lieutenant Colonel Kenneth C. Schow, Jr., *Falcons Against the Jihad*, Air University Press, Maxwell AFB, Alabama, 1995.

103. The attentive reader might well have noticed that punitive uses of force do not necessarily have anything to do with denial or coercion. The idea of strategic bombing in retaliation dates back to WWI. Some commentators argue that punitive bombing is really intended for coercion, otherwise it is senseless. This argument however, ignores the possibility that retaliation might fulfill certain human emotional needs, and could be done for domestic political purposes without regard for future deterrent or compellent effects.

104. The US was, of course, a belligerent in the Vietnam War, whereas in Bosnia NATO was involved in peace support operations, which are considered military operations other than war.

105. As Richard Haass points out in his book *Intervention*, preventive strikes should not be confused with preemptive attacks. In a preemptive attack, one perceives an imminent attack from an enemy who already possesses the means of striking, and one preempts the would be attacker by striking first. In a preventive attack, an enemy attack is not imminent but the enemy's will to attack is established; the preventive attack is designed to keep the enemy from developing the capability to act on his hostile intentions. Richard N. Haass, *Intervention: The Use of American Military Force in the Post-Cold War World*, Carnegie Endowment, Washington, 1994, pp. 51-52.

objective is to deny or delay a potential adversary's ability to do one harm. The Israeli air strike on Iraq's Osirak nuclear facility in 1981 exemplifies this type of strategic bombing.[106] In 1996, US Secretary of Defence William Perry reportedly threatened the same sort of action against Libya's Tarhuna chemical weapons plant. Given the concerns in the US and the UK over nuclear weapons proliferation, strategic bombing as a tool for counter-proliferation could become increasingly viable in the future. Even if the US and UK forego such preventive strikes as stand-alone operations, either state could become involved in a war against an adversary who is in the process of developing WMD. In that case, air strikes against WMD targets would almost certainly constitute an element of any strategic bombing operations, just as in the Gulf War.

Though problematic in many respects, using an airstrike to kill an individual could serve a strategic objective.[107] In the past, the likelihood of success in such an endeavour was so low as to make it practically impossible.[108] Modern technology may have changed that. Some observers believe that killing Saddam Hussein was one goal of the strategic bombing campaign against Iraq, though the US government denies that.[109] Five years after the Gulf War, the Russians may have planned and executed a bombing operation that killed the rebel Chechen leader Dzhokhar Dudayev. Whether this sort of bombing will occur more frequently remains to be seen, but the technology for conducting it exists and the precedence has been set.

---

106. Ibid., p. 51.

107. For a discussion of some of the practical problems associated with killing or unseating an enemy political leader see Pape, *Bombing to Win*, pp. 232-238. See also, Richard K. Betts and Samuel Huntington, 'Dead Dictators and Rioting Mobs: Does the Demise of Authoritarian Rulers Lead to Political Instability', *International Security* 10, no. 3 (Winter 1985/86): pp. 112-146; Lieutenant Commander Bruce A. Ross, USN, 'The Case for Targeting Leadership in War', *Naval War College Review* 46, no. 1 (Winter 1993): 73-93; James L. Taulbee and David A. Head, 'Mercenary Commando Coup Operations: Theory versus Practice', *Journal of Strategic Studies* 16, no. 1 (March 1993): 109-121; and Edward Luttwak, *Coup d'État*, Harvard University Press, Cambridge, Massachusetts, 1979. Robert A. Pape "A Surgical Strike That Could Backfire," *The New York Times*, 27 April 1986, p.15.

108. On 18 August 1943 American fighters shot down Admiral Isoroku Yamamoto as part of a carefully planned and executed operation designed to deprive the Japanese of one of their most able naval leaders. However, this was not a bombing operation, and it took place in the context of a war. I am not aware of any successful bombing operations which specifically targeted a military or civilian leader in peace or war prior to the 1990s.

109. The US has steadfastly denied that killing Saddam Hussein was a goal of the bombing operations during Desert Storm, but as Robert Pape points out, senior military commanders might have advocated such operations. Pape, *Bombing to Win*, pp. 221-222.

LIMITED WARS

The determination of how relevant strategic bombing will be in a limited war cannot be answered very well in general, or abstract, terms; one can, however, meaningfully discuss some of the considerations and processes involved in making such a determination. To the degree that achieving the strategic objectives of a limited war depend on military victory over an adversary who employs conventional forces, strategic bombing is likely to be relevant and useful (see discussion below on total conventional war). The following brief discussion on COG should convey a sense of when strategic bombing might be most useful.

A key to any strategic bombing campaign, whether based on denial or coercion, is to identify an adversary's COG(s). I shall define COGs, in part, as Clausewitz did, as: "the hub of all power and movement, on which everything depends."[110] Clausewitz noted there can be more than one COG, but, ideally, a strategist should narrow these down to the smallest possible number – ideally one. Here, I will part ways with Clausewitz, and expand the concept a bit. I subscribe to the view of a state as a system with multiple sources of power. If possible, it will compensate for any deprivation of power from one source, by attempting to substitute from another source. Each source of power has its own vulnerabilities, as well as its own degree of relevance for sustaining the state's war-making effort. Those sources of power which are of the greatest importance to a state's war-making capabilities constitute COGs.[111] Moreover, COGs exist within the subsystems which make up the state; for instance, the enemy's military forces may have their own COGs. Centres of gravity exist at all levels of war, but the strategic COGs are most important for this discussion.

COGs are an enemy's strengths, not his weaknesses, but an enemy might have an Achilles' heel – a way of undermining his strengths. Small powers are likely to be vulnerable to air attack if they engage in conventional warfare. By definition, small powers lack the ability to substitute for lost sources of power; their lack of depth and resiliency is, in part, what makes them small powers. However, as the Vietnam War showed, other factors – especially superpower sponsorship – can

---

110. Carl von Clausewitz, On War, ed. and trans. by Michael Howard and Peter Paret, Princeton University Press, Princeton, New Jersey, 1984, pp. 595-6.

111. A recent USAF White Paper uses the term 'instruments of power', which it defined as 'the various means a hostile government uses to pursue its national objectives, the machinery of government, military forces, and other constituents of national power.' Strategic Aerospace Warfare Study Panel, "Aerospace Power for the 21st Century a Theory to Fly By," Unpublished USAF White Paper, 4 October 1996, vii.

mitigate disadvantages in traditional forms of national power. In conventional wars, middle powers are perhaps even more vulnerable than small powers to well conceived strategic bombing campaigns, for what they gain in traditional sources of power, tend to be those things which make good targets for airstrikes. Finally, great powers, and especially super powers, are least likely to be vulnerable to strategic bombing, because they tend to be able to draw from more numerous and deeper sources of power.[112] By properly identifying and analysing COGs, military planners can best develop strategies for beating an adversary, great or small.

The fundamental question for formulating an air campaign is: How can one influence an adversary's COG(s) in a way that is most likely to achieve the desired political objective(s)? Air strategy is, as Douhet once noted, essentially a matter of targeting: 'the selection of objectives...and determining the order in which they are to be destroyed is the most difficult and delicate task in aerial warfare, constituting what may be defined as aerial strategy.'[113] More recently, Colonel Phillip Meilinger, whilst Dean of the USAF's School of Advanced Air power Studies, suggested much the same thing: 'Selecting objectives to strike or influence is the essence of air strategy.'[114] Tangible COGs, such as German industry in WWII, the Iraqi Republican Guard, or Bosnian Serb heavy weapons, represent COGs which bombing might be effective at influencing. Intangible COGs, such as North Vietnamese nationalism, fundamentalist Islam, or Somali clan loyalty, are much more difficult to influence usefully via air attack. Tangible COGs do not guarantee successful air strategies, and intangible COGs do not necessarily preclude them. In general, however, it is much easier to formulate and execute a successful strategic bombing campaign around tangible COGs. Military strategists must first identify COGs, then determine how to influence the COGs to achieve the desired objectives.

Properly conceived, then, strategic bombing in war is an attempt to destroy targets that will lead directly to the attainment of one's own strategic objectives. The targets are selected on the basis of the air strategist's analysis of the nature of the war, the political objectives he has been tasked to achieve, his own capabilities and limitations, and the adversary's objectives, capabilities, limitations, and

---

112. For an argument along these lines, see: Colonel Richard Szafranski, USAF, 'Parallel War and Hyperwar: Is Every Want a Weakness?', *Battlefield of the Future: 21st Century Warfare Issues*, Air University Press, Maxwell AFB, Alabama, 1995, pp. 125-148.

113. Giulio Douhet, *Command of the Air*, Coward-McCann, New York, 1942; reprint, Office of Air Force History, Washington, 1983, p. 50.

114. Colonel Phillip S. Meilinger, USAF, *10 Propositions Regarding Air Power*, Air Force History and Museums Program, Np, 1995, p. 21.

COGs. The process of formulating air strategy is neither straightforward nor scientific; it is a dynamic, creative, iterative, and messy process.

TOTAL WAR

Total conventional war between great powers is, almost certainly, a thing of the past. This is not a pacific prediction, it is simply an acknowledgement that we live in an age when most great powers possess nuclear weapons. If great powers were to engage in total war then, by definition, one would expect them to use all of the means at their disposal, including nuclear weapons, in order to win.[115] Assuming for the moment, though, that a future total war could remain conventional, it seems reasonable to suggest that strategic bombing could play a leading role for a belligerent with the wherewithal to win air superiority and the requisite capacity for planning, gathering intelligence, and conducting precision strikes against strategic targets. Any nation wishing to engage in high intensity conventional warfare will be dependent on at least three things, all of which are extremely vulnerable to air attack: electricity, petroleum, and command, control and communications (C3) infrastructure. Significantly disrupting any or all of these things would degrade an enemy's war fighting ability out of all proportion to the level of effort required to mount such attacks. Since the primary strategic objective would be to win the war in the traditional military sense, the side that could best conduct strategic bombing could enjoy a tremendous advantage.

At the high end of the conflict spectrum, we come to nuclear war, and it might be said that nuclear attack represents the epitome of strategic bombing. However, nuclear weapons are so utterly destructive that it is hard to imagine what rational political objective could be served by actually engaging in nuclear war. The destructive means seem to have eclipsed any sensible political ends. This is not the same as suggesting that nuclear weapons are politically useless. As Robert Art noted during the Cold War:

---

115. Perhaps it should be remembered that in the years between WWI and WWII, many military theorists and planners assumed chemical weapons would be used in any future war between the world's leading powers. Yet chemical weapons were not used. Likewise, nuclear-armed belligerents of some future total war might find it in their interest to avoid using their nuclear weapons.

[T]he high degree of security which nuclear deterrence supplies... [in turn provides] three potentially useful political advantages...1) a wide margin of safety for diplomatic manoeuvring (and error); 2) a capacity to trade its nuclear protection for those things that each superpower values highly and wants from others; 3) a security so efficiently provided that many resources are freed up for other pursuits.[116]

The end of the Cold War has altered the context in which one views such conclusions, but not the fundamental truth behind them. A state capable of conducting a nuclear attack will be able to directly achieve certain political objectives merely by the existence of that capability – not through a nuclear compellent threat but, as Art suggests, by acting within the bounds of the security provided by nuclear deterrence. Since the credibility of one's deterrent threat hinges on an adversary's perception of one's capacity to act on that threat, air power is essential to credible, hence effective, nuclear deterrence. An international actor, especially a state, with a nuclear weapon and no air power (planes or missiles) will find it difficult to extract the sort of political advantages described by Robert Art. If we move beyond deterrence and into planning for actual prosecution of nuclear war, the relevance of strategic bombing becomes a basic assumption, which needs no elaboration here.

IMPLICATIONS

Defence of the nation is a fundamental responsibility of any government, and the citizens of the UK and the US are fortunate that the relatively low threat environment they currently enjoy allows their governments to spend less national treasure on defence than in previous decades. Still, whatever military capabilities a nation retains in this era of declining defence budgets must satisfy the basic *raison d'être* of military forces, that is, the ability to make a significant contribution toward fighting and winning in time of war. Though other security threats will certainly emerge (e.g. socio-cultural, economic, or information warfare), the military must stand ready in case a potential adversary resorts to that supreme tribunal – military force. To the degree military forces can serve political objectives in situations other than a major war, they will be valued by governments and military leaders alike. As the Gulf War and the air strikes over Bosnia in September 1995 illustrated, strategic bombing capabilities can be used to good effect in a variety of circumstances.

---

116. Robert Art, "To What Ends Military Power," *International Security* 4, no. 4 (Spring 1980): 22.

The implication of the continuities and changes in strategic bombing suggest that, properly understood, it is likely to be of continuing relevance outside the total war context in which it was initially forged. Moreover, trends in increased precision, decreased exposure of friendly forces, and reduced logistical demands could make strategic bombing a highly attractive option whenever force is needed. Continued technological advances will probably reduce the constraints on strategic bombing and broaden the range of circumstances where it is deemed useful. To this end, whether a nation wishes to have a seat at the table in a coalition operation, or desires an independent capability for employing force on its own, it will advance its interests by pursuing increased precision and survivability for its air forces.[117] The convergence of trends in technology, the geopolitical environment, and new concepts of strategic bombing suggest that air power is an increasingly powerful and flexible instrument for the pursuit of political objectives. If one is to exploit the potential of strategic bombing to its best effect, one must first understand it, see how it has changed, and in the process, one must discard some long-lived notions that tend to confuse discussions about strategic bombing.

---

117. Survivability can be pursued through stand-off munitions, suppression of enemy air defence (SEAD) capabilities, stealth, or some combination of these elements.

CHAPTER 12

CHALLENGES FACING MILITARY POWER
"Beyond this Place there be Dragons"...............*Early Sea Charts*[1]
Mr A C Williamson

Far from being unique to air power, many of the issues considered in this paper are of concern to the other services. It therefore has a comparative aspect. However, the main focus is on the ways in which the issues in question pose challenges to the use of air power.

---

1. A note frequently found on early English sea charts; it indicated uncharted or dangerous areas.

INTRODUCTION

THE CHALLENGES FACING MILITARY POWER that are addressed in this chapter take the form of vulnerabilities and constraints. A vulnerability is a weakness which can be exploited by an opponent, so it is an area in which the users of military power can be seriously wounded by their opponents; in the context of air power, for example, the destruction of expensive aircraft, communications satellites or computer software could be extremely damaging. A constraint, on the other hand, is a factor which narrows down the options open to an attacker, so it is a limitation which reduces the effectiveness of military power when its users are *on* the attack rather than *under* attack; classic examples are the Geneva Convention and Rules of Engagement (ROE), but geography (in particular topography, terrain and weather), technology and the media can also impose restrictions. The emphasis will be more on vulnerabilities when military power is considered in a passive capacity, and more on constraints when it is viewed in an active role. However, vulnerabilities and constraints are really two sides of the same coin. Users of military power need to take precautions in all circumstances, during offensive operations as well as in defensive situations. Just as attack is also a form of defence, so defence plays its part in attack – only those who adapt a 'Kamikaze' approach do not try to protect themselves when they launch an attack.

Military power is now routinely used in both conventional and unconventional warfare and also in peace support or enforcement actions[2]. In such circumstances, potential aggressors try to compensate for their lack of air superiority, for example, by developing ways of emasculating air power. A consequence of the growing concentration of military power in fewer and fewer hands is that conventional conflict between nation states is becoming the exception rather than the rule. The increasing likelihood of unconventional conflict or operations other than war (OOTW)[3] means that identifying potential opponents is more difficult than in the past. A short list of possible future aggressors could perhaps include: ethnic or religious groups, criminal organisations, drug cartels and, generically, the global mafia. Alliances of any of the above cannot be excluded, and there is also the possibility of multi-national corporations working through third parties to accom-

---

2. See Chapter 3 on *Coalition Warfare* by Group Captain Peach for a generic model.
3. Warfare can no longer be defined in purely military terms. An attack on a national currency by flooding world markets with a deluge of forged banknotes, for example, could be interpreted as an act of war. The term used to describe these forms of conflict in the past was post-conventional warfare.

plish their aims.[1] All these groups will share two characteristics: ruthlessness and the ability to purchase and deploy whatever weaponry they consider necessary to achieve their objectives. Furthermore, they will exploit to the full any vulnerabilities and constraints they are able to identify in the forces ranged against them. In OOTW there is often an asymmetry: "...dissatisfied locals are likely to avoid the strengths of the intervening forces while exploiting [their] weaknesses."[5]

It is also worth emphasising at the outset that users of military power cannot assume that unconventional opponents will share their values, abide by the code of international law or heed the exhortations of the UN. The standards they apply to themselves will not necessarily be upheld by the enemy. The latter may well have a completely different mind-set, and if each side approaches the conflict with different assumptions, the question of who makes the rules becomes extremely important. In such a context, it is not inconceivable that the most effective planning tool may prove to be a good understanding of history and psychology and an open mind. It is a fact of life that we do not all think the same way.[6]

As has been indicated, this chapter takes a leap into the unknown. One of the hazards of sailing in these uncharted waters is that the 'dragons' that lurk there do not fit neatly into conventional categories. It would be misleading to classify the media, for example, as either political or psychological, since it is clearly both and something else as well. Coalitions impose logistical as well as political constraints and the environment is as much a political as a physical vulnerability. These three 'dragons' all have a technological dimension too. In such circumstances, conventional categories can themselves become a constraint. This chapter is concerned with the ways in which the military may need to adapt to a context which is continually changing. Its purpose is to identify areas for which charts are needed, not to provide the charts.

---

4. Gray specifically queries the use of the term 'superpower' on the grounds that major nation states no longer have a monopoly of nuclear and other weapons of mass destruction. Chris Hables Gray, *Postmodern War*, Routledge, London 1997, note 3, p.263.

5. Andrew P.N. Lambert, Group Captain RAF, and Arthur C.Williamson, (eds.), *The Dynamics of Air Power*, MOD RAF Staff College, Bracknell, 1996, p.157. An example of asymmetry occurred during October 1983 when the battleship USS *New Jersey*, in support of Lebanese government troops, heavily shelled military positions in the hills around Beirut. This was effectively countered by a suicide bomb attack on the US Marine compound and French Headquarters of the Multi-National Force (MNF) which caused a withdrawal of the US forces, including the naval presence.

6. Witness the treatment of captured air crew by the Japanese during World War II , by the Viet Cong in the Vietnam War, and by the Mujaheddin during the Soviet involvement in Afghanistan.

USE OF FORCE

Use of the military, and in particular of air power, in peace support operations (PSOs) could easily be seen as an escalation of a crisis or conflict and an inappropriate response, no matter how logical it may be. Indeed, as Gray states, "The problem is that the reasons for using most weapons are often not logical or utilitarian, sometimes they are emotional and political"[7]. Lack of clear political and military objectives can seriously inhibit the use of military power and hand the initiative to the enemy: the question of who makes the rules immediately rears its head. In the recent past the lack of clearly defined objectives and fudged ROE have resulted in some operations, for example, peace support operations (PSOs) being conducted with one hand tied behind the back. When neither the aggressor nor the enforcer is clear as to what actions will or will not be acceptable, the advantage will inevitably lie with the aggressor, who is frequently prepared, if past OOTW are any thing to go by, to operate outside the accepted rules of warfare. Classic examples are the loss of the 'safe havens' in Bosnia and the taking of Peacekeepers as hostages; although these situations arose as a result of having small military units scattered in indefensible positions, it may well have been possible to avoid them with an appropriate use of air power had political direction been more forthcoming and military objectives more clearly defined. The response of air power to a military threat or the need for humanitarian aid can be almost immediate, and in a military confrontation the perceived human and financial cost of air power might well be less than that of the alternatives.[8]

LEGALITY

Legal considerations, together with constraints arising from differing national ROE, have posed problems in the past and will continue to do so. Legal constraints and those relating to the question of who makes the rules are probably the most difficult to identify at the present moment in time, largely because so few serious attempts have been made to clarify issues which will undoubtedly pose problems in the future. Legal constraints in war date back to the Geneva

---

7. Gray, *op.cit.* p. 57.
8. See Dr. Philip A.Towle, *Pilots and Rebels*, Brassey's UK,1989, *passim*. Air control was used by the British government between the two world wars and was arguably cost effective in terms of finance and lives.

Convention of 1864 and were reinforced by the Hague Peace Conference of 1907 and numerous international agreements thereafter. However, the constraints which were internationally agreed prior to the Second World War were concerned with surface warfare, even if many of the principles can also be applied to present-day uses of air power. The legal issues raised by the use of military power will affect the conduct of all future operations, not least because participating nations will be operating outside their national boundaries. Seeking and obtaining permission to overfly or use air bases in another country, for example, is never straightforward, and neither are the problems associated with logistics, basing and the execution of military operations. All are likely to be affected by a multiplicity of legal issues.

With regard to the crucial issue of overseas bases, politico-legal considerations can materially affect at least four factors that are fundamental to their use:[9]

- Security of tenure in the base; this may be limited by treaty,[10] or lost altogether following a change of policy on the part of the host state.[11]
- Freedom of overflight and freedom of movement within and around the base; these may be curbed, for example by the imposition of operational constraints.[12]
- Freedom to defend, weaponise and deploy forces within the base.[13]
- Freedom to mount military operations from the base; freedom of action may be restricted by treaty, by threats or by proclamations issued by the host government.[14]

---

9. These considerations are discussed in: K.A.Kyriakides, *British Cold War Strategy and the Struggle to Maintain Military Bases in Cyprus 1951-1960*, (University of Cambridge Ph.D. Dissertation, October 1996).

10. The United Kingdom's right to military bases in Egypt for a twenty year period was established by treaty in 1936.

11. When France decided to leave NATO, US bases there were closed down at the request of the French government. The USA and the UK departed from their bases in Libya following the change of government in 1969. Similarly, the UK withdrew from Malta under pressure from the government of Mr. Dom Mintoff.

12. In 1973 the governments of Greece and Turkey refused to permit the USA to supply military aid to Israel from bases within these countries. Greece and Turkey argued that under the terms of their respective agreements, the US bases could only be used for North Atlantic Treaty Organisation (NATO) purposes. John Woodliffe, *The Peacetime Use of Foreign Military Installations under Modern International Law*, Martinus Nijhoff Publishers, The Netherlands 1992, p. 274.

13. During the Cold War the Norwegian government forbade US forces from deploying nuclear weapons in Norway.

14. On 15 January 1993 The Daily Telegraph reported that air strikes against Iraqi airfields by RAF Jaguars based at Incirlik would be restricted: the Turkish government had made it clear that its Muslim sensibilities made a strike against Iraq from Incirlik politically difficult.

More particularly, the above are likely to be conditioned by the following:

- The policies of the government of the host state.
- The United Nations Charter and the laws regarding the use of force by states, the Laws of Armed Conflict, the Law of the Sea and International Air Law. See Dr K.A. Kyriakides in Chapter 4 for a full description of International Air Law.
- The specific treaty (or bilateral agreement) governing the use of the base.
- The domestic legislation of both the host and user nation.
- Mandatory constraints, if the base is used in a PSO.
- Cultural sensitivities.[15]

Legalities pertaining to the overflight of non-participating nations, in order to carry out reconnaissance or air-to-air refuelling (AAR) for example, will have to be considered before any international operation is undertaken.

John Woodliffe states that the stationing of foreign forces overseas in peacetime has also become affected by the emergence of what Harkavy calls "...a complex web of essentially subjective, psychological factors revolving around issues of sovereignty, national dignity/humiliation", and he goes on to say that the relevance of these factors is evident.[16] Under these circumstances there is clearly a case for the use of aircraft carriers. The liberation of the Falkland Islands in 1982, for example, would have been inconceivable without the air power provided by the Royal Navy aircraft carriers that were operating as part of the British Task Force, and the value of aircraft carriers was underlined again during the Gulf crisis of 1997/8. However, carriers also have their own vulnerabilities and limitations, particularly in terms of strike rate and aircraft capacity.

The sovereignty of the area used for a military base is, for reasons of security, a major political and legal concern for the user as well as the host nation. And it necessarily raises the question of what purpose the base serves, and whether it is temporary or permanent. At the moment, these issues tend to be dealt with on a purely ad hoc basis in a number of places, but they ought to be given further consideration. For many years the UK has benefited strategically from the availability of bases within several of its dependent territories, especially Ascension Island, the Cyprus Sovereign Base Areas, Gibraltar and Diego Garcia. The fact that these territories are under British sovereignty has facilitated their use and limited any political complications. By contrast, the use of bases within the

---

15. During the 1950s the government of Saudi Arabia reportedly refused to allow any Jewish American military personnel to serve on US bases within their territory.

16. Woodliffe, *op. cit.* p. 324; he quotes R. Harkavy, *Great Power Competition for Overseas Bases, The Geopolitics of Access Diplomacy,* 1982, p. 9.

The liberation of the Falkland Islands would have been inconceivable without
the use of air power provided by the Royal Navy aircraft carriers

sovereign territory of another state is often fraught with difficulties. However,
states which do not enjoy the advantage of forward basing are likely to be at a
serious disadvantage and dependent upon the goodwill of other states.[17]

Legal questions also arise in connection with the following:

- Space, which is already of great importance. See General Jones' exposition on air
  power in space in Chapter 7.
- The formulation of ROE, for example when it is necessary to suppress hostile air
  activity or neutralise the threat of surface-to-air missiles (SAMs).

These questions are complex, but they need to be addressed: if answers are not
found, future operations will be unable to count on uninhibited military support.
Some of these issues are analysed elsewhere in this volume.[18]

---

17. The rescue of Israeli hostages from Entebbe Airport in Uganda illustrates how facilities can be
made available temporarily in exceptional circumstances.
18. See Chapter 4 on *Air Power and International Air Law* by Dr. K.A. Kyriakides and Chapter 3 on
Coalition Operations by Group Captain Peach.

COSTS AND FINANCE FOR MILITARY FORCE

The political face of the financial problem is the belief that privatisation of military functions produces a budgetary saving. At first sight the proposition appears to be valid, but more careful consideration shows that it fails to think things through.[19] A few examples should suffice:

- Objections from airline owners and crews could well make it difficult to order aircraft of the Civil Air Fleet into a militarily hostile environment.
- How will the relevant authorising body provide insurance cover for civilian equipment or crews in wartime situations?
- On occasion, ground maintenance staff may be required to work unusual shifts for unusual lengths of time yet may be unwilling to do so.

The potential problems of employing civilian staff for military duties are legion,[20] and a report on a security failure in the United States provides a good illustration: "Contract guards were expensive, especially considering their lack of training and poor reliability in comparison with their military counterparts."[21]

Government cut-backs in the military budget seem to have two consequences for the military: the reserves of equipment logistically necessary to keep a modern air force in the air are run down and the number of technical support staff is reduced. The consequent lowering of morale among the remaining service personnel makes them more inclined to explore the prospects of a civilian career before age becomes a factor in employment.

The fundamental problem is that defence budgets which are susceptible to cut-backs can lead to short-sighted decisions. The development costs of modern technology are invariably high, but the latest equipment is not necessarily the most expensive option. At least three other factors should be taken into account when evaluating off-the-shelf prices:

---

19. The most recent manifestation was the failure on 6 November 1997 of three out of four engines on an aircraft of the RAF Royal Flight after being serviced by civilian contractors. *BBC News*, Radio 4, 18 November 1997.

20. During the Falklands War a problem with Merchant Navy ships and their crews was successfully resolved thanks largely to the cooperation of the relevant trade unions and the patriotic feelings of the time, but such factors cannot necessarily be taken for granted in future conflict situations.

21. James K. Mathews and Cora J. Holt, *So Many, So Much, So Far, So Fast.*, Joint History Office, Office of the Joint Chiefs of Staff and Research Center, United States Transport Command, Washington DC, 1995, p.205.

- The length of time the piece of equipment is expected to be in front-line operational service.
- The operating costs.
- The lead time over possible opponents and hence the advantage gained.

Taken at face value, for example, the off-the-shelf price of a C-17 airlift aircraft, which has four times the cargo capacity of a Lockheed C-130 Hercules, appears to be extremely high, but it probably represents the best value for money in that particular category: a C-17 can be expected to be in service for at least twenty years with a minimum of maintenance, and is the most efficient aircraft in the world at performing the tasks for which it has been designed.[22] In 1996 the C-17 flew in the region of a quarter of the missions for support of the United Nations peace keepers in Bosnia yet brought in approximately 50 per cent of the Cargo.[23] As Mathews and Holt point out,

"...by replacing 117 C-141s with 80 C-17s during the first 45 days of the operations [Desert Shield and Desert Storm], the command [the Military Air Command] could have increased strategic lift capability by 28 percent... the C-17 would mean fewer inter-theater missions, fewer crew members , less maintenance as well as additional intra-theater capability, and a faster rate of cargo delivery."[24]

The growing use of airlift by all forces makes the choice of aircraft for this role particularly important for all future military operations. Furthermore, the use of airlift can counter the piracy threat to which surface ships are exposed to. The same argument could probably be made in respect of AAR tankers, which are also increasingly important; indeed they are almost indispensable in the context of maintaining global reach.

In his book on air power, Meilinger's ninth proposition states: "Technology and air power are integrally and synergistically related."[25] Air power is sophisticated technology and there are no low-cost options.

---

22. *ibid.* Mathews and Holt. As well as requiring significantly less personnel to operate them, an analysis of airlift during the Gulf War showed that the necessary turn-around and maintenance time would have been considerably less for C-17s than for other heavy lift aircraft.

23. 'Airlift assets', *Global Defence Review 1997*, London, pp. 141-2.

24. *ibid.*, Mathews and Holt, p.77.

25. Philip S. Meilinger, Colonel, USAF, *10 Propositions Regarding Air Power*, Air Force History and Museums Program, Washington DC, 1995.

BASES

Military bases overseas are, as John Woodliffe points out, expensive to maintain.[26] They also have to be defended, as do home bases. The defence of military bases must encompass both aerial threats and ground attacks. The problems of air defence through the use of anti-aircraft systems are well understood, but ground defence poses a more complex set of problems, particularly for air bases. Aircraft are arguably in their most vulnerable state when they are on the ground, and personnel are equally difficult to protect in this regard. Such targeting could be geared to the destruction of expensive aircraft on the ground or key personnel, so base security on an unprecedented scale may be a necessity if suicide satchel-bombers are not to destroy valuable assets; there is certainly no shortage of fanatical volunteers willing to operate this kind of weapon.[27] The danger may be particularly serious during PSO, since the commitment of the public could easily waver under an assault of this kind, especially with a hostile media calling the value of the operation into question. In such circumstances, the risk of maintaining an in-theatre operational air base is likely to be considered too great, and bases outside the theatre of operations may be the only possible answer. However, transport aircraft will still face considerable risks when making essential deliveries, whether by conventional means or by low-level air delivery. In the Vietnam War a significant number of US helicopters and fixed-wing aircraft were destroyed on the ground by the Viet Cong, who repeatedly penetrated the defences of the US air bases in South Vietnam and neighbouring countries.[28] Referring to those air bases outside Vietnam, Kries states:

"In Thailand United States Air Force (USAF) and Royal Australian Air Force (RAAF) units were found at Don Muang Airport, Korat, Takhili and Udorn Royal Thai Air Force bases after 1962. Although the risk of air attack was small, these aircraft were exposed to serious ground attacks that on occasion caused heavy damage..."[29].

---

26. Woodliffe, *op.cit.* p.323.

27. See footnote 67 to this chapter.

28. In Vietnam between June 1966 and December 1971, the US military lost 4,869 helicopters of which 375 were destroyed on the ground. See John Everett-Heath, *Helicopters in Combat*, Arms and Armour, London, 1992 (reprint 1993), p.111.

29. John Kries, *Air Warfare and Air Bases*, Office of Air Force History, Washington, DC, 1988. p.279. He also points out that, although no US air defence system was actually put to the test, US air bases in Vietnam would also have been vulnerable to air attack.

The dangers of this problem were recognised during the Gulf War, and a post-conflict report stated:

"Obvious terrorist targets were aircraft and airports. Military Airlift Command (MAC) reinforced already stringent flightline security procedures at MAC bases .... security forces guarded airlift aircraft and crews."[30]

There are numerous other historical precedents for this kind of counter-air action. The RAF air base at Habbinya was attacked by the Iraqi Army in April 1941, and a scratch force of RAF training aircraft and RAF Iraqi levies on the ground defended the base for some two months until a British relieving force could arrive overland.[31] In May of the same year, the German airborne invasion of Crete began with an attack on the British airfield at Maleme, first by Luftwaffe glider-borne troops and then by paratroops.[32] It was to thwart this kind of assault that the RAF Regiment was established in the spring of 1941; fear of a German invasion of the United Kingdom was at its height, and the capture of key RAF airfields was assumed be a high priority for the Luftwaffe.[33] More recently, a British Special Air Service (SAS) party raided the Argentinean air base at Pebble Island during the Falklands War; all the aircraft stationed at the base were destroyed without loss to the SAS. Ethell and Price describe the attack as "... a serious blow to Argentinean air strength on the Islands."[34]

TERRAIN AND WEATHER

Although it is clear that modern technology is now overcoming many of the problems which formerly beset the operational use of aeroplanes in geographically hostile regions, terrain and weather still pose problems. In the area of surveillance and the use of uninhabited air vehicles (UAVs), the atmosphere and weather are extremely important when attempting to monitor the movement of ground forces, because cloud cover inhibits the use of satellites for observation. As

---

30. Mathews and Holt, *op.cit.*, p.206.

31. The importance of this air base at the time cannot be over-emphasised: it was a major air base on the overland air route to India and the Far East. For further information on this incident see Denis Richards, *Royal Air Force 1939-1945, Volume 1: The Fight at Odds*, HMSO, London, 1953, pp.311-24.

32. *ibid.*, pp. 334-336.

33. German airborne forces were an integral component of the Luftwaffe.

34. Jeffrey Ethell, and Alfred Price, *Air War South Atlantic*, Sidgwick & Jackson, London 1983, pp. 91-92. Forty-five men of 'D' Squadron SAS were landed from two Sea King helicopters. They destroyed eleven Argentinean aircraft without loss to themselves.

observation platforms, satellites are also limited by their fixed flight paths and their regular timed and predictable appearances,[35] so a place still exists for surveillance aircraft like the U-2, the comings and goings of which cannot be so readily predicted by an opponent. The constraints of terrain and weather also apply to operational aircraft. As the Soviet Air Force discovered in Afghanistan, flying in mountainous terrain in a militarily hostile environment is extremely hazardous, and in difficult meteorological conditions the risks are even greater. Poor weather can often prevent aircraft from flying at a low altitude or in mountainous terrain. To quote a Soviet source on the subject of air operations in Afghanistan, "Mountains are a harsh schoolmaster".[36] Military operations in mountainous terrain are difficult at the best of times, and in the absence of air support, ground forces can incur heavy casualties: there is perhaps a lesson to be learnt from the experience of Soviet ground forces in Afghanistan, and also from the earlier experiences of the British both in Afghanistan and on the north west frontier of India.[37] With regard to Afghanistan, Everett-Heath states that, "Because of the mountainous terrain communications were often difficult, if not impossible.... (other) aircraft were then used as relay stations."[38]

So far as targeting is concerned, Peter Almond reported that cloud cover "affected the ability of some aircraft to use lasers on their targets for precision bombing" in the USAF and RAF air strikes against Iraqi anti-aircraft defence in January 1993.[39] Infra-red observation can be limited by heavy rainfall, and the terrain also has an effect on which operations are possible and which are not. Low-level air-delivery in mountainous areas is hazardous in the extreme and could therefore have a limited role in the future use of air power until new technical solutions have been devised.

---

35. See Lambert and Williamson, *op. cit.* pp.10-13. During the Gulf War, for example, the Iraqis hid assets like Scud missiles whenever satellites were overhead. Scuds were also transported in buses, making recognition from the air virtually impossible.

36. See Towle, *op cit.* p.199; quoted from *Aviatsiya 1 Kosmonavtika* No.11, 1984, pp. 4-5.

37. Over 15,000 lives were lost during the withdrawal of the British Army from Kabul in the winter of 1842. See Patrick Macrory, *Signal Catastrophe*, Book Club Associates, London (Reprint)1972 passim, and George Pottinger and Patrick Macrory, *The Ten-Rupee Jezail*, Michael Russell, Norwich 1993, *passim*, for an excellent account of this disaster. For a more recent description of fighting on the north west frontier of India and the casualty costs see John Masters, *Bugles and a Tiger*, Michael Joseph, London 1956, pp.219-47. For an overall view of these military actions including the Soviet entry into Afghanistan see Victoria Schofield, *Every Rock, Every Hill*, Buchan & Enright, London 1984, *passim*.

38. Everett-Heath, *op.cit.* pp.128-9.

39. Peter Almond, Defence Correspondent, 'Weather caused targeting problems', *Daily Telegraph*, London, 15 January, 1993.

Mountains are a harsh schoolmaster

THE ENVIRONMENT

A new constraint of growing concern is the environmental lobby, which is increasingly affecting the levels of operational training that military forces can undertake. Such is the perceived strength of the environmental lobby that a French government agency was adjudged responsible for the sinking of the Greenpeace ship 'Rainbow Warrior' in Auckland Harbour, New Zealand, to stop it sailing to the French Nuclear test area in the South Pacific. In respect of air forces, environmental restrictions on low-level and night flying exercises often severely limit the amount of operational training that can be undertaken and hence the level of military preparedness. Although the precise level of military preparedness will vary and be determined by the nature of the perceived threat, the ability of air power to respond rapidly makes a state of readiness a constant requirement in the air force, even more so than in the other two Services. The training problem is being partially resolved by the use of simulation techniques, but the latter will always be a less than satisfactory substitute for the real thing.[10]

---

40. Tim Ripley, 'Military simulation', *Global Defence Review 1997*, London 1997, pp. 152-154.

As Everett-Heath states, "...basic theatre training and familiarisation are necessary if unnecessary casualties are to be avoided."[11] The levels of operational training directly affect all military casualty rates, and it will probably be necessary to find new training areas in regions where the possibility of an environmental backlash is minimal in order to overcome this threat to operational efficiency.

Environmental concerns have frequently been expressed in the past. Israel was criticised during the invasion of the Lebanon in 1982 when, in the midst of the conflict, serious fires broke out in the world-famous cedar forests. During and after the Vietnam War the United States was condemned for using defoliants[12]. In the Gulf War in 1991 the contamination caused by oil slicks and burning oil wells was a public relations disaster for the Iraqi government. This is perhaps not too surprising given that the "...Gulf War was one of the most disastrous ever for the environment." [13] In Germany, concerns about noise pollution caused restrictions to be placed on RAF air exercises, and aircraft were not allowed to fly below one thousand feet.[14] These examples raise the question of who makes the rules with regard to the environment and how the military operates within them.

THE MEDIA

With the advent of the Precision Guided Missile (PGM) or 'smart bomb', the response of air power to aggression can be very precise and almost instantaneous. However, there is always a risk of collateral damage, if for no other reason than that, particularly in OOTW, potential aggressors may use civilian populations either to cloak their actions or to inhibit an effective response to them. Placing a missile launch site in the middle of a school or hospital complex, for instance, makes that site an almost impossible target, even for the most sophisticated PGM; the risk of causing at least some collateral damage cannot be discounted.

Under these circumstances, the accidental maiming and killing of innocent civilians on the opposing side can easily be amplified by the media and dramatically increase sensitivities in the outside world. A classic example of this phenomenon occurred during the Gulf War when the Al Firdos Bunker in

41. Everett-Heath, *op.cit.*, p.195.
42. Neville Brown, *The Strategic Revolution*, Brassey's, London 1992, p. 127.
43. T.M.Hawley, *Against the Fires of Hell: The Environmental Disaster of the Gulf* War, Harcourt Brace Jovanovich 1992, p.183, quoted in Gray, *op.cit.* p.43.
44. *ibid.*, Brown, p.130.

Baghdad was destroyed by a Coalition PGM. Numbers of civilians were killed and injured and the world-wide television coverage produced an adverse reaction which was to result in a halt being called to this kind of weapon strike.[45] This kind of 'mistake', which despite Herculean efforts to the contrary can so often occur in warfare, exposes a disadvantage which could constrain the aggressive use of air power in future operations. By its very nature, the media will have an extensive agenda, and false information can easily be fed by aggressors to reporters and journalists anxious to meet a deadline. Such information can have extensive repercussions, and the speed of electronic communications is such that unless false information is corrected at birth, it is difficult to refute later. Furthermore, it can raise questions such as "...is the use of aggressive air power escalating the conflict?" or "...is the use of air power an overreaction to what has mistakenly been presented by the media as a limited threat?" Rarely is the global media neutral, and it is as well to remember that "...the media have their own interests and imperatives, not necessarily connected with those of the public."[46] The dangers of this kind of misrepresentation have been emphasised by the respected journalist Martin Bell; with reference to television reporting, he stated that "...the temptation to pervert the truth is there"[47]. It is not simply the reporting of facts but also the way in which they are reported that shapes public opinion. The effect of the media on public opinion is an issue which military and political leaders will have to assess very carefully before commencing any future actions. Gray suggests that in modern war, "The home front is more important than ever. The media must be guided to keep support high."[48] This is especially so in relation to the application of air power, both because it can provide such a rapid response and because in an aggressive stance it can so easily be misinterpreted as an overreaction. Conversely, the media might also question why air power had not been used in a given situation.

Undoubtedly these are very difficult problems to deal with, particularly where the response needs to be immediate. The ever present risk of a critical public opinion or an unfavourable political reaction may mean that the military will need to refer vital decisions to the political leadership, a situation requiring almost

---

45. This was reportedly due to faulty intelligence information, 300 civilians were killed. Bruce W. Watson, (ed.), *Military Lessons of the Gulf War*, Greenhill Books, London 1991, p. 75.

46. Dr. Stephen Badsey, 'Twenty things you thought you knew about the media', *Dispatches No. 5*, Spring 1995, Office of the Director of Public Relations (Army), London, 1995, pp. 55-61.

47. Martin Bell, 'The Truth is our Enemy', *BBC Radio 4*, 6th June 1997. Martin Bell MP is now an Independent Member of the House of Commons

48. Gray, *op.cit.* p.41.

instantaneous communications. In these circumstances the communications network will itself become an obvious target for an opponent. Of course, it is a matter of balancing the benefits that might be obtained from the aggressive use of military power against the costs that might be incurred politically from an adverse reaction.

CASUALTY SENSITIVITY

Casualty sensitivity is an issue which faces all the services, and it is arguably the area in which military power is most vulnerable. It is also one of the most difficult areas to assess since it brings psychological pressure to bear on both governments and participants and presupposes a willingness to sacrifice for the cause. In a case of national survival there is likely to be a degree of casualty insensitivity, but if the cause is essentially idealistic, for instance enforcing a United Nations (UN) mandate, the national sensitivity to casualties could increase dramatically. Casualty sensitivity will vary in proportion to the scale of the casualties and whether the lives of nationals are at risk. Potential aggressors are also well aware of that the fact that, the further the area of conflict is from an opponent's home country, the greater also is the degree of sensitivity.[49]

One of the possible advantages of the use of air power is that in a conflict situation fewer casualties are likely to be incurred by an air force than by a ground force, and in that sense it represents a low risk option. However, the political and psychological damage if aeroplanes are brought down, for whatever reason, can be considerable. Casualty sensitivity featured prominently in the conflicts in Afghanistan, Somalia and Bosnia. Russian military forces entered Afghanistan in 1979 to help maintain a new communist government, and more than 500 helicopters and 250 fixed-wing aircraft were eventually supporting Soviet ground troops. Despite having complete air superiority over the opposing force of devout Muslim tribesmen, the Mujaheddin, the Soviet Air Force had lost some 600 aircraft by the summer of 1987, and thereafter losses rose to around 500 a year. These losses, combined with the loss of some 14,500 military personnel, clearly

---

49. The sensitivity of the British public to casualties during the Falklands War, for example, was more pronounced than its sensitivity to Police and British Army casualties in Northern Ireland, although in the latter case there is also a degree of habituation. However, in neither case were conscripted forces involved; if they had been, the situation in respect of casualty sensitivity may have been heightened.

affected the Soviet leadership and also Soviet families,[50] but perhaps of more interest is the effect that the aircraft losses had on Soviet aircrew, whose morale appears to have been severely damaged by the treatment meted out by the rebels to their captured colleagues, and it could be argued that the Soviet Air Force failed to learn from history in this regard.[51] The deciding factor in the air-war was the gradual acquisition by the rebel Mujaheddin of the shoulder launched Stinger surface-to-air missiles (SAMs) from 1986 "...which was to have a profound effect on the course of the war."[52] Over one hundred helicopters were lost in the first eighteen months after the introduction of Stingers, significantly inhibiting air actions.[53] The Soviets tried to counter these by high-level bombing, jamming techniques and spotting the launch sites, but with only limited success.[54] The result was to emasculate the ability of the Soviet Air Force to adequately support the Soviet and Afghan government ground forces. The reduction in air support for the ground forces probably explains the increase in casualties on the ground, and it must therefore be regarded as a major contributory factor in the decision to withdraw Soviet forces.

In an air power-related incident during UN operations in Somalia, television viewers in the United States (US) were exposed to the sight of the bodies of US servicemen being dragged through the streets of Mogadishu after a US helicopter had been shot down. The public reaction to this incident was to cause the White House, shortly thereafter, to order a complete change of mission for the entire US force involved.[55] In Bosnia, the taking of peacekeeping troops as hostages and the

---

50. The Soviet Mothers movement was an important influence during the war in Afghanistan. Between 1979 and 1989 some 14,453 military personnel were lost. See Col. General G.F. Krivosheev, (ed.), *Soviet Casualties and Combat Losses in the Twentieth Century*, Greenhill, London,1997. pp.285-289.

51. In the 1930s all RAF aircrew operating on the north west frontier of India carried what were then known as 'Goolie Chits', notes which promised a substantial reward to tribesmen who returned any captured aircrew in one piece, i.e. without their testicles having been removed. It is important to note that in conflicts with certain kinds of enemy the normal rules of warfare do not apply. See Dr. Philip A.Towle, *op.cit. passim*, and also David E.Omissi, *Air Power and Colonial Control*, Manchester University Press, 1990, for general treatments of this subject. For more specific detail on 'Goolie Chits' see Norman L.R. Franks, *First in the Indian Skies*, Life Publications, Lincoln, 1981, pp. 14,82 & 140. For similar notes (Blood Notes) used in the Far East during World War II see C.G.Sweating, *Combat Flying Equipment*, Airlife, England, 1989, pp. 193-4. For the Gulf War see Pablo Mason, Sqn. Ldr., RAF, *Pablo's War*, Bloomsbury, London, 1992, p. 8.

52. Everett-Heath, *op.cit.* p.118.

53. Everett-Heath, *op.cit.* p.146.

54. 300 Stingers were supplied to the Mujaheddin in 1986 and 600 in 1987, Towle, *op.cit.* p.198.

55. Kenneth Allard, *Somalia Operations*, National Defense University Press, Washington, 1995, p. 20 and *passim*.

shooting down of French and US aircraft had repercussions on subsequent peace enforcement activities. The successful recovery of US pilot Scott O'Grady received news coverage worldwide, was a fillip to the morale of the forces involved in Bosnia, and illustrates the importance of casualty sensitivity. However, the sight of peacekeeping troops being held hostage offended the sensibilities of those nations involved, particularly in France: the sight of members of the French military chained to sensitive targets in May 1995 provoked an immediate public outcry in France, and the situation was exacerbated three months later in August when two French air crewmen were shot down over the former Yugoslavia.

A further aspect of casualty sensitivity is the possibility of counter-air action in the form of attacks on soft targets such as key personnel. The reduction in numbers occasioned by the efficiency and effectiveness of modern aircraft has made key personnel easier to identify and hence to target. Being based in home territory, for instance, no longer guarantees security when air crew and other key military personnel are seen as legitimate targets[56]. Ruthless fanatics who are prepared to sacrifice themselves for the cause can be unstoppable assassins[57].

ATTRITION

Losses are likely to impose greater constraints than in the past, not least because the financial and political costs involved are so much higher today. During the Falklands War, for example, six ships of the British Task Force were sunk and ten badly damaged by Argentine aircraft.[58] So far as air power is concerned, a dilemma will be how many aircraft and their crews represent an acceptable loss for any given operation. Looked at in the cold light of day, this is clearly a vital question and one which should not be avoided. Not only are expensive aeroplanes involved but also valuable and highly trained aircrew. The off-the-shelf price of a US C-17, one of the world's most sophisticated and effective transport aircraft, makes it one of the world's most expensive aircraft, yet without adequate

---

56. It is worth noting here that, before the start of the Russo-Finnish War of 1939, Finnish pilots had been targeted for assassination by Soviet agents. In the event the plan was never put into practice.

57. The assassination of the Israeli Olympic team in Germany and the bombing of the US Marine compound in Beirut in 1983 are typical examples of this kind of operation. Although occurring over a decade ago and not air power-related, they demonstrate the lengths to which fanatics will go if necessary.

58. The determination of Argentine pilots to press home their air attacks was underestimated by the British and was a major surprise of the Falklands War.

defensive equipment it would be just as vulnerable to attack as that ubiquitous airlift workhorse the Lockheed C-130 Hercules, or for that matter any other airlift transport. This is of particular importance in PSO where airlift provides the majority of sorties; for example, supplying humanitarian aid. Air transports are an early, tempting and opportune target for any ruthless aggressor and, since the target is unable to retaliate, it is not one which he will readily overlook. Those nations which are the providers of airlift must therefore consider their possible losses and the need to suppress any hostile actions of an aggressor group. Sensitivity to losses of this kind may well be a critical issue in future operations, even more so than in the past. However, whereas in the past any risks have been assessed in the context of conventional warfare, the increase in unconventional conflicts has brought casualty sensitivity much more to the fore. The Soviet involvement in Afghanistan is an extremely good illustration, not least because air power was an important element in the Soviet military strategy. The area was land-locked, and in a terrain which favoured attacks on surface lines of communication, Soviet air transport and helicopters became particular targets for the Mujaheddin once they had acquired Stinger SAMs. As Everett-Heath points out, an inadequate road network and the absence of a railway system are typical of much mountainous terrain, and air-supply is therefore of paramount importance in any military operation. He also notes that losses do not always occur in combat: in the Vietnam War "...very roughly, one [Helicopter] loss in two was not due to combat [which] points probably to the fatigue and stress suffered by air and ground crews ...attention needs to be paid to finding ways to reduce non-combat losses."[59]

Clearly this discussion does not simply relate to transport aircraft and helicopters. However, the fact remains that airlift will be a major constituent in all future air power operations, especially as so many of the countries in the world where there is potential for conflict are landlocked and the principal surface lines of communication could well prove hazardous. Airlift is now an important factor in most ground force operations and it must be dependable when it is required. One implication is that aircraft engaged in airlift should be capable of defending themselves. It is unlikely that all available transport aircraft would be required in a particular operational area at any one time, so 'bolt-on' defensive equipment which is capable of being quickly attached to those aircraft exposed to risk would seem to be a possible solution to the problem[60]. The vulnerability of transport

---

59. Everett-Heath, *op.cit* p.112.
60. For an excellent treatment of this subject see John A. Skorupa, Lt. Col. USAF, *Self-Protective Measures to Enhance Airlift Operations in Hostile Environments*, Air University Press, Maxwell A.F.B., Al., 1989.

The C-17 of the USAF, one of the world's most sophisticated
and effective airlift vehicles.

aircraft makes the need for defensive equipment a prime requirement if future air operations in a conflict situation are not to collapse in the same manner as did those of the Soviet Air Force in Afghanistan.

RETENTION AND RECRUITMENT

An additional vulnerability in the future will be the retention and recruitment of personnel for the more technical roles in the services. The democratic countries of the West now generally eschew the concept of conscription, and the future economic and political climate may well exacerbate the issue of military recruitment. The problem is not simply one of numbers for, as the level of the technology used in modern military equipment increases, so does the demand for a higher calibre of recruit. Recruitment is also related to the desirability of a particular function and to general levels of employment. The USAF, for example, is apparently facing a lack of applicants for the U-2 surveillance aircraft training programme due to this aircraft being declassified from 'fighter' status.[61] The services will increasingly find themselves in competition with industry and commerce for the same type of recruits. Add to this a climate in which being a serviceman or woman is unfashionable, and it is relatively easy to see why recruitment might well become a vulnerability. The British Army already has a shortfall in recruits at the time of writing. In the words of George Robertson, the British Defence Secretary "...there is a recruitment crisis in the Services."[62]

TECHNOLOGY

A technical constraint on the use of air power now emerging is the breakdown in global Air Traffic Control (ATC) coverage. The growing threat of ATC 'black holes' is particularly worrying. The latter could affect military as well as civilian air fleets and could quite conceivably inhibit humanitarian relief operations into landlocked or remote areas during which there will be intensive air activity. The problem was highlighted on the African continent in 1997. On 13 September 1997 an outbound USAF C-141 Starlifter from Windhoek collided in mid-air with an inbound German Air Force (GAF) Tupolev Tu-154: no ATC contact had been established with the GAF transport after Accra. An International Civil Aviation Organisation (ICAO) report described the ATC in all but seven African countries as "...critically deficient", but it noted that Namibia complied with international standards.[63] Such a situation necessarily imposes constraints on the use of air power in certain parts of the world, and new forms of ATC may need to be developed in order to prevent tragic accidents in the future. It is also possible that an opponent will deliberately interfere with ATC communications in order to disrupt air traffic. In these circumstances, a military ATC system might have to be deployed. It may also be necessary to devise ATC systems which have their own in-built defence mechanisms to protect them from this form of attack.

Good communications are also essential for another reason, demonstrated in the Battle of Britain by the RAF operations room Fighter Controllers who were

---

61. 'US casts net for high-flying spy pilots', *Sunday Times*, 16 November 1997, Section 2, p.19.
62. George Robertson, British Defence Secretary, in a broadcast on BBC Radio 4, Saturday 26th July 1997.
63. Report in *Flight International*, 24 September, 1997, p.8.

immediately able to exploit the information provided by Radar. In the area of surveillance, the 'long-dwell' Predator UAV is now equipped with Synthetic Aperture Radar (SAR), which can penetrate clouds, smoke and fog, so an opponent can no longer depend on these elements to cloak his activities. However, the near real time information obtained by SAR is transmitted via satellite to a control station, and this communication system may well be vulnerable to electronic attack. The most critical feature of a Predator UAV is therefore its "...ability to transfer the very data rates through modern high-band width data links".[64] As Gray has pointed out, "Sound and image surveillance is... a crucial source of accurate intelligence. Current systems are totally dependent on advanced computer techniques and the control of satellites and other collection systems."[65] Another vulnerability of UAVs is that they are controlled by software packages. It has been suggested that most of the remaining development work required will be in the sensor area, but if the software is susceptible to attack, should not software defence be a priority? If this issue is not resolved, it may also affect the next generation of surveillance aircraft, the US high altitude endurance UAVs Dark Star and Global Hawk. The problem of Year 2000 compliability in respect of software is also of growing concern, as discussed in the chapter on Information Warfare by Peter Emmett.

In the same chapter, Emmett identifies another vulnerability: "...the preferred weapon of influence of rogue states may be cruise missiles and their derivatives equipped with on-board computers programs which will give them the capability of 'smartness'."[66] It is difficult for manned aircraft to intercept or defend themselves against this kind of threat, and the way forward might lie in the ability of satellites to first detect the missiles and then direct a ground- or air-based defence. Once again, however, software and communications are the vital component.

High Energy Radio Frequency (HERF) weapons which can disable unprotected electronics are also becoming an increasing concern. Electronic equipment used by the services will be vulnerable to attack if such threats cannot be countered. It has been suggested that the Gulf War demonstrated, "...in modern war electronic superiority over the enemy has become the most important single

---

64. Aeronautical systems, *Global Defence Review 1997*, p.106.
65. Gray, *op. cit.*, p.59.
66. Peter Emmett, Squadron Leader , Ph.D., RAF. See the chapter on *Air Power in the Information Age* in this volume.

factor in determining victory."[67] Clearly this is debatable and the view of Watson and others is that, "The air campaign virtually won the war in that it so devastated Iraq that the ground campaign was over in hours."[68] However, electronic warfare is undeniably of major importance in a conflict situation. The advent of Laser weapon technology, exposure to which can cause temporary or permanent blinding, could affect all three services in varying degrees, so countermeasures are essential.[69] "Low energy lasers are a threat to human eyes and, for example, thermal sensors. Canopies can be yellowed and crazed by laser damage weapons."[70]

INFORMATION WARFARE (IW)

As Peter Emmett points out in his chapter the term 'information warfare' (IW) is perhaps misleading.[71] IW threatens to constrain military power in a number of ways, but the principal concern is software attacks. Indeed, in an environment which is saturated with information, software does not even have to be attacked. The sheer quantity of information available to commanders during the Gulf War swamped the available means to sift and disseminate it, thereby causing delays in an area where response time could be all important. As Gray says, "No matter how much information machines collect, it is useless unless it is understood."[72]

The fact that many military and civilian communications networks are shared and software-based could also be a potential vulnerability. At the time of the Japanese invasion of Malaya in 1941, a critical failure of the British defence was that military and civilian communications networks were shared: it meant that during the withdrawal of British forces from the peninsular there was a constant conflict of priorities. The communications network in question was relatively primitive, but the principle may still hold good today. There can be no doubt that communications are essential to all military operations, especially those involving air power, and if they are interrupted or destroyed, a precarious situation will ensue. All satellite communications systems are computer-operated and therefore software-based, so they will be vulnerable to 'hacking' - when an opponent is able

---

67. Pimlott and Badsey, *op.cit.* pp.271-2.
68. Watson, *op.cit.* p. 216.
69. NATO maritime reconnaissance air crews have already experienced temporary blindness after 'buzzing' Russian naval vessels.
70. Everett-Heath, *op.cit* . p.160.
71. *ibid.*, Emmett.
72. Gray. *op.cit.*,p.59.

to distort or read the information being transmitted - and the use of malicious software or viruses. Software attacks are difficult to detect but of critical importance. Most Command, Control, Communications, Computers, Intelligence and Interoperability (C^4I^2) systems are computer-based, and in addition to the danger of attacks, there is also the risk of systems failures. As Gray states, "...there are still systems failures."[73]

CONCLUSION

Although the emphasis in this chapter has been on air power, many of the issues outlined above have implications for all the services. Military preparedness is an evolutionary process, and the ways in which military power is likely to be used in the future pose a number of new challenges. As pressures on the environment and sustainable development increase, so do the dangers of new kinds of conflict. Military forces are sailing into uncharted waters in this regard, and coming to terms with the 'dragons' at large there may well involve challenging conventional assumptions. Vision will be needed in abundance, so it is perhaps appropriate to conclude by suggesting that predictability is dangerous. In the following quotations, Neil Sheehan describes how the Viet Cong were vulnerable in this respect at the start of the Vietnam War, and Max Hastings argues that the importance of expecting the unexpected was brought home to Britain yet again during the Falklands War:

"For all their cleverness, the Viet Cong had a weak point. They had fallen into regular patterns of behavior. They had done so, despite a doctrine that they must never lapse into such dangerous predictability, because they were human and human beings are creatures of habit. These guerrillas had been fighting the same war against the same enemy in the same paddies for too long not to succumb to their humanity."[74]

"For the hundredth time in her history, Britain was reminded that there is always an unexpected military threat which defence planning must be flexible enough to provide for."[75]

Air power is by no means omnipotent however, and this chapter has focused on vulnerabilities and constraints. These need to be identified so that appropriate

---

73. *ibid.* Gray, p.62.

74. Neil Sheehan, *A Bright Shinning Lie*, Picador, London 1990, pp. 69-70.

75. Max Hastings and Simon Jenkins, *The Battle for the Falklands*, Michael Joseph, London, 1983, p. 322.

counter measures can be taken: otherwise the considerable advantages of air power could be lost.

If the full potential of air power is to be exploited in such situations, air forces will need to retain their independent status. In Russia, during WWII, the Luftwaffe gradually became subservient to the daily needs of the German Army, with dire consequences for both; in the view of Paul Deichmann, "...the Wehrmacht High Command, deprived itself of an immensely powerful weapon." [76] The very first battle of the Cold War, the Berlin Airlift of the winter of 1948, demonstrated the value of air power. Following the closure of the road corridor to Berlin through the Soviet Zone of occupied Germany, an airlift operation by the RAF and United States Army Air Force (USAAF) kept the besieged city supplied for several months. Air power has unique properties and will often be the preferred instrument of national or international policy when diplomatic efforts fail and military force is used.

---

76. Paul Deichmann, General der Flieger and Dr. Alfred Price (ed.), *Spearhead for Blitzkreig: Luftwaffe Operations in Support of the Army, 1939-1945*, Greenhill Books, London 1996, pp. 154-5.

BIOGRAPHIES

Biography – *Professor M Clarke*
Professor Michael Clarke is Executive Director of the Centre for Defence Studies and Professor of Defence Studies at King's College London. He has served as Specialist Adviser to both the House of Commons Foreign Affairs Committee and, more recently, the House of Commons Defence Committee. He has also been a member of the High Level Group of Experts to advise Commissioner van den Broek of the European Commission. He has previously held teaching posts at the Universities of Manchester and Newcastle upon Tyne and he has been a Guest Fellow of the Brookings Institution, Washington DC, and a Visiting Fellow at the Royal Institute of International Affairs in London

Biography – *Dr D Gates*
Dr David Gates is the Deputy Director of The Centre for Defence and International Security Studies at Lancaster University, having previously been the MOD Lecturer in Defence Studies at Aberdeen University. One of the relatively few academics who specialise in both military history and contemporary strategic studies, he holds a doctorate from Oxford University, is a Fellow of the Royal Historical Society, and has held Visiting Fellowships at the Miltärgeschichtliches Forschungsamt and The Albert Ludwigs University, Freiburg, Germany and at Gonville and Caius College and The Centre of International Studies, Cambridge University. His numerous books and other publications include several pieces on air power topics.

Biography – *Group Captain S W Peach*
Group Captain Stuart Peach joined the RAF from the University of Sheffield in 1977 and completed a masters degree at Cambridge in 1997. He has completed five front line fast jet flying tours, has 3500 flying hours and commanded IX (Bomber) Squadron from 1994 to 1996. Staff experience as a personal staff officer has included tours with the RAF and NATO and he has completed three

operational tours in the Middle East. He has had a number of articles published in *'Air Clues'* and *'The Hawk'* and was the author of *'Pathfinder Station', A History of RAF Wyton*. He has been Director of Defence Studies (RAF) since July 1997.

Biography – *Dr K A Kyriakides*
Dr K A Kyriakides is an independent academic member of the Air Power Workshop. He holds an LL.B. Hons (Law and Politics) Degree from the University of Birmingham and an MPhil (International Relations) Degree from the University of Cambridge. In October 1993 he began his doctoral research at Cambridge, but from January to September 1995 he interrupted his studies to be the Research Fellow at the RAF Staff College, Bracknell. In this capacity, he lectured on behalf of the Director of Defence Studies (RAF), acted as Secretary to the Air Power Workshop, and contributed articles to *The Hawk* and *Air Clues*. After leaving Bracknell, he successfully completed his PhD degree in January 1997. His PhD dissertation is entitled 'British Cold War Strategy and the Struggle to Maintain Military Bases in Cyprus, 1951-60'.

Biography – *Air Vice-Marshal Professor R A Mason*
Air Vice-Marshal Tony Mason is Professor of Aerospace Security in the Department of Political Science and International Security, University of Birmingham. He is a graduate of the United States Air Force Air Warfare Course and of the RAF Staff College. He was the first Director of Defence Studies for the Royal Air Force and his last appointment before retirement in 1989 was Air Secretary. From 1989 to 1994 he was Air Power Research Director of the UK-based foundation for International Security and from 1989 a senior Research Fellow at the University of Birmingham, before being appointed to a personal Chair in 1996. For twenty years he has published and lectured world-wide on air power, strategy and international security. His last book, *'Air Power: A Centennial Appraisal'* was published by Brasseys in 1994 and reprinted in 1997. His most recent study. *'The Aerospace Revolution: Role Revision and Technology'* published by Brasseys in 1998. In the last three years he has contributed to forward policy studies for the Royal Air Force and United States, German, Swedish, Netherlands and Australian Air Forces. He is currently working on the aerospace implications for European Security of NATO enlargement.

Biography – *Squadron Leader P C Emmett*
Squadron Leader Emmett is a communications-electronics engineer officer in the RAF with extensive experience of the software-intensive defence programmes, communications and air command and control. His writings on the subject of

Information Warfare and operational software have won him major essay awards on both sides of the Atlantic. From July 1998 he will be based at the Defence Intelligence Staff, London.

Biography – *Major General W E Jones*
General Jones served in the United States Air Force for over 30 years. His responsibilities included command at numbered air force, wing, group and squadron levels, three tours of duty at the HQ USAF in force structure planning and budgeting. He served for 5 years in Europe in USAFE in various command and staff positions. General Jones also served at HQ Air Force Space Command in separate capacities as the Director of Operations, Director of Requirements and Director of Plans. General Jones retired from the USAF in 1995 and currently consults with the USAF and Lockheed Martin Corporation.

Biography – *Wing Commander D Foster.*
Wing Commander David Foster entered the Royal Air Force Supply branch in 1972. He has a BSc in Mathematics and Aeronautical Engineering from Southampton University and an MSc in Management from UMIST. Service on operational stations has been interleaved with appointments concerned with logistic research, simulation modelling, and the design, implementation and management of logistic systems. An exchange assignment with the United States Air Force (1993-1996) was spent as an internal consultant to the Lean Logistics and Business Process Reengineering projects throughout Air Force Materiel Command. He is currently instructing at the Joint Services Command and Staff College, Bracknell.

Biography – *Dr P A G Sabin*
Dr Philip Sabin MA PhD is a Senior lecturer in the Department of War Studies, King's College London, where he has taught since 1985. His recent publications include a co-edited volume on British Defence Choices for the Twenty-First Century, and several contributions to this Study Group's previous book, *'The Dynamics of Air Power'*. At the other chronological extreme, he also teaches and researches Greek and Roman warfare! Dr Sabin designed the MA upgrade programme which has been running at the various British Staff Colleges since 1992. He is now closely involved in developing King's College's role in providing academic support for the new Joint Services Command and Staff College, where he teaches on air power theory and other aspects of strategy.

Biography – *Group Captain A P N Lambert*
Group Captain Andrew Lambert was educated at Wellington College and the RAF College Cranwell. He joined his first squadron, No 54(F) equipped with F4M Phantoms, in April 1971. After tours in Germany in the Strike Role, and a tour on No23 Squadron at Wattisham, in the Air Defence Role, he passed out top of the Qualified Weapons Instructors Course in 1978, winning the Nicolson Trophy. In 1981, now instructor on the Weapons Instructor Course, he was co-author of a paper on Mixed Fighter Forces which won the Wilkinson Battle of Britain Memorial Sword. After a tour in the Falkland Islands, and a tour as OC Weapons Instructor School, he attended Staff College in 1986 and was posted, on promotion to wing commander, to HQ Strike Command in 1987. There he participated in the UK Battle Planning for Op Granby/Desert Storm before commanding No23 Squadron in 1991. On relinquishing command he completed a Masters' course in International Relations at the University of Cambridge in 1993/94. His most recent tour was as Director of Defence Studies (RAF) where he published monographs on the Psychological Impact of Air Power and Coercion theory. He is also co-editor of *'The Dynamics of Air Power'* and is currently Chief of Staff and Air Commander British Forces Falkland Islands.

Biography – *Lieutenant Colonel M Bucknam USAF*
Lieutenant Colonel Mark Bucknam began his USAF career in 1982 after completing a bachelors degree in physics and a masters in materials science at Virginia Tech. His first operational assignment was at RAF Bentwaters where he flew the A-10. Following a year as an Air Staff officer at the Pentagon, he became a Fighter Lead-In training instructor. He then went on to fly the latest models of the F-16. Before coming to London, he attended Air Command and Staff College, followed by a year at the School of Advanced Air Power Studies. He is currently a PhD candidate at King's College, London researching the use of air power in Bosnia, 1992-95.

Biography – *Mr A C Williamson*
Arthur C Williamson MA(Cantab.) MPhil read History at Cambridge University and is a former Research Fellow of the RAF Staff College. He has served in an Intelligence section in the British Army and also served in the Kenya Police. He has worked for a British International Transportation consultancy, travelled widely, and worked in Africa and the Middle East. His flying experience is as an enthusiastic glider pilot. Research projects include RAF Bomber Command losses, Sir Arthur Harris and Bomber Command decisions during World War II, and a study of logistic support during the Boer War. He has written for the RAF

magazine, contributed to a Deutsche Welle radio programme on the bombing of Dresden and co-edited, with Andrew Lambert, *'The Dynamics of Air Power'*. He is an independent member of the RAF Air Power Workshop and is currently working towards a PhD at Cambridge University.

SELECT BIBLIOGRAPHY

Books

1. Amirov, Oleg, et al, *Disarmament and Security, 1987 Yearbook*, Moscow, Novosti Press, 1988.

2. Armitage, Sir Michael, and Mason R A, *Air Power in the Nuclear Age, 1945-84 – Theory and Practice*, Macmillan, London, 1985.

3. Bailey, J B A, *Field Artillery and Firepower*, Military Press, Oxford, 1989.

4. Barnett, Correlli, *The Sword Bearers*, Eyre & Spottiswoode, London, 1963.

5. Baumbach, George, *Broken Swastika – The Defeat of the Luftwaffe*, George Mann, Maidstone, 1974.

6. Bergquist, Ronald E, *The Roles of Airpower in the Iran-Iraq War*, Air University Press, Maxwell Air Force Base, 1988.

7. Bialer, U, *The Shadow of the Bomber*, Bowie, Christopher J, *Concept of Operations and USAF Planning for Southwest Asia*, Rand Corporation, Santa Monica, 1984.

8. Boyle, A, *Trenchard*, Collins, London, 1962.

9. Brookes, A, *V-Force: The History of Britain's Airborne Deterrent*, Jane's London, 1982.

10. Builder, Carl H, *The Icarus Syndrome – The Role of Air Power Theory in the Evolution and Fate of the US Air Force*, Transaction Publishers, 1994.

11. *Chamber's Encyclopaedia,* International Learning Systems Corporation Ltd, London, 1973.

12. Chapman, Keith, *Military Air Transport Operations,* Brassey's, London, 1989.

13. Churchill, Winston S, *The Crisis on the Eastern Front,* London, 1931.

14 Clausewitz, Carl von, *On War,* edited and translated by Howard, Michael and Paret, Peter, Princeton University Press, N J, 1976.

15. Clodfelter, Mark, *The Limits of Air Power: The American Bombing of North Vietnam,* New York, Free Press, 1989.

16. Collier, Basil, *The Air Defence of the United Kingdom,* HMSO, London, 1957.

17. Cooper, M, *The Birth of Independent Air Power,* Allen & Unwin, London, 1986.

18. Dean, David J, *Airpower in Small Wars – The British Air Control Experience,* CADRE Papers, Air University Press, Maxwell Air Force Base, Alabama 1985.

19. Darby, P, *British Defence Policy East of Suez 1947-1968,* Oxford University Press, Oxford, 1973.

20. Detter de Lupin, Ingrid, *The Law of War,* Cambridge University Press, Cambridge, 1987.

21. Douhet, G, *The Command of the Air,* translated by Dino Ferrari, London, 1942.

22. Dutton, Lyn, et al, *Military Space,* Brassey's, London, 1990.

23. Drew, Dennis M, and Snow, Donald M, Making Strategy, Air University Press, Maxwell Air Force Base, Alabama, 1988.

24. Earle, Edward Meade, *Makers of Modern Strategy,* Princeton University Press, Princeton, N J, 1971.

25. Elsam, M B, *Air Defence,* Brassey's, London, 1989.

26. Emme, Eugene M, *The Impact of Air Power*, Van Nostrand, Princeton, N J, 1959.

27. Ethel, Jeffrey and Price, Alfred, *Air War South Atlantic*, Sidgwick & Jackson, London, 1983.

28. Evans,D, War: *A Matter of Principles*, RUSI Defence Studies Series, 1997

29. Faber, Harold, *Luftwaffe – An Analysis by Former Luftwaffe Generals*, Sidgwick & Jackson, London, 1979.

30. Fall, Bernard B, *Hell in a Very Small Place – The Siege of Dien Bien Phu*, Pall Mall Press, Oxford, 1966.

31. Fuller, J F C, *The History of the Second World War*, Eyre & Spottiswoode, London, 1948.

32. Futrell, Frank, *Ideas, Concepts, Doctrine – Basic Thinking in the United States Air Force 1907-1960*, Vols I and II, Air University Press, Maxwell Air Force Base, Alabama, 1989.

33. Garden, Timothy, *Can Deterrence Last?* Buchan & Enright, London 1984.

34. Garden, Timothy, *The Technology Trap – Science and the Military*, Brassey's, London, 1989.

35. Gross, Charles J, *Prelude to the Total Force: The Air National Guard 1943-1969*, Office of Air Force History, USAF, Washington DC, 1985.

36. Hallion, Richard P, *The Rise of the Fighter Aircraft*, Nautical & Aviation Publishing Company of America, Baltimore, Md, 1988.

37. Hallion, Richard P, *Air Power Confronts an Unstable World*, Brasseys, 1997

38. Hastings, Max, and Jenkins, Simon, *The Battle for the Falklands*, Book Club Associates, London, 1983.

39. Holly, J R, *Ideas and Weapons*, Office of Air Force History, USAF, Washington, DC, 1983.

40. Jane's *All the World's Aircraft*, 1991 and 1992.

41. Johnson, J E, *Wing Leader*, Chatto & Windus, London, 1956.

42. Keaney, Thomas A, *Strategic Bombers and Conventional Weapons – Airpower Options*, NDU Press, Washington DC, 1984.

43. Kenney, George C, *General Kenney Reports*, Office of Air Force History, USAF, Washington, DC, 1987.

44. Knight, Sir Michael, *Strategic Offensive Air Operations*, Brassey's, Exeter, 1989.

45. Kreis, John F, *Air Warfare and Air Base Defence*, Office of Air Force History, USAF, Washington, DC, 1988.

46. Kross, Walter, *Military Reform – The High -Tech Debate on Tactical Air Forces*, NDU Press, 1985.

47. Lambeth, Benjamin, *Desert Storm and Its Meaning – The View from Moscow*, Rand Corporation, Santa Monica, 1992.

48. Lambeth, Benjamin, *Moscow's Lessons from the 1982 Lebanon Air War*, Rand Corporation, Santa Monica, 1984.

49. Lewin, Ronald, *Rommel as Military Commander*, Ballatine Books, New York, 1977.

50. Liddell Hart, Sir Basil, *History of the First World War*, Cassell, London, 1971.

51. Liddell Hart, Sir Basil, *History of the Second World War*, Pan, London, 1970.

52. Liddell Hart, Sir Basil, *T E Lawrence: In Arabia and After*, Jonathan Cape, London, 1965.

53. Liddell Hart, Sir Basil, *Thoughts on War*, Faber & Faber, London, 1944.

54. Lorrell, Mark A, *Air Power in Peripheral Conflict – The French Experience in Africa*, Rand Corporation, Santa Monica, 1988.

55. Mason, R A, Air Power – *An Overview of Roles*, Brassey's, Exeter, 1987.

56. Mason, R A, *Air Power – A Centennial Appraisal*, Brassey's, 1994.

57. Mason, R A, *Readings in Air Power*, RAF Staff College, Cranwell, 1980.

58. Mason, R A, *Warfare in the Third Dimension*, Brassey's, London, 1986.

59. Meir, Golda, *My Life*, Putnam's, New York, 1975.

60. Meilinger, P S, *The Paths of Heaven – The Evolution of Air Power Theory*, Air University Press, Maxwell Air Force Base, Alabama, 1997.

61. Mets, David R, *Land-Based Air Power in Third World Crises*, Air University Press, Maxwell Air Force Base, Alabama, 1986.

62. Middlebrook, Martin, *The Schweinfurt-Regensburg Mission*, Allen Lane, 1983.

63. Miller, Charles E, *Airlift Doctrine*, Air University Press, Maxwell Air Force Base, Alabama, 1988.

64. Montgomery Hyde, H, *British Air Policy between the Wars, 1918-1939*, Heinemann, London, 1976.

65. Mrozek, Donald J, *Air Power in the Ground War in Vietnam*, Air University Press, Maxwell Air Force Base, Alabama, 1988.

66. Murray, Professor Williamson, *Strategy for Defeat – The Luftwaffe 1933-45*, Air University Press, Maxwell Air Force Base, Alabama, 1983.

67. Myers, George E, *Aerospace Power – The Case for Indivisible Application*, Air University Press, Maxwell Air Force Base, Alabama, 1986.

68. *Nuclear Weapons Databook*, Vols II and III, Ballinger, Cambridge, Mass, 1987.

69. Omissi, David E, *Air Power and Colonial Control, 1919-1939*, Manchester University Press, Manchester, 1990.

70. Overy, R J, *The Air War 1939-1945*, Macmillan, London, 1980.

71. Price, Alfred, *Air Battle Central Europe*, Sidgwick & Jackson, London, 1986.

72. Richard, Dennis, and Saunders, Hilary St G, *Royal Air Force 1939-1945*, Vols I-III, London, HMSO, 1953.

73. Scales, Robert H, *Firepower in Limited War*, NDU Press, Washington DC, 1990.

74. Slessor, Sir John, *The Great Deterrent*, Cassell, London, 1957.

75. Slessor, Sir John, *The Central Blue*, Cassell, London, 1956.

76. Slessor, Sir John, *Air Power and Armies*, Oxford University Press, Oxford, 1936.

77. Schlight, John, *The War in South Vietnam – The Years of the Offensive 1965-1968*, Office of Air Force History, USAF, Washington DC, 1988.

78. Slim, Viscount, *Defeat into Victory*, Corgi Books, London, 1971.

79. Smith, M, 'British Air Strategy between the Wars', Clarendon Press, Oxford, 1984.

80. Stephens, Alan, *Power Plus Attitude – Ideas, Strategy and Doctrine in the Royal Australian Air Force 1921-1991*, Australian Government Publishing Service, Canberra, 1992.

81. Stephens, Alan, *Smaller but Larger – Conventional Air Power into the 21st Century*, P J Grills, Commonwealth Government Printer, Canberra, 1991.

82. Stephens, Alan, *The War in the Air 1914-1994*, Air Power Studies Centre, RAAF Base, Fairbairn, Canberra, Australia, 1994.

83. Tedder, Lord, *Air Power in War*, Hodder & Soughton, London, 1949.

84. Terraine, John, *The Right of the Line*, London, 1985.

85. Terraine, John, *White Heat – The New Revolution in Warfare*, 1914-18, Sidgwick & Jackson, London, 1982.

86. Tilford, Jr, Earl H, *Setup – What the Air Force Did in Vietnam and Why*, Air University Press, Maxwell Air Force Base, Alabama, 1991.

87. Towle, Philip Anthony, *Pilots and Rebels – The Use of Aircraft in Unconventional Warfare, 1918-1988*, Brassey's, London, 1989.

88. Vallance, Andrew, *Air Power – Collected Essays in Doctrine*, HMSO, London, 1990.

89. Vallance, Andrew, *Doctrines of Air Power Strategy – and Operational Art*, MacMillan Press, 1996

90. Van Creveld, Martin, *Command in War*, Harvard University Press, Cambridge, Mass, 1985.

91. Van Creveld, Martin, *Technology and War*, Free Press, New York, 1989.

92. Walker, J R, *Air Superiority Operations*, Brassey's London, 1989.

93. Walker, J R, *The Future of Air Power*, Royal United Services Institute, London, 1986.

94. Warden III, John A, *The Air Campaign*, Brassey's, Washington DC, 1991.

95. Waterman, J, *The Fleet Air Arm History*, Surrey Fine Art Press, Redhill, 1970.

96. Waters, Gary, *Gulf Lesson One – The Value of Air Power*, Air Power Studies Centre, RAAF Base Fairbairn, Canberra, 1992.

97. Watts, Barry D, *The Foundations of US Air Doctrine – The Problem of Friction in War*, Air University Press, Maxwell Air Force Base, Alabama, 1984.

98. Webster, Sir Charles, and Frankland, Noble, *The Strategic Air Offensive against Germany 1939-1945*, Vols 1-4, HMSO, London, 1961.

99. Werrell, Kenneth P, *Archie, Flak, AAA and SAM – A Short Operational History of Ground-Based Air Defence*, Air University Press, Maxwell Air Force Base, Alabama, 1988.

100. Westenhoff, Charles M, *Military Air Power*, Air University Press, Maxwell Air Force Base, Alabama, 1990.

101. Wilmot, Chester, *The Struggle for Europe*, Collins, London, 1952.

102. Winnefeld/Johnson, Joint air Operations – Pursuit of Unity in Command and Control, 1942-1991, Airlife Publishing Ltd., 1993.

103. Woodward, Sandy, *One Hundred Days – The Memoirs of the Falklands Battle Group Commander*, Harper Collins, London, 1992.

104. Wrigley, H N, *The Decisive Factor – Air Power Doctrine*, edited by Stephens, Alan and O'Loughlin, Brendan, Australian Government Publishing Service, Canberra, 1990.

Magazine and Journals

105. Air Clues – The RAF Magazine.

106. Air Power History.

107. Air University Review/Airpower Journal.

108. Armed Forces Journal International.

109. Aviation Week and Space Technology.

110. Flight Magazine.

111. The Hawk, Journal of the RAF Staff College.

112. Interavia.

113. International Defence Review.

114. International Institute for Strategic Studies:
    a. The Military Balance.
    b. Strategic Survey.